JavaScript

NINTH EDITION

TOM NEGRINO • DORI SMITH

Peachpit Press

Visual QuickStart Guide
JavaScript, Ninth Edition
Tom Negrino and Dori Smith

Peachpit Press

Find us on the web at www.peachpit.com
To report errors, send a note to errata@peachpit.com
Peachpit Press is a division of Pearson Education

Copyright © 2015 by Tom Negrino and Dori Smith

Project Editor: Nancy Peterson
Development Editor: Scholle Sawyer McFarland
Production Editor: Danielle Foster
Copyeditor: Scout Festa
Indexer: Emily Glossbrenner
Cover Design: RHDG / Riezebos Holzbaur Design Group, Peachpit Press
Interior Design: Peachpit Press
Logo Design: MINE™ www.minesf.com

ISBN 13: 978-0-321-99670-1
ISBN 10:   0-321-99670-4

0 9 8 7 6 5 4 3 2 1

Printed in the United States of America

Dedication

To the memory of Bill Horwitz and Dorothy Negrino, because they loved learning.

Special Note

Way back in 1997, when we were writing Chapter 1 of our first edition of this book, we were searching for a way to make the concept of JavaScript objects clear, and found inspiration in the then-newest member of our family, our cat Pixel. Over the years since then, countless readers have told us how our "cat object" helped them to understand JavaScript better. Pixel became the mascot for many of our books. In the Fall of 2013, after a long and happy life, we lost him to old age. We miss him very much.

Pixel, on his last day with us.

Special Thanks to:

Big thanks to our editor Nancy Peterson; her expert touch, serenity, and compassion made this edition a pleasant one to create. Extra-special thanks for her above-the-call understanding when we were faced with a personal crisis.

Thanks also go to our other editor, Scholle McFarland, who stepped in and kept the project on an even keel when Nancy was overscheduled.

Thanks to Scout Festa for her skillful copy-editing. Our heartfelt thanks to Danielle Foster, the book's production editor, who laid out the book and pulled off the job with grace and aplomb, and to the indexer, Emily Glossbrenner, who should be thanked for doing a thankless job.

As always, we're grateful to Peachpit's Nancy Ruenzel and Nancy Davis for their support.

We'd like to express our special thanks to all of the high school, college, and university instructors who chose to use the previous editions of this book as a textbook for their classes.

Contents at a Glance

Table of Contents

Introduction

Welcome to JavaScript! Using this easy-to-learn programming language, you'll be able to add interest and interaction to your webpages and make them more useful for you and for your site's visitors. We've written this book as a painless introduction to JavaScript, so you don't have to be a geek or a nerd to write a script. Pocket protectors will not be necessary at any time. As a friend of ours says, "We're geeky, so you don't have to be!"

We wrote this book for you

We figure that if you're interested in JavaScript, then you've already got some experience in creating HTML pages and websites, and you want to take the next step by adding some interactivity to your sites. We don't assume that you know anything about programming or scripting. We also don't assume that you are an HTML expert (though if you are, that's just fine). We do assume that you've got at least the basics of building webpages down, and

that you have some familiarity with common HTML, such as links, images, and forms. Similarly, we assume basic knowledge of the other major building block of modern websites: CSS.

We include some extra explanation of HTML in sidebars called "Just Enough HTML." You won't find these sidebars in every chapter, just the ones where we think you'll need a quick reference. Having this information handy means you won't need multiple books or webpages open just to remember the syntax of a particular HTML attribute.

If you already know something about programming, you should be aware that we don't take the same approach to JavaScript as you might have seen in other books. We don't delve deeply into JavaScript's syntax and structure, and we don't pretend that this book is a comprehensive language reference (though you'll find some valuable reference material in Appendix A in the back of the book). There are several other books on the market that do that job admirably, and we list them in Appendix D at the end of this book. The difference between those books and this one is that instead of getting bogged down in formalism, we concentrate on showing you how to get useful tasks done with JavaScript without a lot of extraneous information.

In previous editions we added coverage of Ajax and jQuery, which use JavaScript and other common web technologies to add extra interactivity to webpages and to improve the user experience of your websites. In this edition, we've added even more examples and techniques using the popular jQuery framework.

How to use this book

Throughout the book, we've used some devices that should make it easier for you to work both with the book and with JavaScript itself.

In the step-by-step instructions that make up most of the book, we've used a special type style to denote either HTML, CSS, or JavaScript code, like this:

```
<div id="thisDiv">
→ window.onload = initLinks;
```

You'll also notice that we show the HTML and the JavaScript in lowercase. We've done that because all of the scripts in this edition are compliant with the HTML5 standard from the W3C, the World Wide Web Consortium. Whenever you see a quote mark in a JavaScript, it is always a straight quote (like ' or "), never curly quotes (aka "smart" quotes, like ' or "). Curly quotes will prevent your JavaScript from working, so make sure that you avoid them when you write scripts.

In the illustrations accompanying the step-by-step instructions, we've highlighted the part of the scripts that we're discussing in red, so you can quickly find what we're talking about. We often also highlight parts of the screen shots of web browser windows in red, to indicate the most important part of the picture.

Because book pages are narrower than computer screens, some of the lines of JavaScript code are too long to fit on the page. When this happens, we've broken the line of code up into one or more segments, inserted this gray arrow → to indicate that it's a continued line, and indented the rest of the line. Here's an example of how we show long lines in scripts.

```
dtString = "Hey, just what are you
→ doing up so late?";
```

You say browser, we say kumbaya

Beginning with the sixth edition of this book, we made a big change: we ended our support for browsers that are very old or that don't do a good job of supporting web standards. We'd found that virtually all web users have upgraded and are enjoying the benefits of modern browsers, ones that do a good-to-excellent job of supporting commonly accepted web standards like HTML, CSS2, and the Document Object Model. That covers Internet Explorer 9 or later; all versions of Firefox; all versions of Safari and Chrome; and Opera 7 or later.

We've tested our scripts in a wide variety of browsers, on several different operating systems, including Windows (mostly

Windows 7 and, in a few cases, Windows 8; like Microsoft, we've dropped support for Windows XP and Vista), OS X (10.8.5 and later), and Ubuntu Linux (we tested scripts in Firefox, Ubuntu's default browser).

We used the former 600-pound gorilla of the browser world, Microsoft Internet Explorer for Windows, to test virtually everything in the book (we used versions 9, 10, and 11). For this edition, we added testing in the frequently updated versions of Google Chrome for both Mac and Windows. We also tested the scripts with recent versions of Firefox (which updated every few weeks, ending with version 29) for Mac and Windows, and with Safari for Mac versions 6 and 7 (as Apple has discontinued development of Safari for Windows, we've dropped it from our testing regimen). Working with the latter browser means that our scripts should also work in any browsers based on the WebKit engine, and on browsers (such as Konqueror for Linux) based on KHTML, the open-source rendering engine from which Safari got its start. WebKit is also the basis for browsers in mobile operating systems, such as Apple's iOS, Google's Android, the Amazon Kindle Fire tablets, and BlackBerry Limited's Blackberry 10. So far as mobile devices go, we mainly tested scripts on iPhones and iPads.

Don't type that code!

Some JavaScript books print the scripts and expect you to type in the examples. We think that's way too retro for this day and age. It was tough enough for us to do all that typing, and there's no reason you should have to repeat that work. So we've prepared a companion website for this book—one that includes all of the scripts in the book, ready for you to just copy and paste into your own webpages. If we discover any mistakes in the book that got through the editing process, we'll list the updates on the site, too. You can find our companion site at **javascriptworld.com**.

If for some reason you do plan to type in some script examples, you might find that the examples don't seem to work, because you don't have the supporting files that we used to create the examples. For example, in a task where an onscreen effect happens to an image, you'll need image files. No problem. We've put all of those files up on the book's website, nicely packaged for you to download. You'll find one downloadable file that contains all of the scripts, HTML files, CSS files, and any media files we used. If you have any questions, please check the FAQ (Frequently Asked Questions) page on the companion website. It's clearly marked.

If you've read the FAQ and your question isn't answered there, you can contact us via email at **js9@javascriptworld.com**. We regret that because of the large volume of email that we get, we cannot, and will not, answer email about the book sent to our personal email addresses. We can only guarantee that messages sent to the **js9@javascriptworld.com** address will be answered.

On the other hand, typing code by hand is likely to give you a more thorough learning experience—so don't rule it out entirely!

Time to get started

One of the best things about JavaScript is that it's easy to start with a simple script that makes cool things happen on your webpage, then add more complicated stuff as you need it. You don't have to learn a whole book's worth of information before you can start improving your webpages. But by the time you're done with the book, you'll be adding advanced interactivity to your sites with JavaScript and jQuery.

Of course, every journey begins with the first step, and if you've read this far, your journey into JavaScript has already begun. Thanks for joining us; please keep your hands and feet inside the moving vehicle. And please, no flash photography.

1

Getting Acquainted with JavaScript

For website creators, the evolution of HTML has been a mixed blessing. In the early days of the World Wide Web, HTML was fairly simple, and it was easy to learn everything you needed to put together webpages.

As the web grew, page designers wanted their pages to interact with users, and it soon became obvious that HTML was insufficient to handle the demand. Netscape invented JavaScript as a way to control the browser and add visual interest and interactivity to webpages.

Since its creation, JavaScript has evolved quite a bit, although occasionally in different directions, depending on the browser. Later, we'll discuss JavaScript's evolution in detail.

In this chapter, you'll learn what JavaScript is (and what it isn't); what it can do (and what it can't); some of the basics of the language; and you'll get an introduction to Ajax, the combination of JavaScript with other technologies that has enabled a wave of interactivity and creativity for websites.

In This Chapter

What JavaScript Is

JavaScript is a programming language that you can use to add interactivity to your webpages. But if you're not a programmer, don't panic; there are lots of JavaScripts available on the web that you can copy and modify for your own use with a minimum of effort. In fact, standing on the shoulders of other programmers in this way is a great technique for getting comfortable with JavaScript.

To make it easier for you to get up and running with JavaScript, we have a website that supplements this book. We've included all the scripts in the book (so you don't have to type them in yourself!), as well as additional notes, addenda, and updates. You can find our site at **javascriptworld.com**.

You'll often see JavaScript referred to as a "scripting language," with the implication that it is somehow easier to script than to program. It's a distinction without a difference, in this case. A JavaScript script is a program that either is contained internally in an HTML page (the original method of scripting) or resides in an external file (the now-preferred method). On HTML pages, because it is enclosed in the **<script>** tag, the text of the script doesn't appear on the user's screen, and the web browser knows to run the JavaScript. The **<script>** tag is most often found within the **<head>** section of the HTML page, as in **Listing 1.1**, though you can, if you wish, have scripts in the **<body>** section.

If you're unfamiliar with these HTML concepts and you need more information about HTML, we suggest that you check out Elizabeth Castro and Bruce Hyslop's *HTML and CSS: Visual QuickStart Guide (8th Edition)*, also available from Peachpit Press. If you only need a mini-refresher, many chapters in this book include a section called "Just Enough HTML," which will give you a brief reminder of the relevant tags.

Listing 1.1 This very simple script types "Hello, Cleveland!" into the browser window.

```
<!DOCTYPE html>
<html>
<head>
    <title>Barely a script at all</title>
    <script type="text/javascript">
        window.onload = function() {
            document.getElementById("myMessage").innerHTML = "Hello, Cleveland!";
        }
    </script>
</head>
<body>
<h1 id="myMessage">
</h1>
</body>
</html>
```

JavaScript Isn't Java

Despite the names, JavaScript and Java have almost nothing to do with one another. Java is a full-featured programming language developed by Sun Microsystems and marketed by Oracle (since their purchase of Sun). With Java, a descendant of the C and C++ programming languages, programmers can create entire applications and control consumer electronic devices. Unlike other languages, Java promises cross-platform compatibility; that is, a programmer should be able to write one Java program that can then run on any kind of machine, whether that machine is running Windows, OS X, or any of the different flavors of Unix. In practice, Java hasn't always realized that dream, due in no small part to bickering between Sun and Microsoft as to the direction of the language. Microsoft got involved because it first wanted to integrate Java into Windows in its own way (a way that Sun said would make Java work one way on Windows, and another way on other machines, thereby defeating Java's main purpose); then Microsoft dropped Sun's Java from Windows altogether, after creating its own Java-like language, C#. After a flurry of lawsuits between the two companies (and a big settlement in favor of Sun), Microsoft removed its Java from Windows. No matter what platform you're on, you can download the latest version of Java from **java.com/getjava/**.

Besides standalone applications, Java's main use on the *client side*, that is, in the user's browser, is to create *applets*, small programs that download over the Internet and run inside web browsers. Because of Java's cross-platform nature, these applets should run identically on any Java-enabled browser. In recent years, we've seen many Java applets for browsers replaced first by Adobe Flash animations, which are generally easier to create than Java applets. In recent years, the increase of computer processing speeds and improved JavaScript implementations in browsers have further eroded Java's (and Flash's) use on the client side in favor of web apps written with HTML, CSS, and JavaScript. However, Java has become a popular language for applications written for use on the server side.

You embed Java applets in your webpages using the **<object>** HTML tag, with additional information specifying the applet. When the browser sees the **<object>** tag, it downloads the Java applet from the server, and the applet then runs in the area of the screen specified in the tag Ⓐ.

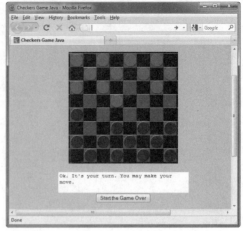

Ⓐ This Java applet plays a mean game of checkers.

Where JavaScript Came From

If JavaScript isn't related to Java, then why do they have such similar names? It's another example of one of the computer industry's most annoying traits: the triumph of marketing over substance.

Long ago, when Netscape added some basic scripting abilities to its Navigator web browser, it originally called that scripting language LiveScript. Around the same time, Java was getting lots of press as the Next Big Thing In Computing. When Netscape revised Navigator to run Java applets in Navigator 2, it also renamed LiveScript to JavaScript, hoping that some of Java's glitter would rub off. The mere fact that JavaScript and Java were very different programming languages didn't stop Netscape's marketing geniuses, and ever since then, writers like us have made good money explaining that JavaScript and Java are very different things. Come to think of it, maybe we should be thanking those marketers.

When Microsoft saw that JavaScript was becoming popular with web developers, it realized that it would have to add some sort of scripting capabilities to Internet Explorer. It could have adopted JavaScript, but as is so often the case, Microsoft instead built its own language, which works much like JavaScript but is not exactly the same. Microsoft's version of JavaScript is called JScript.

What JavaScript Can Do

There are many things that you can do with JavaScript to make your webpages more interactive and provide your site's users with a better, more exciting experience. JavaScript lets you create an active user interface, giving the users feedback as they navigate your pages. For example, you've probably seen sites that have buttons that highlight as you move the mouse pointer over them. That's done with JavaScript, using a technique called a *rollover* .

You can use JavaScript to make sure that your users enter valid information in forms, which can save your business time and money. If your forms require calculations, you can do them in JavaScript on the user's machine without any server-side processing. That's a distinction you should know: programs that run on the user's machine are referred to as *client-side* programs; programs running on the server are called *server-side* programs.

With JavaScript, you have the ability to create customized webpages, depending on actions that the user takes. Let's say that you are running a travel site, and the user clicks Hawaii as a destination. You can have the latest Hawaii travel deals appear in a new window. JavaScript controls the browser, so you can open up new windows, display alert boxes, and put custom messages in the status bar of the browser window. Because JavaScript has a set of date and time features, you can generate clocks, calendars, and timestamp documents.

You can also use JavaScript to deal with forms, set cookies, build HTML pages on the fly, and create web-based applications.

A A rollover is an image that changes when you move the mouse pointer over it.

The Snap-Together Language

Here's another buzzword that we should get out of the way: JavaScript is an *object-oriented* language. So what does that mean?

Objects

First, let's think about objects. An *object* is some kind of a thing. A cat, a computer, and a bicycle are all objects  in the physical world. To JavaScript, there are objects it deals with in web browsers, such as windows and forms, and the elements of the form, such as buttons and check boxes .

Because you can have more than one cat, or more than one window, it makes sense to give them names. While you could refer to your pets as Cat #1 and Cat #2, it's a bad idea for two reasons: first, it's easier to tell the cats apart if they have unique names, and second, it's just plain impolite. In the same way, most of the examples in this book give objects their own unique names.

> **TIP** Be aware that scripts you might see on the Internet will refer to objects like `window[0]` and `form[1]`. This is poor style for the reasons given above, and you'll find that it's much easier for you to keep track of the different objects in your scripts if you give them names instead of numbers.

> **TIP** Some persnickety programmers will argue that JavaScript isn't really object-oriented, but rather, that it's actually object-based. For the purposes of this book, the two meanings are close enough that it makes no difference.

A The cat object (this one's name is Pixel).

B The buttons and check box are browser objects, which can be manipulated by JavaScript.

Properties

Objects have *properties*. A cat has fur, the computer has a keyboard, and the bicycle has wheels. In the JavaScript world, a document has a title, and a form can have a check box.

Changing a property of an object modifies that object, and the same property name can be a part of completely different objects. Let's say that you have a property called **empty**. It's okay to use **empty** wherever it applies, so you could say both that the cat's tummy is empty and that the cat's bowl is empty.

Note that the computer's keyboard and the bicycle's wheels aren't only properties; they are also objects in their own right, which can have their own properties. So objects can have sub-objects.

Methods

The things that objects can do are called *methods*. Cats purr, computers crash, and bicycles roll. JavaScript objects also have methods: buttons **click()**, windows **open()**, and text can be **selected()**. The parentheses signal that we're referring to a method, rather than a property.

TIP It might help to think of objects and properties as nouns, and methods as verbs. The former are things, and the latter are actions that those things can do, or have done to them.

Putting the pieces together

You can put together objects, properties, and methods to get a better description of an object, or to describe a process. In JavaScript, these pieces are separated by periods (also known as dots, as in Internet addresses). This is called *dot syntax*. Here are some examples of objects and their properties written in this way:

```
bicycle.wheels
cat.paws.front.left
computer.drive.dvd
document.images.name
window.status
```

And here are some examples of objects and methods written in dot syntax:

```
cat.purr()
document.write()
forms.elements.radio.click()
```

Introducing the Document Object Model

On a webpage, the objects that make up the page (or *document*) are represented in a tree structure. You've seen this sort of thing before when building HTML pages; the top level of the page is contained in the `<html>` tag, and inside that you'll find the `<head>` and `<body>` tags, with other tags within each of those, and so on. Some browsers can show you representations of this tree structure, as in 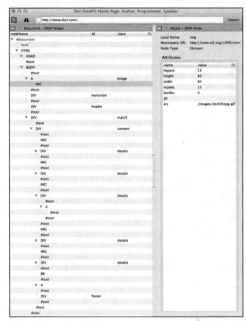. JavaScript considers each of the items in the document tree to be objects, and you can use JavaScript to manipulate those objects. The representation of the objects within the document is called the *Document Object Model* (DOM).

Each of the objects on the tree is also called a *node* of the tree. We can use JavaScript to modify any aspect of the tree, including adding, accessing, changing, and deleting nodes on the tree. Each object on the tree is a node. If the node contains an HTML tag, it's referred to as an *element node*. Otherwise, it's referred to as a *text node*. Of course, element nodes can contain text nodes. That's all you need to know about the DOM and nodes for now; you'll learn more about them throughout the book, especially in Chapter 10.

C You can see a document's tree structure using the DOM Inspector, which is an add-on for Firefox (shown here); there are similar features in Safari, Chrome, and Internet Explorer.

Handling Events

Events are actions that the user performs while visiting your page. Submitting a form and moving a mouse over an image are two examples of events.

JavaScript deals with events using commands called *event handlers*. An action by the user on the page triggers an event handler in your script. The 12 most common JavaScript event handlers are listed in **Table 1.1**. We deal with other, more advanced event handlers in Chapter 8.

For example, let's say that our cat handles the event **onpetting** by performing the actions **purr** and **stretch**.

In JavaScript, if the user clicks a button, the **onclick** event handler takes note of the action and performs whatever duties it was assigned.

When you write a script, you don't have to anticipate every possible action that the user might take, just the ones where you want something special to occur. For instance, your page will load just fine without an **onload** event handler. But you need to use the **onload** handler if you want to trigger a script as soon as the page loads.

TABLE 1.1 Event Handlers

Event	What it handles
onabort	The user aborted loading the page
onblur	The user left the object
onchange	The user changed the object
onclick	The user clicked an object
onerror	The script encountered an error
onfocus	The user made an object active
onload	The object finished loading
onmouseover	The cursor moved over an object
onmouseout	The cursor moved off an object
onselect	The user selected the contents of an object
onsubmit	The user submitted a form
onunload	The user left the page

TABLE 1.2 Value Types

Type	Description	Example
Number	Any numeric value	3.141592654
String	Characters inside quote marks	"Hello, world!"
Boolean	True or False	true
Null	Empty and meaningless	
Object	Any value associated with the object	
Function	Value returned by a function	

TABLE 1.3 Operators

Operator	What it does
x + y (Numeric)	Adds x and y together
x + y (String)	Concatenates x and y together
x - y	Subtracts y from x
x * y	Multiplies x and y together
x / y	Divides x by y
x % y	Modulus of x and y (i.e., the remainder when x is divided by y)
x++, ++x	Adds one to x (same as x = x + 1)
x--, --x	Subtracts one from x (same as x = x - 1)
-x	Reverses the sign on x

Values and Variables

In JavaScript, a piece of information is a *value*. There are different kinds of values; the kind you're most familiar with are numbers. A *string* value is characters—such as a word or words—enclosed in quotes. Other kinds of JavaScript values are listed in **Table 1.2**.

Variables contain values. For example, the variable **myName** is assigned the string "Dori". Another way to write this is **myName = "Dori"**. The equals sign can be read as "is set to." In other words, the variable **myName** now contains the value "Dori".

> **TIP** JavaScript is case sensitive. This means that myname is not the same as myName, and neither is the same as MyName.

> **TIP** Variable names cannot contain spaces or other punctuation, or start with a digit. They also can't be one of JavaScript's reserved words. See Appendix B for a list of JavaScript reserved words.

Operators

Operators are the symbols used to work with variables. You're already familiar with operators from simple arithmetic; plus and minus are operators. See **Table 1.3** for a list of the most common operators.

> **TIP** While both x++ and ++x add one to x, they are not identical; the former increments x after the assignment is complete, and the latter before. For example, if x is 5, y=x++ results in y set to 5 and x set to 6, while y=++x results in both x and y set to 6. The operator -- (minus signs) works similarly.

> **TIP** If you mix numeric and string values when adding two values together, the result is a string. For example, "cat" + 5 results in "cat5".

Assignments and comparisons

When you put a value into a variable, you are assigning that value to the variable, and you use an assignment operator to do the job. For example, you use the equals operator to make an assignment, such as `hisName = "Tom"`. There are a whole set of assignment operators, as listed in **Table 1.4**.

Other than the equals sign, the other assignment operators serve as shortcuts for modifying the value of variables. For example, a shorter way to say **x=x+5** is to say **x+=5**. For the most part, we've used the longer version in this book for clarity's sake.

Comparisons

You'll often want to compare the value of one variable with another, or the value of a variable against a literal value (i.e., a value typed into the expression). For example, you might want to compare the value of the day of the week to "Tuesday", and you can do this by checking if **todaysDate == "Tuesday"** (note the two equals signs). A list of comparisons is in **Table 1.5**.

TIP If you are comparing strings, be aware that "a" is greater than "A" and that "abracadabra" is less than "be".

TABLE 1.4 Assignments

Assignment	What it does
x = y	Sets x to the value of y
x += y	Same as x = x + y
x -= y	Same as x = x - y
x *= y	Same as x = x * y
x /= y	Same as x = x / y
x %= y	Same as x = x % y

TABLE 1.5 Comparisons

Comparison	What it does
x == y	Returns true if x and y are equal
x === y	Returns true if x and y are identical
x != y	Returns true if x and y are not equal
x !== y	Returns true if x and y are not identical
x > y	Returns true if x is greater than y
x >= y	Returns true if x is greater than or equal to y
x < y	Returns true if x is less than y
x <= y	Returns true if x is less than or equal to y
x && y	Returns true if both x and y are true
x || y	Returns true if either x or y is true
!x	Returns true if x is false

Writing JavaScript-Friendly HTML

Because you'll be using JavaScript to manipulate the objects within a document, you want to write your HTML in a way that can be easily used by your scripts. That basically means writing modern, standards-compliant HTML and using CSS to separate the document's structure from its presentation.

When we say modern HTML, we don't just mean documents that pass W3C validation using the web tool at **validator.w3.org**. We also recommend thinking ahead to what you are likely to do with a page and adding appropriate tags and attributes that will make it easy to access objects with JavaScript. What sort of markup, you wonder? Glad you asked.

Structure, presentation, and behavior

CSS (Cascading Style Sheets) is a standard layout language for the web that controls typography, colors, and the size and placement of elements and images. Your HTML documents should have external style sheets defining the styles used within the document. Your JavaScript should also be in an external document, one that contains only JavaScript code.

When split up this way, your sites will contain three types of text files:

- HTML: contains the content and structure of the page
- CSS: controls the appearance and presentation of the page
- JavaScript: controls the behavior of the page

When you do this, it becomes straightforward to make changes to your site—even changes with site-wide effects.

Divs and spans

HTML contains two tags that are finally getting the attention they deserve: `<div>` and `<span>`. They're used to break up your content into *semantic* chunks, that is, chunks that have a similar *meaning*. Things inside a single table cell or paragraph may or may not have anything in common, but the content within each `<div>` and `<span>` should.

Why use one over the other? A `<div>` is a block-level element; that is, there's a physical break between it and the elements above and below it. A `<span>` isn't block-level; instead, it's *inline*, so you can apply it to, for instance, a single phrase within a sentence.

Classes and ids

Inside your HTML document, you'll mark up your content by breaking it down into those meaningful chunks. From there, you'll still need to identify those pieces of content where you want to change their presentation or behavior. For that, you'll primarily use two attributes: `class` and `id`. These attributes can be used by both CSS and JavaScript; a CSS style sheet uses those attributes as part of rules to define the appearance of a page, and the JavaScript file can use those attributes in code that affects the behavior of elements on the page.

- A *class* identifies an element that you may want to use more than once. For example, let's say that you're creating a page for a movie theater. You can define a class for the movie titles, specifying that the titles should be 14 pixels, bold, and dark blue.

  ```
  .movieTitle {
    font: bold 14px;
    color: #000099;
  }
  ```

You should then wrap each movie title on your page with a tag specifying the **class** of the title style, like so:

```
<p>We're currently showing
→ <span class="movieTitle">
→ The Aviator</span> and
→ <span class="movieTitle">
→ The Outlaw</span>.</p>
```

- An *id* identifies an element that is unique to that document. For example, if you only use the name of the movie theater once on your page, you can create a style rule using an **id** to define how the theater's name will look, like this:

```
#theaterName {
    font: bold 28px;
    color: #FF0000;
}
```

Then, when it's time to show the name of the theater, all you do is add that **id** attribute to the tag to get the effect:

```
<h1 id="theaterName">The Raven
→ Theater Presents:</h1>
```

What goes for CSS in the above examples also applies to JavaScript. Once we've assigned classes and **id**s to our divs and spans (and to any other elements as well), we can then modify those elements: not just their appearance with CSS, but also their behavior with JavaScript. And that's a topic that will take up the rest of this book.

TIP Having trouble remembering when to use # versus . in your CSS because you can't recall which one goes with class and which with id? Here's our method: an id can be on any given page one time, and only one time. One is a number, and the hash symbol (#) is also called a number sign—so it's the one that goes with id.

What Tools to Use?

Since JavaScript is just plain text, you could use almost any kind of text editor. You could even use a word processor like Microsoft Word, though you would always have to make sure that Word saved the file as Text Only, instead of in its native file format. HTML, JavaScript, and CSS files must always be in plain text format so web servers can understand them.

You're better off using a program that has plain text as its standard format. On Windows, many people get away with using Notepad Ⓐ. On the Mac, you can use TextEdit, though a favorite of professionals is BBEdit, by Bare Bones Software Ⓑ. On Unix machines, Emacs is one of the best text editors available. No matter what program you use, don't forget to save your plain text files with the proper extension (**.html**, **.css**, or **.js**) so that things will go smoothly when you upload the file to a web server.

You can also use some of the WYSIWYG (What You See Is What You Get) HTML editors available, such as Dreamweaver. Just switch to their HTML Source mode and script away.

> **TIP** If you're a Mac user, try TextWrangler, also from the Bare Bones folks (barebones.com). It's not as full-featured as **BBEdit**, but it has a big point in its favor: it's free.

> **TIP** If you are interested in learning more about using the code tools in Dreamweaver, we recommend *Dreamweaver CC: Visual QuickStart Guide*, written by, uh, us.

Ⓐ Notepad on Windows 7.

Ⓑ BBEdit on OS X.

2

Start Me Up!

Enough of the warm-up; it's time to get scripting. In this chapter, you'll learn where to put your scripts in your HTML; how you can leave comments in your scripts so that you can more easily understand them at a later time; and how you can use scripts to communicate with the user. You'll also see how to make the page automatically change to another page (called *redirection*). Let's get to it!

In This Chapter

TABLE 2.1 Just Enough HTML—The Basics

Tag	Attribute	Meaning
`html`		Contains the HTML part of the webpage
`head`		Contains the header part of the webpage
`script`		Contains the webpage's script or a reference to the external script file. Usually JavaScript, but not always.
	`src`	The location of an external script
`title`		Contains the title of the webpage
`body`		Contains the body part of the webpage
`h1 ... h6`		Contents of this tag are emphasized as heading information; **h1** is the largest heading size, down to **h6** as the smallest heading
`a`		Links to another webpage
	`href`	Specifies where the user should go when the link is clicked

A The "Hello, world" example is *de rigueur* in code books. We'd probably lose our union card if we left it out.

Listing 2.1 Scripts inside HTML files always need to be enclosed inside the **<script>** and **</script>** tags.

```
<!DOCTYPE html>
<html>
<head>
    <title>My first script</title>
</head>
<body>
    <h1>
        <script>

            document.write("Hello, world!");

        </script>
    </h1>
</body>
</html>
```

Where to Put Your Scripts

Scripts can be put in one of two places on an HTML page: between the **<head>** and **</head>** tags (called a *header script*), or between the **<body>** and **</body>** tags (a *body script*). **Listing 2.1** is an example of a body script.

There is an HTML container tag that denotes scripts, which, as you would guess, begins with **<script>** and ends with **</script>**.

To write your first script:

1. **<script>**

   Here's the opening **script** tag. This tells the browser to expect JavaScript instead of HTML.

2. **document.write("Hello, world!");**

   Here's the first line of JavaScript: It takes the document window and writes "Hello, world!" into it **A**. Note the semi-colon at the end of the line; this tells the browser's JavaScript interpreter that the line is ending. With rare exceptions, we'll be using semicolons at the end of each line of JavaScript in this book.

3. **</script>**

   This ends the JavaScript and tells the browser to start expecting HTML again.

TIP The `language` and `type` attributes of the `script` tag (which we're not using here) have been *deprecated*, which means that the W3C, the standards body responsible, has marked the attributes as ones that will not necessarily be supported in future versions of the standard. There are plenty of older scripts that still use it, though.

TIP Using a semicolon at the end of a JavaScript line is optional, so long as you have only one statement per line. We've included them in this book for clarity, and we suggest that you get into the habit of including them in your code for the same reason.

TIP For most of the rest of this book, we've left the `<script>` tags out of our code explanations. As you'll see from the listings themselves, they're still there and still needed, but we won't be cluttering our explanations with them.

TIP You can have as many `<script>` tags (and therefore, multiple scripts) on a page as you'd like.

About Functions

Before you get into the next example, you need to learn a bit about functions, which you'll use often when writing JavaScript. A *function* is a set of JavaScript statements that performs a task. Every function must be given a name (with one very rare exception, which we'll discuss much later in this book) and can be invoked, or *called*, by other parts of the script.

Functions can be called as many times as needed during the running of the script. For example, let's say that you've gotten some information that a user typed into a form, and you've saved it using JavaScript (there's more about this sort of thing in Chapter 6, "Form Handling"). If you need to use that information again and again, you could repeat the same code over and over in your script. But it's better to write that code once as a function and then call the function whenever you need it.

A function consists of the word `function` followed by the function name. There are always parentheses after the function name, followed by an opening brace. The statements that make up the function go on the following lines, and then the function is closed by another brace. Here's what a function looks like:

```
function saySomething() {
    alert("Four score and seven years
    → ago");
}
```

Notice that the line with `alert` is indented? That makes it easier to read your code. All of the statements between the first brace and the last one (and you probably noticed that those two lines are not indented) are part of the function. That's all you need to know for now about functions. You'll learn more about them in subsequent chapters.

Using External Scripts

The problem with using scripts on the HTML page, as in the last example, is that the script is only available to that particular page. That's why those kinds of scripts are sometimes called *internal* scripts. But often, you'll want multiple HTML pages to share a script. You do this by including a reference to an *external* script; that is, a separate file that just contains JavaScript. This external file is called a **.js** file, because whatever it's called, the file name should end with the suffix **.js**. Individual pages call the **.js** file simply by adding a new attribute, **src**, to the **script** tag.

This saves a lot of code on every page and, more importantly, makes it easier to maintain your site. When you need to make changes to a script, you just change the **.js** file, and all HTML pages that reference that file automatically get the benefit of your changes.

In this first example of an external script, **Listing 2.2** contains the HTML with the reference to the external file, and **Listing 2.3** is the external JavaScript file.

To use an external script:

1. `<script src="script02.js"></script>`

   This line is in Listing 2.2. Adding the **src** attribute to the **script** tag causes browsers to look for that file. The resulting webpages will look just as though the scripts were in their usual place inside the page's **script** tags, when really the script resides in the external **.js** file.

   By itself, this line is all we need to do to use an external script. Next, let's work through what is in that script.

Listing 2.2 The simple HTML puts a reference to the external JavaScript file inside the **script** tag.

```
<!DOCTYPE html>
<html>
<head>
    <title>My second script</title>
    <script src="script02.js"></script>
</head>
<body>
    <h1 id="helloMessage">
    </h1>
</body>
</html>
```

Listing 2.3 Your first external JavaScript file.

```
window.onload = writeMessage;

function writeMessage() {
    document.getElementById("helloMessage").
    → innerHTML = "Hello, world!";
}
```

A The result of moving your JavaScript to an external file looks eerily unchanged from the previous example. But it's still a better way of doing things.

2. `window.onload = writeMessage;`

   Moving to Listing 2.3, the first part of this line, `window.onload`, is an event handler, which we discussed in Chapter 1. After the equals sign there is the name of a function, `writeMessage`. In English, this line can be read as "When the window finishes loading, tell the `writeMessage` function to run."

3. `function writeMessage() {`

   This line creates the `writeMessage()` function.

4. `document.getElementById`
   `→("helloMessage").innerHTML =`
   `→"Hello, world!";`

   Refer back to Listing 2.2, and you'll see that there is an `<h1>` tag there with an `id` of `helloMessage`. You'll learn more about `id`s later, but for now, suffice it to say that an `id` is a unique identifier on a page for whatever it is attached to. In other words, on a given page, there can be only one element with any particular `id`. That makes it easy for JavaScript to retrieve and modify the element using the `getElementById()` method. The `innerHTML` property simply takes the string that is on the right-hand side of the equals sign and drops it directly into the page, just as if we'd written it into the HTML itself. So, reading the JavaScript line from right to left in English, we could say "Take the string 'Hello, world!' and put it into the document, inside the element on the page named `helloMessage`." The result **A** looks an awful lot like **A** of "Where to Put Your Scripts."

continues on next page

TIP Browsers that support external JavaScript files include Microsoft Internet Explorer 4 and later, Netscape 3 and later, and just about every other browser that's shipped since then, including modern browsers like Firefox, Safari, and Chrome.

TIP Using external JavaScript files is sometimes used to try to hide JavaScript from users. It doesn't work if the user is technically savvy enough to check their browser cache files—everything that the browser has seen is stored there.

TIP In Listing 2.1 (and much earlier editions of this book), we used a technique for inserting information into the HTML page called `document.write()`. In later editions, we've mostly replaced that approach with setting `innerHTML`, because it is more versatile. Some people object to the use of the `innerHTML` property because it hasn't been blessed by the W3C. But even those people with issues agree that it's the simplest cross-browser way to work, so that's what we're primarily showing in this book. The "official" way to add or change an HTML page is covered in Chapter 10, "Objects and the DOM."

TIP If you've seen functions before, you might be expecting the `writeMessage` reference in step 2 to instead be `writeMessage()`. It's not, because the two mean different things: a function shown with parentheses means that the function is being called, right then and there. When it's without parentheses (as it is here), we're assigning it to the event handler, to be run later when that event happens.

Listing 2.4 Here's how you can annotate your script with comments, which helps you and others understand your code.

```
/*
    This is an example of a long JavaScript
    → comment. Note the characters at the
    → beginning and ending of the comment.

    This script adds the words "Hello,
    → world!" into the body area of the
    → HTML page.
*/

window.onload = writeMessage; // Do this when
→ page finishes loading

function writeMessage() {
    // Here's where the actual work gets
    → done

    document.getElementById("helloMessage").
    → innerHTML = "Hello, world!";
}
```

Putting Comments in Scripts

It's a good idea to get into the habit of adding comments to your scripts. You do this by inserting comments that JavaScript won't interpret as script commands. While your script may seem perfectly clear to you when you write it, if you come back to it a couple of months later it may seem as clear as mud. Comments help to explain why you solved the problem in a particular way. Another reason to comment your script is to help other people who may want to re-use and modify your script.

Listing 2.4 shows examples of two kinds of script comments. The first kind is for longer, multi-line comments. The second example shows how to do single-line comments.

Note that we haven't included the HTML for this example, as it is (virtually) identical to Listing 2.2. From now on in the book, when the HTML hasn't changed from a previous example, we won't be printing it again.

To comment your script:

1. ```
   /*
   This is an example of a long
   → JavaScript comment. Note the
   → characters at the beginning and
   → ending of the comment.
   This script adds the words
   → "Hello, world!" into the body
   → area of the HTML page.
   ```

   For multi-line comments, the **/*** at the beginning of the line tells JavaScript to ignore everything that follows until the end of the comment.

   continues on next page
   ```

2. `*/`

   This is the end of the comment.

3. `window.onload = writeMessage;`

   ```
   // Do this when page finishes
   → loading
   function writeMessage() {
     // Here's where the actual work
     → gets done
     document.getElementById
     → ("helloMessage").innerHTML =
     → "Hello, world!";
   }
   ```

   And here's the script again, as in the previous example, with single-line comments. As you can see here, single-line comments can be on a line by themselves, or they can follow a line of code. You can't have any code on the same line after a single-line comment, nor can you have a multi-line comment on the same line as code.

   Yes, we're as tired of seeing this one as you are, but it's traditional for all code books to start off with the "Hello, world!" example.

   So much for tradition.

Listing 2.5 The HTML for this example includes `<script>` and `<noscript>` tags.

```
<!DOCTYPE html>
<html>
<head>
    <title>My JavaScript page</title>
    <script src="script04.js"></script>
</head>
<body>
<noscript>
    <h2>This page requires JavaScript.</h2>
</noscript>
</body>
</html>
```

Listing 2.6 Alert dialog boxes help you communicate with the user.

```
alert("Welcome to my JavaScript page!");
```

Alerting the User

One of the main uses of JavaScript is to provide feedback to people browsing your site. You can create an alert window that pops up and gives users the vitally important information that they need to know about your page.

In user interface design, less is generally more. For example, you could get the user's attention with loud alarm sirens and big animated banners, but that would be just a bit over the top. Instead, **Listings 2.5** (HTML, which just calls the external script) and **2.6** (JavaScript) show how to create a nice, tasteful alert window. Now you know why we're writers, not designers.

To alert a user:

- alert("Welcome to my JavaScript
  → page!");

  Yes, that's all there is to it . Just put
  the text that you want to have appear
  within the **alert()** method in straight
  quotes.

TIP In most JavaScript alert boxes, you'll see
some indication telling the user that the alert
box was put up by a JavaScript command.
This is a security feature to keep unscrupulous
scripters from fooling hapless users. You can't
code around this. On Safari, for example, it
shows the URL of the site that opened the
alert . Chrome on both Windows and Mac
does the same thing. In Internet Explorer,
the window title is always "Message from
webpage." Firefox, on the other hand, doesn't
show a message; instead, it shows the alert as
an overlay on top of the window that put up
the alert.

TIP You'll also see the <noscript> tag
used here. On non-JavaScript browsers (older
browsers and browsers with JavaScript turned
off), a message appears saying that this page
requires JavaScript.

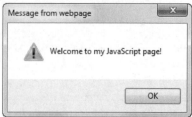

Ⓐ This script only puts up one dialog box; the
three shown are examples of how the dialog box
looks in, from top to bottom, Firefox 26; Microsoft
Internet Explorer 11; and Safari 6 for OS X.

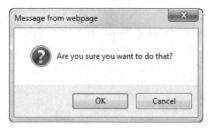

(A) You can capture the result of a user's action and confirm the result in an alert box, as seen here. The top image asks the user a question, and the result of pressing the OK or Cancel button is shown below.

Listing 2.7 You can put up different replies, depending on how the user reacts to a prompt.

```
if (confirm("Are you sure you want to do
→that?")) {
    alert("You said yes");
}
else {
    alert("You said no");
}
```

Confirming a User's Choice

While it's useful to give information to a user, sometimes you'll want to also get information back in return. **Listing 2.7** shows how to find out if the user accepts or rejects your question. This script also introduces the idea of *conditionals*, which is where the script poses a test and performs different actions depending on the results of the test.

Introducing conditionals

Conditionals break down into three parts: the *if* section, where we do our test; the *then* section, where we put the part of the script we want to do if the result is true; and an optional *else* section, which contains the part of the script we want to have happen if the result of the test is not true. The contents of what we're testing in the *if* section are in parentheses, and the contents of the other two sections are each contained in braces.

To confirm a choice:

1. `if (confirm("Are you sure you`
   `→ want to do that?")) {`

   The `confirm()` method takes one *parameter* (the question we want to ask the user) and returns either true or false, depending on the user's response **(A)**.

2. `alert("You said yes");`

   If the user clicked the OK button, `confirm()` returns true, and an alert displays, saying, "You said yes". As you can see, this is the *then* section of the code, even though there's no *then* operator in JavaScript. The braces serve as the delineation of the *then* area.

   continues on next page

3. `}`

This brace ends the part that occurs when `confirm()` returned a value of true.

4. `else {`

Here, we begin the section that only happens when the user hits the Cancel button.

5. `alert("You said no");`

If the user clicked the Cancel button, `confirm()` returns false, and the message "You said no" is displayed.

6. `}`

This curly brace ends the entire **if/else** conditional statement.

TIP You can put as many statements as you wish inside the *then* and *else* braces.

There's No One Right Way

There are a million ways to write any given script and still have it work correctly. For instance, braces are not required on conditionals if (and only if) there is only one statement in that code block.

In addition, there's an alternate method of writing a conditional that takes the form:

```
(condition) ? truePart :
 falsePart;
```

which is the rough equivalent of:

```
if (condition) {
    truePart;
}
else {
    falsePart;
}
```

That same shorthand method can also be used to set variables; for instance:

```
myNewVariable = (condition) ?
 trueValue : falseValue;
```

is equivalent to:

```
if (condition) {
    myNewVariable = trueValue;
}
else {
    myNewVariable = falseValue;
}
```

There's also no requirement that the braces have to be at the end or beginning of lines, or that the true and false code blocks need to be indented. It's all a matter of style, and the correct style to use is the one you've found to work best for you.

In this book, for the most part and for clarity's sake, we've included the braces in the examples and chosen to use the longer form for conditionals.

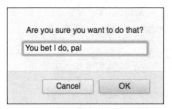

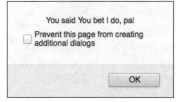

A You can prompt a user for a text string, then act on that string.

Listing 2.8 You can use a dialog box to query the user and work with the reply.

```
var ans = prompt("Are you sure you want to do
→ that?","");
if (ans) {
    alert("You said " + ans);
}
else {
    alert("You refused to answer");
}
```

Prompting the User

Sometimes, instead of just asking a Yes/No question, you'll want to get a more specific response. In that case, **Listing 2.8** allows you to ask a question (with a default answer) and receive the reply in turn **A**.

To prompt a user for a response:

1. `var ans = prompt("Are you sure` `→ you want to do that?","");`

   Here, we're declaring a variable (as discussed in Chapter 1). We use the **var** keyword to declare variables. In this case, the variable is called **ans** and assigned the result of the **prompt()**; i.e., whatever the user types into the prompt dialog.

   The **prompt()** method is passed two pieces of information (officially called *parameters*), separated by a comma: the question for the user and the default answer. It returns either the user's response or *null*; "null" occurs when the user hits Cancel, when there is no default and the user hits OK, or when the user clears the default answer and hits OK. For those browsers where a prompt shows a close box control, using that also returns a null result.

2. `if (ans) {` `    alert("You said " + ans);` `}`

   This conditional uses the variable that we just set. If **ans** exists (that is, if the user typed in a response), then the script puts up an alert window that says, "You said " (and note the extra space at the end of that text string above) and concatenates (appends to the end) the value of **ans**.

   continues on next page

3. ```
   else {
       alert("You refused to answer");
   }
   ```

   If **ans** is null, because the user didn't enter anything or clicked the Cancel button in the prompt dialog, then the **else** block of the condition is executed, and the alert pops up.

   TIP Using var does two things:

   It tells JavaScript to create a variable (that is, to set aside some space in memory for this new object).

   It defines the *scope* of the variable, that is, where JavaScript needs to know about this particular object (see the "What Is Scope?" sidebar). If a variable is created inside a function, other functions don't have access to it, as it's *local* to that function. If it's created outside any function, it's *global*, and everything has access to it. In this script, we're creating the ans global variable.

   TIP In some browsers, if you leave off prompt's second parameter (the default response), everything works fine. However, in others, the prompt window will display a default of "undefined." The answer is to always include *some* default, even if it's an empty string (as shown in Listing 2.8).

   TIP Chrome and Firefox allow visitors to prevent pages from creating additional dialogs **A**. Consequently, it's a bad idea to make your page dependent on users viewing the dialogs.

What Is Scope?

In most of the world, when you talk about "Broadway," people know that you're referring to a street in New York City. While the street itself is in New York, people globally understand your reference. You can think of Broadway as a *global*.

However, if you're in San Diego, California, and you refer to "Broadway," people will think that you're referring to a major street in their downtown area. This is a *local* value. In San Diego, not being clear about whether you're referring to the locally known "Broadway" or the globally known "Broadway" can lead to confusion.

If you're in San Diego, the default is the local version, and you have to explicitly state "New York City's Broadway" in order to refer to the other. Outside of San Diego, people will think of New York's Broadway first, unless they have some other local version of Broadway.

The *scope* of each of these streets is where each is the default, that is, the one that will be automatically thought of if no other identifying information is given. The scope of San Diego's Broadway is local—inside the city and a few outlying suburbs. The scope of New York's Broadway is global; that is, people anywhere in the world will know to where you're referring.

With JavaScript code, the easiest way to avoid questions and confusion about a variable's scope is to avoid using two variables with the same name in two different places doing two different things. If you must go down this slippery slope, be clear about your variable's scope!
   ```

A This page has the link that contains the redirection code.

Listing 2.9 This HTML allows you to redirect the user based on a link.

```
<!DOCTYPE html>
<html>
<head>
    <title>Welcome to our site</title>
    <script src="script07.js"></script>
</head>
<body>
    <h2>
        <a href="script04.html" id="redirect">
        → Welcome to our site... c'mon in!</a>
    </h2>
</body>
</html>
```

Listing 2.10 By embedding the redirection inside the code, the user doesn't even know your script intervened in the link.

```
window.onload = initAll;

function initAll() {
    document.getElementById("redirect").
    → onclick = initRedirect;
}

function initRedirect() {
    window.location = "jswelcome.html";
    return false;
}
```

Redirecting the User with a Link

You can check for the existence of JavaScript and then seamlessly *redirect*, or send users to another page, depending on if they have JavaScript turned on. This example shows you how to embed the redirection in a link. We'll use two HTML pages and one JavaScript file. The first HTML page, **Listing 2.9**, gives the user the link to click. **Listing 2.10** is the JavaScript file, and **Listing 2.11** is the HTML page the user is redirected to if they have JavaScript enabled. When users click the link **A**, they'll be taken to one of two pages, depending on whether or not they have JavaScript.

Listing 2.11 This is the HTML for the page the JavaScript-enabled user ends up on.

```
<!DOCTYPE html>
<html>
<head>
    <title>Our site</title>
</head>
<body>
    <h1>Welcome to our web site, which
    → features lots of cutting-edge
    → JavaScript</h1>
</body>
</html>
```

To redirect a user:

1. `<a href="script04.html"`
   `→id="redirect">Welcome to our`
   `→site... c'mon in!</a>`

   In Listing 2.9, this is the link the user clicks. If users don't have JavaScript and they click the link, they'll follow the usual **href** path and end up on a page that looks like Ⓑ. If users have JavaScript and they click the link, the script (down in step 4) takes over and loads a new page.

2. `window.onload = initAll;`

   Now we're in Listing 2.10. When the page finishes loading, it triggers the **initAll()** function.

3. `function initAll() {`
   `    document.getElementById`
   `    →("redirect").onclick =`
   `    →initRedirect;`
   `}`

   This function simply tells the element with the **id redirect** that it should call the **initRedirect()** function when a user clicks that link (that is, the link from step 1).

4. `function initRedirect() {`
   `    window.location =`
   `    →"jswelcome.html";`
   `    return false;`
   `}`

   If this function is called, it sets **window.location** (the page loaded in the browser) to a new page. The **return false** says to stop processing the user's click, so the **href** page doesn't also get loaded.

   What's so cool about this is that we've done a redirection without users having any idea that it happened. They're just on one of two different pages, depending on what they came in with. If they have JavaScript, they end up on a page shown in Ⓒ.

Ⓑ This message gives the user the heave-ho, if you've decided that JavaScript is essential to your site.

Ⓒ JavaScript-savvy browsers see this page instead.

TIP On first glance, we might think that we could just set the `onclick` handler globally—that is, as the page is loading—but we can't. There's a chance, particularly for a large and complex page, that the browser will not yet have come across that `redirect id`, and if that happens, JavaScript won't be able to assign the `onclick` handler. Instead, we have to wait until the page has completed loading, and that's done via `onload`.

TIP Keep in mind that some users may object to being sent to a different page than the one they saw when they put their mouse over the link.

Listing 2.12 The HTML, as usual, contains an **id** in the link tag that JavaScript can use.

```
<!DOCTYPE html>
<html>
<head>
    <title>Welcome to our site</title>
    <script src="script08.js"></script>
</head>
<body>
    <h2>
        Hey, check out <a href="http://
        → www.pixel.mu" id="redirect">
        → my cat's Web site</a>.
    </h2>
</body>
</html>
```

Listing 2.13 The link enhancement script.

```
window.onload = initAll;

function initAll() {
    document.getElementById("redirect").
    → onclick = initRedirect;
}

function initRedirect() {
    alert("We are not responsible for the
    → content of pages outside our site");
    window.location = this;
    return false;
}
```

Using JavaScript to Enhance Links

Sometimes, you may want to perform some sort of action after the user clicks a link, but before the browser loads the new page. A typical example would be when you want to put up an alert before the user goes to a particular page on your site, or to make it clear when the user leaves your site. In this example, we'll put up an alert dialog before continuing on to the ultimate destination. **Listing 2.12** shows the HTML, and **Listing 2.13** shows the small number of changes we need to make to previous scripts.

To enhance links:

1. **Hey, check out <a href="http://**
   → www.pixel.mu" id="redirect">
   → my cat's Web site</a>.

   This line in Listing 2.12 shows the link, with the **href** for the link's destination, and the **id** for the link, which will be used by Listing 2.13. The page is shown in .

2. **alert("We are not responsible for**
   → the content of pages outside
   → our site");

   This alert appears after the link has been clicked 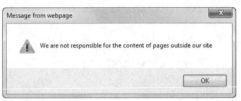.

3. **window.location = this;**

   This line allows us to set the browser window to the location specified by the keyword **this**, which contains the link. For now, just think of **this** as a container—if you want to know more, see the "What Is 'this'?" sidebar. When the user reaches their final destination, it looks like  (at least, using our cat's webpage as the destination).

Ⓐ Clicking the link will redirect the user to our cat's website.

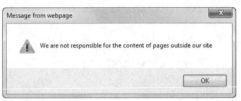

Ⓑ If the user has a JavaScript-capable browser, they'll see this warning message as they leave.

Ⓒ In this case, we'll admit that we actually are responsible for this cat's page. (What, you think he does it himself?)

What Is "this"?

In the example, you see the word **this** used, but it's not completely clear what **this** is.

The JavaScript keyword **this** allows the script to pass a value to a function, solely based on the context where the keyword is used. In this case, **this** is used inside a function triggered by an event attached to an **a** tag, so here, **this** is a link object. In later examples, you'll see **this** used elsewhere, and you should be able to tell what **this** is, simply based on the context where it's being used.

TIP You may have noticed that nowh the code does it refer to a particular web page—that's part of the power of **this**. On of the things the **this** keyword does for us is grab the URL from the HTML link (that is, the value of the a tag's **href** attribute). Because we're using this approach, we don't have to touch Listing 2.13 if we someday change Listing 2.12 to point to our kid instead of our cat. In fact, we could have links all over our website calling this same script, and that one line of code would automatically grab *their* **href** values as well.

TIP If that previous tip wasn't enough, think about it this way: with this approach, your HTML pages can be modified by WYSI-WYG editors and people who know nothing about JavaScript—and so long as they only change the HTML pages, they can't screw up your script.

TIP That wasn't enough for you either? Here's another benefit: if the user's browser doesn't understand JavaScript, it loads in only the HTML page. When they click the link, it loads just as it normally would: no errors, no confusing "you must have some other browser," no problems.

TIP This kind of coding style—where the code is separated out from the HTML, so that both are more flexible—is referred to as *unobtrusive scripting*. If you want to know more about how this fits in with all the other buzzwords you hear about code on the web, check out the "Just Enough Terminology" sidebar.

...ology

pt for any length of time, you may start to feel overwhelmed by the
...at gets thrown around—and much of it, at its root, is about what
...ere's a quick rundown of where we stand on these burning issues
...y're burning issues, hang out with some scripters for a while!):

...ially this term is owned by AOL (via Netscape), it's commonly used to
cover all JavaScript-like scripting technologies such as Microsoft's JScript. We'll continue that
trend in this book.

- **DHTML:** This stands for *Dynamic HTML*, but in real life, what *that* actually means depends
  on who's doing the talking. The Web Standards Project defined DHTML as "...an outdated
  scripting technique that is mainly characterized by the changes it makes to the style properties of certain elements, and by the use of the browser-specific DOMs `document.layers` and
  `document.all`." Thankfully, the term isn't used much anymore.

- **DOM scripting:** An approach to scripting webpages using JavaScript, in which the code
  only modifies pages via manipulation of the W3C DOM (that is, no use of proprietary,
  non-standard, or deprecated properties). When Listings 2.10 and 2.13 refer to
  `document.getElementById("redirect").onclick`, that's DOM scripting in action.

- **Unobtrusive scripting:** An approach to scripting webpages using JavaScript in which the
  behavior of the webpage is kept separate from its content—that is, the HTML is in one file, and
  the JavaScript is in another. As a best-practices recommendation, it's comparable to the split
  between HTML and CSS, where the presentation (CSS) is in one file and the content (HTML)
  is in another.

- **Progressive enhancement:** This addition to unobtrusive scripting is used when code is written
  such that visitors without JavaScript (or with less-capable browsers) get all the functionality of
  a site, just with a less-rich user experience. Listings 2.10 and 2.13 are examples of progressive
  enhancement, in that you don't need JavaScript in order to click the links, but you'll have a
  richer experience when you do.

Throughout this book, we use a variety of scripting techniques. While we recommend the unobtrusive scripting/progressive enhancement approach wholeheartedly (and we try to demonstrate it
whenever possible), we also know that you, as a budding scripter, will frequently need to be able
to understand and support older, less rigorously written code. And finally, this being the real world,
we also know that sometimes the simplest way to hammer in a nail is to grab a rock and pound the
nail into the wall. This, for instance, is why we used **innerHTML** back in Listing 2.3, even though it's
not part of the W3C DOM.

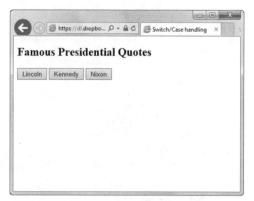

A Calling the function with each of the three buttons in the top window results in three different responses, as shown in the three dialog boxes.

Using Multi-Level Conditionals

There are times when you need more than two choices in a conditional test; **then** and **else** sometimes just aren't enough. While you can have nested levels of **if**s, it's often simpler to just use a **switch**/**case** statement instead. The **switch**/**case** construct allows you to check a variable against multiple values. As you can see in **A**, this script returns one of three different Presidential quotes as alert dialogs, depending on which button the user clicks. **Listing 2.14** shows the HTML, which is fairly simple. **Listing 2.15**, the JavaScript, uses the **switch**/**case** construct to differentiate between presidents.

Listing 2.14 The HTML sets up the page for multi-level conditionals.

```
<!DOCTYPE html>
<html>
<head>
    <title>Switch/Case handling</title>
    <script src="script09.js"></script>
</head>
<body>
<h2>Famous Presidential Quotes</h2>
<form action="#">
    <input type="button" id="Lincoln"
    → value="Lincoln">
    <input type="button" id="Kennedy"
    → value="Kennedy">
    <input type="button" id="Nixon"
    → value="Nixon">
</form>
</body>
</html>
```

To use a switch/case statement:

1. `window.onload = initAll;`

   When the page loads, call the **initAll()** function.

2. ```
   function initAll() {
       document.getElementById
   → ("Lincoln").onclick =
   → saySomething;
       document.getElementById
   → ("Kennedy").onclick =
   → saySomething;
       document.getElementById
   → ("Nixon").onclick =
   → saySomething;
   ```

   In the function, we set the **onclick** handler for each of the buttons on the page. Because we set the **id** attribute along with the **value** attribute in the HTML, we're able to use **getElementById()** to set the event handler. If it existed, it would have been nice to be able to use a **getElementByValue()** call—then, we wouldn't have had to set the **id** attribute.

3. `function saySomething() {`

   This begins the **saySomething()** function.

4. `switch(this.id) {`

   The **id** of the **this** object is used as the parameter to **switch()**. Its value will decide which of the below **case** statements gets executed.

5. ```
   case "Lincoln":
      alert("Four score and seven
   → years ago...");
      break;
   ```

   If the **id** of the **this** object is "Lincoln", this alert appears. Regarding **break**, if the user clicked Lincoln, we're in this section of code. However, we've done

Listing 2.15 This type of conditional allows you to check against multiple possibilities.

```
window.onload = initAll;

function initAll() {
     document.getElementById("Lincoln").
   → onclick = saySomething;
     document.getElementById("Kennedy").
   → onclick = saySomething;
     document.getElementById("Nixon").
   → onclick = saySomething;
}

function saySomething() {
     switch(this.id) {
        case "Lincoln":
           alert("Four score and seven years
   → ago...");
           break;
        case "Kennedy":
           alert("Ask not what your country
   → can do for you...");
           break;
        case "Nixon":
           alert("I am not a crook!");
           break;
        default:
     }
}
```

everything we want to do, and so we want to get out of the **switch**. In order to do that, we need to **break** out. Otherwise, we'll execute all of the code below, too. While that continued execution can be handy in certain circumstances, this isn't one of them.

6. ```
   case "Kennedy":
       alert("Ask not what your
       → country can do for you...");
       break;
   ```

   If the user clicked Kennedy, we end up in this **case** block.

7. ```
   case "Nixon":
       alert("I am not a crook!");
       break;
   ```

   And finally, if the user clicked Nixon, we end up here, popping up another alert and then breaking out of the **switch**.

8. ```
   default:
   ```

   If you were wondering what would happen if the user's entry didn't meet one of the above criteria, you're in the right place. The **default** section is where we end up if our **switch** value didn't match any of the **case** values. The **default** block is optional, but it's always good coding practice to include it, just in case (so to speak). In this script, there's no code here to execute, because we shouldn't ever get here.

9. ```
   }
   ```

   This closing brace ends the **switch** statement.

> **TIP** A **switch** statement can be passed other values besides strings. You can use it with a numeric value or even have it evaluate a mathematical result. If its result should be numeric, though, be sure that the **case** statements match—your **case** statements would then need to check for numbers, not strings (e.g., 5, not "5").

Handling Errors

While you may have years of experience working with computers, it's a good bet that many of your site's visitors won't. Consequently, you'll want to give them meaningful error messages instead of the technobabble that most browsers return if they object to something the user does. **Listing 2.16** shows how to use JavaScript's **try/throw/catch** commands to produce a friendly, useful error message. We've built this into a simple square root calculator.

To handle errors gracefully:

1. `var ans = prompt("Enter a number",` `→ "");`

   Here's an ordinary, everyday prompt, which stores its returned value in the **ans** variable for later use. In this case, we want the user to enter a number. If they do that successfully, JavaScript displays the square root of whatever they entered.

2. `try {`

   However, if they didn't enter a number 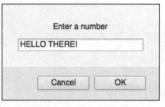, we want to be able to catch it gracefully and display something meaningful. Yes, we'll be polite about it, even though the user entered words when the alert asked for a number. We start off by using the **try** command. Inside its block of code, we'll check to see if the user's entry was valid.

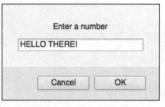

A We want a number, but the user could enter anything, like this non-numeric entry.

Listing 2.16 Use this script to have JavaScript gracefully handle errors.

```
window.onload = initAll;

function initAll() {
    var ans = prompt("Enter a number","");
    try {
        if (!ans || isNaN(ans) || ans<0) {
            throw new Error("Not a valid
            → number");
        }
        alert("The square root of " + ans + "
        → is " + Math.sqrt(ans));
    }
    catch (errMsg) {
        alert(errMsg.message);
    }
}
```

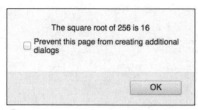

The square root of 256 is 16

☐ Prevent this page from creating additional dialogs

OK

B Here's the result of the script acting on a number.

3. ```
if (!ans || isNaN(ans) || ans<0) {
    throw new Error("Not a valid
    → number");
}
```

There are three things we care about: no entry at all, or if the user entered something but it was non-numeric, or if the entry was numeric but was a negative number (because the square root of a negative number is an imaginary number, and that's beyond this example). If **!ans** is true, that means that the user didn't enter anything. The built-in **isNaN()** method checks to see if the parameter it was passed is "Not a Number." If **isNaN()** returns true, we know that something invalid was entered. And if **ans** is less than 0, it's a negative number. In any of these cases, we want to **throw** an error; in this case, it says "Not a valid number". Once an error is thrown, JavaScript jumps out of the **try** block and looks for a corresponding **catch** statement. Everything between here and there is skipped over.

4. ```
alert("The square root of " +
→ ans + " is " + Math.sqrt(ans));
```

If something valid was entered, the square root is displayed **B**.

continues on next page

5. `}`

This closing brace ends the **try** block.

6. `catch (errMsg) {`
    `alert(errMsg.message);`
`}`

Here's the promised and looked-for **catch** statement. The **error** is passed in as a parameter, and the **message** part of the error is displayed 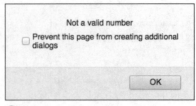. If no error was thrown, the code inside the catch will never be executed.

Ⓒ If bad data was entered, let the user know.

TIP There's another, optional part to this: the `finally {}` block. That would go after the `catch` and would contain code that should be executed whether the `try` threw an error or not.

TIP There's more about the `Math` object in the next chapter.

3

Your First Web App

Now that you've gotten your feet wet, let's wade a bit deeper into the JavaScript language. In this chapter, we'll go into more detail about the basic elements of JavaScript and introduce you to other aspects of the JavaScript language, such as loops, arrays, and more about functions (don't let your eyes glaze over; we promise that it'll be easy).

You'll see how you can use JavaScript to write your webpages for you, learn how JavaScript handles errors that the user makes, and much more.

In This Chapter

Around and Around with Loops

It's common in programming to test for a particular condition and repeat the test as many times as needed. Let's use an example you probably know well: doing a search and replace in a word processor. You search for one bit of text, change it to a different text string, and then repeat the process for all of the instances of the first string in the document. Now imagine that you have a program that does it for you automatically: the program would execute a *loop*, which lets it repeat an action a specified number of times. In JavaScript, loops are a vital part of your scripting toolbox.

More about loops

The kind of loop that we mostly use in this book is the **for** loop, named after the command that begins the loop. This sort of loop uses a *counter*, which is a variable that begins with one value (usually 0) and ends when a conditional test inside the loop is satisfied.

The command that starts the loop structure is immediately followed by parentheses. Inside the parentheses you'll usually find the counter definition and the way the counter is incremented (i.e., the way the counter's value is increased).

A This Bingo card has randomly generated numbers, but it isn't a valid Bingo card. Yet.

TABLE 3.1 Just Enough HTML—Tables

Tag	Meaning
table	Presents tabular data on a webpage
tr	Begins a row inside the table
th	Heading cells for the columns in the table
td	Contains each cell in the table

Listing 3.1 This HTML page creates the skeleton for the Bingo card.

```
<!DOCTYPE html>
<html>
<head>
    <title>Make Your Own Bingo Card</title>
    <link rel="stylesheet"
    → href="script01.css">
    <script src="script01.js"></script>
</head>
<body>
<h1>Create A Bingo Card</h1>
<table>
    <tr>
        <th>B</th>
        <th>I</th>
        <th>N</th>
        <th>G</th>
        <th>O</th>
    </tr>
    <tr>
        <td id="square0"> </td>
        <td id="square5"> </td>
        <td id="square10"> </td>
        <td id="square14"> </td>
        <td id="square19"> </td>
    </tr>
    <tr>
        <td id="square1"> </td>
        <td id="square6"> </td>
        <td id="square11"> </td>
        <td id="square15"> </td>
        <td id="square20"> </td>
    </tr>
    <tr>
        <td id="square2"> </td>
        <td id="square7"> </td>
        <td id="free">Free</td>
        <td id="square16"> </td>
        <td id="square21"> </td>
    </tr>
    <tr>
        <td id="square3"> </td>
        <td id="square8"> </td>
        <td id="square12"> </td>
        <td id="square17"> </td>
        <td id="square22"> </td>
    </tr>
    <tr>
        <td id="square4"> </td>
        <td id="square9"> </td>
        <td id="square13"> </td>
        <td id="square18"> </td>
        <td id="square23"> </td>
    </tr>
</table>
<p><a href="script01.html" id="reload">Click
→ here</a> to create a new card</p>
</body>
</html>
```

In the next several examples we're going to build a simple yet familiar application: a Bingo card. We'll use each example to show you a new aspect of JavaScript. We begin with an HTML page, **Listing 3.1**. It contains the table that is the Bingo card's framework Ⓐ. Take a look at the listing, and you'll see that the first row contains the letters at the top of the card, and each subsequent row contains five table cells. Most cells contain just a non-breaking space (using the HTML entity ** **); however, the third row contains the Free space, so one table cell in that row contains the word "Free". Note that each cell has an **id** attribute, which the script uses to manipulate the cell contents. The **id** is in the form of **square0**, **square1**, **square2**, through **square23**, for reasons that we'll explain below. At the bottom of the page, there's a link that generates a new card.

Listing 3.2 is the CSS file that we're using to style the contents of the Bingo card. If you don't know CSS, don't worry about it, as it doesn't matter much here anyway. The HTML and CSS pages won't change for the rest of the Bingo card examples, so we're only going to print them once here.

This example shows you how to set up and use a loop to populate the contents of the Bingo card with randomly generated numbers. **Listing 3.3** contains the JavaScript you need to make it happen. The card that is generated from this script is not a valid Bingo card, because there are constraints on which numbers can be in particular columns. Later examples add to the script until the resulting Bingo card is valid.

What's in a Bingo Card?

Sure, you've seen them, but maybe you haven't looked carefully at a Bingo card lately. Bingo cards in the United States are 5 x 5 squares, with the columns labeled B-I-N-G-O and with spots containing numbers between 1 and 75. The center square typically is a free spot and often has the word "free" printed on it. Each column has a range of allowable numbers:

- Column B contains numbers 1–15
- Column I contains numbers 16–30
- Column N contains numbers 31–45
- Column G contains numbers 46–60
- Column O contains numbers 61–75

Listing 3.2 This CSS file adds style to the Bingo card.

```css
body {
    background-color: white;
    color: black;
    font-size: 20px;
    font-family: "Lucida Grande", Verdana,
    ➝ Arial, Helvetica, sans-serif;
}

h1, th {
    font-family: Georgia, "Times New Roman",
    ➝ Times, serif;
}

h1 {
    font-size: 28px;
}

table {
    border-collapse: collapse;
}

th, td {
    padding: 10px;
    border: 2px #666 solid;
    text-align: center;
    width: 20%;
}

#free, .pickedBG {
    background-color: #f66;
}

.winningBG {
    background-image:
    ➝ url(images/redFlash.gif);
}
```

Listing 3.3 Welcome to your first JavaScript loop.

```javascript
window.onload = initAll;

function initAll() {
    for (var i=0; i<24; i++) {
        var newNum = Math.floor
        ➝ (Math.random() * 75) + 1;

        document.getElementById
        ➝ ("square" + i).innerHTML = newNum;
    }
}
```

Looping the Loop

A **for** loop has three parts **B**:

1. **The initialization step.** The first time through the loop, this is what the loop variable (**i**, in this case) is set to.

2. **The limiting step.** This is where we say when to stop looping. While normal people count from one to ten, it's common in programming languages to count from zero to nine. In both cases, the code inside the loop is run ten times, but the latter method works better with languages (like JavaScript) where arrays start with a zeroth position. That's why you'll see loops have a limitation of "less than **userNum**" instead of "less than or equal to **userNum**." Let's say that the variable **userNum** is 10, and you want the loop to run ten times. If you count from 0 to 9 (using the "less than" test), the loop runs ten times. If you count from 0 to 10 (using the "less than or equals to" test), the loop runs 11 times.

3. **The increment step.** This is where we say by how much to increase the loop counter on each pass through the loop. In this case, we add one each time through, using **++** to add one to **i**'s value.

```
   i=0;  i<userNum;  i++
   ‾‾‾‾  ‾‾‾‾‾‾‾‾‾‾‾  ‾‾‾
Initialization  Limiting  Increment
```

B The three parts of a loop.

To use a loop to create the table's contents:

1. `window.onload = initAll;`

   This is in Listing 3.3. This line calls the **initAll()** function when the window finishes loading. It's common to use an event handler to call a function.

2. `function initAll() {`

   This line begins the function.

3. `for (var i=0; i<24; i++) {`

   This line begins the loop. Programmers traditionally use the variable **i** to denote a variable used as a counter inside a loop. First **i** is set to 0. A semicolon signals the end of that statement and allows us to put another statement on the same line. The next part is read as "if **i** is less than 24, do the following code inside the braces." The final bit (after the second semicolon) adds 1 to the value of **i**. Because this is new, let's break that down a bit. The **i++** part uses the **++** operator you saw in Chapter 1 to increment the value of **i** by 1. The loop will repeat 24 times, and the code inside the loop will execute 24 times. On the first go-through, **i** will be 0, and on the last go-through **i** will be 23.

   continues on next page

4. `var newNum = Math.floor`
`→ (Math.random() * 75) + 1;`

Inside the loop, we create a new variable, **newNum**, and fill it with the result of the calculation on the right side of the equals sign. The built-in JavaScript command **Math.random()** (as shown in **Table 3.2**) gives us a number between 0 and 1, such as 0.12345678. Multiplying **Math.random()** by the maximum value (remember, values in Bingo cards can be from 1 to 75) gives us a result between 0 and one less than the max value. The **floor** of that result gives us the integer portion; i.e., an integer between 0 and (one less than the maximum value). Add one, and we have a number between 1 and our maximum value.

5. `document.getElementById`
`→ ("square" + i).innerHTML =`
`→ newNum;`

This is where we write into the table the value of the random number we just got. We get the element with the **id** named **square** with the current value of **i** concatenated onto it. For example, the first time through the loop, the value of **i** will be zero, so the line gets the element with the **id** of **square0**. Then the line sets the **innerHTML** property of the **square0** object to the current value of **newNum**. Then, because we're still inside the loop, steps 4 and 5 happen again, until the whole Bingo card is filled out.

TABLE 3.2 JavaScript's Math Functionality

Function	Description
abs	Absolute value
sin, cos, tan	Standard trigonometric functions; arguments in radians
acos, asin, atan	Inverse trigonometric functions; return values in radians
exp, log	Exponential and natural logarithm, base e
ceil	Returns least integer greater than or equal to argument
floor	Returns greatest integer less than or equal to argument
min	Returns lesser of two arguments
max	Returns greater of two arguments
pow	Exponential; first argument is base, second is exponent
random	Returns a random number between zero and one
round	Rounds argument to nearest integer
sqrt	Square root

Passing a Value to a Function

You'll often want to take some information and give it to a function to use. This is called *passing* the information to the function. For example, look at this function definition:

```
function playBall(batterup)
```

The variable **batterup** is a *parameter* of the function. When a function is called, a value can be passed into the function. Then, when you're inside the function, that data is in the **batterup** variable. Functions can be passed just about any data you want to use, including text strings, numbers, or even other JavaScript objects. For example, the **batterup** variable could be passed a player's name as a text string (**"Mantle"**) or his number in the lineup (7) (although mixing the two can be a very bad idea unless you really know what you're doing). Like all variables, give the ones you use as function parameters names that remind you what the variable is being used for.

A function can have more than one parameter; just separate them inside the parentheses with commas, like this:

```
function currentScore
→ (hometeam,visitors)
```

so these code fragments are all equivalent:

```
currentScore(6,4);
```

```
var homeScore = 6;
var visitingScore = 4;
currentScore(homeScore,visitingScore);
```

```
currentScore(6,3+1);
```

For all three examples, once we're inside **currentScore()**, the value of **hometeam** is 6, and the value of **visitors** is 4 (which is great news for the home team).

In this example, we'll clean up some of the calculations from Listing 3.3 by taking them out of the **initAll()** function, restating them a bit, and putting them into a function with passed values in order to make it more obvious what's going on. It all happens in **Listing 3.4**.

To pass a value to a function:

1. **setSquare(i);**

   This is inside the **initAll()** function. We're passing the value of **i** into the **setSquare()** function.

2. **function setSquare(thisSquare) {**

   This defines the **setSquare()** function, and it's being passed the current square number that we want to update. When we pass it in, it's the loop variable **i**. When the function receives it, it's the parameter **thisSquare**. What is a little tricky to understand is that this function is passed **i**, and does stuff with that value, but doesn't actually see **i** itself. Inside the function, all it knows about is the **thisSquare** variable.

3. **var currSquare =**
   → "square" + thisSquare;

   In order to make the **getElementById()** call later in the script clearer, we're creating and setting a new variable: **currSquare**. This is the current square that we're working on. It takes the text string **"square"** and concatenates it with the **thisSquare** variable.

4. **document.getElementById**
   → (currSquare).innerHTML = newNum;

   This line gets the element with the name specified by **currSquare** and changes it to display **newNum**.

Listing 3.4 By passing values to the **setSquare()** function, the script becomes easier to read and understand.

```
window.onload = initAll;

function initAll() {
    for (var i=0; i<24; i++) {
        setSquare(i);
    }
}

function setSquare(thisSquare) {
    var currSquare = "square" + thisSquare;
    var newNum = Math.floor
    → (Math.random() * 75) + 1;

    document.getElementById(currSquare).
    → innerHTML = newNum;
}
```

A Object detection rejected this ancient browser (Netscape 4 for Mac) and displayed this error message.

Listing 3.5 Object detection is an important tool for scripters.

```
window.onload = initAll;

function initAll() {
    if (document.getElementById) {
        for (var i=0; i<24; i++) {
            setSquare(i);
        }
    }
    else {
        alert("Sorry, your browser
        → doesn't support this script");
    }
}

function setSquare(thisSquare) {
    var currSquare = "square" + thisSquare;
    var newNum = Math.floor
    → (Math.random() * 75) + 1;

    document.getElementById(currSquare).
    → innerHTML = newNum;
}
```

Detecting Objects

When you're scripting, you may want to check to see if the browser is smart enough to understand the objects you want to use. There is a way to do this check, which is called *object detection*.

What you do is pose a question for the object you're looking for, like this:

if (document.getElementById) {

If the object exists, the **if** statement is **true**, and the script continues on its merry way. But if the browser doesn't understand the object, the test returns **false**, and the **else** portion of the conditional executes. **Listing 3.5** gives you the JavaScript you need, and you can see the result in an obsolete browser **A**.

To detect an object:

1. **if (document.getElementById) {**

   This line begins the conditional. If the object inside the parentheses exists, the test returns **true**, and the rest of this block in the **initAll()** function runs.

2. **else {**
   alert("Sorry, your browser
   → doesn't support this script");
   }

   If the test in step 1 returns **false**, this line pops up an alert, and the script ends.

   In a production environment, it's better to give users something else to do, or at least some version of the page that doesn't require this capability. Here, though, there's nothing to be done.

TIP It's important to understand that you won't always check for `document.getElementById`. What objects you check for depends on what objects your script uses. If your scripts use objects with less than 100% support, always check first if the browser can handle it—never assume that it can. We aren't showing object detection throughout this book to save space, but in the real world, it's vital.

Washed-Up Detectives

An alternate way to try to figure which objects a browser supports is to do a *browser detect*, which tries to identify the browser being used to view the page. It gets this by requesting the user agent string from the browser, which reports the browser name and version. The idea is that you would then write your scripts to work one way with particular browsers and another way for other browsers. This is an obsolete approach to scripting because it doesn't work well.

Browser detection relies on you knowing that a particular browser supports the script you're writing, and another browser doesn't. But what about obscure browsers that you've never used? Or browsers that are released after your script is done?

Worse, many browsers try to get around browser detection by intentionally misrepresenting themselves. For example, Apple's Safari browser claims that it is a Mozilla browser, even though it is not. And most browsers, such as Safari, Chrome, and Opera, allow some way for you to set which browser you want it to report itself as.

There's just no way that you can retrofit your script fast enough to keep up with all of the possible browser permutations. It's a losing game.

The same goes for attempting to detect which version of JavaScript a browser supports. We strongly suggest that you do not use these detection methods, and that you use object detection instead.

Working with Arrays

A This Bingo card is improved, but not quite right yet, because there are duplicate numbers in some of the columns.

Listing 3.6 This script limits the range of values that can go into each column.

```
window.onload = initAll;

function initAll() {
    if (document.getElementById) {
        for (var i=0; i<24; i++) {
            setSquare(i);
        }
    }
    else {
        alert("Sorry, your browser
        → doesn't support this script");
    }
}

function setSquare(thisSquare) {
    var currSquare = "square" + thisSquare;
    var colPlace = new Array(0,0,0,0,0,1,1,
    → 1,1,1,2,2,2,2,2,3,3,3,3,3,4,4,4,4,4);
    var colBasis = colPlace[thisSquare] * 15;
    var newNum = colBasis + Math.floor
    → (Math.random() * 15) + 1;

    document.getElementById(currSquare).
    → innerHTML = newNum;
}
```

In this example, we're introducing another useful JavaScript object, the *array*. An array is a kind of variable that can store a group of information. Like variables, arrays can contain any sort of data: text strings, numbers, other JavaScript objects, whatever. You declare an array with the elements of the array inside parentheses, separated by commas, like so:

`var newCars = new Array("Toyota",`
`→ "Honda", "Nissan");`

After this, the **newCars** array contains the three text strings with the car makes. To access the contents of the array, you use the variable name with the *index number* of the array member you want to use in square brackets. So **newCars[2]** has the value **"Nissan"**, because array numbering, like most other numbering in JavaScript, begins at zero. Notice in the example above we're using text strings as elements of the array. Each text string needs to be contained within straight quotes, and the commas that separate each element of the array go outside of the quotes.

In this example, shown in **Listing 3.6**, we begin making sure the Bingo card is valid. On a real Bingo card, each column has a different range of numbers: B is 1–15, I is 16–30, N is 31–45, G is 46–60, and O is 61–75. If you look back at **A** in "More about loops," you'll see that it is not a valid card, because it was generated with a version of the script that simply put a random number between 1 and 75 in each square. This example fixes that with only three lines of changed or new code. When we're done it's still not a valid Bingo card (note how there are duplicate numbers in some of the columns), but we're getting there **A**.

To use an array:

1. ```
   var colPlace = new Array
       (0,0,0,0,0,1,1,1,1,1,2,2,2,2,
       3,3,3,3,3,4,4,4,4,4);
   ```

   We're concerned with limiting which random numbers go into which columns. The simplest way to keep track of this is to give each column a number (B: 0, I: 1, N: 2, G: 3, O: 4) and then calculate the numbers that can go into each column as (the column number × 15) + (a random number from 1–15).

   For each square, the **colPlace** array keeps track of which column it's in. It's the numbers 0–4 repeated five times (minus the Free space; notice that the digit 2 representing the N column is only used four times).

2. ```
   var colBasis =
       colPlace[thisSquare] * 15;
   var newNum = colBasis + Math.
       floor(Math.random() * 15) + 1;
   ```

   We start off by calculating the column basis: the number stored in **colPlace[thisSquare]** multiplied by 15. The **newNum** variable still generates the random numbers, but instead of coming up with a number from 1–75, it now calculates a random number from 1–15, and then adds that to the column basis. So, if our random number is 7, it would be 7 in the B column, 22 in the I column, 37 in the N column, 52 in the G column, and 67 in the O column.

Listing 3.7 A function can return a value, which can then be checked.

```
window.onload = initAll;

function initAll() {
    if (document.getElementById) {
        for (var i=0; i<24; i++) {
            setSquare(i);
        }
    }
    else {
        alert("Sorry, your browser
        → doesn't support this script");
    }
}

function setSquare(thisSquare) {
    var currSquare = "square" + thisSquare;
    var colPlace = new Array(0,0,0,0,0,1,1,
    → 1,1,1,2,2,2,2,2,3,3,3,3,3,4,4,4,4,4);
    var colBasis = colPlace[thisSquare] * 15;
    var newNum = colBasis + getNewNum() + 1;

    document.getElementById(currSquare).
    → innerHTML = newNum;
}

function getNewNum() {
    return Math.floor(Math.random() * 15);
}
```

Working with Functions That Return Values

Up to this point, all the functions that you've seen simply do something and then return. Sometimes, though, you want to return a result of some kind. **Listing 3.7** makes the overall script more understandable by breaking out some of the calculations in previous examples into a function which returns the random numbers for the cells on the Bingo card. Another function then uses this result.

To return a value from a function:

1. `var newNum = colBasis +`
   `→ getNewNum() + 1;`

   This line is again just setting the **newNum** variable to our desired number, but here we've moved that random number generator into a function, called **getNewNum()**. By breaking the calculation up, it makes it easier to understand what's going on in the script.

2. `function getNewNum() {`
   `   return Math.floor`
   `   → (Math.random() * 15);`
   `}`

   This code calculates a random number between 0 and 14 and returns it. This function can be used anywhere a variable or a number can be used.

> **TIP** Any value can be returned. Strings, Booleans, and numbers work just fine.

Updating Arrays

As you saw in Ⓐ in "Working with Arrays," the Bingo card script doesn't yet have a way to make sure that duplicate numbers don't appear in a given column. This example fixes that problem, while simultaneously demonstrating that arrays don't have to be just initialized and then read—instead, they can be declared and then set on the fly. This gives you a great deal of flexibility, since you can use calculations or functions to change the values in the array while the script is running. **Listing 3.8** shows you how, with only a few new lines of code.

Listing 3.8 Changing the contents of arrays to store the current situation is a very powerful technique.

```
window.onload = initAll;
var usedNums = new Array(76);

function initAll() {
    if (document.getElementById) {
        for (var i=0; i<24; i++) {
            setSquare(i);
        }
    }
    else {
        alert("Sorry, your browser
        → doesn't support this script");
    }
}

function setSquare(thisSquare) {
    var currSquare = "square" + thisSquare;
    var colPlace = new Array(0,0,0,0,0,1,1,
    → 1,1,1,2,2,2,2,2,3,3,3,3,3,4,4,4,4,4);
    var colBasis = colPlace[thisSquare] * 15;
    var newNum = colBasis + getNewNum() + 1;

    if (!usedNums[newNum]) {
        usedNums[newNum] = true;
        document.getElementById(currSquare).
        → innerHTML = newNum;
    }
}

function getNewNum() {
    return Math.floor(Math.random() * 15);
}
```

Create A Bingo Card

B	I	N	G	O
3	29	34	55	74
5	27	41	54	65
13		Free	58	62
	20	45	53	
8		38	56	64

Click here to create a new card

Ⓐ We've gotten rid of the duplicate numbers, but some of the spaces are now blank. Time to go back to the drawing board.

To update an array on the fly:

1. `var usedNums = new Array(76);`

   Here is a new way of declaring an array. We're creating **usedNums**, a new array with 76 objects. As mentioned before, those objects can be *anything*. In this case, they're going to be Booleans; that is, true/false values.

2. `if (!usedNums[newNum]) {`
   `    usedNums[newNum] = true;`

   If the **newNum** slot in the **usedNums** array is false (represented by the ! before the statement, meaning "not"), then we set it to true and write it out to the card. If it's true, we don't do anything at all, leaving us with no duplicates, but possibly blank spaces on our card Ⓐ. That's not good either, which leads us to the next task.

TIP Why is the array defined as containing 76 items? Because we want to use the values 1 to 75. If we initialized it to contain 75 items, the numbering would go from 0 to 74. 76 lets us use 1 through 75, and we'll just ignore item 0.

TIP If you don't do anything to initialize Booleans, they'll automatically be false.

Using Do/While Loops

Sometimes you'll need to have a loop in your code that loops around a number of times, but there's no way of knowing in advance how many times you'll want to loop. That's when you'll want to use a **do/while** loop: you want to **do** something, **while** some value is true. **Listing 3.9** writes out each row of numbers as always, but this time it checks first to see if a number has been used already before putting it in a cell. If it has, the script generates a new random number and repeats the process until it finds one that's unique. **Ⓐ** shows the working, finally valid Bingo card.

Create A Bingo Card

B	I	N	G	O
15	16	43	46	63
5	23	36	48	66
8	20	Free	49	67
6	26	42	60	74
12	28	44	57	72

Click here to create a new card

Ⓐ Finally, we've ended up with a valid Bingo card!

Listing 3.9 This script prevents numbers in a given column from being used more than once.

```
window.onload = initAll;
var usedNums = new Array(76);

function initAll() {
    if (document.getElementById) {
        for (var i=0; i<24; i++) {
            setSquare(i);
        }
    }
    else {
        alert("Sorry, your browser
         → doesn't support this script");
    }
}

function setSquare(thisSquare) {
    var currSquare = "square" + thisSquare;
    var colPlace = new Array(0,0,0,0,0,1,1,
     → 1,1,1,2,2,2,2,3,3,3,3,4,4,4,4);
    var colBasis = colPlace[thisSquare] * 15;
    var newNum;

    do {
        newNum = colBasis + getNewNum() + 1;
    }
    while (usedNums[newNum]);

    usedNums[newNum] = true;
    document.getElementById(currSquare).
     → innerHTML = newNum;
}

function getNewNum() {
    return Math.floor(Math.random() * 15);
}
```

To use a do/while loop:

1. `var newNum;`

   In the previous task, we initialized the **newNum** variable when we created it. Because we're going to be setting it multiple times, we're instead going to create it just the once, before we get into the loop.

2. `do {`

   This line starts the **do** block of code. One of the things you have to remember about this type of loop is that the code inside the **do** block will always be executed at least once.

3. `newNum = colBasis +`
   `→ getNewNum() + 1;`

   This line inside the loop sets the **newNum** variable to our desired number, as in previous examples.

4. `}`

   The closing brace signals the end of the **do** block.

5. `while (usedNums[newNum]);`

   The **while** check causes the **do** block of code to repeat until the check evaluates to **false**. In this case, we're checking **newNum** against the **usedNums[]** array, to see if **newNum** has already been used. If it has, control is passed back to the top of the **do** block and the whole process starts again. Eventually, we'll find a number that hasn't been used. When we do, we drop out of the loop, set the **usedNums[]** item to true, and write it out to the card, as in the last task.

> **TIP** A common use for a do/while loop would be to strip blanks or invalid characters off data entered by a user. But again, remember that the do block of code always gets executed at least once, whether the while check evaluates to true or false.

Calling Scripts Multiple Ways

Up to this point in the book, you've seen scripts that usually run automatically when the page loads. But in the real world, you'll often want to give the user more control over your scripts, even allowing them to run a script whenever they want. In this example (**Listing 3.10**), the script still runs when the page loads. But we also allow the user to click the link at the bottom of the page to rerun the script that generates the Bingo card entirely in their browser, *without* needing to reload the page from the server. This gives the user fast response with zero server load.

To call a script multiple ways:

1. ```
   document.getElementById("reload").
   → onclick = anotherCard;
   newCard();
   ```

   The **initAll()** function we've seen before has one change and one addition. All it does that's new is set the link on the HTML page (the one with the **id** of **reload**; refer back to Listing 3.1) to call the **anotherCard()** function when it's clicked. All the calculations that used to be in this function have now been moved to our new **newCard()** function—and that's all that's done there, so there's nothing new in that function for us to look at.

Listing 3.10 Give your user the ability to run scripts themselves.

```
window.onload = initAll;
var usedNums = new Array(76);

function initAll() {
    if (document.getElementById) {
        document.getElementById("reload").
        → onclick = anotherCard;
        newCard();
    }
    else {
        alert("Sorry, your browser
        → doesn't support this script");
    }
}

function newCard() {
    for (var i=0; i<24; i++) {
        setSquare(i);
    }
}

function setSquare(thisSquare) {
    var currSquare = "square" + thisSquare;
    var colPlace = new Array(0,0,0,0,0,1,1,
    → 1,1,1,2,2,2,2,3,3,3,3,3,4,4,4,4,4);
    var colBasis = colPlace[thisSquare] * 15;
    var newNum;

    do {
        newNum = colBasis + getNewNum() + 1;
    }
    while (usedNums[newNum]);

    usedNums[newNum] = true;
    document.getElementById(currSquare).
    → innerHTML = newNum;
}

function getNewNum() {
    return Math.floor(Math.random() * 15);
}

function anotherCard() {
    for (var i=1; i<usedNums.length; i++) {
        usedNums[i] = false;
    }

    newCard();
    return false;
}
```
```

2.
```
function anotherCard() {
    for (var i=1; i<usedNums.
    → length; i++) {
        usedNums[i] = false;
    }

    newCard();
    return false;
}
```

Here's the **anotherCard()** function that's called when someone clicks the link. It does three things:

▸ Sets all the items in the **usedNums[]** array to false (so that we can reuse all the numbers again)

▸ Calls the **newCard()** function (generating another card)

▸ Returns a value of false so that the browser won't try to load the page in the **href** in the link (we covered this in Chapter 2)

TIP If you've gotten this far, you now know how to do something that many people consider to be a fundamental part of Ajax—using JavaScript to reload a part of a page instead of hitting the server and requesting an entirely new page. We'll be going into Ajax in much more detail in Chapters 13 and up.

Combining JavaScript and CSS

If you've been following along this far with the Bingo example, you may well be wondering, "Hey, they said that JavaScript was all about the interactivity—why haven't we seen any user interaction?" That's a reasonable question, and here we show how to now let the user actually play that Bingo card you generated. To do that, **Listing 3.11** uses some JavaScript to leverage the power of CSS.

To apply a style using JavaScript:

1. ```
   document.getElementById
   → (currSquare).className = "";
   document.getElementById
   → (currSquare).onmousedown =
   → toggleColor;
   ```

   Because our Bingo card can be used and reused, we're going to make sure that we start off with a clean slate: for every square that's set in **setSquare()**, we're going to set the class attribute to **""** (the empty string), and the **onmousedown** event handler to call the new **toggleColor()** function.

2. ```
   function toggleColor(evt) {
   ```

   If you're a CSS wiz, you may have noticed back in Listing 3.2 that we declared styles that we've never used. Now, inside the new **toggleColor()** function we're going to change that. The user can now click any of the squares on the card, and that square's background will change color to show that that number was called.

Listing 3.11 Adding a class via JavaScript allows our code to leverage the power of CSS.

```
window.onload = initAll;
var usedNums = new Array(76);

function initAll() {
    if (document.getElementById) {
        document.getElementById("reload").
        → onclick = anotherCard;
        newCard();
    }
    else {
        alert("Sorry, your browser
        → doesn't support this script");
    }
}

function newCard() {
    for (var i=0; i<24; i++) {
        setSquare(i);
    }
}

function setSquare(thisSquare) {
    var currSquare = "square" + thisSquare;
    var colPlace = new Array(0,0,0,0,0,1,1,
    → 1,1,1,2,2,2,2,3,3,3,3,3,4,4,4,4,4);
    var colBasis = colPlace[thisSquare] * 15;
    var newNum;

    do {
        newNum = colBasis + getNewNum() + 1;
    }
    while (usedNums[newNum]);

    usedNums[newNum] = true;
    document.getElementById(currSquare).
    → innerHTML = newNum;
    document.getElementById(currSquare).
    → className = "";
    document.getElementById(currSquare).
    → onmousedown = toggleColor;
}

function getNewNum() {
    return Math.floor(Math.random() * 15);
}
```

listing continues on next page

Listing 3.11 *continued*

```
function anotherCard() {
    for (var i=1; i<usedNums.length; i++) {
        usedNums[i] = false;
    }

    newCard();
    return false;
}

function toggleColor(evt) {
    if (evt) {
        var thisSquare = evt.target;
    }
    else {
        var thisSquare = window.event.
        → srcElement;
    }
    if (thisSquare.className == "") {
        thisSquare.className = "pickedBG";
    }
    else {
        thisSquare.className = "";
    }
}
```

3. ```
if (evt) {
    var thisSquare = evt.target;
}
else {
    var thisSquare = window.event.
    → srcElement;
}
```

First off, we need to figure out which square was clicked. Unfortunately, there are two ways to do this: the Internet Explorer way, and the way every other browser handles events.

If a value called **evt** was passed into this function, we know we're in a non-IE browser, and we can look at its target. If we're in IE, we instead need to look at the **event** property of the **window** object, and then at its **srcElement** property. Either way, we end up with the **thisSquare** object, which we can then examine and modify.

4. ```
if (thisSquare.className == "") {
    thisSquare.className =
    → "pickedBG";
}
else {
    thisSquare.className = "";
}
```

Here, we check to see if the class attribute of the clicked square has a value. If it doesn't, we want to give it one: **pickedBG**, named because the background of the square shows that the number has been picked.

Now normally, just changing a **class** attribute wouldn't actually change anything visually on the page—but remember the CSS back in Listing 3.2? Any tag with a class of **pickedBG** gets the same background color as the Free square.

continues on next page

Changing the class here automatically makes that style apply to this square, causing it to also have a pink background 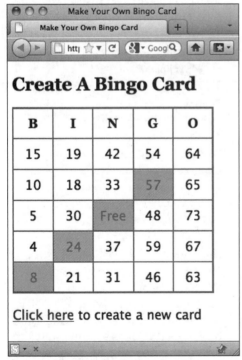.

Of course, squares can be picked accidentally, and we need to make sure there's a way to reset the value. Click the square again, and this time around, `className` has a value, so we toggle it to once again be the empty string.

Instead of changing the `class` attribute on the square, we could instead change its `style` attribute, and then we wouldn't have to worry about the CSS file. That's the wrong approach, though—because we're leveraging the CSS file, it's simple to change the page's visual appearance without having to touch its behavior.

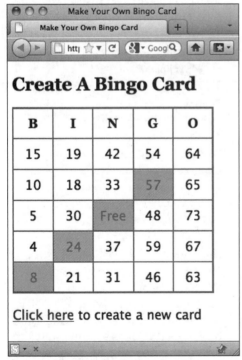

A Being able to mark squares when numbers are called lets the user interact with the card.

A Bit About Bits

Whenever you use a Boolean, you're dealing with a value that's either **true** or **false**. Another way to think about these variables is as containing either zero or one, which is how computers handle everything internally (**true** being **1** and **false** being **0**).

Those values—**0** and **1**—are called *bits*. They're single *bits* of information that the computer keeps track of. If it helps, you can instead think of each bit as a light switch that's either on or off.

Because everything on a computer is just a whole bunch of bits, you need to be able to do things with those bits. And in particular, you need to be able to compare them to each other. Here's some of what's going on inside:

- **and (&)**

  When we **and** two bits together, if they're both true (that is, both 1), the result is true. Otherwise, the result is false.

- **or (|)**

  When we **or** two bits together, if either is true (that is, either is 1), then the result is true. If they're both false, the result is false.

When you use **and** and **or** on numbers greater than one, it's referred to as *bitwise arithmetic*. Internally, your computer converts each number to its binary value and then compares the bits against each other. Because it's done internally, you don't have to do the conversion yourself (whew!).

Listing 3.12 Complex math makes this script simple: a winning combination.

```
window.onload = initAll;
var usedNums = new Array(76);

function initAll() {
    if (document.getElementById) {
        document.getElementById("reload").
        → onclick = anotherCard;
        newCard();
    }
    else {
        alert("Sorry, your browser
        → doesn't support this script");
    }
}

function newCard() {
    for (var i=0; i<24; i++) {
        setSquare(i);
    }
}

function setSquare(thisSquare) {
    var currSquare = "square" + thisSquare;
    var colPlace = new Array(0,0,0,0,0,1,1,
    → 1,1,1,2,2,2,2,3,3,3,3,3,4,4,4,4,4);
    var colBasis = colPlace[thisSquare] * 15;
    var newNum;

    do {
        newNum = colBasis + getNewNum() + 1;
    }
    while (usedNums[newNum]);

    usedNums[newNum] = true;
    document.getElementById(currSquare).
    → innerHTML = newNum;
    document.getElementById(currSquare).
    → className = "";
    document.getElementById(currSquare).
    → onmousedown = toggleColor;
}

function getNewNum() {
    return Math.floor(Math.random() * 15);
}
```

listing continues on next page

Checking State

Along with interaction to let the user set a square, we can also check to see if the squares form a winning pattern. In this penultimate example, the user checks off which numbers have been called, and then **Listing 3.12** lets the user know when they've won.

There's some powerful math going on in this example; if you've never had to deal with binary before, you'll want to read the sidebar "A Bit About Bits." And if you want to get into the details, check out the sidebar "Getting Wise About Bits" (but you can skip that one if you feel your eyes glazing over!).

To check for the winning state:

1. `checkWin();`

   Any time the user toggles a square, it's possible that the winning status has changed, so here's a call to **checkWin()** at the end of **toggleColor()**.

2. `var winningOption = -1;`
   `var setSquares = 0;`
   `var winners = new Array(31, 992,`
   `→ 15360, 507904, 541729, 557328,`
   `→ 1083458, 2162820, 4329736,`
   `→ 8519745, 8659472, 16252928);`

   Three new variables are created at the beginning of **checkWin()**:

   ▸ **winningOption**, which stores which of the possible winning options the user has hit (if any),

   ▸ **setSquares**, which stores which squares have been clicked, and

   ▸ **winners**, an array of numbers, each of which is the encoded value of a possible winning line.

continues on next page

3.
```
for (var i=0; i<24; i++) {
    var currSquare = "square" + i;
    if (document.getElementById
    ⇢ (currSquare).className
    ⇢ != "") {
```

For each square on the card, we need to check to see whether or not its number has already been called. We'll use the square's **class** attribute as a flag—if it's empty, then it hasn't been clicked. If there is a **class** attribute, do the following lines.

4.
```
document.
getElementById(currSquare).
⇢ className = "pickedBG";
setSquares = setSquares |
⇢ Math.pow(2,i);
```

The first line here is straightforward, and in fact, should be redundant—the **class** attribute should already be set to **pickedBG**. However, there's a chance it might not be, such as when someone clicks a square they didn't mean to click, gets a win (resetting the attribute to **winningBG** instead of **pickedBG**), and then clicks it again to turn it off. If it actually is a winner, that'll be reset later.

The second line uses *bitwise* arithmetic to set **setSquares** to a number based on each possible state of the card. The single bar (|) does a bitwise **or** of two values: **setSquares** itself and the number 2^i, which is the result of **Math.pow(2,i)**. That is, 2^0 is 1, 2^1 is 2, 2^2 is 4, and so on. **Or**'ing each of these numbers together results in a unique variable storing which of the 16-some million possible states we're in.

Listing 3.12 *continued*

```
function anotherCard() {
    for (var i=1; i<usedNums.length; i++) {
        usedNums[i] = false;
    }

    newCard();
    return false;
}

function toggleColor(evt) {
    if (evt) {
        var thisSquare = evt.target;
    }
    else {
        var thisSquare = window.event.
        ⇢ srcElement;
    }
    if (thisSquare.className == "") {
        thisSquare.className = "pickedBG";
    }
    else {
        thisSquare.className = "";
    }
    checkWin();
}

function checkWin() {
    var winningOption = -1;
    var setSquares = 0;
    var winners = new Array(31,992,15360,
    ⇢ 507904,541729,557328,1083458,2162820,
    ⇢ 4329736,8519745,8659472,16252928);

    for (var i=0; i<24; i++) {
        var currSquare = "square" + i;
        if (document.getElementById
        ⇢ (currSquare).className != "") {
            document.getElementById
            ⇢ (currSquare).className =
            ⇢ "pickedBG";
            setSquares = setSquares |
            ⇢ Math.pow(2,i);
        }
    }
```

listing continues on next page

Listing 3.12 *continued*

```
    for (var i=0; i<winners.length; i++) {
        if ((winners[i] & setSquares) ==
        → winners[i]) {
            winningOption = i;
        }
    }

    if (winningOption > -1) {
        for (var i=0; i<24; i++) {
            if (winners[winningOption] &
            → Math.pow(2,i)) {
                currSquare = "square" + i;
                document.getElementById
                → (currSquare).className =
                → "winningBG";
            }
        }
    }
}
```

5. ```
   for (var i=0; i<winners.length;
   → i++) {
       if ((winners[i] & setSquares) ==
       → winners[i]) {
           winningOption = i;
       }
   }
   ```

Here's the second complex section: now that we know just what state the card is currently in, we want to know if it's a winning state. In a common Bingo game, there are 12 winning states, and this section compares our card's current state to each. We do a bitwise **and** between each winning state and the current state, which results in a new state that only has true values for each square that is in both of the two. Comparing that back to the same winning state allows us to see if we've fully hit this pattern—that is, the result will have no hits outside the winning state (as they aren't found in the winning state) and so long as everything found in the winning pattern is also in the current pattern, we've got ourselves a winner. In that case, set **winningOption** to **i**, the pattern we matched.

continues on next page
   ```

6.
```
if (winningOption > -1) {
    for (var i=0; i<24; i++) {
        if (winners[winningOption] &
        ↪ Math.pow(2,i)) {
            currSquare = "square" + i;
            document.getElementById
            ↪ (currSquare).className =
            ↪ "winningBG";
        }
    }
}
```

Finally, if **winningOption** is a number greater than −1, we know we've got a winner. In that case, we want to loop through each square and check to see if it's found in the winning pattern. If it is, we set the **class** attribute to **winningBG**, and we're done .

A Looks like we've got a winner! (In print, you can't see the pulsing colors.)

TIP Again, just setting the **class** attribute of the winning squares to match a particular **CSS** style is enough to change the card's appearance. Because this is paper, though, you can't see how it truly looks: the **winningBG** rule sets the background to an animated gif which slowly flashes between red and white. A friend of ours described it as "delightfully obnoxious."

TIP There are a number of different Bingo games, each with different winning patterns. By modifying the single line of code that initializes the **winners** array, your script can fit any result someone might want.

TIP If you've ever wondered why conditionals use **&&** and **||** (for *and* and *or*, respectively), now you know: the single version of those operators tells JavaScript that you're doing binary math, not decimal math.

Getting Wise About Bits

(As we said above, this is the sidebar for geeks, so please be advised to p
beanie *and* pocket protector before continuing. If you don't already own t
feel free to just skip this section.)

Given that there are (at least in this version of Bingo) only 12 possible winni
easily write code that would check for each of those. Because of the many
though, that would mean that any time you wanted to play a different versi
the entire way the script checks for wins.

Instead, we're using what's called bitwise arithmetic (see the sidebar "A Bit About Bits") to store
the winning patterns. That means that we're taking advantage of the way computers internally
keep track of everything as 1s and 0s. So, we create the programming equivalent of making a list:

0	✔	1
1		2
2		4
3		8
4		16
5	✔	32
6		64
7		128
8		256
9		512
10	✔	1024
11		2048
12		4096
13		8192
14	✔	16384
15		32768
16		65536
17		131072
18		262144
19	✔	524288
20		1048576
21		2097152
22		4194304
23		8388608

If you compare the numbers in the left-hand column next to the checked boxes, you'll see that
we've picked the top row of the card: **square0**, **square5**, **square10**, **square14**, and **square19**.
The right-hand column is 2 to the power of the left-hand number.

To figure out the numeric equivalent of a winning pattern, we just add up the right-hand numbers
that are part of the pattern. In this case, that's 1+32+1024+16384+524288, or 541729—which you'll
see is included in the list of winners.

continues on next page

...o calculate what you get with a vertical line in the B column, you add up 1+2+4+8+16, for a result of 31. That's another winner. And so on, for each possible winning pattern.

Here's the secret: if you flip that chart on its side so that it goes from 23 to 0, replace the check marks with 1s and the blanks with 0s, you'll have a 24-digit binary number. So, you could (if you wanted to) think of our first winning pattern as **000010000100010000100001** and our second as **000000000000000000011111**—although why you'd want to, we have no idea. But take our word for it: the first is the binary representation of 541729, and the latter of 31.

When we go through each square and check to see if it's set, we store the result in **setSquares**. That value is the sum of all the squares the player has selected, which, again, you could think of as a line of 24 ones and zeros if you prefer.

We get **setSquares** by **or**'ing all those values together. When a zero and a zero are **or**'ed together (using a single bar |), the result is a zero. Any other combination and the result is a one.

Let's say that our end result in **setSquares** is 561424—that means that the player set squares 4, 8, 12, 15, and 19, for a binary value of **000010001001000100010000**. Now, 561424 isn't on our list of winners. But when we **and** the number above with 557328 (which is a winner), we get:

000010001001000100010000 and
000010001000000100010000

000010001000000100010000

When a one and a one are **and**'ed together (using a single ampersand, **&**), the result is a one. Any other combination and the result is a zero.

Looking at the code, we then compare the resulting value back to the winning value, and if they're the same (as they are in this case), we've got a winner; here, it's the diagonal going from the bottom left to the top right.

If you're now wondering if this is really easier than calculating everything out manually, think about it this way: in order to play a round where getting all four corners also counts as a win, all you have to do is add the number 8912913 to the array of winners—and everything else just works (that's squares 0, 4, 19, and 23, by the way).

Listing 3.13 A private game of Buzzword Bingo will
liven up that next deadly dull staff meeting—just
add your own text strings.

```
var buzzwords = new Array ("Aggregate",
    "Ajax",
    "API",
    "Bandwidth",
    "Beta",
    "Bleeding edge",
    "Convergence",
    "Design pattern",
    "Disruptive",
    "DRM",
    "Enterprise",
    "Facilitate",
    "Folksonomy",
    "Framework",
    "Impact",
    "Innovate",
    "Long tail",
    "Mashup",
    "Microformats",
    "Mobile",
    "Monetize",
    "Open social",
    "Paradigm",
    "Podcast",
    "Proactive",
    "Rails",
    "Scalable",
    "Social bookmarks",
    "Social graph",
    "Social software",
    "Spam",
    "Synergy",
    "Tagging",
    "Tipping point",
    "Truthiness",
    "User-generated",
    "Vlog",
    "Webinar",
    "Wiki",
    "Workflow"
);

var usedWords = new Array(buzzwords.length);
window.onload = initAll;
```

listing continues on next page

Working with String Arrays

Up to this point, all the arrays we've dealt
with have consisted of Booleans or numbers. As our final Bingo-related example,
Listing 3.13 combines everything we've
done previously with a string array to create the popular "Buzzword Bingo" game.

Listing 3.13 *continued*

```
function initAll() {
    if (document.getElementById) {
        document.getElementById("reload").onclick = anotherCard;
        newCard();
    }
    else {
        alert("Sorry, your browser doesn't support this script");
    }
}

function newCard() {
    for (var i=0; i<24; i++) {
        setSquare(i);
    }
}

function setSquare(thisSquare) {
    do {
        var randomWord = Math.floor(Math.random() * buzzwords.length);
    }
    while (usedWords[randomWord]);

    usedWords[randomWord] = true;
    var currSquare = "square" + thisSquare;
    document.getElementById(currSquare).innerHTML = buzzwords[randomWord];
    document.getElementById(currSquare).className = "";
    document.getElementById(currSquare).onmousedown = toggleColor;
}

function anotherCard() {
    for (var i=0; i<buzzwords.length; i++) {
        usedWords[i] = false;
    }

    newCard();
    return false;
}

function toggleColor(evt) {
    if (evt) {
        var thisSquare = evt.target;
    }
    else {
        var thisSquare = window.event.srcElement;
    }
    if (thisSquare.className == "") {
        thisSquare.className = "pickedBG";
    }
```

listing continues on next page

Listing 3.13 *continued*

```
        else {
            thisSquare.className = "";
        }
        checkWin();
}

function checkWin() {
    var winningOption = -1;
    var setSquares = 0;
    var winners = new Array(31,992,15360,
    → 507904,541729,557328,1083458,2162820,
    → 4329736,8519745,8659472,16252928);

    for (var i=0; i<24; i++) {
        var currSquare = "square" + i;
        if (document.getElementById
        → (currSquare).className != "") {
            document.getElementById
            → (currSquare).className =
            → "pickedBG";
            setSquares = setSquares |
            → Math.pow(2,i);
        }
    }

    for (var i=0; i<winners.length; i++) {
        if ((winners[i] & setSquares) ==
        → winners[i]) {
            winningOption = i;
        }
    }

    if (winningOption > -1) {
        for (var i=0; i<24; i++) {
            if (winners[winningOption] &
            → Math.pow(2,i)) {
                currSquare = "square" + i;
                document.getElementById
                → (currSquare).className =
                → "winningBG";
            }
        }
    }
}
```

To use string arrays:

1. ```
var buzzwords = new Array
→ ("Aggregate", "Ajax", "API",
→ "Bandwidth", "Beta",
→ "Bleeding edge", "Convergence",
→ "Design pattern", "Disruptive",
→ "DRM", "Enterprise",
→ "Facilitate", "Folksonomy",
→ "Framework", "Impact",
→ "Innovate", "Long tail",
→ "Mashup", "Microformats",
→ "Mobile", "Monetize",
→ "Open social", "Paradigm",
→ "Podcast", "Proactive", "Rails",
→ "Scalable", "Social bookmarks",
→ "Social graph",
→ "Social software", "Spam",
→ "Synergy", "Tagging",
→ "Tipping point", "Truthiness",
→ "User-generated", "Vlog",
→ "Webinar", "Wiki", "Workflow");
```

```
var usedWords = new Array
→ (buzzwords.length);
```

This game of Buzzword Bingo has a "Web 2.0" theme, but you can put strings based around any topic inside the **buzzwords** array. You'll need to have at least 24 entries (more is better), and you won't want them to be too lengthy (or they won't fit in the squares), but other than those restrictions, the only limit is your imagination.

Along with initializing the string array, we also need to initialize the new **usedWords** array of Booleans. Giving it a size of **buzzwords.length** means that nothing needs to change when we add new entries—it will automatically be the right length.

continues on next page
```

2.
```
   do {
      var randomWord = Math.floor
      → (Math.random() * buzzwords.
      → length);
   }
   while (usedWords[randomWord]);

   usedWords[randomWord] = true;
   var currSquare = "square" +
   → thisSquare;
   document.getElementById
   → (currSquare).innerHTML =
   → buzzwords[randomWord];
```

Figuring out what strings to put in what squares is actually simpler, as any string can go in any square (unlike the number restrictions in standard Bingo). All we're doing here is making sure that we're getting an as-yet-unused word, marking it as used, and then writing it into the square.

3.
```
   for (var i=0; i<buzzwords.length;
   → i++) {
      usedWords[i] = false;
   }
```

When a new card is generated, just like with the standard Bingo card, we have to set all the flags in **usedWords** back to false so they're once again available.

A With a mobile browser and a little imagination, you can write a Bingo game of your own for almost any occasion.

TIP When Apple still attended the annual Macworld Expo in San Francisco, it was traditional for Steve Jobs to give the opening keynote—which was, therefore, referred to as the "SteveNote." Also somewhat traditional was audience members playing "SteveNote Bingo," seeing which of Steve's pet phrases (such as "Boom!" and "One more thing...") were said and which of the rumored products actually appeared.

Because the iPhone comes with the standard Safari browser, I was able to easily come up with an interactive version of this game **A** for the Macworld following the iPhone's introduction. It was very well received, although no one actually yelled out "Bingo!" during the keynote. I've also adapted this same Bingo example for other breaking news events, such as televised US political debates.

4

Working with Images

One of the best (and most common) uses of JavaScript is to add visual interest to webpages by animating graphics, and that's what this chapter is all about. Making an image on a webpage change when the user moves the mouse over the image, thereby making the page react to the user, is one of the most common—and effective—tricks you can learn in JavaScript. This *rollover*, as it is called, is easy to implement yet has many applications, as you'll see.

Rollovers are a great tool, but you can do much more than rollovers with JavaScript, such as automatically change images, create ad banners, build slideshows, and display random images on a page.

In this chapter, you'll learn how to make JavaScript do all of these image tricks. Let's get started.

In This Chapter

TABLE 4.1 Just Enough HTML—Images

Tag	Attribute	Meaning
`img`		Contains the attributes that describe the image to be displayed by the browser
	`src`	Contains the URL of the image, relative to the URL of the webpage
	`width`	Contains the width (in pixels) at which the browser will display the image
	`height`	Contains the height (in pixels) at which the browser will display the image
	`alt`	Used for non-visual browsers in place of the image

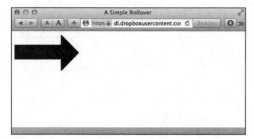

A The first image, before the user moves the mouse over it.

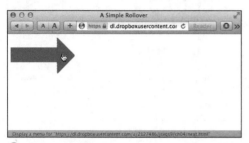

B When the mouse is over the image, the script replaces the first image with the second image.

Listing 4.1 Here's the simplest way to do a rollover, within a link tag.

```
<!DOCTYPE html>
<html>
<head>
    <title>A Simple Rollover</title>
    <link rel="stylesheet"
    → href="script01.css">
</head>
<body>
    <a href="next.html" onmouseover=
    → "document.images['arrow'].src=
    → 'images/arrow_on.gif'" onmouseout=
    → "document.images['arrow'].src=
    → 'images/arrow_off.gif'"><img src=
    → "images/arrow_off.gif" id="arrow"
    → alt="arrow"></a>
</body>
</html>
```

Creating Rollovers

The idea behind rollovers is simple. You have two images. The first, or *original,* image is loaded and displayed along with the rest of the webpage by the user. When the user moves the mouse over the first image, the browser quickly swaps out the first image for the second, or *replacement,* image, giving the illusion of movement or animation.

Listing 4.1 gives you the bare-bones rollover; the whole thing is done within a standard image link. First a blue arrow is loaded **A**, and then it is overwritten by a red arrow when the user moves the mouse over the image **B**. The blue arrow is redrawn when the user moves the mouse away.

Some styles get applied to elements on the page, and we've broken those styles out into a separate CSS file, as seen in **Listing 4.2.**

To create a rollover:

1. `<a href="next.html"`

   The link begins by specifying where the browser will go when the user clicks the image, in this case to the page `next.html`.

2. `onmouseover="document.`
   `→ images['arrow'].src=`
   `→ 'images/arrow_on.gif'"`

   When the user moves the mouse over the image (the `src` of the arrow `id`), the replacement image `arrow_on.gif`, which is inside the `images` directory, is swapped into the document.

3. `onmouseout="document.`
   `→ images['arrow'].src=`
   `→ 'images/arrow_off.gif'">`

   Then, when the mouse moves away, the image `arrow_off.gif` is swapped back in.

continues on next page

4. `<img src="images/arrow_off.gif"` `↪id="arrow" alt="arrow">`

The image link defines the source of the original image for the page.

TIP We have included the alt attribute inside the image tag because `alt` attributes (which give non-graphical browsers a name or description of an image) are required if you want your HTML to be compliant with the W3C standards, and because using `alt` attributes helps make your page accessible to disabled users, such as visually impaired users who browse using screen readers.

TIP Make sure that the "on" versions of all your images exist—if they don't, your page will display a broken image icon when the user hovers over the link.

TIP This example uses both single and double quotes, so you might be wondering what the difference is. Basically, it's the same rule as English: if you're quoting something inside a phrase that's already within double quotes, switch to single quotes.

Outside of that restriction, JavaScript doesn't care if you use single or double quotes. Just keep in mind that quotes need to come in pairs; that is, an opening double quote needs to be ended with another double quote, and the same goes for single quotes.

Listing 4.2 This CSS file is used to style elements throughout many of the examples in this chapter.

```
body {
    background-color: #FFF;
}

img {
    border-width: 0;
}

img#arrow, img#arrowImg {
    width: 147px;
    height: 82px;
}

#button1, #button2 {
    width: 113px;
    height: 33px;
}

.centered {
    text-align: center;
}

#adBanner {
    width: 400px;
    height: 75px;
}
```

Disadvantages to This Kind of Rollover

This method of doing rollovers is very simple, but you should be aware that there are several problems and drawbacks with it.

- Because the second image is downloaded from the server at the time the user rolls over the first image, there can be a perceptible delay before the second image replaces the first one, especially for people browsing your site with a slower connection.

- Using this method causes an error message in ancient browsers, such as Netscape 2.0 or earlier, Internet Explorer 3.0 or earlier, or the America Online 2.7 browser. Since there are so few of these vintage browsers still in use, it's not much of a problem these days.

Instead of using this method, we suggest that you use the following way to create rollovers, in the "Creating More Effective Rollovers" section, which solves all these problems and more.

Listing 4.3 The only JavaScript on this HTML page is the pointer to the external **.js** file.

```
<!DOCTYPE html>
<html>
<head>
     <title>A More Effective Rollover</title>
     <script src="script02.js"></script>
     <link rel="stylesheet"
   → href="script01.css">
</head>
<body>
     <a href="next1.html"><img src=
   → "images/button1_off.gif" alt="button1"
   → id="button1"></a>  
     <a href="next2.html"><img src=
   → "images/button2_off.gif" alt="button2"
   → id="button2"></a>
</body>
</html>
```

Listing 4.4 This is a better way to do rollovers than in Listing 4.1, because it is much more flexible.

```
window.onload = rolloverInit;

function rolloverInit() {
     for (var i=0; i<document.images.length;
   → i++) {
        if (document.images[i].parentNode.
   → tagName == "A") {
           setupRollover(document.images[i]);
        }
     }
}

function setupRollover(theImage) {
     theImage.outImage = new Image();
     theImage.outImage.src = theImage.src;
     theImage.onmouseout = function() {
        this.src = this.outImage.src;
     }

     theImage.overImage = new Image();
     theImage.overImage.src =
   → "images/" + theImage.id + "_on.gif";
     theImage.onmouseover = function() {
        this.src = this.overImage.src;
     }
}
```

Creating More Effective Rollovers

To make the illusion of animation work, you need to make sure that the replacement image appears immediately, with no delay while it is fetched from the server. To do that, you use JavaScript to place the images into variables used by your script, which preloads all the images into the browser's cache (so that they are already on the user's hard disk when they are needed). Then, when the user moves the mouse over an image, the script swaps out one variable containing an image for a second variable containing the replacement image. **Listing 4.3** shows how it's done. The visible result is the same as in Ⓐ and Ⓑ from the previous exercise, but the apparent animation is smoother.

To keep your JavaScript more manageable, we'll extract the JavaScript code from the HTML page and put it in an external **.js** file, as in **Listing 4.4** (see Chapter 2 for more about **.js** files).

To create a better rollover:

1. `<script src="script02.js"></script>`

   This tag is in Listing 4.3, the HTML page. It uses the **src** attribute to tell the browser where to find the external **.js** file, which is where the JavaScript resides.

2. `<a href="next1.html"><img src=`
   `⟶ "images/button1_off.gif"`
   `⟶ alt="button1" id="button1">`
   `⟶ </a>  `
   `<a href="next2.html"><img`
   `⟶ src="images/button2_off.gif"`
   `⟶ alt="button2" id="button2"></a>`

   Still in Listing 4.3, these are two typical link tags for the buttons, with image tags embedded in them. The **href** attribute describes the destination of the link when the user clicks it. In the **img** tag, the **src** attribute provides the path to the image before the user rolls over it. The link tags also define the image's **alt** text. Note that each of the two buttons also has an **id** attribute; as described in Chapter 1, the **id** must be unique for each object. The script uses the image's **id** to make the rollover work.

3. `window.onload = rolloverInit;`

   Moving to Listing 4.4, the **window.onload** event handler is triggered when the page has finished loading. The handler calls the **rolloverInit()** function.

   This handler is used here to make sure that the script doesn't execute before the page is done loading. That's because referring to items on the page before the page has finished loading can cause errors if some of the page's elements haven't yet been loaded.

4.
```
function rolloverInit() {
   for (var i=0; i<document.
  → images.length; i++) {
```

The **rolloverInit()** function scans each image on the page, looking to see if the tag around the image is an **<a>** tag, indicating that it is a link. The first of these two lines begins the function. The second begins a **for…next** loop that goes through all of the images. The loop begins by setting the counter variable **i** to 0. Then, each time the loop goes around, if the value of **i** is less than the number of images in the document, increment **i** by 1.

5.
```
if (document.images[i].parentNode.
  → tagName == "A") {
```

This is where we test to see if the tag surrounding the image is an anchor tag. We do it by looking at an object and seeing if the object's value is **A** (the anchor tag). Let's break that object apart a bit. The first part of the object, **document.images[i]**, is the current image. Its **parentNode** property is the container tag that surrounds it, and **tagName** then provides the name of that container tag. So in English, you can read the part of the line in the parentheses as "For this particular image, is the tag around it an 'A'?"

6.
```
setupRollover(document.images[i]);
```

If the result of the test in step 5 is true, then the **setupRollover** function is called and passed the current image.

continues on next page

7. `function setupRollover(theImage) {`

Take a minute to look at the whole function before we go through it line by line. Here's the overview: this function adds two new properties to the image object that's passed in. The new properties are **outImage** (the version of the image when you're not on it) and **overImage** (the version of the image when you are on it), both of which are image objects themselves. Because they're image objects, once they're created, we can add their **src** property. The **src** for **outImage** is the current (off) image **src**. The **src** value for **overImage** is calculated based on the **id** attribute of the original image.

This line starts off the function with the image that was passed to it by the **rolloverInit()** function.

8. `theImage.outImage = new Image();`

This line takes the image object that was passed in and adds the new **outImage** property to it. Because you can add a property of any kind to an object, and because properties are just objects themselves, what's happening here is that we're adding an image object to an image. The parentheses for the new image object are optional, but it's good coding practice to include them; if needed, you can set properties of the new image object by passing certain parameters.

9. `theImage.outImage.src =`
   `→ theImage.src;`

   Now we set the source for the new **outImage** to be the same as the source of **theImage**. The default image on the page is always the version you see when the cursor is off the image.

10. `theImage.onmouseout =`
    `→ function() {`
    `    this.src = this.outImage.src;`
    `}`

    The first line here starts off what's called an *anonymous function*—that is, it's a function without a name. We could name it (say, **rollOut**), but as it's only one line, why bother?

    In this section, we're telling the browser to trigger what should happen when the user moves the mouse away from the image. Whenever that happens, we want to set the image source back to the initial source value, that is, the **outImage** version of the image.

11. `theImage.overImage = new Image();`
    `theImage.overImage.src =`
    `→ "images/" + theImage.id +`
    `→ "_on.gif";`

    In the first line, we create a new image object that will contain the **overImage** version of the image. The second line sets the source for **overImage**. It builds the name of the source file on the fly, concatenating "**images/**" with the **id** of the image (remember, in Listing 4.3, we saw that those **ids** were **button1** and **button2**) and adding "**_on.gif**".

continues on next page

12. `theImage.onmouseover =`
   `→ function() {`
   `    this.src = this.overImage.src;`
   `}`

Here we have another anonymous function. This one tells the browser that when the user moves the cursor over the image, it should reset the current image's source to that of the **overImage** version, as seen in  Ⓐ and Ⓑ.

Ⓐ You can also put multiple rollovers on the same page.

Ⓑ Hovering over the second rollover.

TIP When you prepare your graphics for rollovers, make sure that all your GIF or PNG images are not transparent. If they are, you will see the image you are trying to replace beneath the transparent image—and that's not what you want.

TIP Both the original and the replacement images need to have identical dimensions. Otherwise, some browsers resize the images for you, and you probably won't like the distorted result.

TIP In the previous example, the rollover happened when you moved the cursor over the link; here, the rollover happens when you move the cursor over the image—that is, the `onmouseover` and `onmouseout` are now attached to the image, not the link. While these methods usually give the same effect, there's one big difference: some older browsers (Netscape 4 and earlier, IE 3 and earlier) don't support `onmouseover` and `onmouseout` on the `img` tag.

TIP You might think that, because all of the tags on the HTML page are lowercase, `tagName` should be compared to a lowercase "a". That's not the way it works; `tagName` always returns an uppercase value.

TIP There are many different ways to script rollovers. We prefer this one due to its flexibility: images can be added to or subtracted from associated HTML pages without any code needing to be changed.

Building Three-State Rollovers

A When the button is clicked, you get a third image (hard to see in this grayscale image; check our companion website for the full effect).

Listing 4.5 By putting your JavaScript in an external file, the HTML for a three-state rollover is virtually identical to a two-state rollover.

```
<!DOCTYPE html>
<html>
<head>
    <title>Three-state Rollovers</title>
    <script src="script03.js"></script>
    <link rel="stylesheet"
    → href="script01.css">
</head>
<body>
    <a href="next1.html"><img src=
    → "images/button1_off.gif" alt="button1"
    → id="button1"></a>  
    <a href="next2.html"><img src=
    → "images/button2_off.gif" alt="button2"
    → id="button2"></a>
</body>
</html>
```

A three-state rollover is one where the rollover has three versions. Besides the original image and the version that appears when the user places the cursor over the image, there is a third version of the image when the button itself is clicked, as shown in **A**.

Listing 4.5, the HTML file, looks almost exactly the same as Listing 4.3 from the previous task. In fact, the only differences are the document's title and the name of the external JavaScript file that is being called. That's it. This is an example of why putting all your JavaScript into an external file is so powerful; you can add functionality to your pages without having to rework your HTML pages.

In **Listing 4.6**, the external JavaScript file, there are only a few changes from Listing 4.4. Rather than go through the whole script again, we'll just focus on the changes. Remember, the parts of the script that we're covering are shown in red in the code.

To build a three-state rollover:

1. `theImage.clickImage = new Image();`
   `theImage.clickImage.src =`
   `→"images/" + theImage.id +`
   `→"_click.gif";`

   In the **setupRollover()** function, we now need to add a third image property for the click state. In the first line, we create a new image object that will contain the **clickImage** version of the image. The second line sets the source for **clickImage**. It builds the name of the source file on the fly, concatenating **"images/"** with the **id** of the image, and adding **"_click.gif"**.

2. `theImage.onclick = function() {`
   `    this.src = this.clickImage.src;`
   `}`

   This tells the browser what to do when the user clicks the mouse on the image: in this case, we want to set the image source to its **clickImage** version.

> **TIP** If you're thinking about using a script like this on your own site, a more complete version is Listing 7.9, in "Replacing Elements Using Regular Expressions," and its final version is Listing 13.19, in "Checking Whether a File Exists."

Listing 4.6 This script powers the three-state rollover.

```
window.onload = rolloverInit;

function rolloverInit() {
    for (var i=0; i<document.images.length;
    → i++) {
        if (document.images[i].parentNode.
        → tagName == "A") {
            setupRollover(document.images[i]);
        }
    }
}

function setupRollover(theImage) {
    theImage.outImage = new Image();
    theImage.outImage.src = theImage.src;
    theImage.onmouseout = function() {
        this.src = this.outImage.src;
    }

    theImage.clickImage = new Image();
    theImage.clickImage.src = "images/" +
    → theImage.id + "_click.gif";
    theImage.onclick = function() {
        this.src = this.clickImage.src;
    }

    theImage.overImage = new Image();
    theImage.overImage.src = "images/" +
    → theImage.id + "_on.gif";
    theImage.onmouseover = function() {
        this.src = this.overImage.src;
    }
}
```

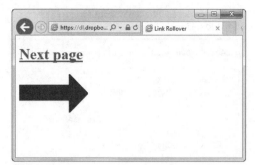

A The text link is the triggering device for this rollover.

B When the user points at the link, the graphic below changes.

Listing 4.7 This script shows the HTML for a rollover from a text link.

```
<!DOCTYPE html>
<html>
<head>
    <title>Link Rollover</title>
    <script src="script04.js"></script>
    <link rel="stylesheet"
    → href="script01.css">
</head>
<body>
    <h1><a href="next.html" id="arrow">
    → Next page</a></h1>
    <img src="images/arrow_off.gif"
    → id="arrowImg" alt="arrow">
</body>
</html>
```

Triggering Rollovers from a Link

In earlier examples, the user triggered the rollover by moving the mouse over an image. But you can also make a rollover occur when the user hovers over a text link, as in **A** and **B**. The HTML is an unexciting page with one link and one image, shown in **Listing 4.7**. We'll do the rollover by modifying the script used in previous examples, as in **Listing 4.8**.

To trigger a rollover from a link:

1. `function rolloverInit() {`
   `    for (var i=0; i<document.links.`
   `    ⇢ length; i++) {`

   After beginning the **rolloverInit()** function, we start a loop, much like previous examples in this chapter. But there we were looking for images (**document.images.length**), and here we're looking for links (**document.links.length**). The loop begins by setting the counter variable **i** to zero. Every time around, if the value of **i** is less than the number of links in the document, increment **i** by 1.

2. `var linkObj = document.links[i];`

   We create the **linkObj** variable and set it to the current link.

3. `if (linkObj.id) {`
   `    var imgObj = document.`
   `    ⇢ getElementById(linkObj.id +`
   `    ⇢ "Img");`

   If **linkObj** has an **id**, then we check to see if there's another element on the page that has an **id** that's the same plus **Img**. If so, put that element into the new variable **imgObj**.

4. `if (imgObj) {`
   `    setupRollover(linkObj,imgObj);`

   If **imgObj** exists, then call the **setupRollover()** function, passing it the link object and the image object.

Listing 4.8 Here is the JavaScript for a rollover from a text link.

```
window.onload = rolloverInit;

function rolloverInit() {
    for (var i=0; i<document.links.length;
    ⇢ i++) {
        var linkObj = document.links[i];
        if (linkObj.id) {
            var imgObj = document.
            ⇢ getElementById(linkObj.id +
            ⇢ "Img");
            if (imgObj) {
                setupRollover(linkObj,imgObj);
            }
        }
    }
}

function setupRollover(theLink,theImage) {
    theLink.imgToChange = theImage;
    theLink.onmouseout = function() {
        this.imgToChange.src =
        ⇢ this.outImage.src;
    }
    theLink.onmouseover = function() {
        this.imgToChange.src =
        ⇢ this.overImage.src;
    }

    theLink.outImage = new Image();
    theLink.outImage.src = theImage.src;

    theLink.overImage = new Image();
    theLink.overImage.src = "images/" +
    ⇢ theLink.id + "_on.gif";
}
```

5.
```
function setupRollover
→(theLink,theImage) {
    theLink.imgToChange = theImage;
```

The **setupRollover()** function begins with the link and image parameters that were passed to it in step 4. Then we add a new property, **imgToChange**, to the link object. JavaScript needs some way of knowing what image is to be changed when the link is moused over, and this is where it's stored.

6.
```
theLink.onmouseout = function() {
    this.imgToChange.src =
    →this.outImage.src;
}
theLink.onmouseover = function() {
    this.imgToChange.src =
    →this.overImage.src;
}
```

When the **mouseover** and **mouseout** are triggered, they're slightly different from the previous examples in this chapter: now, **this.imgToChange.src** is being reset instead of **this.src** itself.

TIP This technique is useful when you want to provide the user with a preview of what they will see if they click the link at which they are pointing. For example, say you have a travel site describing trips to Scotland, Tahiti, and Cleveland. On the left of the page could be a column of text links for each destination, while on the right could be a preview area where an image appears. As the user points at the name of a destination, a picture of that place appears in the preview area. Clicking the link takes the user to a page detailing their fabulous vacation spot.

Making Multiple Links Change a Single Rollover

Up to now, you've seen how mousing over a single area can trigger a rollover effect. But you can also have several different areas that trigger a rollover. This can be very useful, for example, when you have several images that you want to annotate; that is, where rolling over each of the images makes the description of that image appear. In this example, we've done just this with images of three of Leonardo da Vinci's inventions. As you roll over each image, the description of that image appears elsewhere. The description itself is another image. Actually, it's three images, one for each of the three inventions. 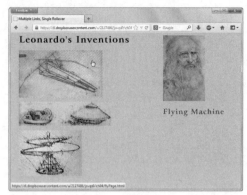 shows **Listing 4.9**

Ⓐ This page has three interactive images: a flying machine, a tank, and a helicopter. When you roll over an image, its description appears under Leonardo's face.

Listing 4.9 Note that the links and images on this page all have unique **id**s.

```
<!DOCTYPE html>
<html>
<head>
    <title>Multiple Links, Single Rollover</title>
    <script src="script05.js"></script>
    <link rel="stylesheet" href="script02.css">
</head>
<body>
    <div id="captionDiv">
        <img src="images/DaVinci.jpg" width="144" height="219" alt="DaVinci">
        <img src="images/bg.gif" id="captionField" alt="Text Field">
    </div>
    <div id="inventionDiv">
        <img src="images/leoText.gif" id="heading" alt="Leonardo's Inventions">
        <a href="flyPage.html" class="captionField" id="flyer"><img src="images/flyer.gif"
        → width="293" height="165" alt="Flying Machine" id="flyerImg"></a>
        <a href="tankPage.html" class="captionField" id="tank"><img src="images/tank.gif"
        → width="325" height="92" alt="Tank" id="tankImg"></a>
        <a href="heliPage.html" class="captionField" id="helicopter"><img src="images/helicopter.gif"
        → width="224" height="160" alt="Helicopter" id="helicopterImg"></a>
    </div>
</body>
</html>
```

Listing 4.10 In this CSS file, we define the classes we reference in the HTML.

```css
body {
    background-color: #EC9;
}

img {
    border-width: 0;
}

#captionDiv {
    float: right;
    width: 210px;
    margin: auto 50px;
}

#captionField {
    margin: 20px auto;
    width: 208px;
    height: 27px;
}

#inventionDiv {
    width: 375px;
    margin-left: 20px;
}

#heading {
    margin-bottom: 20px;
    width: 375px;
    height: 26px;
}
```

(HTML), **Listing 4.10** (CSS), and **Listing 4.11** (JavaScript) in action. As with most of the scripts in this book, it builds on previous examples, so we'll just explain the new concepts. There are just a few lines that are different between Listing 4.8 and Listing 4.11.

To make multiple links change a single rollover:

1. ```
   if (linkObj.className) {
       var imgObj = document.
       → getElementById(linkObj.
       → className);
   ```

   We can't use the **id** of the rolled-over images to calculate the **id** of the changed image—that's because an **id** has to be unique, and all of the rolled-over images have to come up with the same value for the changed image destination. Instead, we're using the **class** attribute (because you can have multiple page elements sharing the same **class**). In this line, we're looking for the **className** of the link object.

2. ```
   function setupRollover(theLink,
   → textImage) {
       theLink.imgToChange = textImage;
   ```

   The **setupRollover()** function is passed the current link object (**theLink**) and the image object, which we're calling **textImage**. Note that when we passed these objects (which can also be referred to as variables) in, we called them **linkObj** and **imgObj**, respectively.

   The rest of the script works the same way as the previous examples in this chapter.

Listing 4.11 This script shows you how to use multiple links to trigger a single rollover.

```
window.onload = rolloverInit;

function rolloverInit() {
    for (var i=0; i<document.links.length;
    → i++) {
        var linkObj = document.links[i];
        if (linkObj.className) {
            var imgObj = document.
            → getElementById(linkObj.
            → className);
            if (imgObj) {
                setupRollover(linkObj,imgObj);
            }
        }
    }
}

function setupRollover(theLink,textImage) {
    theLink.imgToChange = textImage;
    theLink.onmouseout = function() {
        this.imgToChange.src =
        → this.outImage.src;
    }
    theLink.onmouseover = function() {
        this.imgToChange.src =
        → this.overImage.src;
    }

    theLink.outImage = new Image();
    theLink.outImage.src = textImage.src;

    theLink.overImage = new Image();
    theLink.overImage.src = "images/" +
    → theLink.id + "Text.gif";
}
```

Working with Multiple Rollovers

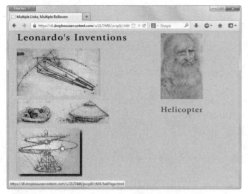

A When you roll over one of the images, a description appears and a drop shadow appears around the image itself.

What if you want the image that triggers the rollover to also be a rollover itself? **A** builds on the last example and shows how we've added this feature. When you roll over one of the invention images, it makes the description image appear, as before, but this time also swaps out the invention image for another image with a drop shadow. This gives the user visual feedback about what they're pointing at (as if the mouse pointer isn't enough!). **Listing 4.12** is the HTML page (no changes except for the title and the name of the external JavaScript file being called), and **Listing 4.13** shows the additions to the JavaScript from the previous example.

Listing 4.12 This HTML is identical to Listing 4.9, except for the title and reference to the external script.

```
<!DOCTYPE html>
<html>
<head>
    <title>Multiple Links, Multiple Rollovers</title>
    <script src="script06.js"></script>
    <link rel="stylesheet" href="script02.css">
</head>
<body>
    <div id="captionDiv">
        <img src="images/DaVinci.jpg" width="144" height="219" alt="DaVinci">
        <img src="images/bg.gif" id="captionField" alt="Text Field">
    </div>
    <div id="inventionDiv">
        <img src="images/leoText.gif" id="heading" alt="Leonardo's Inventions">
        <a href="flyPage.html" class="captionField" id="flyer"><img src="images/flyer.gif"
        → width="293" height="165" alt="Flying Machine" id="flyerImg"></a>
        <a href="tankPage.html" class="captionField" id="tank"><img src="images/tank.gif"
        → width="325" height="92" alt="Tank" id="tankImg"></a>
        <a href="heliPage.html" class="captionField" id="helicopter"><img src="images/helicopter.gif"
        → width="224" height="160" alt="Helicopter" id="helicopterImg"></a>
    </div>
</body>
</html>
```

Listing 4.13 This script handles the multiple rollovers.

```
window.onload = rolloverInit;

function rolloverInit() {
    for (var i=0; i<document.links.length; i++) {
        var linkObj = document.links[i];
        if (linkObj.className) {
            var imgObj = document.getElementById(linkObj.className);
            if (imgObj) {
                setupRollover(linkObj,imgObj);
            }
        }
    }
}

function setupRollover(theLink,textImage) {
    theLink.imgToChange = new Array;
    theLink.outImage = new Array;
    theLink.overImage = new Array;

    theLink.imgToChange[0] = textImage;
    theLink.onmouseout = rollOut;
    theLink.onmouseover = rollOver;

    theLink.outImage[0] = new Image();
    theLink.outImage[0].src = textImage.src;

    theLink.overImage[0] = new Image();
    theLink.overImage[0].src = "images/" + theLink.id + "Text.gif";

    var rolloverObj = document.getElementById(theLink.id + "Img");
    if (rolloverObj) {
        theLink.imgToChange[1] = rolloverObj;

        theLink.outImage[1] = new Image();
        theLink.outImage[1].src = rolloverObj.src;

        theLink.overImage[1] = new Image();
        theLink.overImage[1].src = "images/" + theLink.id + "_on.gif";
    }
}

function rollOver() {
    for (var i=0;i<this.imgToChange.length; i++) {
        this.imgToChange[i].src = this.overImage[i].src;
    }
}

function rollOut() {
    for (var i=0;i<this.imgToChange.length; i++) {
        this.imgToChange[i].src = this.outImage[i].src;
    }
}
```

To work with multiple rollovers:

1. `theLink.imgToChange = new Array;`
   `theLink.outImage = new Array;`
   `theLink.overImage = new Array;`

   These lines were added because the script has more images to work with (two for each rollover). In each line, we're creating a new property of **theLink**, each of which is an array.

2. `theLink.imgToChange[0] =`
   `→ textImage;`

   In the previous task, **imgToChange** was an image, but in this task, it's an array that will contain images. Here, **textImage** is stored in the first element of **imgToChange**.

3. `theLink.outImage[0] = new Image();`
   `theLink.outImage[0].src =`
   `→ textImage.src;`

   As previously, we need to store the out (off) version of the image, but this time it's stored in the first element of the **outImage** array.

4. `theLink.overImage[0] =`
   `→ new Image();`
   `theLink.overImage[0].src =`
   `→ "images/" + theLink.id +`
   `→ "Text.gif";`

   Similarly, the over (on) version of the image is calculated and stored in the first element of **overImage**.

continues on next page

5.
```
var rolloverObj = document.
→ getElementById(theLink.id +
→ "Img");
if (rolloverObj) {
```

Now we need to figure out if this roll-over will trigger multiple images, not just an individual image. If that's the case, there will be an element on the HTML page whose **id** is the same as this one, but with **Img** appended. That is, if we're working on **flyer**, we'll be checking to see if there's a **flyerImg** element on the page. If there is, it's saved in **rolloverObj**, and we should do the next three steps.

6.
```
theLink.imgToChange[1] =
→ rolloverObj;
```

In the same way that we set **imgToChange[0]** above, we now set **imgToChange[1]** (the second element in the array) to the new **rolloverObj**. When the **onmouseout** and **onmouseover** event handlers are triggered, both images swap to their alternate versions, as we'll see later.

7.
```
theLink.outImage[1] = new Image();
theLink.outImage[1].src =
→ rolloverObj.src;
```

This sets the second array element of **outImage** to the out (off) version of the image.

8.
```
theLink.overImage[1] =
→ new Image();
theLink.overImage[1].src =
→ "images/" + theLink.id +
→ "_on.gif";
```

And here, the over (on) version of the image is calculated and stored in the second element of **overImage**.

If, for some reason, we wanted a third image to also change during this same rollover, we'd repeat steps 6–8 with the third image object.

9.
```
for (var i=0; i<this.imgToChange.
→ length; i++) {
   this.imgToChange[i].src =
   → this.overImage[i].src;
}
```

Here inside the **rollOver()** function is where the images get swapped. Because one or more images can be changed, we need to start by asking how many images we have stored—that's the value of **this.imgToChange.length**. Here, the value is 2, because we want two images to change. We then loop through two times, setting the source of **imgToChange[0]** and then **imgToChange[1]** to their respective over values.

10.
```
for (var i=0; i<this.imgToChange.
→ length; i++) {
   this.imgToChange[i].src =
   → this.outImage[i].src;
}
```

This code in the **rollOut()** function is virtually the same as that in the previous step; the only difference is that we're now resetting those images to their out source values.

TIP It's important to remember that every image that ever gets rolled over must have a unique **id**.

TIP What if you want some of the links on your page to trigger multiple rollovers, but others to be individual rollovers? No problem—you don't even need to change a line of JavaScript. So long as the check in step 5 doesn't find the alternate **id** on the page, no second element is stored, and the **rollOver()** and **rollOut()** loops only animate the initial image.

Creating Cycling Banners

When you surf the web, it's common to see advertising banners that periodically switch between images. Some of these are animated GIF files, which are GIF files that contain a number of frames that play in succession; others are Flash animations. If you want to have a page that cycles through a number of GIFs (either animated or not), you can use JavaScript to do the job, as in **Listing 4.15**. This example uses three GIFs and cycles repeatedly through them, as shown in **Ⓐ**, **Ⓑ**, and **Ⓒ**. The simple HTML page is shown in **Listing 4.14**.

To create cycling banners:

1. ```
   var theAd = 0;
   var adImages = new Array
   →("images/reading1.gif",
   →"images/reading2.gif",
   →"images/reading3.gif");
   ```

   Our script starts by creating **theAd**, which is given its beginning value in this code. The next line creates a new array called **adImages**. In this case, the array contains the names of the three GIF files that make up the cycling banner.

2. ```
   function rotate() {
   ```

   We start off with a new function called **rotate()**.

3. ```
   theAd++;
   ```

   Take the value of **theAd**, and add one to it.

4. ```
   if (theAd == adImages.length) {
      theAd = 0;
   ```

   This code checks to see if the value of **theAd** is equal to the number of items in the **adImages** array; if it is, then set the value of **theAd** back to zero.

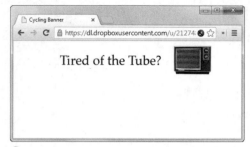

Ⓐ The first image, which starts the cycling banner...

Ⓑ ...the second image...

Ⓒ ...the final image. Once the page loads and the banner begins cycling, the animation continues with no user intervention required.

Listing 4.14 The HTML loads the first image in the cycling banner; the JavaScript handles the rest.

```
<!DOCTYPE html>
<html>
<head>
    <title>Cycling Banner</title>
    <script src="script07.js"></script>
    <link rel="stylesheet"
    → href="script01.css">
</head>
<body>
    <div class="centered">
        <img src="images/reading1.gif"
        → id="adBanner" alt="Ad Banner">
    </div>
</body>
</html>
```

Listing 4.15 You can use JavaScript to cycle between images in a banner.

```
window.onload = rotate;

var theAd = 0;
var adImages = new Array("images/
→ reading1.gif","images/reading2.gif",
→ "images/reading3.gif");

function rotate() {
    theAd++;
    if (theAd == adImages.length) {
        theAd = 0;
    }
    document.getElementById("adBanner").
    → src = adImages[theAd];

    setTimeout(rotate, 3 * 1000);
}
```

5. **document.getElementById
→ ("adBanner").src =
→ adImages[theAd];**

   The image on the web that is being cycled has the **id adBanner**; you define the name as part of the **img** tag, as shown in Listing 4.14. This line of code says that the new sources for **adBanner** are in the array **adImages**, and the value of the variable **theAd** defines which of the three GIFs the browser should use at this moment.

6. **setTimeout(rotate, 3 * 1000);**

   This line tells the script how often to change GIFs in the banner. The built-in JavaScript command **setTimeout()** lets you specify that an action should occur on a particular schedule, always measured in milliseconds. In this case, the function **rotate()** is called every 3000 milliseconds, or every 3 seconds, so the GIFs will cycle in the banner every three seconds.

TIP You might be wondering why you would want to use JavaScript for a cycling banner, rather than just create an animated GIF. One good reason is that it lets you use JPEGs or PNGs in the banner, which gives you higher-quality images. With these higher-quality images, you can use photographs in your banners.

TIP Unlike in some of the previous examples in this chapter, the images in this task are not pre-cached. Each downloads from the server the first time that it's displayed. This is because you might have any number of images in your ad array, and it's not polite to force users to download, for example, 100 images if they're only going to see 2 or 3 of them.

Adding Links to Cycling Banners

Banners are often used in advertising, and you'll want to know how to make a banner into a link that will take a visitor somewhere when the visitor clicks the banner. **Listing 4.16** shows the HTML page, which differs from the last example only in that it adds a link around the **img** tag. **Listing 4.17** shows a variation of the previous script. In this script, we'll add a new array. This new array contains destinations that users will be sent to when they click the banner. In this case, the "Eat at Joe's" banner takes you to **negrino.com**, "Drink More Java" goes to **sun.com**, and "Heartburn" goes to **microsoft.com**, as shown in Ⓐ. No editorial comments implied, of course.

To add links to cycling banners:

1. **window.onload = initBannerLink;**

   When the window finishes loading, trigger the **initBannerLink()** function.

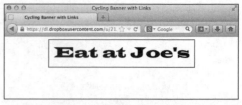

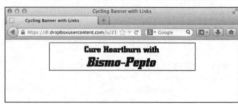

Ⓐ Each of these three images is a link, and clicking each image takes you to one of three different websites.

Listing 4.16 The HTML needed for an ad banner.

```
<!DOCTYPE html>
<html>
<head>
    <title>Cycling Banner with Links</title>
    <script src="script08.js"></script>
    <link rel="stylesheet"
    → href="script01.css">
</head>
<body>
    <div class="centered">
        <a href="linkPage.html"><img src=
        → "images/banner1.gif" id="adBanner"
        → alt="ad banner"></a>
    </div>
</body>
</html>
```

Listing 4.17 This script shows how you can turn cycling banners into real, clickable ad banners.

```
window.onload = initBannerLink;

var theAd = 0;
var adURL = new Array("negrino.com",
→ "sun.com","microsoft.com");
var adImages = new Array("images/
→ banner1.gif","images/banner2.gif",
→ "images/banner3.gif");


function initBannerLink() {
    if (document.getElementById("adBanner").
    → parentNode.tagName == "A") {
        document.getElementById("adBanner").
        → parentNode.onclick = newLocation;
    }

    rotate();
}

function newLocation() {
    document.location.href = "http://www." +
    → adURL[theAd];
    return false;
}

function rotate() {
    theAd++;
    if (theAd == adImages.length) {
        theAd = 0;
    }
    document.getElementById("adBanner").
    → src = adImages[theAd];

    setTimeout(rotate, 3 * 1000);
}
```

2. `if (document.getElementById` `→ ("adBanner").parentNode.tagName` `→ == "A") {` `document.getElementById` `→ ("adBanner").parentNode.` `→ onclick = newLocation;` `}` `rotate();`

   This code, inside the **initBannerLink()** function, first checks to see if the **adBanner** object is surrounded by a link tag. If so, when the link is clicked, the **newLocation()** function will be called. Finally, the **rotate()** function is called.

3. `document.location.href =` `→ "http://www." + adURL[theAd];` `return false;`

   Inside **newLocation()**, we set the **document.location.href** object (in other words, the current document window) to the value of the text string **"http://www."** (notice the period), plus the value of one item from **adURL.** Since **adURL** is an array, you need to specify a member of the array. That's stored in **theAd**, and the resulting string can be any of the three links, depending on when the user clicks. Last, it returns false, which tells the browser that it should *not* also load in the **href**. Otherwise, the browser would do both. We've handled everything within JavaScript, so the **href** doesn't need to be loaded.

   TIP The adURL array needs to have the same number of array items as the adImages array for this script to work correctly.

Building Wraparound Slideshows

Slideshows on websites present the user with an image and let the user control the progression (either forward or backward) of the images. JavaScript gives the user the interactive control needed. **Listing 4.18** shows the HTML needed, and the JavaScript in **Listing 4.19** has what you need to add slideshows to your pages.

This script builds a slideshow that wraps around—that is, if you go past the end of the list you go back to the beginning and vice versa. **A** shows the new slideshow.

Listing 4.18 This HTML page creates a slideshow.

```
<!DOCTYPE html>
<html>
<head>
    <title>Image Slideshow</title>
    <script src="script09.js"></script>
    <link rel="stylesheet"
    → href="script01.css">
</head>
<body>
    <div class="centered">
        <h1>Welcome, Robot Overlords!</h1>
        <img src="images/robot1.jpg"
        → id="myPicture" width="200"
        → height="400" alt="Slideshow">
        <h2><a href="previous.html"
        → id="prevLink">&lt;&lt; Previous
        → </a>  <a href="next.html"
        → id="nextLink">Next &gt;&gt;</a></h2>
    </div>
</body>
</html>
```

Listing 4.19 This script builds a slideshow that the user can click through using links to control movement forward and back.

```
window.onload = initLinks;

var thePic = 0;
var myPix = new Array("images/robot1.jpg","images/robot2.jpg","images/robot3.jpg");

function initLinks() {
    document.getElementById("prevLink").onclick = processPrevious;
    document.getElementById("nextLink").onclick = processNext;
}

function processPrevious() {
    if (thePic == 0) {
        thePic = myPix.length;
    }
    thePic--;
    document.getElementById("myPicture").src = myPix[thePic];
    return false;
}

function processNext() {
    thePic++;
    if (thePic == myPix.length) {
        thePic = 0;
    }
    document.getElementById("myPicture").src = myPix[thePic];
    return false;
}
```

To build a wraparound slideshow:

1. `window.onload = initLinks;`

   When the window finishes loading, trigger the **initLinks()** function.

2. ```
   function initLinks() {
       document.getElementById
       → ("prevLink").onclick =
       → processPrevious;
       document.getElementById
       → ("nextLink").onclick =
       → processNext;
   }
   ```

   This function sets up the **onclick** event handlers for the Previous and Next links.

   continues on next page

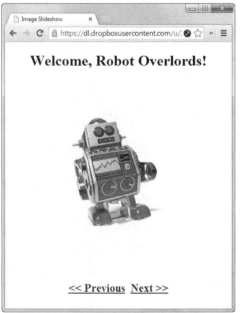

Ⓐ Clicking the Previous or Next link calls the **processPrevious()** or **processNext()** function, respectively.
   ```

3.
```
function processPrevious() {
   if (thePic == 0) {
      thePic = myPix.length;
```

This function makes the slideshow run in the Previous direction. This first part checks to see if **thePic** is equal to 0. If it is, the function gets the number of pictures in the **myPix** array.

4.
```
thePic--;
document.getElementById
→ ("myPicture").src =
→ myPix[thePic];
```

The first line reduces the value of **thePic** by 1. The next line sets the **src** of **myPicture** to the element of the **myPix** array represented by the current value of **thePic**.

5.
```
thePic++;
if (thePic == myPix.length) {
   thePic = 0;
}
document.getElementById
→ ("myPicture").src =
→ myPix[thePic];
```

This code, inside the **processNext()** function, makes the slideshow run in the Next direction and is much like the **processPrevious()** function. The first thing it does is increment the value of **thePic** by 1. Then it checks to see if the value of **thePic** is the same as the number of items in the **myPix** array. If so, it sets **thePic** back to 0. The next line sets the **src** of **myPicture**.

Displaying a Random Image

If your site is rich with graphics, or if you are displaying digital artwork, then you may want to have a random image from your collection appear when the user enters your site. Once again, JavaScript to the rescue! The extremely simple **Listing 4.20** shows the required HTML, and **Listing 4.21** provides the JavaScript. **Ⓐ** shows the result of the script, in this case images of a stuffed lion, tiger, and bear (oh, my!).

Ⓐ Depending on the value of the random number generated by the script, the user is presented with the lion, the tiger, or the bear.

To display a random image:

1. `var myPix = new Array`
   `→ ("images/lion.jpg", "images/`
   `→ tiger.jpg", "images/bear.jpg");`

   Here we build an array of three images, and stuff it into the variable **myPix**.

2. `var randomNum = Math.floor`
   `→ (Math.random() * myPix.length);`

   The variable called **randomNum** gets the value of a math expression that's best read from the inside outwards. **Math.random** generates a random number between 0 and 1, which is then multiplied by **myPix.length**, which is the number of items in the array (in this case, it's 3). **Math.floor** rounds the result down to an integer, which means that the number must be between 0 and 2.

3. `document.getElementById`
   `→ ("myPicture").src =`
   `→ myPix[randomNum];`

   This says that the source of the image **myPicture** is set based on the array **myPix**, and the value at this moment is dependent on the value of **randomNum**.

Listing 4.20 This simple HTML creates the page for a random image.

```
<!DOCTYPE html>
<html>
<head>
    <title>Random Image</title>
    <script src="script10.js"></script>
    <link rel="stylesheet"
    → href="script01.css">
</head>
<body>
    <img src="images/spacer.gif" width="305"
    → height="312" id="myPicture"
    → alt="some image">
</body>
</html>
```

Listing 4.21 You can display random images on your page with this script, which uses JavaScript's **Math.random** method to generate a random number.

```
window.onload = choosePic;

var myPix = new Array("images/lion.jpg",
→ "images/tiger.jpg","images/bear.jpg");

function choosePic() {
    var randomNum = Math.floor
    → (Math.random() * myPix.length);
    document.getElementById("myPicture").
    → src = myPix[randomNum];
}
```

Listing 4.22 There's a spacer GIF in the HTML file, which is a placeholder until the ad banner appears.

```
<!DOCTYPE html>
<html>
<head>
    <title>Cycling Random Banner</title>
    <script src="script11.js"></script>
    <link rel="stylesheet"
    → href="script01.css">
</head>
<body>
    <div class="centered">
        <img src="images/spacer.gif"
        → id="adBanner" alt="Ad Banner">
    </div>
</body>
</html>
```

Cycling Images with a Random Start

If you have a number of images that you want to display, you may not want to display them beginning with the same image each time the page is loaded. **Listing 4.22** has the HTML, and **Listing 4.23** combines the code used earlier for the cycling ad banners with the random image code.

Listing 4.23 This script allows you to start your cycling image show with a random image.

```
window.onload = choosePic;

var theAd = 0;
var adImages = new Array("images/reading1.gif","images/reading2.gif","images/reading3.gif");

function choosePic() {
    theAd = Math.floor(Math.random() * adImages.length);
    document.getElementById("adBanner").src = adImages[theAd];

    rotate();
}

function rotate() {
    theAd++;
    if (theAd == adImages.length) {
        theAd = 0;
    }
    document.getElementById("adBanner").src = adImages[theAd];

    setTimeout(rotate, 3 * 1000);
}
```

To start images cycling from a random start:

1. `var adImages = new Array("images/`
   `→ reading1.gif", "images/reading2.`
   `→ gif", "images/reading3.gif");`

   As in previous examples, set up the array and the variable that contains the number of items in the array.

2. `function rotate() {`

   This function is similar to the **rotate()** function in Listing 4.15. See that explanation for the details of how it works.

5

Windows and Frames

The window is the most important interface element in a web browser, and as you might expect, JavaScript provides you with many tools to manipulate windows.

JavaScript deals with windows similarly to the way it deals with frames. This makes perfect sense, since frames are just other document windows within the overall browser window.

However, frames have fallen out of favor over the past few years—to the point that (except for iframes) they've been removed from HTML5 entirely. Consequently, the frames portion of this chapter will focus on using JavaScript to make iframes even more useful.

In This Chapter

TABLE 5.1 Just Enough HTML—Frames

Tag	Attribute	Meaning
`iframe`		An internal frame, displayed inside the calling HTML page
	`name`	JavaScript can alternatively use this (instead of the `id`) to refer to the iframe
	`src`	The URL of the iframe page

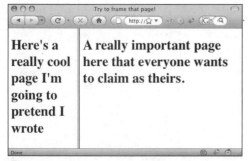

A Our page, buried in someone else's frameset.

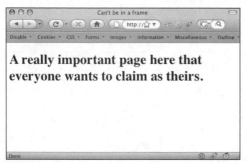

B Our page, after escaping from the evil hijacking frameset.

Listing 5.1 Here is an HTML page that people want to hijack.

```
<!DOCTYPE html>
<html>
<head>
     <title>Can't be in a frame</title>
     <script src="script01.js"></script>
</head>
<body>
     <h1>A really important page here that
     → everyone wants to claim as
     → theirs.</h1>
</body>
</html>
```

Listing 5.2 JavaScript provides a way to force our page to always appear on a separate page.

```
if (top.location != self.location) {
     top.location.replace(self.location);
}
```

Keeping a Page out of a Frame

Other people can put one of your pages inside a frame on their site, making it appear that your page is part of their content. In JavaScript, windows appear in a hierarchy, with the parent window at the top of the heap. When someone hijacks your page, they are forcing it to be a child frame to their parent window. **A** shows how the page would appear as part of someone else's site. With the following script, you can prevent page-hijacking and force your page to always be in a browser window by itself. There are two files; **Listing 5.1** is the HTML page that should always stand alone and has the **<script>** tag that calls the JavaScript; **Listing 5.2** is the JavaScript document, which we'll describe next.

To isolate a page:

1. `if (top.location != self.location) {`

   First, check to see if the location of the current page (**self**) is the top-most in the browser window hierarchy. If it is, there's no need to do anything.

2. `top.location.replace(self.location);`

   If the current page isn't at the top, replace the top page with the location of the current page. This forces the current window to be our page and our page only. **B** shows our page as we designed it.

   TIP We could just set `top.location` to `self.location`, but this has one nasty side effect: users can no longer use the browser's back button. If they try to, going back to the previous page automatically jumps them back to the current page. Using the `replace()` method shown above replaces the current page in the history, which allows the back button to display the previous page.

Setting a Target

An *iframe* is an inline frame; that is, a frame that can be embedded within a regular HTML page instead of needing to be inside a frameset. Like a regular frame, an iframe is a separate HTML document. You can use an iframe as the target of a script, so you can create content on the fly under script control and display it in the page.

In this task, we have a regular HTML page with a small area that is an iframe. Links in the main content area can *target* the iframe—that is, to load that iframe using HTML, you can use the **target** attribute of the **<a>** tag. Or, you can set the **target** attribute by scripting, as we're doing here.

The HTML page (**Listing 5.3**) allows you to load your choice of page into the iframe, just by clicking a link. The CSS is **Listing 5.4**; the initial page loaded into the iframe is **Listing 5.5**; and the JavaScript required to set the target is **Listing 5.6** (detailed next). There are also three other simple HTML pages (not shown) that can be loaded into the iframe. The result is shown in .

A Clicking a link in the main window causes the iframe to update.

Listing 5.3 This page creates the iframe and calls the external JavaScript.

```
<!DOCTYPE html>
<html>
<head>
    <title>iframe 1</title>
    <script src="script02.js"></script>
    <link rel="stylesheet"
    → href="script01.css">
</head>
<body>
    <iframe src="iframe01.html"
    → id="icontent" name="icontent"></iframe>
    <h1>Main Content Area</h1>
    <h2>
    <a href="page1.html">Link 1</a><br>
    <a href="page2.html">Link 2</a><br>
    <a href="page3.html">Link 3</a>
    </h2>
</body>
</html>
```

Listing 5.4 This CSS styles the main page and positions the iframe.

```
body {
    background-color: #FFF;
}

iframe#icontent {
    float: right;
    border: 1px solid black;
    width: 350px;
    height: 300px;
    margin-top: 100px;
}
```

Listing 5.5 The initial page that goes in the iframe.

```
<!DOCTYPE html>
<html>
<head>
    <title>Content iframe</title>
</head>
<body>
    Please load a page
</body>
</html>
```

Listing 5.6 There are a number of reasons why you might need JavaScript to set frame targets.

```
window.onload = initLinks;

function initLinks() {
    for (var i=0; i<document.links.length;
    → i++) {
        document.links[i].target = "icontent";
    }
}
```

To set the target for a frame:

1. `window.onload = initLinks;`

   When the page loads, call the `initLinks()` function.

2. `for (var i=0; i<document.links.` `→length; i++) {` `document.links[i].target =` `→"icontent";` `}`

   The `initLinks()` function loops through all of the links on the page. When the loop finds a link, it sets the `target` property to the string `"icontent"`. And that's all it takes.

TIP If JavaScript is turned off, visitors will find that the first link that gets clicked loads into the main window, not the `icontent` iframe. Sorry, but that's the way iframes work.

TIP While setting the target via a script isn't necessary, it can still be handy to set the target programmatically. Often, the people working on the main content area have no idea what the iframe workers want, and vice versa. Putting the name of the target into one line of JavaScript code allows for much more flexibility than hardcoding it into numerous `<a>` tags throughout a site.

TIP In Listing 5.3, it ought to be sufficient for the `id` of the iframe to be set. Some browsers (e.g., Firefox and Internet Explorer) require that the `name` attribute be used, though, so we've set them both here.

Loading iframes with JavaScript

Of course, you can do more with iframes than just setting the target, such as loading other HTML pages, and this example shows you how. Once again, we'll have a main page that sets up the iframe and will be virtually identical to Listing 5.3, and a page with the initial content of the iframe, like Listing 5.5. The JavaScript required is shown in **Listing 5.7**.

To load an iframe with JavaScript:

1. ```
   for (var i=0; i<document.links.
   → length; i++) {
     document.links[i].onclick =
     → setContent;
   }
   ```

   As with Listing 5.6, the **initLinks()** function is called when the page loads. This time, though, we tell all the links on the page that, when they're clicked, they're to call the **setContent()** function.

Listing 5.7 This script loads HTML pages into the **icontent** iframe.

```
window.onload = initLinks;

function initLinks() {
    for (var i=0; i<document.links.length;
    → i++) {
        document.links[i].onclick =
        → setContent;
    }
}

function setContent() {
    document.getElementById("icontent").
    → contentWindow.document.location.href =
    → this.href;
    return false;
}
```
```

A The **icontent** iframe gets loaded when you click a link in the main window.

2. ```
function setContent() {
    document.getElementById
    → ("icontent").contentWindow.
    → document.location.href =
    → this.href;
```

In this example, clicking any of the links triggers the **setContent()** function, which loads the new page into the iframe A. We do this by finding the **icontent** element on the page, and resetting its **contentWindow.document.location.href** to **this.href**. That is, we find an element with a given **id** (in this case, **icontent**) and then get that element's **contentWindow**. Then we get the **document** it contains. Then we get the **location** of that **document**, and then we reset **href**, which is the URL the user chose to load.

3. ```
return false;
```

Lastly, **setContent()** returns false, which tells the browser that it should *not* also load the **href**s into the main window. Otherwise, the browser would do both. We've handled everything within JavaScript, so the **href** doesn't need to be loaded.

Working with iframes

Because JavaScript can create page content on the fly, it's useful for loading pages into iframes based on a user's choice elsewhere. **Listing 5.8** is an HTML page that loads our usual dummy iframe page. **Listing 5.9**, detailed next, creates a page and loads it into the **icontent** iframe. The result looks like 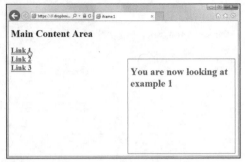.

A Here's the result of Listing 5.9, an iframe written by JavaScript.

To create the content for an iframe:

1.  ```
    for (var i=0; i<document.links.
    → length; i++) {
      document.links[i].onclick =
      → writeContent;
      document.links[i].thisPage =
      → i+1;
    }
    ```

    The **initLinks()** function begins by looping through the links on the page. Then, for each link, two things are set: the **onclick** handler for that link, and a new property, **thisPage**. The latter contains the page number to be displayed when that link is clicked; that is, link 0 is "page 1", link 1 is "page 2", and so on. The **onclick** handler in the loop sets every link to call the **writeContent()** function when they're clicked.

Listing 5.8 This page has an iframe on the right, along with instructions to click a link.

```
<!DOCTYPE html>
<html>
<head>
    <title>iframe 3</title>
    <script src="script04.js"></script>
    <link rel="stylesheet"
    → href="script01.css">
</head>
<body>
    <iframe src="iframe01.html" id="icontent"
    → name="icontent"></iframe>
    <h1>Main Content Area</h1>
    <h2>
    <a href="#">Link 1</a><br>
    <a href="#">Link 2</a><br>
    <a href="#">Link 3</a>
    </h2>
</body>
</html>
```
```

Listing 5.9 This script adds content to the **icontent** iframe.

```
window.onload = initLinks;

function initLinks() {
    for (var i=0; i<document.links.length;
    → i++) {
        document.links[i].onclick =
        → writeContent;
        document.links[i].thisPage = i+1;
    }
}

function writeContent() {
    var newText = "<h1>You are now looking
    → at example " + this.thisPage +
    → ".<\/h1>";

    document.getElementById("icontent").
    → contentWindow.document.body.
    → innerHTML = newText;
    return false;
}
```

2. ```
   var newText = "<h1>You are now
   → looking at example " +
   → this.thisPage + ".<\/h1>";

   document.getElementById
   → ("icontent").contentWindow.
   → document.body.innerHTML =
   → newText;
   ```

   Here is the meat of the **writeContent()** function, which first declares and sets a variable, **newText**, and assigns it some text. Given the **icontent** element (as in the previous task), we reset its **contentWindow.document.body. innerHTML** to **newText**.

   TIP Why is there a backslash ("\") before the slash ("/") in step 2? According to the standards, the browser may interpret the beginning of a closing tag ("</") as the end of the line. The backslash "escapes" the slash, allowing us to write out HTML without the chance of causing an error.
   ```

Creating Dynamic iframes

Building on the previous example, we can use JavaScript to create content for our iframe that's obviously dynamic. That content will be generated by **Listing 5.10**; when the user clicks one of the links, JavaScript writes out new code to the iframe. In this case, it's displaying the name of the page and how many times the user has gone to that page in this session.

To load a dynamic iframe:

1. `var pageCount = new Array(0,0,0,0);`

   In order to show how many times we load a page, we have to somehow keep track of that information. The **pageCount** array is what we'll use.

2. `pageCount[this.thisPage]++;`

   This line increments the **pageCount** array, so that we can keep track of how many times we've visited this particular page.

Listing 5.10 This script calculates the content of the iframe and writes it into the window.

```
window.onload = initLinks;
var pageCount = new Array(0,0,0,0);

function initLinks() {
    for (var i=0; i<document.links.length;
    → i++) {
        document.links[i].onclick =
        → writeContent;
        document.links[i].thisPage = i+1;
    }
}

function writeContent() {
    pageCount[this.thisPage]++;

    var newText = "<h1>You are now looking
    → at example " + this.thisPage;
    newText += ".<br>You have been to this
    → page ";
    newText += pageCount[this.thisPage] +
    → " times.<\/h1>";

    document.getElementById("icontent").
    → contentWindow.document.body.
    → innerHTML = newText;
    return false;
}
```

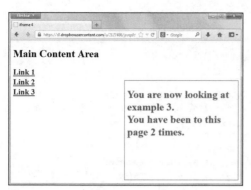

Ⓐ Each time you click a link in the main window, the content in the iframe updates.

3. `var newText = "<h1>You are now`
   `→ looking at example " +`
   `→ this.thisPage;`
   `newText += ".<br>You have been to`
   `→ this page ";`
   `newText += pageCount[this.`
   `→ thisPage] + " times.<\/h1>";`

   These lines create on the fly what will be the content of the iframe.

4. `document.getElementById`
   `→ ("icontent").contentWindow.`
   `→ document.body.innerHTML =`
   `→ newText;`
   `return false;`

   As with previous examples, we get the **icontent** element and reset the **innerHTML** property of its **body**. Resetting **innerHTML** writes the two lines of text in the iframe, and the result is shown in Ⓐ. And because that's everything, we end with a **return false** so that the browser doesn't do things it shouldn't.

Sharing Functions Between Documents

So long as both your main window and your iframe are coming from the same domain, it can be handy for them to share a single external JavaScript file. Here, we'll have the iframe load the external JavaScript file to demonstrate how it can be used by the main window **Ⓐ**. **Listing 5.11** is the main HTML page, **Listing 5.12** is the page loaded into the iframe, and **Listing 5.13** is our JavaScript file.

To use a function from another document:

1. `var bannerArray = new Array`
   `→ ("images/reading1.gif",`
   `→ "images/reading2.gif",`
   `→ "images/reading3.gif");`

   Start by creating a new array that contains all the possible banner image names, and assign the array to the **bannerArray** variable.

2. `for (var i=0; i<parent.document.`
   `→ links.length; i++) {`
   `   parent.document.links[i].`
   `   → onclick = setBanner;`

   Now we start the code inside the **initLinks()** function. Because this function is being called from the iframe's context, setting the main window's links is slightly different than in previous examples. This time, we reset the **onclick** handler of the *parent* document for each link.

3. `setBanner();`

   As the last initialization step, the **setBanner()** function is called.

Listing 5.11 This page has an image tag, but nothing to show in it.

```
<!DOCTYPE html>
<html>
<head>
    <title>iframe 5</title>
    <link rel="stylesheet" href="script01.
css">
</head>
<body>
    Today's featured site:
    <img src="images/spacer.gif" width="400"
    → height="75" id="adBanner"
    → alt="banner">
    <iframe src="iframe02.html"
    → id="icontent" name="icontent">
    → </iframe>
    <h1>Main Content Area</h1>
    <h2>
    <a href="#">Link 1</a><br>
    <a href="#">Link 2</a><br>
    <a href="#">Link 3</a>
    </h2>
</body>
</html>
```

Listing 5.12 Whereas this page loads an external JavaScript file that only refers to its parent.

```
<!DOCTYPE html>
<html>
<head>
    <title>Content iframe</title>
    <script src="script06.js"></script>
</head>
<body>
    Please load a page
</body>
</html>
```

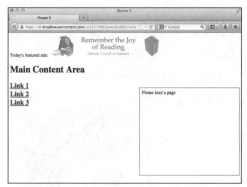

A The image on the main page is updated by code called from the iframe.

4. `var randomNum = Math.floor(Math.` → `random() * bannerArray.length);`

   The **setBanner()** function starts off by calculating a random number. This line uses the **Math.random()** function multiplied by the number of elements in the **bannerArray** array to calculate a random number between 0 and the number of elements in the array. Then it places the result into the **randomNum** variable.

5. `parent.document.getElementById` → `("adBanner").src = bannerArray` → `[randomNum];`

   The main window can refer to an iframe—its child document—just by using its **id**. But for an iframe to refer to the main window, it needs to explicitly refer to its **parent**. Here, we get that element (a **window**), the **document** in that window, and then the **adBanner** element itself. Then, we set the **src** for **adBanner** to the current item in the array. That's the new image name, which will then be displayed on the page. Then, the ad banner in the main window is set to a random ad from the array.

Listing 5.13 This script updates the parent page.

```
window.onload = initLinks;
var bannerArray = new Array("images/reading1.gif", "images/reading2.gif", "images/reading3.gif");

function initLinks() {
    for (var i=0; i<parent.document.links.length; i++) {
        parent.document.links[i].onclick = setBanner;
    }

    setBanner();
}

function setBanner() {
    var randomNum = Math.floor(Math.random() * bannerArray.length);

    parent.document.getElementById("adBanner").src = bannerArray[randomNum];
    return false;
}
```

Opening a New Window

You may want to create a new window to show users additional information without losing the information they're reading. For example, you could open up an annotation window for a technical paper or for a news story. Although it's possible to open a new browser window with HTML, using JavaScript gives you more control over the new window's content and features. **A** shows you a standard browser window with all the parts labeled. You can create windows that have any or all of these parts. **Listing 5.14** shows the HTML, and **Listing 5.15** shows the JavaScript that creates a window from a page **B** where clicking a link brings up a new window (that contains an image of our cat, in this example).

You'll note that there is no JavaScript in Listing 5.14, just a call to the external JavaScript file, and we also include an attribute to the link tag on the page:

B Opening a new window.

A The elements of a browser window. The names in this figure correspond to the parameters you can apply in the **open()** command.

Listing 5.14 The HTML page that calls the external JavaScript that opens a new window.

```
<!DOCTYPE html>
<html>
<head>
     <title>Opening a Window</title>
     <script src="script07.js"></script>
</head>
<body>
     <h1>The Master of the House</h1>
     <h2>Click on His name to behold He Who
     → Must Be Adored</h2>
     <h2><a href="#" class="newWin"
     →>Pixel</a></h2>
</body>
</html>
```

Listing 5.15 Use this script to open a new window.

```
window.onload = newWinLinks;

function newWinLinks() {
     for (var i=0; i<document.links.length;
     → i++) {
          if (document.links[i].className ==
          → "newWin") {
               document.links[i].onclick =
               → newWindow;
          }
     }
}

function newWindow() {
     var catWindow = window.open
     → ("images/pixel1.jpg", "catWin",
     → "resizable=no,width=350,height=260");
     return false;
}
```

TIP Internet Explorer 6 and later does some funky and inconsistent window stuff for security reasons (scripting windows will work, or not; that sort of thing). If security is turned off, everything in this chapter works fine, but we don't recommend turning off security or requiring your site visitors to turn off security. Additionally, some new windows in IE7 and later may open in new tabs instead, based on your tabbed browsing settings.

a class called **newWin**. As with the iframes examples, Listing 5.15 includes an **onload** event handler that calls a function, in this case called **newWinLinks**. The **newWinLinks** function cycles through the links on the page and looks to see if any of the links include a class of **newWin**. If so, when the link is clicked, the function calls the **newWindow** function.

To open a new window:

1. `document.links[i].onclick =`
   `→ newWindow;`

   In the **newWinLinks()** function, we've added the **newWindow()** function call as the **onclick** handler via JavaScript.

2. `function newWindow() {`

   Next, define a function called **newWindow()**.

3. `var catWindow = window.open`
   `→ ("images/pixel1.jpg", "catWin",`
   `→ "resizable=no,width=350,`
   `→ height=260");`

   The variable **catWindow** contains a new window object, referencing the image file **pixel1.jpg**. The name of this new window is **catWin**. Names are required, because we might want to reference this window later in a link or in another script. The new window has a width of 350 pixels and a height of 260 pixels; these parameters are optional.

TIP In step 3, you can't have any spaces between the commas in the width and height parameters. If you do, your script may not work in some browsers. In general, when you get script errors and you need to debug your scripts, look for little problems like this. Syntax errors can be a major cause of frustration, especially when you're new to coding.

Adding Parameters to Windows

To add one or more of the parameters listed in Ⓐ (at the beginning of this section) to your windows, put them in the **open()** command enclosed in quotes, with **=yes** after the name of a feature you want and **=no** after one you don't want (though **=no** is usually the default, so you can often skip even mentioning those features). For example, if you want a window of a specified size with a toolbar, a location box, and scrollbars, you would type

"toolbar=yes,location=yes,scrollbars=yes,width=300,height=300"

as part of the **open()** command. Note that the window created would not have a menu bar or a status bar, and it would not be resizable.

Given that leaving a parameter off entirely is (usually, see below for some exceptions) the same as setting it to **=no**, you can also just use the name of the parameter itself (without the **=yes**) to turn it on. Because there are some exceptions, we prefer to make it a little more obvious what we're turning on and off—that is, we use **"location=yes,scrollbars=yes"**.

Ⓒ shows the results of Listing 5.15 in (from left to right) Firefox for Windows, IE for Windows, Chrome for Mac, and Safari for Mac. As you can see, no two browsers produce identical results. In fact, the only browser that did just what we wanted was Safari. You may get results that differ from ours; for example, Firefox gives the user ultimate control—if they have their options set to require the add-on (status) bar to show, it always will, no matter what your script says to do.

Ultimately, you'll still need to test your scripts in all the browsers that you think your site's users are most likely to be using, which may mean keeping both Windows and Mac (and maybe Linux) machines around for testing. Testing (and if necessary, script revision) will help make sure that your intentions for the script will work with whatever the browser hands you.

Ⓒ Different browsers use different window defaults, so items like the location appear even though you've told it not to.

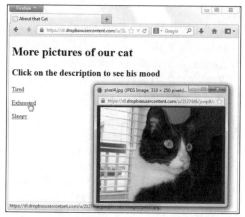

A Clicking any of the three links opens the smaller window and fills it with the appropriate image of our cat.

Listing 5.16 With this script, you can open a new window and fill it with a variety of content, triggered by clicking different links.

```
window.onload = newWinLinks;

function newWinLinks() {
    for (var i=0; i<document.links.length;
    → i++) {
        if (document.links[i].className ==
        → "newWin") {
            document.links[i].onclick =
            → newWindow;
        }
    }
}

function newWindow() {
    var catWindow = window.open(this.href,
    → "catWin","width=350,height=260");
    catWindow.focus();
    return false;
}
```

Loading Different Contents into a Window

In the previous task, clicking a link created a new window filled with an image. But what if you have several links on a page, and you want them all to target a single new window? **Listing 5.16** demonstrates this technique. The main window in **A** has three links. Clicking any of the links opens a new window, filled with the corresponding image of our cat. If you switch back to the main window and click another link, the image in the smaller window is replaced.

To load different contents into a window:

1. `document.links[i].onclick =`
   `→ newWindow;`

   In the **newWinLinks()** function, we've added the **newWindow()** function call as the **onclick** handler via JavaScript. Unlike in the previous task, when **newWindow()** is called, it uses **this.href**—that is, the **href** attribute value from HTML.

2. `function newWindow() {`

   Here, we're defining a new function called **newWindow()**.

   continues on next page

3. ```
var catWindow = window.open
  → (this.href, "catWin",
  → "width=350, height=260");
```

   By setting the variable **catWindow**, we're opening a new window object, followed by the window's parameters. First, we pass it the value of **this.href**. The name of the new window is **catWin**, and the width and height parameters set the size of the window.

4. ```
catWindow.focus();
```

   This line uses the **focus()** method to tell the window we just opened to come to the front. You can use **focus()** whenever you need to make a window visible; if there are several windows open, using **focus()** brings the window to the top.

5. ```
return false;
```

   The function needs to end with **return false** so that the HTML knows to not also load the **href** in.

**TIP** The opposite of the focus() method used in step 4 is blur(). Using blur() pushes a window behind any other windows that are open. The focus() and blur() methods of the window object have associated onfocus and onblur event handlers, which let you take action when a window gains or loses focus.

## Don't Kill Those Pop-Ups!

The last two tasks in this chapter are about creating and working with windows using JavaScript. These particular windows are called pop-up windows, and they've become a bane to many a web surfer. We've shown you some benign uses of pop-up windows, but if you're having trouble getting these examples to work, it may be because you've turned off pop-up windows in your browser, or because you have other software running that kills pop-up windows. While most browsers should open any pop-up that you've explicitly chosen to open, some don't. So while you're working on this chapter, make sure your pop-up killers are turned off.

However, some browsers, allegedly for security reasons (we're looking at *you*, Internet Explorer), will decide they know better than you and will not open pop-up windows from scripts even if you've asked them to.
```

6

Form Handling

Anytime you need to gather information from the users of your websites, you'll need to use a form.

Forms can contain most of the usual graphical interface elements, including entry fields, radio buttons, check boxes, pop-up menus, and entry lists. In addition, HTML forms can contain password fields, shielding the user's input from prying eyes.

Once the form is filled out, a click on the form's Submit button sends the form's information to your web server, where a server-side script interprets the data and acts on it. Often, the data is then stored in a database for later use. It's useful to make sure that the data the user enters is "clean"—that is, accurate and in the correct format—before it gets stored on the server. JavaScript is the perfect way to check the data; this is called *form validation*. Though the server-side script can do the validation (and should as a backup measure, since some people will have JavaScript turned off in their browsers), it's much faster and more efficient for your users to initially do it on their own machines with JavaScript.

In this chapter, you'll learn how to use JavaScript to make sure that your forms contain valid information, to check the data in one field against the data in another field, and to highlight incorrect information to let the user know what needs to be changed.

TABLE 6.1 Just Enough HTML—Forms

Tag	Attribute	Meaning
`form`		A tag that contains any of the following tags, making them into a valid HTML form
	`action`	The name of the server-side script that is run when control is passed back to the web server
`input`		A form field of varying types, depending on the value of the **type** attribute
	`name`	Primarily used to group sets of radio buttons
	`maxlength`	The maximum length entry that the user may enter in this field
	`size`	The number of characters that are displayed on the page
	`type`	The type of input required; possible values include **button**, **checkbox**, **image**, **password**, **radio**, **reset**, **submit**, and **text**
	`value`	The preset value of this form field
`label`		Used to specify labels for controls that do not have built-in labels, such as text fields, check boxes, radio buttons, and menus
	`for`	Associates the label with a specific element's **id**
`option`		The possible options available inside a select tag
	`selected`	Indicates whether this option is selected as the default
	`value`	The preset value of each option
`select`		A form field that is either a pop-up menu or a scrolling list, based on the **size** attribute
	`size`	The number of options that are displayed on the page; if the attribute is set to 1, or this attribute is not present, the result is a pop-up menu

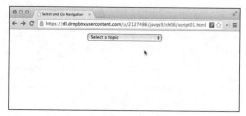

(A) Picking any of the choices in this menu jumps you directly to the page containing that topic, without requiring a separate Go button.

Select-and-Go Navigation

You've probably seen lots of examples of the common navigation menu on the web; you pick a choice from a menu and click a Go button, which takes you to your destination. For example, many online stores use such menus to move you to different departments. But with a bit of JavaScript, you can launch users on their way with just the menu choice, eliminating the Go button **(A)**. This makes your site feel snappier and more responsive, which is always a good idea. We call these JavaScript-enhanced menus select-and-go menus, and they're easy to create. The HTML is in **Listing 6.1**, the CSS is in **Listing 6.2**, and the JavaScript is shown in **Listing 6.3**. You'll never want to use a Go button again!

Listing 6.1 The HTML for a select-and-go menu is fairly simple.

```html
<!DOCTYPE html>
<html>
<head>
    <title>Select and Go Navigation</title>
    <link rel="stylesheet" href="script01.css">
    <script src="script01.js"></script>
</head>
<body>
<form action="gotoLocation.cgi" class="centered">
    <select id="newLocation">
        <option selected>Select a topic</option>
        <option value="script06.html">Cross-checking fields</option>
        <option value="script07.html">Working with radio buttons</option>
        <option value="script08.html">Setting one field with another</option>
        <option value="script09.html">Validating Zip codes</option>
        <option value="script10.html">Validating email addresses</option>
    </select>
    <noscript>
        <input type="submit" value="Go There!">
    </noscript>
</form>
</body>
</html>
```

To create a select-and-go menu:

1. ```
   window.onload = initForm;
   window.onunload = function() {};
   ```

   When the window loads, call the **initForm()** function. The next line needs some explanation, because it is a workaround for the odd behavior of some browsers.

   When the window *unloads* (i.e., when it is closed or the browser goes to another location), we call an anonymous function; that is, a function that doesn't have a name. In this case, it not only doesn't have a name, it doesn't have anything at all. It's here because we have to set **onunload** to *something*—otherwise, the **onload** event isn't triggered when the browser's back button is clicked, because the page is cached in some browsers (e.g., Firefox and Safari). Having **onunload** do anything at all causes the page to be uncached, and therefore, when we come back, the **onload** happens.

Listing 6.2 There's not a lot in this CSS file, but it's here when you want to add more styling.

```
.centered {
    text-align: center;
}
```
```

Listing 6.3 You can use JavaScript and forms for active site navigation.

```
window.onload = initForm;
window.onunload = function() {};

function initForm() {
    document.getElementById("newLocation").
    → selectedIndex = 0;
    document.getElementById("newLocation").
    → onchange = jumpPage;
}

function jumpPage() {
    var newLoc = document.getElementById
    → ("newLocation");
    var newPage = newLoc.options
    → [newLoc.selectedIndex].value;

    if (newPage != "") {
        window.location = newPage;
    }
}
```

2. ```
document.getElementById
→ ("newLocation").
→ selectedIndex = 0;
document.getElementById
→ ("newLocation").
→ onchange = jumpPage;
```

In the **initForm()** function, the first line gets the menu on the HTML page, which has the **id** of **newLocation**, and sets its **selectedIndex** property to zero, which forces it to say "Select a topic."

The second line tells the script to call the **jumpPage()** function when the menu selection changes.

3. ```
var newLoc = document.
→ getElementById("newLocation");
```

Inside the **jumpPage()** function, the **newLoc** variable looks up the value chosen in the menu by the visitor.

4. ```
var newPage = newLoc.options
→ [newLoc.selectedIndex].value;
```

Start from the code inside the brackets and work outward. The object **newLoc.selectedIndex** will be a number from 0 to 5 (because there are six possible menu choices; remember that JavaScript arrays are zero-based). Given that number, we next get the value for the corresponding menu option, which is the name of the webpage we want to jump to. Then we assign the result to the variable **newPage**.

*continues on next page*
```

5. `if (newPage != "") {`
   `   window.location = newPage;`

This conditional first checks to see that **newPage** is not equal to nothing (that is, it's not empty). In other words, if **newPage** has a value, then tell the window to go to the URL specified by the menu option chosen.

TIP One of the nicest things about this script is that once the JavaScript function has been added, there's no need to modify the function when pull-down options are added, modified, or changed. Only the values of the options (i.e., the URLs that the menu options jump to) need to be set. For this reason, this script works well with WYSIWYG page editors.

TIP As mentioned above, Firefox caches pages, causing `onload` events to not be triggered when the back button is clicked. One way to work around this is covered above; another way we can do this is to add the following line:

`window.onpageshow = initForm;`

We didn't use this because it doesn't work in Safari (the other caching troublemaker). But if you are specifically targeting Firefox, it's worth knowing that there are two new non-standard window event handlers, `onpageshow` and `onpagehide`, which can be used to handle events that we only want triggered in Firefox.

TIP We call these "select-and-go" menus, which isn't especially elegant but clearly tells you what's going on. You may see other names for the same functionality; for example, Dreamweaver calls them "jump menus." By the way, if you're a Dreamweaver user and need a great book on getting the most out of Dreamweaver, let us suggest *Dreamweaver: Visual QuickStart Guide* (Peachpit Press), by, uh, us.

Accommodating the JavaScript-impaired User

The point of this task is to use JavaScript to eliminate the need for a Go button when using a form to jump from one page to another. But what if the user has an old, non-JavaScript-capable browser, or just has JavaScript turned off? No problem; Listing 6.1 handles those users just fine, by putting in a Go button that's visible only in the absence of JavaScript.

The only way to get from one page to another with a form but without JavaScript is to use a server-side script, a program running on the web server. Listing 6.1 sets that up in this line:

```
<form action="gotoLocation.cgi">
```

The **form** tag has the **action** attribute, which calls the server-side script. But a **form action** requires the user to click a **submit** button, and there's no such button in Ⓐ at the beginning of this section. Ah, but there is in Ⓑ, which shows what happens when you turn JavaScript off. These lines contain the button, which is wrapped in the **noscript** tags, which are only executed if JavaScript is missing.

```
<noscript>
        <input type="submit" value="Go There!">
</noscript>
```

The really cool thing about all this is that the server-side script only ever gets called if JavaScript is missing; if the user has a JavaScript-enabled browser, then the **submit** button doesn't appear, and the server-side script is unnecessary.

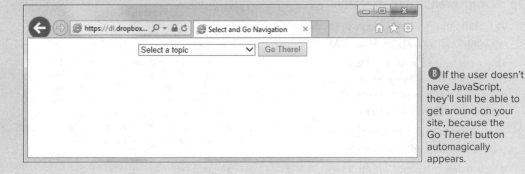

Ⓑ If the user doesn't have JavaScript, they'll still be able to get around on your site, because the Go There! button automagically appears.

Changing Menus Dynamically

It's often useful to offer the user a choice of inputs via pop-up menus, and to be able to change the contents of one or more pop-up menus depending on the choice the user makes in another pop-up menu. You've probably seen this on websites that ask you to choose the country you live in from a pop-up menu and then fill a second menu with state or province names, based on the choice you made. In **Listings 6.4** (HTML) and **6.5** (JavaScript), we're using two pop-up menus **A**. The first menu is for months. When the user picks a month, the script populates the second pop-up menu with the correct number of days for the selected month **B**.

To change menus dynamically:

1. `var monthDays = new Array(31,28,`
   `→ 31,30,31,30,31,31,30,31,30,31);`

   This new array contains 12 values for the 12 months, with the correct number of days in each month. The array is stored in the variable **monthDays**.

2. `var monthStr = this.options`
   `→ [this.selectedIndex].value;`

   We're using **this** (the month the user picked from the first menu) to get the value from the menu, and storing it in **monthStr**.

A The contents of the second menu are filled in automatically when the user makes a selection from the first menu.

Listing 6.4 The HTML for the pop-up menus lists the months but not the days.

```
<!DOCTYPE html>
<html>
<head>
    <title>Dynamic Menus</title>
    <script src="script02.js"></script>
</head>
<body>
<form action="#">
    <select id="months">
        <option value="">Month</option>
        <option value="0">January</option>
        <option value="1">February</option>
        <option value="2">March</option>
        <option value="3">April</option>
        <option value="4">May</option>
        <option value="5">June</option>
        <option value="6">July</option>
        <option value="7">August</option>
        <option value="8">September</option>
        <option value="9">October</option>
        <option value="10">November</option>
        <option value="11">December</option>
    </select>
     
    <select id="days">
        <option>Day</option>
    </select>
</form>
</body>
</html>
```

B The result of choosing a month: the correct number of days in that month appears in the Day menu.

Listing 6.5 By selecting a value from one pop-up menu, you can create the contents of a second pop-up menu.

```
window.onload = initForm;

function initForm() {
    document.getElementById("months").
    → selectedIndex = 0;
    document.getElementById("months").
    → onchange = populateDays;
}

function populateDays() {
    var monthDays = new Array(31,28,31,30,
    → 31,30,31,31,30,31,30,31);
    var monthStr = this.options
    → [this.selectedIndex].value;

    if (monthStr != "") {
        var theMonth = parseInt(monthStr);

        document.getElementById("days").
        → options.length = 0;
        for (var i=0; i<monthDays[theMonth];
        → i++) {
            document.getElementById("days").
            → options[i] = new Option(i+1);
        }
    }
}
```

3. ```
   if (monthStr != "") {
       var theMonth =
       → parseInt(monthStr);
   ```

   If the value of **monthStr** is "", then the user chose the word "Month" in the menu, rather than a month name. What these lines do is check to see that the value of **monthStr** is not ""; if that condition is true, then **monthStr** is turned into a number with the **parseInt()** method, and the variable **theMonth** is set to the result.

4. ```
   document.getElementById("days").
   → options.length = 0;
   for (var i=0; i<monthDays
   → [theMonth]; i++) {
       document.getElementById("days").
       → options[i] = new Option(i+1);
   ```

   Start changing the day menu by setting its options length to zero. That clears out whatever happened to be there before, so we're starting fresh. The loop simply goes through the number of days in whatever the chosen month is, adding a new option to the menu for each day. Option is passed **i**+1, so that it shows 1 to 31 instead of 0 to 30.

TIP The **monthDays** array contains the number of days in each month, which works fine except in the case of leap years. To get your script to work in a leap year, you'll need to change the February value in **monthDays**.

Making Fields Required

When filling out a form, you may want to specify particular fields that are required to be filled out by the user before the form can be submitted. You can use JavaScript to check that some or all fields are filled out. In this example, we use HTML, CSS, and JavaScript (**Listings 6.6**, **6.7**, and **6.8**, respectively) to highlight fields that are not filled out with a red border and a yellow interior. The check occurs when the user clicks the form's Submit button.

Here's the big picture: the **class** attributes in the HTML page store the checks we want JavaScript to do. If a check is failed, we add **invalid** to the list of **class** attributes. Doing that causes (1) the form submission to fail, and (2) the CSS in Listing 6.7 to change the appearance of the field on the page .

To make fields required:

1. ```
   window.onload = function() {
       document.forms[0].onsubmit =
   → validForm;
   ```

   When the page first loads, an anonymous function looks for the first form on the page. For that form, it adds an event handler to that form's **onsubmit**: a call to **validForm**. When an **onsubmit** handler returns a value of false, the form doesn't automatically get passed back to the server. The server only gets the form (running whatever server-side script is stored in the action attribute) when we return a value of true.

Ⓐ Make sure that passwords are entered correctly by highlighting the background to let the user know there's a problem with a particular field.

Listing 6.6 The HTML for the password check example.

```
<!DOCTYPE html>
<html>
<head>
    <title>Password Check</title>
    <link rel="stylesheet"
    → href="script03.css">
    <script src="script03.js"></script>
</head>
<body>
<form action="#">
    <p><label for="userName">Your
    → name: <input type="text" size="30"
    → id="userName" class="reqd"></label></p>
    <p><label for="passwd1">Choose a
    → password: <input type="password"
    → id="passwd1" class="reqd"></label></p>
    <p><label for="passwd2">Verify password:
    → <input type="password" id="passwd2"
    → class="reqd passwd1"></label></p>
    <p><input type="submit" value="Submit">
    →  <input type="reset"></p>
</form>
</body>
</html>
```
```

Listing 6.7 The CSS sets the style for invalid form elements.

```css
body {
    color: #000;
    background-color: #FFF;
}

input.invalid {
    background-color: #FF9;
    border: 2px red inset;
}

label.invalid {
    color: #F00;
    font-weight: bold;
}
```

2. `var allTags = document.forms[0].`
   `→ getElementsByTagName("*");`

   The **document.getElementsByTagName**
   → ("*") object is very useful—that asterisk tells JavaScript to return an array containing *every* tag on the page. It's even more useful when you realize that you can use it to get every tag *inside* a particular element, as we've done here. This line of code finds every tag inside the page's first form. Once we have that, we can then just loop through the **allTags** array looking for things of interest.

3. `for (var i=0; i<allTags.length;`
   `→ i++) {`
   `    if (!validTag(allTags[i])) {`
   `        allGood = false;`

   This loop searches through **allTags**, and the **if** conditional calls the **validTag()** function, which checks each tag to see if there's anything there that should keep the form from submitting this page. It's passed **allTags[i]**, which is the object that we're currently processing. If any tag causes **validTag()** to return false, we set **allGood** to false. However, even if one is false, we still keep going through all the tags.

4. `return allGood;`

   We return **allGood**, to signify whether or not we're good to go.

5. `function validTag(thisTag) {`

   Create the **validTag()** function, and set it to receive the parameter **thisTag**.

   continues on next page

6. `var allClasses = thisTag.`
   `→ className.split(" ");`

For each tag, we want to look at every **class** attribute (remember, **class** can be set to have multiple attributes "like so and so and so"). The **allClasses** array is created and set based on **thisTag.className.split(" "),** which splits a string up into an array, broken up by the string that's passed in. Here, the string is a space, which would, for example, cause the string "this that and the other" to turn into an array of five elements: this, that, and, the, other.

We want to look at each **class** attribute, because **class** is where we're storing what we want each form field to have to provide. In this task, the one we care about is **reqd**—required. If any form field has a **class** that includes **reqd**, it's got to contain something.

7. `for (var j=0; j<allClasses.length;`
   `→ j++) {`
   `   outClass += validBasedOnClass`
   `→ (allClasses[j]) + " ";`

This loop uses **j** as its loop variable because we're inside a loop that's using **i**. We loop around once for each **class** attribute in **allClasses**.

For each class, we set **outClass** to **validBasedOnClass(allClasses[j])**. This calls the **validBasedOnClass()** function (explained below), passing in the current class we're looking at. That function returns something, and that something, plus a space, is appended onto the **outClass** variable.

8. `thisTag.className = outClass;`

When we've finished with the **allClasses** loop, we take the contents of **outClass** and put it into **thisTag.className**, overwriting the current **class** attribute

Listing 6.8 This script serves as the basis for all the rest of the examples in this chapter; it's a framework that you can use to add additional validation checks.

```
window.onload = function() {
    document.forms[0].onsubmit = validForm;
}

function validForm() {
    var allGood = true;
    var allTags = document.forms[0].
    → getElementsByTagName("*");

    for (var i=0; i<allTags.length; i++) {
        if (!validTag(allTags[i])) {
            allGood = false;
        }
    }
    return allGood;

    function validTag(thisTag) {
        var outClass = "";
        var allClasses = thisTag.className.
        → split(" ");

        for (var j=0; j<allClasses.length;
        → j++) {
            outClass += validBasedOnClass
            → (allClasses[j]) + " ";
        }

        thisTag.className = outClass;

        if (outClass.indexOf("invalid") > -1) {
            thisTag.focus();
            if (thisTag.nodeName == "INPUT") {
                thisTag.select();
            }
            return false;
        }
```

listing continues on next page

Listing 6.8 *continued*

```
    return true;

    function validBasedOnClass
→ (thisClass) {
      var classBack = "";

      switch(thisClass) {
        case "":
        case "invalid":
          break;
        case "reqd":
          if (allGood && thisTag.
          → value == "") {
            classBack = "invalid ";
          }
          classBack += thisClass;
          break;
        default:
          classBack += thisClass;
      }
      return classBack;
    }
  }
}
```

for this form field. That's because it can change during this process, as we'll see very shortly.

9. `if (outClass.indexOf("invalid") >`
`→ -1) {`

Something that can be returned in the new **class** attribute is the word "invalid", so we check for it. If that's found anywhere in the new class, do the following, as there's a problem.

10. `thisTag.focus();`

If this form field can take focus (remember, we discussed focus in Chapter 5), we want to put the focus into the field, and that's what this line does. This is a way of forcing the user to know which field is the problem.

11. `if (thisTag.nodeName == "INPUT") {`
`thisTag.select();`

Basically, these lines say, "This tag I'm looking at: is it an **<input>** tag? If so, select its value so that the user has an easier time modifying it."

12. `return false;`

We're still inside the "invalid was returned" block, so we return false back to where we were called.

13. `return true;`

If all is good and valid, we return true.

14. `function validBasedOnClass`
`→ (thisClass) {`
`var classBack = "";`

Begin the new **validBasedOnClass()** function, and set it to receive the value **thisClass**. Next, initialize the **classBack** variable, which will contain the class to be returned; that is, the value we want to send back.

continues on next page

15. `switch(thisClass) {`

The **switch** statement looks at the single **class** attribute that was passed in (in **thisClass**) and does one of the following based on it.

16. `case "":`
`case "invalid":`
`   break;`

If **thisClass** is empty or **invalid**, then break out of the switch/case statement.

17. `case "reqd":`
`    if (allGood && thisTag.value`
`→  == "") {`
`      classBack = "invalid ";`
`    }`
`    classBack += thisClass;`
`    break;`

If the attribute being processed is **reqd** *and* **allGood** is true *and* the value of the current tag is **""** (i.e., nothing), then set **classBack** to be **invalid**, because there's a problem and we want to notify the user. After that, whether there was a problem or not, we append the current class to **classBack** so that it doesn't get lost.

18. `default:`
`    classBack += thisClass;`

The **default** block is executed when-ever something happens that isn't caught by one of the above cases. When that happens, it's a class we don't care about, so we just stick it onto **classBack** and don't fret.

19. `return classBack;`

Finally, we return **classBack**.

TIP It's good UI design to have only a single form on a page, so this script assumes that it only needs to look at the first (i.e., only) form. If you're trying to add validation to pages with multiple forms, you'll need to tweak this script accordingly.

A The two password fields cross-check to make sure their contents are identical. In this case, not so much.

Checking Fields Against Each Other

It's common to want to check one field against another, especially when you're asking the user to type in a password. You want to make them type it in twice for accuracy, and you want to make sure that they typed the same thing both times.

This example reuses Listings 6.6 (HTML) and 6.7 (CSS); only a few lines of JavaScript need to be added to Listing 6.8 (**Listing 6.9**) to give the script the extra cross-checking functionality. The result is shown in **A**; once again, when the check fails, the offending field gets a red border.

Listing 6.9 Use this script to compare the value of one field to another. Do they match?

```
window.onload = function() {
    document.forms[0].onsubmit = validForm;
}

function validForm() {
    var allGood = true;
    var allTags = document.forms[0].getElementsByTagName("*");

    for (var i=0; i<allTags.length; i++) {
        if (!validTag(allTags[i])) {
            allGood = false;
        }
    }
    return allGood;

    function validTag(thisTag) {
        var outClass = "";
        var allClasses = thisTag.className.split(" ");

        for (var j=0; j<allClasses.length; j++) {
            outClass += validBasedOnClass(allClasses[j]) + " ";
```

listing continues on next page

To check one field against another:

1. ```
if (allGood && !crossCheck
→ (thisTag,thisClass)) {
   classBack = "invalid ";
```

   We're now checking to make sure that the two password fields are the same. Because (see Listing 6.6) the second password field has a class containing **passwd1**, this JavaScript knows that it has to cross-check the second field against the first. Here in the **default** block of the conditional is where that's handled. If **allGood** is true *and* the **crossCheck()** function (see below) spotted a problem (and returned false), then we want to set **classBack** to **invalid**.

2. ```
function
crossCheck(inTag,otherFieldID) {
   if (!document.getElementById
→ (otherFieldID)) {
      return false;
   }
   return (inTag.value ==
→ document.getElementById
→ (otherFieldID).value);
```

   Here's the **crossCheck()** function. It takes in the current tag and the **id** of the other field to check against. In this case, the current tag is the **passwd2** **<input>** and the **id** of the other field is **passwd1**. If the other field doesn't exist, no check can be done; that's a problem, so the function returns false. Otherwise, the fields both exist, so we compare their values: if they're equivalent, true is returned; if they aren't, false is returned.

   TIP This script does not check against a master password database to see if the password the user entered is valid; that requires a server-side script. It just makes sure that when a password is entered twice, it has the same value both times.

Listing 6.9 *continued*

```
   }

   thisTag.className = outClass;

   if (outClass.indexOf("invalid") > -1) {
      thisTag.focus();
      if (thisTag.nodeName == "INPUT") {
         thisTag.select();
      }
      return false;
   }
   return true;
}

function validBasedOnClass(thisClass) {
   var classBack = "";

   switch(thisClass) {
      case "":
      case "invalid":
         break;
      case "reqd":
         if (allGood && thisTag.
→ value == "") {
            classBack = "invalid ";
         }
         classBack += thisClass;
         break;
      default:
         if (allGood && !crossCheck
→ (thisTag,thisClass)) {
            classBack = "invalid ";
         }
         classBack += thisClass;
   }
   return classBack;

   function crossCheck
→ (inTag,otherFieldID) {
      if (!document.getElementById
→ (otherFieldID)) {
         return false;
      }
      return (inTag.value ==
→ document.getElementById
→ (otherFieldID).value);
   }
   }
}
```

A When there's a problem, you can make the field's label, as well as the field itself, red and bold.

Identifying Problem Fields

Changing the border of the input field to red is nice and all, but it would be better if we could make it a little clearer which field was the problem. In this example, you'll learn how to set the label next to the field to be red and bold, making it clear where the problem lies **A**. Once again, the HTML and CSS files have not changed (they're still Listings 6.6 and 6.7). In **Listing 6.10**, we've added a few lines of JavaScript to Listing 6.9 to help point out entry errors.

Listing 6.10 This script highlights the incorrect field's label when it finds an error.

```
window.onload = function() {
    document.forms[0].onsubmit = validForm;
}

function validForm() {
    var allGood = true;
    var allTags = document.forms[0].getElementsByTagName("*");

    for (var i=0; i<allTags.length; i++) {
        if (!validTag(allTags[i])) {
            allGood = false;
        }
    }
    return allGood;

    function validTag(thisTag) {
        var outClass = "";
        var allClasses = thisTag.className.split(" ");

        for (var j=0; j<allClasses.length; j++) {
            outClass += validBasedOnClass(allClasses[j]) + " ";
        }

        thisTag.className = outClass;

        if (outClass.indexOf("invalid") > -1) {
```

listing continues on next page

To identify a problem form field:

1. `invalidLabel(thisTag.parentNode);`

   This line of code has been added to the invalid check inside `validTag()`. When the current field fails validation, we want to check to see if we can also highlight the `label` surrounding the problem child. To do this, call the new `invalidLabel()` function (explained below) and pass it the *parent* of our current tag. That is, if there's a problem with the `passwd1 input` field, we want both that tag *and* the `label` tag around it to be assigned a `class` of `invalid`. So, once we know that the `passwd1 input` field has a problem, we pass its parent (the `label` tag) over to `invalidLabel()` to see if it's an appropriate element to mark invalid.

2. ```
   function invalidLabel(parentTag) {
      if (parentTag.nodeName ==
    → "LABEL") {
         parentTag.className +=
    → " invalid";
   ```

   This function takes in a tag and checks to see if that tag is a label. If it is, it adds the attribute `invalid` to its class.

   If we now try to submit the form and there's an error, we'll notice that the field labels for the problem fields turn bold and red when there's a problem. Fix the error, submit the form, and they'll turn black again.

Listing 6.10 *continued*

```
         invalidLabel(thisTag.parentNode);
         thisTag.focus();
         if (thisTag.nodeName == "INPUT") {
            thisTag.select();
         }
         return false;
      }
      return true;
   }
   function validBasedOnClass
 → (thisClass) {
      var classBack = "";

      switch(thisClass) {
         case "":
         case "invalid":
            break;
         case "reqd":
            if (allGood && thisTag.
          → value == "") {
               classBack = "invalid ";
            }
            classBack += thisClass;
            break;
         default:
            if (allGood && !crossCheck
          → (thisTag,thisClass)) {
               classBack = "invalid ";
            }
            classBack += thisClass;
      }
      return classBack;

      function crossCheck
    → (inTag,otherFieldID) {
         if (!document.getElementById
       → (otherFieldID)) {
            return false;
         }
         return (inTag.value ==
       → document.getElementById
       → (otherFieldID).value);
      }
   }
}

function invalidLabel(parentTag) {
   if (parentTag.nodeName == "LABEL") {
      parentTag.className += " invalid";
   }
}
}
```
```

The Car Picker form uses text fields, a pop-up menu, check boxes, and radio buttons—all common form elements.

Putting Form Validation into Action

One interesting thing about the script that we built up in the last few examples is that it is largely independent of the HTML page that we used with it. In other words, you can substitute an entirely different page, with a completely different form, and you need to make only minor changes to the script to have it do all the validation tasks you want.

For example, take a look at **A**, which is a simplistic version of a form that could be used to customize a car that you want to purchase. The form includes a variety of options and interface elements, including radio buttons, menus, check boxes, and text fields that need validation for correct data entry. You'll find the HTML for this form in **Listing 6.11** and the CSS in **Listing 6.12**; we'll be using these files for the rest of the examples in this chapter.

The JavaScript file, **Listing 6.13**, builds on the script that we've used earlier in this chapter. We've added a few lines to the script to handle the new interface elements, but otherwise the form is the same. In this example, you'll see what needed to be added to prepare the script for more validation, and subsequent examples will go deeper into specific types of form elements.

Listing 6.11 Here's the entire HTML page for the Car Picker example.

```html
<!DOCTYPE html>
<html>
<head>
    <title>Car Picker</title>
    <link rel="stylesheet" href="script06.css">
    <script src="script06.js"></script>
</head>
<body>
<h2 class="centered">Car Picker</h2>
<form action="someAction.cgi">
    <p><label for="emailAddr">Email Address:<input id="emailAddr" type="text" size="30"
    → class="reqd email"></label></p>
    <p>Colors:
        <select id="color" class="reqd">
            <option value="" selected>Choose a color</option>
            <option value="Red">Red</option>
            <option value="Green">Green</option>
            <option value="Blue">Blue</option>
        </select>
    </p>
    <p>Options:
        <label for="sunroof"><input type="checkbox" id="sunroof" value="Yes">Sunroof
        → (Two door only)</label>
        <label for="pWindows"><input type="checkbox" id="pWindows" value="Yes">Power Windows</label>
    </p>
    <p>Doors:  
        <label for="twoDoor"><input type="radio" id="twoDoor" name="DoorCt" value="twoDoor"
        → class="radio">Two</label>
        <label for="fourDoor"><input type="radio" id="fourDoor" name="DoorCt" value="fourDoor"
        → class="radio">Four</label>
    </p>
    <p>
        <label for="zip">Enter your Zip code or pick the dealer nearest you:<br>
            Zip: <input id="zip" type="text" size="5" maxlength="5" class="isZip dealerList">
        </label>
        <select id="dealerList" size="4" class="zip">
            <option value="California--Lemon Grove">California--Lemon Grove</option>
            <option value="California--Lomita">California--Lomita</option>
            <option value="California--Long Beach">California--Long Beach</option>
            <option value="California--Los Alamitos">California--Los Alamitos</option>
            <option value="California--Los Angeles">California--Los Angeles</option>
        </select>
    </p>
    <p><input type="submit" value="Submit"> <input type="reset"></p>
</form>
</body>
</html>
```

Listing 6.12 Some of the styles shown here will only be used later on.

```css
body {
    color: #000;
    background-color: #FFF;
}

input.invalid {
    background-color: #FF9;
    border: 2px red inset;
}

label.invalid {
    color: #F00;
    font-weight: bold;
}

select {
    margin-left: 80px;
}

input {
    margin-left: 30px;
}

input+select, input+input {
    margin-left: 20px;
}

.centered {
    text-align: center;
}
```

To validate a form with many elements:

1. ```
   case "radio":
   case "isNum":
   case "isZip":
   case "email":
       classBack += thisClass;
       break;
   ```

   By adding additional blocks to the **switch**/**case** conditional inside the **validBasedOnClass()** function, we allow the script to handle more situations. We've added **radio**, **isNum**, **isZip**, and **email** to the list. Although we're not validating them in this task, they do exist on the HTML page, so we add each to the list of attributes handled by the **switch**/**case**. Because there are no instructions in the first three blocks, all of them fall through to **email**, which just adds the attribute currently being checked onto **classBack**.

2. ```
   return (inTag.value != "" ||
   → document.getElementById
   → (otherFieldID).value != "");
   ```

   This line in **crossCheck()** has changed a bit. Instead of comparing the two fields to make sure they're the same, we're comparing two fields to make sure that at least one of them is set (this is in preparation for dealing with the zip code and list elements at the end of the form). If either field contains a value, we return true. If not, we return false.

Listing 6.13 This script adds several blocks to the **switch**/**case** conditional, setting it up for later examples.

```
window.onload = function() {
    document.forms[0].onsubmit = validForm;
}

function validForm() {
    var allGood = true;
    var allTags = document.forms[0].getElementsByTagName("*");

    for (var i=0; i<allTags.length; i++) {
        if (!validTag(allTags[i])) {
            allGood = false;
        }
    }
    return allGood;

    function validTag(thisTag) {
        var outClass = "";
        var allClasses = thisTag.className.split(" ");

        for (var j=0; j<allClasses.length; j++) {
            outClass += validBasedOnClass(allClasses[j]) + " ";
        }

        thisTag.className = outClass;

        if (outClass.indexOf("invalid") > -1) {
            invalidLabel(thisTag.parentNode);
            thisTag.focus();
            if (thisTag.nodeName == "INPUT") {
                thisTag.select();
            }
            return false;
        }
        return true;

        function validBasedOnClass(thisClass) {
            var classBack = "";

            switch(thisClass) {
                case "":
                case "invalid":
                    break;
                case "reqd":
                    if (allGood && thisTag.value == "") {
                        classBack = "invalid ";
                    }
                    classBack += thisClass;
```

listing continues on next page

Listing 6.13 *continued*

```
                break;
            case "radio":
            case "isNum":
            case "isZip":
            case "email":
                classBack += thisClass;
                break;
            default:
                if (allGood && !crossCheck(thisTag,thisClass)) {
                    classBack = "invalid ";
                }
                classBack += thisClass;
        }
        return classBack;

        function crossCheck(inTag,otherFieldID) {
            if (!document.getElementById(otherFieldID)) {
                return false;
            }
            return (inTag.value != "" || document.getElementById(otherFieldID).value != "");
        }
    }
}

function invalidLabel(parentTag) {
    if (parentTag.nodeName == "LABEL") {
        parentTag.className += " invalid";
    }
}
}
```

Working with Radio Buttons

Radio buttons are an either/or interface element that let the user pick one (and only one) choice within a group of options. Radio buttons should be used when one of those options is required. As shown in 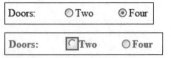, the form uses radio buttons to let the hypothetical car buyer choose between a two-door or four-door automobile. In this case, you can only pick one of these choices, and you must make a choice.

As seen in **Listing 6.14**, it doesn't take much scripting to check that one button is selected. We use a technique where we loop through each button and check its status and then turn the radio buttons' label and buttons red and bold if no button is picked.

Ⓐ Radio buttons are the best way to let the user pick only one choice from a group of options.

Listing 6.14 One radio button must be selected, and this JavaScript is there to enforce the interface law.

```
window.onload = function() {
    document.forms[0].onsubmit = validForm;
}

function validForm() {
    var allGood = true;
    var allTags = document.forms[0].
    → getElementsByTagName("*");

    for (var i=0; i<allTags.length; i++) {
        if (!validTag(allTags[i])) {
            allGood = false;
        }
    }
    return allGood;

    function validTag(thisTag) {
        var outClass = "";
        var allClasses = thisTag.className.
        → split(" ");

        for (var j=0; j<allClasses.length;
        → j++) {
            outClass += validBasedOnClass
            → (allClasses[j]) + " ";
        }

        thisTag.className = outClass;

        if (outClass.indexOf("invalid") > -1) {
            invalidLabel(thisTag.parentNode);
```

listing continues on next page

Listing 6.14 *continued*

```
          thisTag.focus();
          if (thisTag.nodeName == "INPUT") {
             thisTag.select();
          }
          return false;
       }
       return true;

       function validBasedOnClass
     → (thisClass) {
          var classBack = "";

          switch(thisClass) {
             case "":
             case "invalid":
                break;
             case "reqd":
                if (allGood && thisTag.
              → value == "") {
                   classBack = "invalid ";
                }
                classBack += thisClass;
                break;
             case "radio":
                if (allGood && !radioPicked
              → (thisTag.name)) {
                   classBack = "invalid ";
                }
                classBack += thisClass;
                break;
             case "isNum":
             case "isZip":
             case "email":
                classBack += thisClass;
                break;
             default:
                if (allGood && !crossCheck
              → (thisTag,thisClass)) {
                   classBack = "invalid ";
                }
                classBack += thisClass;
          }
          return classBack;

       function crossCheck
     → (inTag,otherFieldID) {
```

listing continues on next page

To make sure that the user picks a radio button:

1. `if (allGood && !radioPicked`
   `→ (thisTag.name)) {`
     `classBack = "invalid ";`

   This goes into the **radio** block of the **switch**/**case** conditional. We want to check to make sure at least one of the radio buttons was picked, and the new **radioPicked()** function handles that. If it returns false, then we set **classBack** to **invalid**.

2. `function radioPicked(radioName) {`
   `var radioSet = document.forms[0]`
   `→ [radioName];`

   Start the new **radioPicked()** function, and initialize the **radioSet** variable.

   This function takes in the name of the *set* of radio buttons—in this case, **DoorCt**, as found in Listing 6.11. Note that that's not the **id** of the current tag, or a **class**, or anything that we usually see. It's its **name**. The **name** attribute of **<input>** tags is how HTML knows which radio buttons are grouped together; that is, all **<input>** tags with the same name attribute are part of one radio button set.

   We then try to set **radioSet** to the name of this set of radio buttons inside the form. If it's found, **radioSet** will then have a value.

   continues on next page

3. `if (radioSet) {`
   `for (k=0; k<radioSet.length;`
    ↪`k++) {`
      `if (radioSet[k].checked) {`
        `return true;`

If **radioSet** has a value, then we've got the radio button set we want to inspect, so we start another loop to look through each button. When we find one that's checked, we return true, because we're done.

4. `return false;`

If we make it to the end of the loop, then either no set was found or we've looked at the entire set and nothing was clicked. In either case, return false to change the radio buttons' label and make the buttons red and bold.

Listing 6.14 *continued*

```
            if (!document.getElementById
            ↪(otherFieldID)) {
               return false;
            }
            return (inTag.value != "" ||
            ↪document.getElementById
            ↪(otherFieldID).value != "");
        }

        function radioPicked(radioName) {
            var radioSet = document.
            ↪forms[0][radioName];

            if (radioSet) {
                for (k=0; k<radioSet.length;
                ↪k++) {
                    if (radioSet[k].checked) {
                        return true;
                    }
                }
                return false;
            }
        }
    }

    function invalidLabel(parentTag) {
        if (parentTag.nodeName == "LABEL") {
            parentTag.className += " invalid";
        }
    }
}
```

Options:	☑ Sunroof (Two door only)	☐ Power Windows
Doors:	⊙ Two ○ Four	

A When the user checks the sunroof option, the script automatically sets the two-door radio button.

Listing 6.15 A sophisticated way to handle user choices lets you control and set field entries based on other choices made by the user.

```
window.onload = initForm;

function initForm() {
    document.forms[0].onsubmit = validForm;
    document.getElementById("sunroof").
    → onclick = doorSet;
}

function validForm() {
    var allGood = true;
    var allTags = document.forms[0].
    → getElementsByTagName("*");

    for (var i=0; i<allTags.length; i++) {
        if (!validTag(allTags[i])) {
            allGood = false;
        }
    }
    return allGood;

    function validTag(thisTag) {
        var outClass = "";
        var allClasses = thisTag.className.
        → split(" ");

        for (var j=0; j<allClasses.length;
        → j++) {
            outClass += validBasedOnClass
            → (allClasses[j]) + " ";
        }

        thisTag.className = outClass;

        if (outClass.indexOf("invalid") > -1) {
```

listing continues on next page

Setting One Field with Another

With forms, you'll often find that if the user makes one choice, that choice dictates the value of other fields on the form. For example, let's say that the sunroof option is only available on a two-door model. You could deal with this in two ways. First, you could check the entry and put up an alert dialog if the user makes the wrong choice. But it's a slicker design to simply make the entry for the user. Here, if they pick the sunroof, the script automatically clicks the two-door button, as in **A**. **Listing 6.15** shows you how.

To set a field value automatically:

1. `document.getElementById`
   `→ ("sunroof").onclick = doorSet;`

   This line of code has been added to **initForm()**, which runs after the page initially loads. When the user clicks the sunroof check box, the **doorSet()** function will be called.

2. `function doorSet() {`
   `    if (this.checked) {`
   `        document.getElementById`
   `        → ("twoDoor").checked = true;`

   This new function checks to see if the sunroof field was checked; if so, it sets the **twoDoor** radio button to true. If we've clicked the sunroof check box to turn it off, nothing happens.

TIP You may have noticed that there's no check to see if the user clicked the sunroof and then reset the **fourDoor** radio button. We'll leave that as an exercise for you, the reader.

Listing 6.15 *continued*

```
        invalidLabel(thisTag.parentNode);
        thisTag.focus();
        if (thisTag.nodeName == "INPUT") {
            thisTag.select();
        }
        return false;
    }
    return true;

    function validBasedOnClass(thisClass) {
        var classBack = "";

        switch(thisClass) {
            case "":
            case "invalid":
                break;
            case "reqd":
                if (allGood && thisTag.value == "") {
                    classBack = "invalid ";
                }
                classBack += thisClass;
                break;
            case "radio":
                if (allGood && !radioPicked(thisTag.name)) {
                    classBack = "invalid ";
                }
                classBack += thisClass;
                break;
            case "isNum":
            case "isZip":
            case "email":
                classBack += thisClass;
                break;
            default:
                if (allGood && !crossCheck(thisTag,thisClass)) {
                    classBack = "invalid ";
                }
                classBack += thisClass;
        }
        return classBack;

    function crossCheck(inTag,otherFieldID) {
        if (!document.getElementById(otherFieldID)) {
            return false;
        }
        return (inTag.value != "" || document.getElementById(otherFieldID).value != "");
    }

    function radioPicked(radioName) {
```

listing continues on next page

Listing 6.15 *continued*

```
                var radioSet = document.forms[0][radioName];

            if (radioSet) {
                for (k=0; k<radioSet.length; k++) {
                    if (radioSet[k].checked) {
                        return true;
                    }
                }
            }
            return false;
        }
    }
}

    function invalidLabel(parentTag) {
        if (parentTag.nodeName == "LABEL") {
            parentTag.className += " invalid";
        }
    }
}

function doorSet() {
    if (this.checked) {
        document.getElementById("twoDoor").checked = true;
    }
}
```

Validating Zip Codes

Those wacky users can type almost anything into a form, so you'll want to make sure that if they entered anything into the zip code field 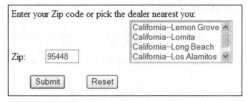 that it contains only numbers. **Listing 6.16** shows you how.

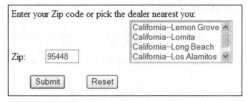

A You can make sure that the user either enters a zip code or makes a selection from the scrolling list.

Listing 6.16 Banish incorrect letters from your zip codes with just a few lines of JavaScript.

```
window.onload = initForm;

function initForm() {
    document.forms[0].onsubmit = validForm;
    document.getElementById("sunroof").onclick = doorSet;
}

function validForm() {
    var allGood = true;
    var allTags = document.forms[0].getElementsByTagName("*");

    for (var i=0; i<allTags.length; i++) {
        if (!validTag(allTags[i])) {
            allGood = false;
        }
    }
    return allGood;

    function validTag(thisTag) {
        var outClass = "";
        var allClasses = thisTag.className.split(" ");

        for (var j=0; j<allClasses.length; j++) {
            outClass += validBasedOnClass(allClasses[j]) + " ";
        }

        thisTag.className = outClass;

        if (outClass.indexOf("invalid") > -1) {
            invalidLabel(thisTag.parentNode);
            thisTag.focus();
            if (thisTag.nodeName == "INPUT") {
                thisTag.select();
            }
            return false;
```

listing continues on next page

Listing 6.16 *continued*

```
      }
      return true;

   function validBasedOnClass(thisClass) {
      var classBack = "";

      switch(thisClass) {
         case "":
         case "invalid":
            break;
         case "reqd":
            if (allGood && thisTag.value == "") {
               classBack = "invalid ";
            }
            classBack += thisClass;
            break;
         case "radio":
            if (allGood && !radioPicked(thisTag.name)) {
               classBack = "invalid ";
            }
            classBack += thisClass;
            break;
         case "isNum":
            if (allGood && !isNum(thisTag.value)) {
               classBack = "invalid ";
            }
            classBack += thisClass;
            break;
         case "isZip":
            if (allGood && !isZip(thisTag.value)) {
               classBack = "invalid ";
            }
            classBack += thisClass;
            break;
         case "email":
            classBack += thisClass;
            break;
         default:
            if (allGood && !crossCheck(thisTag,thisClass)) {
               classBack = "invalid ";
            }
            classBack += thisClass;
      }
      return classBack;

      function crossCheck(inTag,otherFieldID) {
         if (!document.getElementById(otherFieldID)) {
            return false;
```

listing continues on next page

To make sure zip codes are valid:

1. `if (allGood && !isNum`
   `→ (thisTag.value)) {`
   `    classBack = "invalid ";`
   `}`
   `classBack += thisClass;`

This goes into the **isNum** block of the **switch**/**case** conditional. If the entry isn't numeric, **isNum()** returns false.

2. `if (allGood && !isZip`
   `→ (thisTag.value)) {`
   `    classBack = "invalid ";`

This line has been added to the **isZip switch**/**case** block. If the field is not blank and it's not a zip code, **isZip()** returns false.

3. `if (passedVal == "") {`
   `    return false;`

Inside the **isNum()** function, if **passedVal** is empty, then the field we're looking at isn't a number. When that happens, return false, signaling an error.

4. `for (var k=0; k<passedVal.length;`
   `→ k++) {`

Now scan through the length of **passedVal**, incrementing the **k** counter each time it goes through the loop. We're using **k** because we're already inside two other loops (**i** and **j**).

Listing 6.16 *continued*

```
        }
        return (inTag.value != "" ||
        → document.getElementById
        → (otherFieldID).value != "");
    }

    function radioPicked(radioName) {
        var radioSet = document.
        → forms[0][radioName];

        if (radioSet) {
            for (k=0; k<radioSet.length;
            → k++) {
                if (radioSet[k].checked) {
                    return true;
                }
            }
        }
        return false;
    }

    function isNum(passedVal) {
        if (passedVal == "") {
            return false;
        }
        for (var k=0;
        → k<passedVal.length; k++) {
            if (passedVal.charAt(k) <
            → "0") {
                return false;
            }
            if (passedVal.charAt(k) >
            → "9") {
                return false;
            }
        }
        return true;
    }
```

listing continues on next page

Listing 6.16 *continued*

```
        function isZip(inZip) {
            if (inZip == "") {
                return true;
            }
            return (isNum(inZip));
        }
    }
}

    function invalidLabel(parentTag) {
        if (parentTag.nodeName == "LABEL") {
            parentTag.className += " invalid";
        }
    }
}

function doorSet() {
    if (this.checked) {
        document.getElementById("twoDoor").
        → checked = true;
    }
}
```

5.
```
if (passedVal.charAt(k) < "0") {
    return false;
}
if (passedVal.charAt(k) > "9") {
    return false;
```

The **charAt()** operator checks the character at the position **k**. If the character is less than "0" or greater than "9", it isn't a digit, so bail out and declare the input to be non-numeric, or false.

6. return true;

If we make it here, we've got a number, so we return true.

7.
```
function isZip(inZip) {
    if (inZip == "") {
        return true;
    }
    return (isNum(inZip));
```

In the context of this form, it's valid for the zip code field to be empty. Because of that, we first check the field to see if the user entered anything, and if they didn't, we return true—it's a valid entry. If they did enter anything, though, it needs to be numeric, so that's the next check.

TIP If at some later point we want to add a new field to the HTML form that must be numeric, there's no need to write any new JavaScript code. Instead, we'd just use the now-existing isNum() check. However, you would need to modify the code if you wanted users to be able to enter anything other than positive integers.

TIP Remember, it's the World Wide Web, not the American Web. If your site is likely to draw attention from outside the United States, don't require that the user enter a zip code. Addresses outside the United States may or may not have postal codes, and those postal codes may not be numeric.

Validating Email Addresses

Internet addresses can be tricky things for users—especially new users—to type. You can help them out by scanning the email address they enter and checking it for proper form. For example, you can check that there's only one @ sign, and that there are no invalid characters, as there are in **Ⓐ**. The limit, of course, is that your script can't catch misspellings, so if the user meant to type in **joe@myprovider.com** and instead entered **joe@yprovider.com**, the mistake will go through. **Listing 6.17** shows you how to snoop through an address for errors.

Email Address:	badaddress@chalcedony/.com

Ⓐ Here's an example of the kind of entry error that the email validation script will catch.

Listing 6.17 By scanning through the text within an email field on your form, you can ensure that you get proper email addresses.

```
window.onload = initForm;

function initForm() {
    document.forms[0].onsubmit = validForm;
    document.getElementById("sunroof").onclick = doorSet;
}

function validForm() {
    var allGood = true;
    var allTags = document.forms[0].getElementsByTagName("*");

    for (var i=0; i<allTags.length; i++) {
        if (!validTag(allTags[i])) {
            allGood = false;
        }
    }
    return allGood;

    function validTag(thisTag) {
        var outClass = "";
        var allClasses = thisTag.className.split(" ");

        for (var j=0; j<allClasses.length; j++) {
            outClass += validBasedOnClass(allClasses[j]) + " ";
        }
```

listing continues on next page

Listing 6.17 *continued*

```
        thisTag.className = outClass;

    if (outClass.indexOf("invalid") > -1) {
        invalidLabel(thisTag.parentNode);
        thisTag.focus();
        if (thisTag.nodeName == "INPUT") {
            thisTag.select();
        }
        return false;
    }
    return true;

    function validBasedOnClass(thisClass) {
        var classBack = "";

        switch(thisClass) {
            case "":
            case "invalid":
                break;
            case "reqd":
                if (allGood && thisTag.value == "") {
                    classBack = "invalid ";
                }
                classBack += thisClass;
                break;
            case "radio":
                if (allGood && !radioPicked(thisTag.name)) {
                    classBack = "invalid ";
                }
                classBack += thisClass;
                break;
            case "isNum":
                if (allGood && !isNum(thisTag.value)) {
                    classBack = "invalid ";
                }
                classBack += thisClass;
                break;
            case "isZip":
                if (allGood && !isZip(thisTag.value)) {
                    classBack = "invalid ";
                }
                classBack += thisClass;
                break;
            case "email":
                if (allGood && !validEmail(thisTag.value)) {
                    classBack = "invalid ";
                }
                classBack += thisClass;
                break;
```

listing continues on next page

To validate an email address:

1. `if (allGood && !validEmail`
   `→ (thisTag.value)) {`
      `classBack = "invalid ";`

This line has been added to the **email switch/case** block. If the **validEmail()** function returns false, set the **class** to be **invalid**.

2. `var invalidChars = " /:,;";`

Inside the **validEmail()** function, create a variable, **invalidChars**, that contains five likely invalid characters in an email address: blank space, slash, colon, comma, and semicolon.

3. `if (email == "") {`
      `return false;`

This test says, "If the contents of **email** is nothing (or empty), then the result is false."

4. `for (var k=0;`
   `→ k<invalidChars.length; k++) {`

In this **for** statement, start a loop that scans through the **invalidChars** string. Start by initializing the counter **k** to zero; then, each time through the loop that **k** is less than the length of the string, add 1 to **k** with the **++** increment operator.

Listing 6.17 continued

```
    default:
        if (allGood && !crossCheck
        → (thisTag,thisClass)) {
            classBack = "invalid ";
        }
        classBack += thisClass;
}
return classBack;

function crossCheck
→ (inTag,otherFieldID) {
    if (!document.getElementById
    → (otherFieldID)) {
        return false;
    }
    return (inTag.value != "" ||
    → document.getElementById
    → (otherFieldID).value != "");
}

function radioPicked(radioName) {
    var radioSet = document.
    → forms[0][radioName];

    if (radioSet) {
        for (k=0; k<radioSet.length;
        → k++) {
            if (radioSet[k].checked) {
                return true;
            }
        }
    }
    return false;
}

function isNum(passedVal) {
    if (passedVal == "") {
        return false;
    }
    for (var k=0;
    → k<passedVal.length; k++) {
        if (passedVal.charAt(k) <
        → "0") {
            return false;
        }
        if (passedVal.charAt(k) >
        → "9") {
            return false;
```

listing continues on next page

Listing 6.17 *continued*

```
            }
        }
        return true;
    }

    function isZip(inZip) {
        if (inZip == "") {
            return true;
        }
        return (isNum(inZip));
    }

    function validEmail(email) {
        var invalidChars = " /:,;";

        if (email == "") {
            return false;
        }
        for (var k=0;
→ k<invalidChars.length; k++) {
            var badChar = invalidChars.
→ charAt(k);
            if (email.indexOf(badChar) >
→ -1) {
                return false;
            }
        }
        var atPos = email.indexOf
→ ("@",1);
        if (atPos == -1) {
            return false;
        }
        if (email.indexOf("@",atPos+1)
→ != -1) {
            return false;
        }
```

listing continues on next page

5. ```
   var badChar =
→ invalidChars.charAt(k);
   if (email.indexOf(badChar) > -1) {
       return false;
   ```

   The **badChar** variable is set to the invalid character in position **k** in the **invalidChars** string, and we then check to see if that character is in **email**. If so, **indexOf()** returns the position where it was found; if not, it returns a –1. If we get a value other than –1, we've found a bad character, and so we then return a value of false.

6. ```
   var atPos = email.indexOf("@",1);
   if (atPos == -1) {
       return false;
   ```

   The **atPos** variable holds the position of the @ sign. Using **indexOf**, the script checks for the first @ sign, starting at the second character in the address. If the result is that the position of the @ sign is –1, it means that there is no @ sign in the address, and you've got trouble in Address City.

7. ```
   if (email.indexOf("@",atPos+1)
→ != -1) {
       return false;
   ```

   Now the script is making sure that there is only one @ sign and rejecting anything with more than one @, by checking characters beginning at 1 character past where we found the first @.

   *continues on next page*
   ```

8. ```
var periodPos =
→ email.indexOf(".",atPos);
if (periodPos == -1) {
   return false;
```

   Now the script checks that there is a period somewhere after the @ sign. If not, we get a false result.

9. ```
if (periodPos+3 > email.length) {
   return false;
}
return true;
```

   Finally, the script requires that there be at least two characters after the period in the address. If we made it this far without a false result, then the value of the function **validEmail** is true, meaning we have a good email address.

TIP There's a difference between validating an email address and verifying it. This script validates addresses by making sure that what the user entered is in the proper form for an email address. But it doesn't verify that the address really exists. The only way to do that would be to send an email message to the address and see if the message bounces. Besides the fact that you would probably annoy your users a great deal if you sent such a verifying message, it can take hours for a message to bounce, and the user isn't going to wait patiently at your form in the meantime.

TIP This script routine doesn't catch every possible incorrect email address, just some of the most likely errors. A full check for every possible bad email address would take several pages of code. If you think about it a bit, you can probably come up with possible mistakes that fall outside the checks in this script.

Listing 6.17 *continued*

```
                var periodPos =
                → email.indexOf(".",atPos);
                if (periodPos == -1) {
                    return false;
                }
                if (periodPos+3 >
                → email.length) {
                    return false;
                }
                return true;
            }
        }
    }

    function invalidLabel(parentTag) {
        if (parentTag.nodeName == "LABEL") {
            parentTag.className += " invalid";
        }
    }
}

function doorSet() {
    if (this.checked) {
        document.getElementById("twoDoor").
        → checked = true;
    }
}
```

7

Forms and Regular Expressions

Regular expressions are an amazingly powerful way to validate and format text strings. Using regular expressions, you can write a line or two of JavaScript code that can accomplish tasks that otherwise would have taken several dozen lines.

A *regular expression* (often abbreviated as *RegExp* or called by its synonym *grep*) is a pattern—written using special symbols—that describes one or more text strings. You use regular expressions to match patterns of text so that your script can easily recognize and manipulate text. Like an arithmetic expression, you create a regular expression by using *operators*; in this case, operators that work on text rather than numbers. There are many regular expression operators, and we'll look at some of the most common in this chapter. By learning and using these operators, you'll be able to save yourself a huge amount of effort whenever you need to detect and manipulate text strings.

In This Chapter

Regular expressions are also commonly considered to be one of the geekiest parts of programming. If you've gotten to the point where you think that you have a good grasp of JavaScript, you might look at a script that contains a regular expression and be puzzled that it makes no sense at all. If you don't know the syntax, you don't have any way of even guessing what's going on. What does all that gibberish mean?

But the syntax isn't that hard, so long as you break the gibberish down into small, meaningful pieces (at which point it's no longer gibberish). In this chapter, we'll demystify regular expression syntax and discuss how to make your code tighter and more powerful using regular expressions.

Are You Freaking Out Yet?

If this is the first time that you've been exposed to regular expressions, chances are you're feeling a bit intimidated right about now. We've included this chapter here because it makes the most sense to use regular expressions to validate form entries. But the rest of the material in this book doesn't build on this chapter, so if you want to skip to the next chapter until you've got a bit more scripting experience under your belt, we won't mind a bit.

On the other hand, regular expressions are well worth the investment of your time. They're not only useful in JavaScript; regular expressions can also be used everywhere from other programming languages (such as Perl, Java, Python, and PHP) to Apache configuration files to inside text editors such as BBEdit and TextMate. Even Adobe Dreamweaver and (to a certain extent) Microsoft Word use regular expressions to make search and replace more powerful.

```
<!DOCTYPE html>
<html>
<head>
    <title>Email Validation</title>
    <link rel="stylesheet"
    → href="script01.css">
    <script src="script01.js"></script>
</head>
<body>
<h2 class="centered">Email Validation</h2>
<form action="someAction.cgi">
    <p><label for="emailAddr">Email
    → Address:<input id="emailAddr"
    → type="text" size="30"
    ⋯ class="email"></label></p>
    <p><input type="submit" value=
    → "Submit"> <input type="reset"></p>
</form>
</body>
</html>
```

Listing 7.2 Here's the little bit of CSS that the first
few tasks in this chapter require.

```
body {
    color: #000;
    background-color: #FFF;
}

input.invalid {
    background-color: #FF9;
    border: 2px red inset;
}

label.invalid {
    color: #F00;
    font-weight: bold;
}

.centered {
    text-align: center;
}
```

Validating an Email Address with Regular Expressions

Back in Chapter 6, one of the tasks was validating an email address. To do the job, the script needed to be relatively long. **Listing 7.3**, at its heart, does exactly the same thing as Listing 6.17; but by using regular expressions, it takes many fewer lines, and you get a more rigorous result. You'll find the simple HTML in **Listing 7.1**, and the CSS in **Listing 7.2**.

To validate an email address using regular expressions:

1. `var re = /^\w+([\.-]?\w+)*@\w+`
   `→ ([\.-]?\w+)*(\.\w{2,3})+$/;`

   Yow! What on earth is this? Don't panic; it's just a regular expression in the **validEmail()** function. Let's break it apart and take it piece by piece. Like any line of JavaScript, you read a regular expression from left to right.

   First, **re** is just a variable. We've given it the name **re** so that when we use it later, we'll remember that it's a regular expression. The line sets the value of **re** to the regular expression on the right side of the equals sign.

   A regular expression always begins and ends with a slash, **/** (of course, there is still a semicolon here, to denote the end of the JavaScript line, but the semicolon is not part of the regular expression). Everything in between the slashes is part of the regular expression.

   continues on next page

The caret ^ means that we're going to use this expression to examine a string starting at the string's beginning. If the caret were left off, the email address might show as valid even though there was a bunch of garbage at the beginning of the string.

The expression \w means any *one* character, "a" through "z", "A" through "Z", "0" through "9", or underscore. An email address must start with one of these characters.

The plus sign + means *one or more of* whatever the previous item was that we're checking on. In this case, an email address must start with one or more of any combination of the characters "a" through "z", "A" through "Z", "0" through "9", or underscore.

The opening parenthesis (signifies a group. It means that we're going to want to refer to everything inside the parentheses in some way later, so we put them into a group now.

The brackets [] are used to show that we can have any *one* of the characters inside. In this example, the characters \.- are inside the brackets. We want to allow the user to enter either a period or a dash, but the period has a special meaning to regular expressions, so we need to preface it with a backslash \ to show that we really want to refer to the period itself, not its special meaning. Using a backslash before a special character is called *escaping* that character. Because of the brackets, the entered string can have either a period or a dash here, but not both. Note that the dash doesn't stand for any special character, just itself.

Listing 7.3 These few lines of JavaScript go a long way to validate email addresses.

```
window.onload = function() {
    document.forms[0].onsubmit = validForm;
}

function validForm() {
    var allGood = true;
    var allTags = document.forms[0].
    → getElementsByTagName("*");

    for (var i=0; i<allTags.length; i++) {
        if (!validTag(allTags[i])) {
            allGood = false;
        }
    }
    return allGood;

    function validTag(thisTag) {
        var outClass = "";
        var allClasses = thisTag.className.
        → split(" ");

        for (var j=0; j<allClasses.length;
        → j++) {
            outClass += validBasedOnClass
            → (allClasses[j]) + " ";
        }

        thisTag.className = outClass;

        if (outClass.indexOf("invalid") > -1) {
            invalidLabel(thisTag.parentNode);
            thisTag.focus();
            if (thisTag.nodeName == "INPUT") {
                thisTag.select();
            }
            return false;
        }
        return true;

        function validBasedOnClass(thisClass) {
```

listing continues on next page

Listing 7.3 *continued*

```
        var classBack = "";

        switch(thisClass) {
            case "":
            case "invalid":
                break;
            case "email":
                if (allGood && !validEmail
→ (thisTag.value)) {
                    classBack = "invalid ";
                }
            default:
                classBack += thisClass;
        }
        return classBack;
    }

    function validEmail(email) {
        var re = /^\w+([\.-]?\w+)*@\w+
→ ([\.-]?\w+)*(\.\w{2,3})+$/;

        return re.test(email);
    }

    function invalidLabel(parentTag) {
        if (parentTag.nodeName == "LABEL") {
            parentTag.className +=
→ " invalid";
        }
    }
}
}
```

The question mark **?** means that we can have *zero or one* of the previous item. So along with it being OK to have either a period or a dash in the first part of the email address (the part before the **@**), it's also OK to have neither.

Following the **?**, we once again have **\w+**, which says that the period or dash must be followed by some other characters.

The closing parenthesis **)** says that this is the end of the group. That's followed by an asterisk *****, which means that we can have *zero or more* of the previous item—in this case, whatever was inside the parentheses. So while "dori" is a valid email prefix, so is "testing-testing-1-2-3".

The **@** character doesn't stand for anything besides itself, located between the email address and the domain name.

The **\w+** once again says that a domain name must start with one or more of any character "a" through "z", "A" through "Z", "0" through "9", or underscore. That's again followed by **([\.-]?\w+)***, which says that periods and dashes are allowed within the suffix of an email address.

We then have another group within a set of parentheses: **\.\w{2,3}**, which says that we're expecting to find a period followed by characters. In this case, the numbers inside the braces mean *either 2 or 3* of the previous item (in this case the **\w**, meaning a letter, number, or underscore). Following the right parenthesis around this group is a **+**, which again means that the previous item (the group, in this case) must exist *one or more* times. This will match ".com" or ".edu", for instance, as well as "ox.ac.uk".

continues on next page

And finally, the regular expression ends with a dollar sign **$**, which signifies that the matched string must end here. This keeps the script from validating an email address that starts off properly but contains garbage characters at the end. The slash closes the regular expression. The semicolon ends the JavaScript statement, as usual.

2. `return re.test(email);`

This single line takes the regular expression defined in the previous step and uses the **test()** method to check the validity of **email**. If the entered string doesn't fit the pattern stored in **re**, **test()** returns false, and the user sees the incorrect field and its label turn red and bold, as shown in 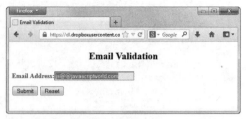. Otherwise, a valid entry returns true , and the form submits the email address to a server-side script, **someAction.cgi**, for additional processing.

Ⓐ Here's the result if the user enters an invalid email address: the label and field turn red and bold.

Ⓑ But this address is just fine.

TIP This code doesn't match every possible legal variation of email addresses, just the ones that you're likely to want to allow a person to enter.

TIP Note that in Listing 7.3, after we assigned the value of **re**, we used **re** as an object in step 2. Like any other JavaScript variable, the result of a regular expression can be an object.

TIP Compare the **validEmail()** functions in Listings 6.17 and 7.3. The former has 27 lines of code; the latter, only four. They do the same thing, so you can see that the power of regular expressions can save you a lot of coding.

TIP You'll see in **Table 7.1** that the special characters (sometimes called meta characters) in regular expressions are case-sensitive. Keep this in mind when debugging scripts that use regular expressions.

TIP There are characters in regular expressions that modify other operators. We've listed them in **Table 7.2**.

TABLE 7.1 Regular Expression Special Characters

Character	Matches
\	Toggles between literal and special characters; for example, "\w" means the special value of "\w" (see below) instead of the literal "w", but "\$" means to ignore the special value of "$" (see below) and use the "$" character instead
^	Beginning of a string
$	End of a string
*	Zero or more times
+	One or more times
?	Zero or one time
.	Any character except newline
\b	Word boundary
\B	Non-word boundary
\d	Any digit 0 through 9 (same as [0-9])
\D	Any non-digit
\f	Form feed
\n	New line
\r	Carriage return
\s	Any single white space character (same as [\f\n\r\t\v])
\S	Any single non–white space character
\t	Tab
\v	Vertical tab
\w	Any letter, number, or the underscore (same as [a-zA-Z0-9_])
\W	Any character other than a letter, number, or underscore
\xnn	The ASCII character defined by the hexadecimal number **nn**
\onn	The ASCII character defined by the octal number **nn**
\cX	The control character **X**
[abcde]	A character set that matches any one of the enclosed characters
[^abcde]	A complemented or negated character set; one that does not match any of the enclosed characters
[a-e]	A character set that matches any one in the range of enclosed characters
[\b]	The literal backspace character (different from \b)
{n}	Exactly *n* occurrences of the previous character
{n,}	At least *n* occurrences of the previous character
{n,m}	Between *n* and *m* occurrences of the previous character
()	A grouping, which is also stored for later use
x|y	Either **x** or **y**

TABLE 7.2 Regular Expression Modifiers

Modifier	Meaning
g	Search for all possible matches (globally), not just the first
i	Search without case-sensitivity

Validating a File Name

There are many things that can be done with regular expressions, but one of the most useful is validating entry fields in forms on your webpages. **Listing 7.4** expects the user to enter a valid URL of an image, and the regular expression helps to make sure that users do as you've requested (specifically, that there has to be a suffix that denotes an image file).  shows the appearance of the page when an invalid entry was accidentally entered, and 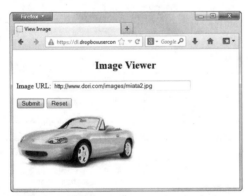 shows the result when the image name was typed correctly.

A If the user enters something that isn't a valid image file name, the page shows an error, thanks to regular expressions.

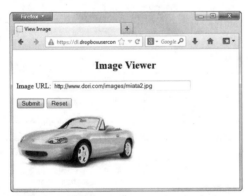

B When the image name is entered correctly, the image is displayed on the page.

Listing 7.4 This script asks for an image location and, if it passes the validation, displays the image on the page.

```
window.onload = function() {
    document.forms[0].onsubmit = validForm;
}

function validForm() {
    var allGood = true;
    var allTags = document.forms[0].
    → getElementsByTagName("*");

    for (var i=0; i<allTags.length; i++) {
        if (!validTag(allTags[i])) {
            allGood = false;
        }
    }
    return false;

    function validTag(thisTag) {
        var outClass = "";
        var allClasses = thisTag.className.
        → split(" ");

        for (var j=0; j<allClasses.length;
        → j++) {
            outClass += validBasedOnClass
            → (allClasses[j]) + " ";
        }

        thisTag.className = outClass;

        if (outClass.indexOf("invalid") > -1) {
            invalidLabel(thisTag.parentNode);
            thisTag.focus();
            if (thisTag.nodeName == "INPUT") {
                thisTag.select();
            }
            return false;
```

listing continues on next page

Listing 7.4 *continued*

```
        }
        return true;

        function validBasedOnClass
        → (thisClass) {
          var classBack = "";

          switch(thisClass) {
            case "":
            case "invalid":
              break;
            case "imgURL":
              if (allGood && !setImgURL
              → (thisTag.value)) {
                classBack = "invalid ";
              }
            default:
              classBack += thisClass;
          }
          return classBack;
        }

        function setImgURL(newURL) {
          var re = /^(file|http):\/\/\S+
          → \/\S+\.(gif|jpg|png)$/i;

          if (re.test(newURL)) {
            document.getElementById
            → ("chgImg").src = newURL;
            return true;
          }
          return false;
        }

        function invalidLabel(parentTag) {
          if (parentTag.nodeName == "LABEL") {
            parentTag.className +=
            → "invalid";
          }
        }
      }
    }
}
```

To validate a URL:

- `var re = /^(file|http):\/\/\S+`
  `→ \/\S+\.(gif|jpg|png)$/i;`

  This is in the **imgURL()** function. As in the previous example, we want to check the full field entered, so the regular expression begins with **/^** and ends with **$/**. The input can begin with either the text "**http**" or "**file**", so the two are grouped together with a | to show that either one or the other value is acceptable. Whether the user is getting the image off of their hard drive or off the web, the next characters have to be "**://**", so that's checked for next. Note that each of the forward slashes must be escaped individually (that's what the two instances of **\/** are, escaped forward slashes), because forward slashes are regular expression special characters.

  After that, nearly anything goes, so **\S+** is used to signify that one or more non–white space characters follow. Then there's another required forward slash (again escaped) to separate the domain from the file name, and then another **\S+** to handle the file name.

  The file name needs to end with a period and then "**gif**", "**jpg**", or "**png**". The period is escaped, and the suffixes are grouped together to test for any match.

  After the regular expression, the modifier **i** is used, to allow the user input to be either upper- or lowercase. This modifier tells the regular expression not to be case-sensitive.

Extracting Strings

String validation isn't the only useful thing you can do with regular expressions. String *extraction* is also useful; being able to take just part of a string and manipulate it allows you to have more control over the final result. In **Listing 7.5**, we'll take a list of names entered in first-name-first order and swap them so that they're in last-name-first order.

To extract strings:

1. `var re = /\s*\n\s*/;`

   Here's a new regular expression, which simply searches for a pattern that consists of any white space **\s***, followed by a new line character **\n**, followed again by any white space **\s***.

2. `var nameList = inNameList.`
   `split(re);`

   The string method **split()** takes the regular expression and applies it to the data entered by the user , stored in **inNameList**. Every new line separates a name, and **split()** cuts up the entered data at each new line. The result is a string array of the entered names, one name per array element, stored in the array **nameList**.

3. `re = /(\S+)\s(\S+)/;`

   Next we'll need another regular expression, which splits each name into first and last names. It looks for any non–white space characters **(\S+)** followed by a single white space character **\s**, followed by any non–white space characters **(\S+)**. The parentheses are required around each group of characters so that the information can be used later.

Ⓐ Here's the before version of the list.

Firefox
Name List Reversal
https://dl.dropbc

Reverse a list of names

Enter a list of names with first name first, one per line:

Ralph Spoilsport
BettyJo Bialovsky
Audrey Farber
Melanie Faber
Porgy Tirebiter
Nick Danger

Submit   Reset

Listing 7.5 This script rearranges an entered list of names.

```
window.onload = function() {
    document.forms[0].onsubmit = validForm;
}

function validForm() {
    var allTags = document.forms[0].
    → getElementsByTagName("*");

    for (var i=0; i<allTags.length; i++) {
        validTag(allTags[i]);
    }
    return false;

    function validTag(thisTag) {
        var allClasses = thisTag.className.
        → split(" ");

        for (var j=0; j<allClasses.length;
        → j++) {
            if (allClasses[j] == "nameList") {
                thisTag.value = setNameList
                → (thisTag.value);
            }
        }
    }

    function setNameList(inNameList) {
        var newNames = new Array;
        var newNameField = "";

        var re = /\s*\n\s*/;
        var nameList = inNameList.
        → split(re);

        re = /(\S+)\s(\S+)/;

        for (var k=0; k<nameList.length;
        → k++) {
            newNames[k] = nameList[k].
            → replace(re, "$2, $1");
        }

        for (k=0; k<newNames.length;
        → k++) {
            newNameField += newNames[k] +
            → "\n";
        }
        return newNameField;
    }
}
```

4. `for (var k=0; k<nameList.length;`
`→ k++) {`

For each name in the **nameList** array, loop through the following line of code.

5. `newNames[k] = nameList[k].`
`→ replace(re, "$2, $1");`

Remember those parentheses in step 3? When the **replace()** method is executed, the regular expression **re** breaks apart **nameList** into first and last names. Those parentheses tell JavaScript to store the first name in the regular expression property **$1** and the last name in the regular expression property **$2**. The **replace()** method then uses the second parameter passed to it to return the last name **$2**, followed by a comma, followed by the first name **$1**. The names, now in last-name-first order, are stored in the new array **newNames**.

6. `for (k=0; k<newNames.length;`
`→ k++) {`
`    newNameField += newNames[k] +`
`    → "\n";`
`}`

This loop sets up a new variable **newNameField**, which will contain the revised version of the user-entered text. For each name in the **newNames** array, append that name followed by a new-line character to **newNameField**.

continues on next page

7. `return newNameField;`

We pass the result back up to update the webpage. This happens in the **switch/case** section: **thisTag.value = nameList(thisTag.value);**. The result is shown in 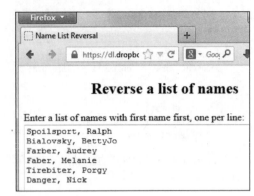.

TIP This script, as shown, handles only first and last names that are separated by a space. You'll have to change it if you want it to handle middle names or multi-part last names.

TIP In this script, the variable **re** gets used more than once, with different values being assigned to it at different parts of the script. That's perfectly OK to do in JavaScript (and that's why we've done it here as an illustration), but you might want to consider using different variable names in your own scripts. It makes them easier to debug or change when you come back to them in a few months.

B Here's the reordered version of the page.

Listing 7.6 This script takes a name entered in any format and replaces it with the capitalization you desire.

```
window.onload = function() {
    document.forms[0].onsubmit = validForm;
}

function validForm() {
    var allTags = document.forms[0].
    ⇢ getElementsByTagName("*");

    for (var i=0; i<allTags.length; i++) {
        validTag(allTags[i]);
    }
    return false;

    function validTag(thisTag) {
        var allClasses = thisTag.className.
        ⇢ split(" ");

        for (var j=0; j<allClasses.length;
        ⇢ j++) {
            if (allClasses[j] == "nameList") {
                thisTag.value = setNameList
                ⇢ (thisTag.value);
            }
        }

        function setNameList(inNameList) {
            var newNames = new Array;
            var newNameField = "";

            var re = /\s*\n\s*/;
            var nameList = inNameList.
            ⇢ split(re);

            re = /^(\S)(\S+)\s(\S)(\S+)$/;

            for (var k=0; k<nameList.length;
            ⇢ k++) {
                if (nameList[k]) {
                    re.exec(nameList[k]);
                    newNames[k] = RegExp.$1.
                    ⇢ toUpperCase() + RegExp.$2.
                    ⇢ toLowerCase() + " " +
                    ⇢ RegExp.$3.toUpperCase() +
                    ⇢ RegExp.$4.toLowerCase();
                }
            }
        }
```

listing continues on next page

Formatting Strings

Those darn users often enter data in a haphazard fashion. If you want entries to follow a standard format, your best bet is to handle the formatting yourself. **Listing 7.6** shows how to take a list of names and convert them to standard capitalization format.

To format a string:

1. **re = /^(\S)(\S+)\s(\S)(\S+)$/;**

   This regular expression again expects to find names in first name, space, last name order, and separates each name into four parts: the first letter of the first name **^(\S)**, the remainder of the first name **(\S+)**, the first letter of the last name **(\S)**, and the remainder of the last name **(\S+)$**. Note that the ^ and **$** force the string to begin at the beginning and end at the ending—we don't want to leave any parts out.

   continues on next page

2. `for (var k=0; k<nameList.length;`
   `→ k++) {`

   We want to look at each name in the
   nameList array, shown in Ⓐ.

3. `re.exec(nameList[k]);`

   This step uses the **exec()** method to
   execute the **re** pattern on the string
   nameList[k], breaking the string into
   four parts and automatically setting
   JavaScript's built-in **RegExp** object.
   These four parts will be stored in
   RegExp.$1, **RegExp.$2**, **RegExp.$3**, and
   RegExp.$4 (respectively).

4. `newNames[k] = RegExp.$1.`
   `→ toUpperCase() + RegExp.$2.`
   `→ toLowerCase() + " " +`
   `→ RegExp.$3.toUpperCase() +`
   `→ RegExp.$4.toLowerCase();`

   The new version of the name is stored
   in the **newNames** array. It consists of the
   first letter of the first name (**RegExp.$1**)
   forced to uppercase, then the remainder of the first name (**RegExp.$2**) forced
   to lowercase, then a space, then the
   first letter of the last name (**RegExp.$3**)
   forced to uppercase, and finally the
   remainder of the last name (**RegExp.$4**)
   forced to lowercase. The name is then
   displayed, as shown in Ⓑ.

Listing 7.6 *continued*

```
        for (k=0; k<newNames.length;
        → k++) {
            newNameField += newNames[k] +
            → "\n";
        }
        return newNameField;
    }
  }
}
```

Ⓐ Here's the before version of the names.

Ⓑ And here's how they look afterwards, just the
way we wanted them.

About the RegExp Object

JavaScript has a built-in **RegExp** object that's automatically set (and reset) every time a script executes a regular expression method (given in **Tables 7.4** and **7.5**). The properties of this object are shown in **Table 7.3** and its methods in Table 7.4. The **RegExp** object isn't a variable that contains the result of the regular expression operation, but rather it contains the *pattern* described by the regular expression, in a form that can be used in your scripts via the **RegExp** object's properties and methods.

TABLE 7.3 Properties of the RegExp Object

Properties	Meaning
$1 (through $9)	Parenthesized substring matches
$_	Same as input
$*	Same as multiline
$&	Same as lastMatch
$+	Same as lastParen
$`	Same as leftContext
$'	Same as rightContext
constructor	Specifies the function that creates an object's prototype
global	Search globally (**g** modifier in use)
ignoreCase	Search case-insensitive (**i** modifier in use)
input	The string to search if no string is passed
lastIndex	The index at which to start the next match
lastMatch	The last matched characters
lastParen	The last parenthesized substring match
leftContext	The substring to the left of the most recent match
multiline	Whether strings are searched across multiple lines
prototype	Allows the addition of properties to all objects
rightContext	The substring to the right of the most recent match
source	The regular expression pattern itself

TABLE 7.4 Methods of the RegExp Object

Methods	Meaning
compile(pattern, [, "g" | "i" | "gi"])	Compiles a regular expression
exec(string)	Executes a search for a match
test(string)	Tests for a match
toSource()	Returns a literal representing the object
toString()	Returns a string representing the specified object
valueOf()	Returns the primitive value of the specified object

TABLE 7.5 String Methods

Methods	Meaning
match(re)	Finds a match for a regular expression pattern (**re**) within a string
replace(re, replaceStr)	Using **re**, performs the desired replacement
search(re)	Searches for a match to **re**
split(re)	Splits a string based on **re**

Formatting and Sorting Strings

Another typical task you might want to do is to sort a group of names. **Listing 7.7** combines the previous two examples and adds a sort. The end result is the list of names in last-name order, properly capitalized, and alphabetized.

To format and sort strings:

1. ```
   newNames[k] = RegExp.$3.
   → toUpperCase() + RegExp.$4.
   → toLowerCase() + ", " +
   → RegExp.$1.toUpperCase() +
   → RegExp.$2.toLowerCase();
   ```

   In this example, we want to sort by last name, so we create the new **newNames** array by appending the uppercased first letter of the last name, the lowercased remainder of the last name, a comma and space, the uppercased first letter of the first name, and the lowercased remainder of the first name.

2. ```
   newNames.sort();
   ```

   The array method **sort()** sorts the elements of an array in place, overwriting the previous contents. Ⓐ shows the "before" version and Ⓑ the "after" version.

Ⓐ Here's the version as the user entered it.

Ⓑ And here's the sorted and cleaned-up list, just the way we want it.

Listing 7.7 This script takes a bunch of names in any format and order and turns them into a neat and orderly list.

```
window.onload = function() {
     document.forms[0].onsubmit = validForm;
}

function validForm() {
     var allTags = document.forms[0].getElementsByTagName("*");

     for (var i=0; i<allTags.length; i++) {
        validTag(allTags[i]);
     }
     return false;

     function validTag(thisTag) {
        var allClasses = thisTag.className.split(" ");

        for (var j=0; j<allClasses.length; j++) {
           if (allClasses[j] == "nameList") {
              thisTag.value = setNameList(thisTag.value);
           }
        }

        function setNameList(inNameList) {
           var newNames = new Array;
           var newNameField = "";

           var re = /\s*\n\s*/;
           var nameList = inNameList.split(re);

           re = /^(\S)(\S+)\s(\S)(\S+)$/;

           for (var k=0; k<nameList.length; k++) {
              if (nameList[k]) {
                 re.exec(nameList[k]);
                 newNames[k] = RegExp.$3.toUpperCase() + RegExp.$4.toLowerCase() + ", " +
              ⸺▸ RegExp.$1.toUpperCase() + RegExp.$2.toLowerCase();
              }
           }

           newNames.sort();
           for (k=0; k<newNames.length; k++) {
              newNameField += newNames[k] + "\n";
           }
           return newNameField;
        }
     }
}
```

Formatting and Validating Strings

Regular expressions can be used to simultaneously format *and* validate an entered value. In **Listing 7.8**, the user enters a phone number in any format. Either the end result will be a formatted phone number or the input box will turn red and the label will turn red and bold.

Listing 7.8 This script validates and formats a user-entered phone number.

```
window.onload = function() {
    document.forms[0].onsubmit = validForm;
}

function validForm() {
    var allTags = document.forms[0].getElementsByTagName("*");

    for (var i=0; i<allTags.length; i++) {
        validTag(allTags[i]);
    }
    return false;

    function validTag(thisTag) {
        var outClass = "";
        var allClasses = thisTag.className.split(" ");

        for (var j=0; j<allClasses.length; j++) {
            outClass += validBasedOnClass(allClasses[j]) + " ";
        }

        thisTag.className = outClass;

        if (outClass.indexOf("invalid") > -1) {
            invalidLabel(thisTag.parentNode);
            thisTag.focus();
            if (thisTag.nodeName == "INPUT") {
                thisTag.select();
            }
        }
    }
```

listing continues on next page

Listing 7.8 *continued*

```
    function validBasedOnClass
→ (thisClass) {
    var classBack = "";

    switch(thisClass) {
        case "":
        case "invalid":
            break;
        case "phone":
            if (!validPhone(thisTag.
→ value)) {
                classBack = "invalid ";
            }
        default:
            classBack += thisClass;
    }
    return classBack;
}

function validPhone(phoneNum) {
    var re = /^\(?(\d{3})\)?[\.\-\/
→ ]?(\d{3})[\.\-\/ ]?(\d{4})$/;

    var phoneArray = re.exec
→ (phoneNum);
    if (phoneArray) {
        document.getElementById
→ ("phoneField").value =
→ "(" + phoneArray[1] + ") " +
→ phoneArray[2] + "-" +
→ phoneArray[3];
        return true;
    }
    return false;
}

function invalidLabel(parentTag) {
    if (parentTag.nodeName ==
→ "LABEL") {
        parentTag.className +=
→ "invalid";
    }
}
    }
}
```

To format and validate a phone number:

1. `var re = /^\(?(\d{3})\)?[\.\-\/`
    `→ ]?(\d{3})[\.\-\/ ]?(\d{4})$/;`

    This regular expression looks for a string that has:

    ▸ An optional left parenthesis `\(?`

    ▸ 3 digits `(\d{3})`

    ▸ An optional right parenthesis `\)?`

    ▸ An optional period, dash, forward slash, or space `[\.\-\/ ]?`

    ▸ 3 digits `(\d{3})`

    ▸ An optional period, dash, forward slash, or space `[\.\-\/ ]?`

    ▸ 4 digits `(\d{4})`

    This pattern is anchored to both the beginning and ending of the string, so extraneous characters aren't valid. The sequences of three digits (the area code), three digits (the prefix), and four digits (the suffix) are saved, if found.

    continues on next page

2. `var phoneArray = re.exec`
`→ (phoneNum);`

The **exec()** method performs the regular expression stored in **re** on **phoneNum**. If the pattern we're searching for isn't found 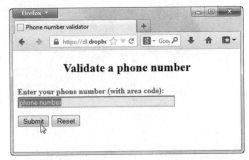, **phoneArray** will be set to null. Otherwise, **phoneArray** will be an array of the values stored by the regular expression.

3. `if (phoneArray) {`
`    document.getElementById`
`    → ("phoneField").value = "(" +`
`    → phoneArray[1] + ") " +`
`    → phoneArray[2] + "-" +`
`    → phoneArray[3];`

If **phoneArray** is true, the test was successfully passed, and the array has been initialized. So, we reset the form field on the page to the area code inside parentheses and a space, followed by the prefix, a dash, and the suffix, as shown in .

Ⓐ Here's the result when an invalid number is entered.

Ⓑ And here's what's displayed when the number is entered correctly.

Listing 7.9 Use regular expressions to save you from writing or retrofitting your HTML files.

```
window.onload = rolloverInit;

function rolloverInit() {
    for (var i=0; i<document.images.length;
    → i++) {
        if (document.images[i].parentNode.
        → tagName.toLowerCase() == "a") {
            setupRollover(document.images[i]);
        }
    }
}

function setupRollover(theImage) {
    var re = /\s*_off\s*/;

    theImage.outImage = new Image();
    theImage.outImage.src = theImage.src;
    theImage.onmouseout = function() {
        this.src = this.outImage.src;
    }

    theImage.overImage = new Image();
    theImage.overImage.src = theImage.src.
    → replace(re,"_on");
    theImage.onmouseover = function() {
        this.src = this.overImage.src;
    }

    theImage.clickImage = new Image();
    theImage.clickImage.src = theImage.src.
    → replace(re,"_click");
    theImage.onclick = function() {
        this.src = this.clickImage.src;
    }

    theImage.parentNode.childImg = theImage;

    theImage.parentNode.onblur = function() {
        this.childImg.src = this.childImg.
        → outImage.src;
    }

    theImage.parentNode.onfocus =
    → function() {
        this.childImg.src = this.childImg.
        → overImage.src;
    }
}
```

Replacing Elements Using Regular Expressions

You've already seen how useful regular expressions are for finding, matching, and replacing strings. But you can also use them to replace the names of page elements, and this can often save you a bunch of time. In this task, we're going to retrofit a regular expression into a script that you've seen before, Listing 4.6. That script built three-state rollovers. It's a useful script, but it has one drawback: it requires you to have tagged every image that you want to manipulate with its own **id**. That's not too difficult, but you can instead let JavaScript build the names of page elements and save yourself some work.

At this point, you should review Chapter 4's image rollovers (Listings 4.5 and 4.6) to see what's going on in this example. Go ahead, we'll wait.

Back so soon? Great. In short, instead of creating the **_click** and **_on** names of an image on the fly based on the **id** of each image, we're instead creating the **_click** and **_on** names on the fly based on the **_off** name of the image. That way, we don't even need the image **id**s. **Listing 7.9** shows you the way. There's no change in the way the page looks or acts from changing the JavaScript; but it saves you work in creating the HTML pages.

To use a regular expression to replace an element:

1. `var re = /\s*_off\s*/;`

This line sets up a new regular expression pattern that looks for the text **_off** anywhere in a string.

2. `theImage.overImage.src =`
`→ theImage.src.replace(re,"_on");`

The line in Listing 4.6 was `theImage.overImage.src = "images/" + theImage.id + "_on.gif";`. The new line uses the **re** pattern to look for that particular bit of a string and, when it's found, replace it with *this* string. In this case, we're looking for **_off** and turning it into **_on**. This allows us to not worry about the **id** attribute being set on this image—it just doesn't matter any more.

3. `theImage.clickImage.src =`
`→ theImage.src.replace`
`→ (re,"_click");`

The line in Listing 4.6 was `theImage.clickImage.src = "images/" + theImage.id + "_click.gif";`. In this case, we're looking for **_off** and turning it into **_click**.

TIP This can also be handy if your images are a mixture of .png, .gif, and .jpg files—now, your JavaScript code doesn't have to ever know what suffix each image has.

TIP You may have noticed that there's some code at the end of this script that isn't in Listing 4.6. We've added a little bit of extra code here to enhance accessibility—now, for those people who use the keyboard instead of a mouse, tabbing onto an image will give the same effect that a hover does for a mousing user.

8

Handling Events

Events are actions that the user performs while visiting your page. When the browser detects an event, such as a mouse click or a key press, it can trigger JavaScript objects associated with that event, called *event handlers*. In most of the previous chapters in this book, you've seen examples of how event handlers are used. But event handling is such an important technique to understand—and it encompasses virtually all of your pages' interaction with the user—that it deserves its own chapter.

In this chapter, you'll see how to use event handlers to work with windows, capture mouse movements and clicks, deal with form events, and react when the user presses keys on the keyboard.

In This Chapter

Handling Window Events

Window events occur when the user does something affecting an entire browser window. The most common window event is simply loading the window by opening a particular webpage. You can also have events that trigger event handlers when windows are closed, moved, or even sent to the background.

When working with event handlers, you'll often find it useful to connect an event handler to an object using dot syntax, like so:

```
window.onfocus
window.onload
document.onmousedown
```

Note that when you use the event handler as part of an object like this, the event handler is written all in lowercase. Also, keep your event handlers in external scripts, rather than placing them inside the HTML tag—this approach is more standards compliant, it separates out the JavaScript code from the HTML code, and it's easier to edit (or replace) all your JavaScript code in an external file.

A The script sets multiple **onload** handlers (in this case, for color formatting) to run when the page loads.

Listing 8.1 The HTML for the multiple **onload** example.

```
<!DOCTYPE html>
<html>
<head>
    <title>Welcome!</title>
    <script src="script01.js"></script>
</head>
<body id="pageBody">
    <h1>Welcome to our Web site!</h1>
</body>
</html>
```

The onload event

We have used the **onload** event frequently throughout this book. It is triggered when the user enters your page and all its elements have completed loading. The epidemic of advertising pop-up windows is an example—though not an especially pleasant one—of the **onload** event handler in action.

Although we've shown **onload** repeatedly, up until now we've skipped one important bit of information: what to do when you have multiple things you need to have happen when the page loads. **Listings 8.1** and **8.2** demonstrate how to do this.

1. **addOnload(initOne);**
   addOnload(initTwo);
   addOnload(initThree);

   In this script, we want three entirely separate things to happen when the page first loads. Setting **window.onload** three times wouldn't work, because the second time would overwrite the first, and then the third would overwrite the second. Instead, we're calling a new function (defined below), **addOnload()**, which handles the **onload** handler for us. For each call, we're passing one parameter: the name of the function we want to run when an **onload** event is triggered. You can see the result in **A**.

   continues on next page

2. `function addOnload(newFunction) {`

This line starts off a new function, much like any other function. What's being passed in is the name of a function.

This can be a bit confusing, so here's an example. Instead of calling:

`window.onload = myNewFunction;`

we'll instead call:

`addOnload(myNewFunction);`

which works out the same in the end.

3. `var oldOnload = window.onload;`

This line declares a new variable, **oldOnload**—if we've already set **window.onload**, we'll store its value here. If we haven't, it doesn't hurt anything.

4. `if (typeof oldOnload ==`
`→"function") {`

In this line, we check to see what kind of variable **oldOnload** is. If we've previously set **window.onload**, it'll be a function call (otherwise, it'll be nothing at all). If it's a function, do the following.

5. `window.onload = function() {`
`    oldOnload();`
`    newFunction();`
`}`

These lines of code reset the value of **window.onload** to do two things: whatever it was doing before, and our new function. The **window.onload** event handler is set to be an anonymous function (one that doesn't have a name). Then, we tell **window.onload** to do what it was already doing. But before the function ends, we add that it needs to *also* do our **newFunction()** as well.

Listing 8.2 Setting multiple **onload** attributes using our new **addOnload()** function.

```
addOnload(initOne);
addOnload(initTwo);
addOnload(initThree);

function addOnload(newFunction) {
    var oldOnload = window.onload;

    if (typeof oldOnload == "function") {
        window.onload = function() {
            oldOnload();
            newFunction();
        }
    }
    else {
        window.onload = newFunction;
    }
}

function initOne() {
    document.getElementById("pageBody").
    → style.backgroundColor = "#00F";
}

function initTwo() {
    document.getElementById("pageBody").
    → style.color = "#F00";
}

function initThree() {
    var allTags = document.getElementById
    → ("pageBody").getElementsByTagName("*");

    for (var i=0; i<allTags.length; i++) {
        if (allTags[i].nodeName == "H1") {
            allTags[i].style.border =
            → "5px green solid";
            allTags[i].style.padding = "25px";
            allTags[i].style.backgroundColor
            → = "#FFF";
        }
    }
}
```

```
6. else {
      window.onload = newFunction;
   }
```

If **oldOnload** wasn't a function—that is, it was **undefined**—we tell it to do our new function when the page completes loading. In this fashion, we can call **addOnload()** multiple times: the first time it assigns its function to **window.onload**; the second and later times it creates that anonymous function, telling JavaScript to do everything it's been told to do previously *and* the new thing as well.

TIP If you want to have an onload handler do more than one thing, the easiest way is to create one function that does everything, and then have the onload handler call that function. But make sure that each function returns—if, for example, your function contains a setTimeout() call to itself, it'll never return and therefore never go on to the rest of the called functions.

TIP If you're working with an existing body of code, it's easy to accidentally reset window.onload—any given HTML page can call multiple external JavaScript files, any of which can set the event handler. If one place sets window.onload directly, but every time after that you call addOnload(), you're fine. But if you set window.onload after you've set it previously (whether directly or via addOnload()), you'll have walked on top of your handler and lost its original value.

TIP This script is (very) loosely based on one by Simon Willison (simonwillison.net) and is used with his permission.

TIP Another way to have one event handler handle multiple events is covered in "Advanced Event Handling," later in this chapter.

The onunload event

The **onunload** handler is triggered when the user leaves your webpage. The most common use for this is advertising windows that pop up when you leave some commercial sites, especially pornographic sites. If you find yourself on one of the latter, you'll often find that it's almost impossible to leave—every time you close a window or attempt to navigate away from the site, window after window appears, re-opening the same or other pages, all of the same genre. Consequently, people have come to hate the **onunload** handler with a passion, so use it sparingly.

That's not to say that there aren't good uses for it; one place where it's useful can be seen back in Listing 6.3, "To create a select-and-go menu."

The onbeforeunload event

At first, the **onbeforeunload** event might seem like a duplicate of **onunload**, but there's an important difference: the former is triggered when a user *starts* to leave a webpage, and the latter is triggered *after* the user has left the webpage. **Listings 8.3** and **8.4** show an example in which the difference matters.

Listing 8.3 It's a simple form, but we want to make sure that no one leaves accidentally.

```
<!DOCTYPE html>
<html>
<head>
    <title>FabulousAirTickets.com</title>
    <script src="script02.js"></script>
</head>
<body>
<h2>FabulousAirTickets.com</h2>
<form action="#">
    <p>
        <label for="from">From:</label>
        <input type="text" id="from">
          
        <label for="to">To:</label>
        <input type="text" id="to">
    </p>
    <p>
        <label for="leavedate">Departure
→ Date:</label>
        <input type="date" id="leavedate">
          
        <label for="returndate">Return
→ Date:</label>
        <input type="date" id="returndate">
    </p>
    <p>
        # of Adults:
        <select>
            <option value="1">1</option>
            <option value="2">2</option>
            <option value="3">3</option>
            <option value="4">4</option>
        </select>
    </p>
    <p>
        <input type="submit" value="Find
→ Flights!">
          
        <input type="reset">
    </p>
</form>
</body>
</html>
```

B Here, we make sure that the user knows what they're doing. Each browser (from top to bottom, Firefox, Chrome, and IE) shows a different version of the warning.

Listing 8.4 When users try to leave the page, this script warns that they'll lose data.

```
window.onbeforeunload = function() {
    return "If you close this window, your
    → flight choices will be lost!";
}
```

- ```
  window.onbeforeunload =
  → function() {
    return "If you close this
    → window, your flight choices
    → will be lost!";
  }
  ```

  Here, we want to warn people leaving a form that they'll lose everything they've entered. If we did this using **onunload**, the entries would already be gone. But because we used **onbeforeunload**, there's still a chance for visitors to change their minds.

  The function needs to return the wording used in the confirmation dialog **B**. Note that each browser shows a unique version of the dialog—in particular, Firefox doesn't use the returned wording at all.

The onresize event

The **onresize** event is triggered when the window is resized.

The onmove event

The **onmove** event handler is triggered when the window is moved.

The onabort event

The **onabort** event handler is triggered when the user cancels an image loading on the webpage. It's not used very often, and not all browsers seem to fully support it.
  ```

The onerror event

The **onerror** event may be triggered when a JavaScript error occurs on the page.

TIP It can be polite to set `onerror = null;` in complex pages you put on the web. With this line of code on your page, *some* error messages will not be displayed to the user in the unfortunate event that there's a problem—but which errors will be hidden depends on the browser.

The onfocus and onblur events

The **onfocus** and **onblur** handlers are mirror images of each other. While they may sound like what happens when you've been working on JavaScript too late at night, in reality, the **onfocus** handler triggers when a page becomes the front-most active window, and the **onblur** handler triggers when a page moves to the background.

Due to rampant misuse of these handlers, most current browsers have stopped supporting them.

The onscroll event

The **onscroll** event is triggered when a user scrolls the webpage (either up or down).

The onDOMContentLoaded event

The **onDOMContentLoaded** event is similar to **onload**, except that it's triggered when only the webpage itself has finished loading, but *not* any related files (such as images).

Listing 8.5 You might be able to view the source of this page, but you'll have to work for it.

```
<!DOCTYPE html>
<html>
<head>
    <title>onMousedown capture</title>
    <script src="script03.js"></script>
</head>
<body>
    <h1>Important source data that someone
    → might want to look at.</h1>
</body>
</html>
```

Listing 8.6 This script will deter some inexperienced users from bringing up the shortcut menu on your pages.

```
if (typeof document.oncontextmenu ==
→ "object") {
    if (document.all) {
        document.onmousedown =
        → captureMousedown;
    }
    else {
        document.oncontextmenu =
        → captureMousedown;
    }
}
else {
    window.oncontextmenu = captureMousedown;
}

function captureMousedown(evt) {
    if (evt) {
        var mouseClick = evt.which;
    }
    else {
        var mouseClick = window.event.button;
    }

    if (mouseClick==1 || mouseClick==3) {
        alert("Menu Disabled");
        return false;
    }
}
```

Mouse Event Handling

Many of the user's interactions with your pages come in the form of mouse movements or mouse clicks. JavaScript provides a robust set of handlers for these events.

The onmousedown and oncontextmenu events

One of the questions most frequently asked by new JavaScripters is, "How do I hide my scripts from anyone coming to my page?" The answer is, simply, you can't. A determined person will always be able find out what's in your code.

If you prefer to hide your code from average surfers, though, **Listings 8.5** and **8.6** can keep them from viewing the page source via a mouse-click that normally brings up the shortcut menu (also known as the context menu).

1. ```
   if (typeof document.oncontextmenu
   → == "object") {
       if (document.all) {
           document.onmousedown =
           → captureMousedown;
       }
   ```

   This first block checks to see if the browser is Firefox, which uses **window.oncontextmenu** (and so doesn't know about **document.oncontextmenu**). If it isn't Firefox, we next look for **document.all**, which is an easy way of checking to see if the browser is Internet Explorer (IE). If it is, we want to set **captureMousedown()** to run whenever **onmousedown** is triggered.

   continues on next page
   ```

2. ```
else {
    document.oncontextmenu =
    → captureMousedown;
}
```

If we're here, it's because your visitor is using Safari or Chrome, and they need **oncontextmenu** set on the document object.

3. ```
else {
    window.oncontextmenu =
    → captureMousedown;
}
```

And finally, if the browser is Firefox, we want **oncontextmenu** events for the window to call the **captureMousedown()** function.

4. ```
function captureMousedown(evt) {
```

The function that handles the **onmousedown** and **oncontextmenu** events begins here. Chrome, Safari, and Firefox generate the **evt** parameter being passed in automatically whenever an event is triggered, and this variable contains information about the event.

5. ```
if (evt) {
    var mouseClick = evt.which;
}
else {
    var mouseClick =
    → window.event.button;
}
```

If the **evt** variable exists, we can determine which button the user clicked by checking **evt.which**. If the user has IE, the results of the user's action will be found in **window.event.button**. Either way, we'll store the result in the **mouseClick** variable.

A This alert box scares off the timid (and annoys the rest).

TABLE 8.1 Mouse Click Codes

Code	Event	Browsers
1	Left-click	Internet Explorer
		All Mac browsers
3	Right-click	All browsers

6. ```
if (mouseClick==1 ||
→ mouseClick==3) {
   alert("Menu Disabled");
   return false;
}
```

If **mouseClick** is 1 or 3, put up an alert **A** saying that that functionality is disabled, and return false. Returning false keeps the menu window from being displayed.

**TIP** You're probably asking yourself why we're checking for two different mouse clicks. Shouldn't one be enough? In theory, yes, but in practice, no. The issue is that on the Mac, it's possible to trigger the shortcut menu by left-clicking while holding down the Ctrl key, so we have to check for both right and left clicks, as shown in **Table 8.1**.

Unfortunately, this approach can backfire: you may successfully block left-click and right-click input, but it also means that you might be keeping people from clicking any links on your page.

**TIP** It's very simple for savvy surfers to work around this: all they have to do is turn JavaScript off in their browser, and their clicking ability returns. Putting your JavaScript code into an external .js file seems like a tricky workaround, but users can look in their cache folder on their hard disk. Or they can look at the source of your page, find the name of the external file, and then enter the URL of the external file in their browser, which obediently displays the file's contents. If you really worry about your source code being stolen, the only method that's guaranteed to keep it from being looked at is to never put it on the web.

**TIP** Internet Explorer understands document.oncontextmenu, so you'd think that setting it would cause it to handle those events—not so. IE is the only browser that needs document.onmousedown to be set. And if you set both window.oncontextmenu and document.onmousedown, Firefox triggers every event twice, once for each action.

Handling Events **203**
```

The onmouseup event

Similar to the **onmousedown** event, the **onmouseup** event is triggered when the user clicks the mouse and then releases the button.

The onmousemove event

The **onmousemove** event is triggered whenever visitors to your page move their mouse. In this example, users get the feeling that someone's watching their every move **B**. Listings **8.7**, **8.8**, and **8.9** show how to use JavaScript to display eyeballs that follow visitors around.

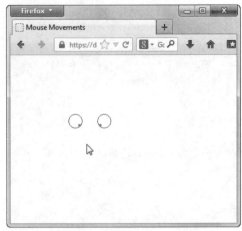

B The eyeballs will follow the cursor no matter where it goes.

Listing 8.7 The HTML for the following-eyes example.

```
<!DOCTYPE html>
<html>
<head>
    <title>Mouse Movements</title>
    <link rel="stylesheet"
    → href="script04.css">
    <script src="script04.js"></script>
</head>
<body>
    <img src="images/circle.gif"
    → alt="left eye" id="lEye">
    <img src="images/circle.gif"
    → alt="right eye" id="rEye">
    <img src="images/lilRed.gif"
    → alt="left eyeball" id="lDot">
    <img src="images/lilRed.gif"
    → alt="right eyeball" id="rDot">
</body>
</html>
```

Listing 8.8 The CSS for the following-eyes example.

```css
body {
    background-color: #FFF;
}

#lEye, #rEye {
    position: absolute;
    top: 100px;
    width: 24px;
    height: 25px;
}

#lDot, #rDot {
    position: absolute;
    top: 113px;
    width: 4px;
    height: 4px;
}

#lEye {
    left: 100px;
}

#rEye {
    left: 150px;
}

#lDot {
    left: 118px;
}

#rDot {
    left: 153px;
}
```

1. ```
   document.onmousemove =
   → moveHandler;
   ```

   For all browsers, if a **mousemove** event is triggered, call the **moveHandler()** function.

2. ```
   function moveHandler(evt) {
       if (!evt) {
           evt = window.event;
       }
       animateEyes(evt.clientX,
       → evt.clientY);
   }
   ```

   The **moveHandler()** function will be triggered whenever a **mousemove** event occurs. If the visitor has Internet Explorer, we need to initialize **evt**, and then for all browsers, we call the **animateEyes()** function and pass it the X and Y cursor coordinates.

3. ```
   function animateEyes(xPos,yPos) {
   ```

   Here's where the actual eyeball movement is done, based on the X and Y coordinates passed in.

4. ```
   var rightEye = document.
   → getElementById("rEye");
   var leftEye = document.
   → getElementById("lEye");
   var rightEyeball = document.
   → getElementById("rDot").style;
   var leftEyeball = document.
   → getElementById("lDot").style;
   ```

   This section assigns variables that match up with the **id**s of the images of the circles of the eyeballs and the dots of the eyeballs.

continues on next page

5. ```
leftEyeball.left = newEyeballPos
  →(xPos, leftEye.offsetLeft);
leftEyeball.top = newEyeballPos
  →(yPos, leftEye.offsetTop);
rightEyeball.left = newEyeballPos
  →(xPos, rightEye.offsetLeft);
rightEyeball.top = newEyeballPos
  →(yPos, rightEye.offsetTop);
```

This block draws the eyeballs based on the mouse pointer's position, using the results of the **newEyeballPos()** function defined in the next step.

6. ```
function newEyeballPos
  →(currPos,eyePos) {
  return Math.min(Math.max
    →(currPos, eyePos+3),
    →eyePos+17) + "px";
}
```

We never want the eyeball to go outside the eye, do we? So, for each eyeball, we check to make sure that it gets as close to the cursor as possible, while still appearing within the circle of the eye.

TIP There was a once-common JavaScript widget where a bunch of dots (or whatever the designer desired) followed the cursor around the page. We didn't want to re-create an existing effect, so we used eyeballs instead. If you want to put tag-along dots on your page, just tweak this script.

Listing 8.9 Keep an eye (OK, two eyes) on your users with this script.

```
document.onmousemove = moveHandler;

function moveHandler(evt) {
    if (!evt) {
        evt = window.event;
    }
    animateEyes(evt.clientX, evt.clientY);
}

function animateEyes(xPos,yPos) {
    var rightEye = document.
      →getElementById("rEye");
    var leftEye = document.
      →getElementById("lEye");
    var rightEyeball = document.
      →getElementById("rDot").style;
    var leftEyeball = document.
      →getElementById("lDot").style;

    leftEyeball.left = newEyeballPos
      →(xPos, leftEye.offsetLeft);
    leftEyeball.top = newEyeballPos
      →(yPos, leftEye.offsetTop);
    rightEyeball.left = newEyeballPos
      →(xPos, rightEye.offsetLeft);
    rightEyeball.top = newEyeballPos
      →(yPos, rightEye.offsetTop);

    function newEyeballPos(currPos,eyePos) {
        return Math.min(Math.max(currPos,
          →eyePos+3), eyePos+17) + "px";
    }
}
```

The onmouseover event

By now, you should be familiar with this event: it's our good buddy from image rollovers. This event will be triggered whenever the mouse is moved into any area for which the **onmouseover** has been registered.

The onmouseout event

And unsurprisingly by now, where there's an **onmouseover**, there's usually an **onmouseout**. This is triggered when the user moves the mouse out of an area for which the event has been registered.

The onmousemove event

The **onmousemove** event is triggered every time the user moves the mouse.

The ondblclick event

One of the drawbacks of the Internet is that the familiar user interface elements you're used to encountering on your computer all change on the web. For instance, one of the first things that new computer users learn how to do is double-click with the mouse. There's no double-clicking on the web, or at least, there wasn't until now. With **Listings 8.10**, **8.11**, and **8.12**, you'll be able to check for double mouse clicks.

■ `document.images[i].ondblclick =`
→ `newWindow;`

The `newWindow()` function is triggered when a user double-clicks one of the thumbnail images. In that case, a new window pops up ⓒ, showing the same image in a larger format.

The onclick event

The `onclick` handler works in a similar fashion to the `ondblclick` handler, except that a single click triggers it instead of a double click. The `onmouseup` handler is also similar, except that `onclick` requires that the user press the mouse button both down and up in order to be triggered, while `onmouseup` requires just the latter.

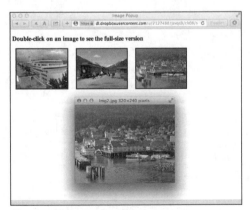

ⓒ A double-click on a thumbnail opens the larger version of the image.

Listing 8.10 This HTML helps you work with double clicks.

```
<!DOCTYPE html>
<html>
<head>
    <title>Image Popup</title>
    <link rel="stylesheet"
    → href="script05.css">
    <script src="script05.js"></script>
</head>
<body>
    <h3>Double-click on an image to see the
    → full-size version</h3>
    <img src="images/Img0_thumb.jpg"
    → alt="Thumbnail 0" id="Img0">
    <img src="images/Img1_thumb.jpg"
    → alt="Thumbnail 1" id="Img1">
    <img src="images/Img2_thumb.jpg"
    → alt="Thumbnail 2" id="Img2">
</body>
</html>
```

Listing 8.11 This CSS makes your images look good.

```
body {
    background-color: #FFF;
}

img {
    margin: 0 10px;
    border: 3px #00F solid;
    width: 160px;
    height: 120px;
}
```

Listing 8.12 Capture and handle double clicks with this script.

```
window.onload = initImages;

function initImages() {
    for (var i=0; i<document.images.length;
    → i++) {
        document.images[i].ondblclick =
        → newWindow;
    }
}

function newWindow() {
    var imgName = "images/" + this.id +
    → ".jpg"
    var imgWindow = window.open(imgName,
    → "imgWin", "width=320,height=240,
    → scrollbars=no")
}
```

Form Event Handling

You'll want to use form event handling mainly for validating forms. With the events listed below, you can deal with just about any action the user takes with forms.

The onsubmit event

The `onsubmit` handler (as seen in Chapter 6) is triggered when the user clicks the Submit button to complete a form. In addition, depending on the browser, it can also be triggered when a user exits the last text entry field on a form. If a script contains an `onsubmit` handler, and the result of the handler is false, the form will not be sent back to the server.

The onreset event

The `onreset` handler is triggered when the user clicks the Reset button (if one is present) on a form. This can be handy if your form has default values that are set when the page loads—if the user clicks Reset, you'll need to handle this situation with a script that resets the default values dynamically.

The onchange event

As shown in Listing 6.3, the `onchange` event handler is triggered when users change a form field. This can be used to verify that they entered information immediately, or to respond to the user's choice before they click the Submit button.

The onselect event

The `onselect` handler is triggered if the user selects text in either an `input` or a `textarea` form field.

The onclick event

While the **onclick** handler is mentioned earlier under "Mouse Event Handling," it's listed here again because it's most commonly used when dealing with forms. This event is triggered when the user clicks a check box or radio button, as in Listing 6.15. Listing 2.10 also uses the **onclick** handler; in that case, it allows a single link to do one action for JavaScript-enabled browsers and another, entirely different action for browsers without JavaScript.

The onblur event

While **onblur** can be used for browser windows (as mentioned above), it's more common for it to be used in forms. **Listings 8.13**, **8.14**, and **8.15** show the **onblur** handler being used to force the user to enter data into a field.

1. ```
   if (allTags[i].className.indexOf
   → ("reqd") > -1) {
   ```

   We're using a class attribute (of **reqd**) to decide on the fly when the **onblur** event handler should be used. Simply adding **class="reqd"** to an input tag triggers the event. You don't have to put the **onblur** handler on fields individually.

2. ```
   allTags[i].onblur = fieldCheck;
   ```

   This event handler on the field causes the **fieldCheck()** function to be called whenever the user leaves a required field.

Listing 8.13 This HTML creates the simple form.

```
<!DOCTYPE html>
<html>
<head>
    <title>Requiring an entry</title>
    <link rel="stylesheet"
    → href="script06.css">
    <script src="script06.js"></script>
</head>
<body>
    <form action="#">
    <h3>
        Email address: <input type="text"
        → class="reqd"><br><br>
        Name (optional): <input type="text">
    </h3>
    </form>
</body>
</html>
```

Listing 8.14 A little bit of CSS goes a long way with JavaScript.

```
body {
    background-color: #FFF;
}

.highlight {
    background-color: #FF9;
}
```

A When the user tabs out of the Email address field without entering anything, the field turns yellow and remains active until data is present.

Listing 8.15 The **onblur** handler can be used in forms to trigger actions when the user leaves a field.

```
window.onload = initForm;

function initForm() {
    var allTags = document.forms[0].
    → getElementsByTagName("*");

    for (var i=0; i<allTags.length; i++) {
        if (allTags[i].className.indexOf
        → ("reqd") > -1) {
            allTags[i].onblur = fieldCheck;
        }
    }
}

function fieldCheck() {
    if (this.value == "") {
        this.className += " highlight";
        this.focus();
    }
    else {
        this.className = "reqd";
    }
}
```

3. ```
function fieldCheck() {
    if (this.value == "") {
        this.className +=
        →" highlight";
        this.focus();
    }
    else {
        this.className = "reqd";
    }
}
```

The **fieldCheck()** function checks to make sure that something (anything) was entered in the current field. If the field has no value, the field's background is colored pale yellow by adding **" highlight"** to its class attribute **A**, and the cursor gets put back into the form field with **focus()**. When the error is corrected, simply resetting the class attribute back to its initial value resets the background to white.

**TIP** Both the **onblur** and **onchange** events are triggered when the user leaves a field after changing it. If the user leaves a field without changing it, just the **onblur** handler is triggered.

**TIP** Some versions of Firefox have had a problem with **focus()**: even though you tell the browser to stay in a field, it doesn't. Changing the background color gives the user a visual cue that something's wrong, though, so they'll still know that there was a problem.
```

The onfocus event

Sometimes you'll have a form field on a page with data that you want to display as part of the form, without the user being able to modify that field. You can use the **readonly** HTML attribute to try to keep users out, but not all browsers support it. **Listings 8.16** and **8.17** show how to use the **onfocus** event to bump users right back out of this field, on the off chance they made it to where they shouldn't be.

- ```
  allTags[i].onfocus = function() {
     this.blur();
  }
  ```

When the user attempts to enter this field, the focus (in this case the active field) will automatically be kicked right back out again **B**. This happens because the **onfocus** event handler is set to call an anonymous function (one without a name) that does just one thing: call **blur()** on the current field, bouncing the user out.

B The user can't type anything into the bottom field.

Listing 8.16 The HTML creates the form, which won't allow entries in the email field.

```
<!DOCTYPE html>
<html>
<head>
    <title>Forbidding an entry</title>
    <script src="script07.js"></script>
</head>
<body>
    <form action="#">
    <h3>
        Your message: <textarea rows="5"
        → cols="30">Enter your message
        → here</textarea>
        <br><br>
        Will be sent to: <input type="text"
        → value="js9@javascriptworld.com"
        → readonly size="25">
    </h3>
    </form>
</body>
</html>
```

Listing 8.17 Prevent wayward field entries with the **onfocus** handler in a form.

```
window.onload = initForm;

function initForm() {
    var allTags = document.forms[0].
    → getElementsByTagName("*");

    for (var i=0; i<allTags.length; i++) {
        if (allTags[i].readOnly) {
            allTags[i].onfocus = function() {
                this.blur();
            }
        }
    }
}
```
```

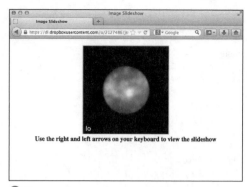

Use the right and left arrows on your keyboard to view the slideshow

A This slideshow is controlled with key presses rather than mouse clicks on navigation buttons.

Listing 8.18 Here's the HTML for the slideshow.

```
<!DOCTYPE html>
<html>
<head>
    <title>Image Slideshow</title>
    <link rel="stylesheet"
    → href="script08.css">
    <script src="script08.js"></script>
</head>
<body>
    <h3 class="centered">
        <img src="images/callisto.jpg"
        → id="myPicture" alt="Slideshow"><br>
        Use the right and left arrows on
        → your keyboard to view the
        → slideshow
    </h3>
</body>
</html>
```

Key Event Handling

Besides the mouse, the other main input device is the keyboard, at least until they get that cool computer thought-control device working. Just as with the mouse, JavaScript has the mojo to handle the keyboard.

The onkeydown event

It's handy to allow users to control your webpage via keyboard as well as via mouse. With the key event handlers, you can trigger events to happen when the appropriate keys are pressed. In **Listings 8.18**, **8.19**, and **8.20**, a standard slideshow (similar to the one in Listing 4.19) can be viewed by pressing the left and right arrow keys on the keyboard **A**.

1. `document.onkeydown = keyHit;`

   Here we register the **keyHit()** function as the one to handle **onkeydown** events.

2. `var thisPic = 0;`

   The variable **thisPic** is initialized and set globally, so it's stored and available for use every time **keyHit()** is called.

3. `function keyHit(evt) {`

   The **keyHit()** function handles the event when keys are hit.

4. `var ltArrow = 37;`
   `var rtArrow = 39;`

   We need to store the appropriate values for when a key is hit. The left arrow key generates a 37, and the right arrow key triggers a 39.

5. `if (evt) {`
   `    var thisKey = evt.which;`
   `}`
   `else {`
   `  var thisKey =`
   `   ` → `window.event.keyCode;`
   `}`

   How we know which key the user hit depends on which browser they're using. If it's Firefox, Chrome, or Safari, we look at **evt.which**, which contains the code for the key hit. If it's IE, that same value will be in **window.event.keyCode**. Either way, the result is saved in **thisKey**.

Listing 8.19 Once again, the CSS makes our images look good.

```
body {
     background-color: #FFF;
}

.centered {
     text-align: center;
}

img#myPicture {
     width: 262px;
     height: 262px;
}
```

Listing 8.20 Use the **onkeydown** handler in this script to trigger a slide change.

```
document.onkeydown = keyHit;
var thisPic = 0;

function keyHit(evt) {
    var myPix = new Array("images/callisto.
    → jpg", "images/europa.jpg","images/
    → io.jpg", "images/ganymede.jpg");
    var imgCt = myPix.length-1;
    var ltArrow = 37;
    var rtArrow = 39;

    if (evt) {
        var thisKey = evt.which;
    }
    else {
        var thisKey = window.event.keyCode;
    }

    if (thisKey == ltArrow) {
        chgSlide(-1);
    }
    else if (thisKey == rtArrow) {
        chgSlide(1);
    }

    function chgSlide(direction) {
        thisPic = thisPic + direction;
        if (thisPic > imgCt) {
            thisPic = 0;
        }
        if (thisPic < 0) {
            thisPic = imgCt;
        }
        document.getElementById("myPicture").
        → src = myPix[thisPic];
    }
}
```

6. `if (thisKey == ltArrow) {`
   `chgSlide(-1);`
`}`
`else if (thisKey == rtArrow) {`
   `chgSlide(1);`
`}`

If the user pressed the left arrow, then go backward through the slideshow. If they pressed the right arrow, go forward. If they chose any other key, don't do anything at all.

TIP If you're not sure what the key values are for a particular key, you can find out by putting the line `alert(thiskey);` in between the lines of code in steps 5 and 6 and then pressing the key for which you want to find the value. The alert box contains the numeric key value.

The onkeyup event

The **onkeyup** event handler is identical to the **onkeydown** handler, except that (big surprise) it gets called when the user has completed pressing the key down and is now letting it come back up again.

The onkeypress event

The **onkeypress** event is triggered when the user both presses a key down and also lets the key back up again—just for the sake of completeness.

Advanced Event Handling

Along with the event handling you've seen up till now in this book, there's another model, usually referred to as DOM Level 2 event handlers. This new, more flexible approach has a number of advantages:

- There's one common way to set every type of event handler.

- Multiple event handlers can be easily registered for the same event—that is, adding another event handler doesn't overwrite the previous version.

- You can control whether events are *bubbled* or *captured* (see the sidebar "Bubbling and Capturing").

- Events can trigger other events.

- Event handlers can be easily removed.

TIP Chapter 10, "Objects and the DOM," will go into further detail about the Document Object Model (the DOM).

The addEventListener method

This task is identical to the last task, except that here the event handler is set via **addEventListener()**, as shown in Listing 8.21. The result can be seen in **Ⓐ**.

- **document.addEventListener**
  → ("keydown",keyHit,false);

  Again, we're registering the **keyHit()** function as the one to handle **onkeydown** events. The **addEventListener()** function has three parameters: the event itself (the target), the function to be called when that event is triggered (the listener), and a Boolean value that specifies whether events should be captured (true) or bubbled (false).

Listing 8.21 The very similar JavaScript code, now using the **addEventListener()** function.

```
document.addEventListener("keydown",keyHit,
→ false);
var thisPic = 0;

function keyHit(evt) {
    var myPix = new Array("images/
    → catseyenebula.jpg", "images/crabnebula.
    → jpg","images/eskimonebula.jpg",
    → "images/ringnebula.jpg");
    var imgCt = myPix.length-1;
    var ltArrow = 37;
    var rtArrow = 39;

    if (evt) {
        var thisKey = evt.which;
    }
    else {
        var thisKey = window.event.keyCode;
    }

    if (thisKey == ltArrow) {
        chgSlide(-1);
    }
    else if (thisKey == rtArrow) {
        chgSlide(1);
    }

    function chgSlide(direction) {
        thisPic = thisPic + direction;
        if (thisPic > imgCt) {
            thisPic = 0;
        }
        if (thisPic < 0) {
            thisPic = imgCt;
        }
        document.getElementById("myPicture").
        → src = myPix[thisPic];
    }
}
```

TIP The target event passed to addEventListener() is the same as the events used elsewhere in this chapter, minus the leading "on".

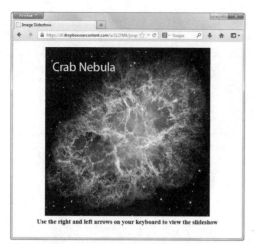

A This slideshow works the same as the previous slideshow, except now we're using a different way to register an event handler.

The removeEventListener method

This method allows the removal of an event listener from its target. It takes the same three parameters as `addEventListener()`.

The dispatchEvent method

This method allows an event handler to be triggered from elsewhere in the code. It is passed one parameter: an **Event** object. For example, to create, initialize, and dispatch an event to click a link, your code might say:

```
var evt = document.createEvent
→ ("Event");
evt.initEvent("click", true, false);
document.getElementById("theLink").
→ dispatchEvent(evt);
```

The initEvent method

This method initializes an already-created event (usually done by calling `document.createEvent("Event");`). It is passed three parameters: the type of event, a Boolean indicating whether the event should bubble, and a Boolean indicating whether the event can be canceled.

TIP Everywhere *but* initEvent(), the Boolean used to declare an event bubbleable is set to false. Here, it's set to true.

The stopPropagation method

This method prevents any further events from being triggered during event flow. It takes no parameters.

The preventDefault method

This method cancels the event in progress (if it's cancelable). It takes no parameters.

Bubbling and Capturing

Think of the structure of a webpage being like a tree. For instance **B**, the body of a webpage can contain a table, which itself contains rows, each of which contains cells.

Say that you wrote a script that popped up an alert every time you moused over elements on the page. If you moused over a cell, you'd expect to get an alert saying that you're over that cell—and you would. But then you'd also get alerts saying that you were over a row, and a table, and finally the body. This is called *event bubbling*: that is, events bubble up from the bottom to the top of the tree. It's the normal way that webpages work.

But what if you wanted events to go in the opposite direction; that is, from the top down? In that case, you want *event capturing*, and your script would put up alerts saying that you were over the body, then the table, then the row, and finally the cell.

This is one of the major advantages of using advanced event handling: when you call **addEventListener()**, you get to decide which direction your events will flow.

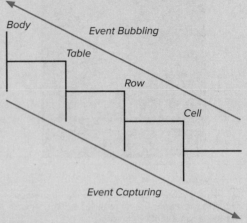

B Events can be triggered going from bottom to top (bubbling), or from top to bottom (capturing).

9

JavaScript and Cookies

In web terms, a *cookie* is a unique nugget of information that a web server gives to your browser when the two first meet and which they then share with each return visit. Your browser saves the cookie—and the information it contains about you—as a plain text file stored on your computer's drive.

As a JavaScript coder, you can do many useful things with cookies. If your site requires registration, you can set cookies to store your readers' user names and passwords on their drives so that they don't need to enter them every time they visit. You can keep track of which parts of your site the user has visited and count the number of visits from that user.

There are many common misconceptions about cookies, so it's important to note what you can't do with them: you can't get any real information about the user, such as their email address; you can't use cookies to check out the contents of their drives; and cookies can't transmit computer viruses. A cookie is just a simple text file on the user's computer in which you, the JavaScript programmer, can store some information.

In This Chapter

A cookie always includes the address of the server that sent it. That's the primary idea behind cookie technology: identification. Think of it as Caller ID for the web, with variations on the theme—each website using cookies gives your browser a personalized ID of some sort so that it can recognize you on the next visit. When you return to the web server that first passed you a particular cookie, the server queries your browser to see if you are one of its many cookie holders. If so, the server retrieves the information stored in the original cookie. Keep in mind that cookies identify the computer being used, not the individual using the computer.

A It doesn't look like much, but the content of the form's text field has just been written to a cookie.

Listing 9.1 The HTML for our first cookie page.

```
<!DOCTYPE html>
<html>
<head>
    <title>Set a cookie based on a
    → form</title>
    <script src="script01.js"></script>
</head>
<body>
    <form id="cookieForm" action="#">
        <h1>Enter your name: <input
        → type="text" id="nameField"></h1>
    </form>
</body>
</html>
```

Baking Your First Cookie

A cookie is a text string with a particular format:

```
cookieName=cookieValue;expires=
→ expirationDateGMT;path=URLpath;
→ domain=siteDomain
```

Breaking this down, the first part of the string gives the cookie a name and assigns it a value. This is the only mandatory part of a cookie; the rest of the string is optional. Next is the expiration date. When this date is reached, the browser automatically deletes the cookie. The expiration date is followed by the path, which stores the directory structure (below the domain) where the webpage resides. Finally, the domain you're on is saved in the cookie.

Listing 9.1, the HTML file, calls the JavaScript in **Listing 9.2**, which sets a cookie from a value entered by the user into a form. When you try this one out **A**, it won't appear to do that much, but the cookie is actually being created. Later examples in this chapter build on this one.

To set a cookie:

1. `function nameFieldInit() {`

    First, set up the function **nameFieldInit()** to define the value of the cookie. This function is called when the window has completed loading.

2. `var userName = "";`

    Next, we initialize the variable **userName** with a null value.

    continues on next page

3. `if (document.cookie != "") {`
    `userName = document.cookie.`
    `⇢ split("=")[1];`

We begin by checking that the object **document.cookie** contains something. The method **split("=")** splits a cookie into an array, where **cookieField[0]** is the cookie name and **cookieField[1]** is the cookie value. Note that **cookieField** can be any variable that you want to use to store a particular cookie's fields. So you assign **userName** the value returned by **document.cookie.split("=")[1]**; that is, the cookie value.

4. `document.getElementById`
    `⇢ ("nameField").value = userName;`

Setting **nameField**'s value puts the user's name into the text field when the page loads if there's a name stored in the cookie file.

5. `document.getElementById`
    `⇢ ("nameField").onblur =`
    `⇢ setCookie;`
    `document.getElementById`
    `⇢ ("cookieForm").onsubmit =`
    `⇢ setCookie;`

In the first line, the **onblur** event handler (see Chapters 1 and 8) calls the **setCookie()** function when the user leaves the text field. In the second, we do the same thing for the form's **onsubmit** handler. If you press Enter after you've typed your name, certain versions of Internet Explorer, for some reason, don't trigger the **onblur** handler. Adding the **onsubmit** handler catches all the variants.

6. `function setCookie() {`

Now begin a new function, called **setCookie()**.

Listing 9.2 Use this script to set a browser cookie.

```
window.addEventListener("load",nameFieldInit,
⇢ false);

function nameFieldInit() {
    var userName = "";
    if (document.cookie != "") {
        userName = document.cookie.
        ⇢ split("=")[1];
    }

    document.getElementById("nameField").
    ⇢ value = userName;
    document.getElementById("nameField").
    ⇢ onblur = setCookie;
    document.getElementById("cookieForm").
    ⇢ onsubmit = setCookie;
}

function setCookie() {
    var expireDate = new Date();
    expireDate.setMonth(expireDate.
    ⇢ getMonth()+6);

    var userName = document.getElementById
    ⇢ ("nameField").value;
    document.cookie = "userName=" +
    ⇢ userName + ";expires=" +
    ⇢ expireDate.toGMTString();

    document.getElementById("nameField").
    ⇢ blur();
    return false;
}
```

7. `var expireDate = new Date();`

Get the current date, and put it into the new variable **expireDate**.

8. `expireDate.setMonth(`
   `↪ expireDate.getMonth()+6);`

This line gets the month portion of **expireDate**, adds 6 to the month, and then sets the month portion of **expireDate** to the new value. In other words, it sets the expiration date of the cookie we're creating to six months in the future.

9. `var userName = document.`
   `↪ getElementById("nameField").`
   `↪ value;`

This line creates a new **userName** variable and assigns it whatever the user typed into the text field. The **userName** variable has to be created twice (once inside each function) because it's not a global; that is, we're using it inside each function, but we're not expecting it to keep its value across functions—it's new each time.

continues on next page

A Fistful of Cookies

You can have multiple cookies on a page, and the format for this is:

```
"cookieName1=cookieValue1;expires=expirationDateGMT1;path=sitePath1;
↪ domain=siteDomain1";
↪ "cookieName2=cookieValue2;expires=expirationDateGMT2;path=sitePath2;
↪ domain=siteDomain2"
```

Again, the only mandatory fields are the name and value pair.

The **split("; ")** command splits the multiple cookie record into an array, with each cookie in a cookie record numbered from 0 on. Note that there is a space after the semicolon in this command. So **cookieArray[0]** would be the first cookie in the multiple cookie record, **cookieArray[1]** would be next, and so on. For more, see the "Handling Multiple Cookies" example later in this chapter.

10. `document.cookie = "userName=" +`
`→ userName + ";expires=" +`
`→ expireDate.toGMTString();`

Here's where we write the cookie. We're setting **document.cookie** (remember, a cookie is just a text string, so you can use the same text string techniques to build it, like using the + sign to combine things) to contain the user's name and the cookie expiration date. The **toGMTString()** method converts the **expireDate Date** object into a text string so that it can be written into the cookie.

11. `document.getElementById`
`→ ("nameField").blur();`
`return false;`

Remember when we set up the form so that **setCookie()** could be called in one of two ways? Here's where we handle the fallout of that choice:

- ▶ If we're in IE, the first line causes the focus to leave the name field, so it's clear that something has occurred, and the second (returning a value of false) keeps the form from actually submitting.

- ▶ If we're not in IE, the first line does nothing (that is, we've already left the name field, so leaving it again doesn't matter) and the second line keeps the form submission from being triggered.

TIP This script assumes that the first cookie contains the user name. Later scripts show how to handle multiple cookies and get a cookie by name instead of number.

TIP If you're in the second half of the year, don't worry if you encounter problems resetting the date. Adding 6 to the month always produces the correct result; that is, if necessary, the year is incremented by one and the month is decremented by six.

TIP The scripts in this chapter are ordered in such a way that they'll work fine if you run them in the order in which they appear. If you skip around, though, you may encounter some weird results (such as the browser thinking that your name is a number). If you want to run them out of sequence, try running Listing 9.7 ("Deleting Cookies") in between scripts.

A This cookie had my name on it.

Listing 9.3 JavaScript uses the **id** in this HTML page to insert the cookie result.

```
<!DOCTYPE html>
<html>
<head>
    <title>I know your name!</title>
    <script src="script02.js"></script>
</head>
<body>
    <h1 id="nameField"> </h1>
</body>
</html>
```

Listing 9.4 This short script reads a previously set cookie and sends it to the document window.

```
window.addEventListener("load",nameFieldInit,
→ false);

function nameFieldInit() {
    if (document.cookie != "") {
        document.getElementById("nameField").
        → innerHTML = "Hello, " +
        → document.cookie.split("=")[1];
    }
}
```

Reading a Cookie

Once you've set a cookie, you'll need to retrieve it in order to do anything useful. The last example set the cookie with the text string "Tom". The very simple **Listings 9.3** and **9.4** show you how to get that value from the cookie and display it on the screen (of course, you normally wouldn't show off your cookies; this script just displays the cookie as an example).

To read a cookie:

1. `if (document.cookie != "") {`

   Make sure that the value in the object **document.cookie** isn't null.

2. `document.getElementById`
   `→ ("nameField").innerHTML =`
   `→ "Hello, " + document.cookie.`
   `→ split("=")[1];`

   If the cookie isn't empty, then write a text string (the "Hello, " and note the extra space after the comma) and combine it with the split of the cookie value **A**.

> **TIP** Did you notice that you don't need to specify which of the cookies in the cookie file you are reading? That's because a cookie can only be read by the server that wrote it in the first place. The internal cookie mechanisms in the browser won't let you read or write cookies written by someone else. You only have access to your own cookies.

Showing Your Cookies

In the previous example, we read the value of one cookie from the server. Now we'll see how to write a script that reads all the cookies that came from your server and displays their names and values. If there are no cookies, the script says, "There are no cookies here" . If there are cookies, it displays a line per cookie showing what's in the cookie 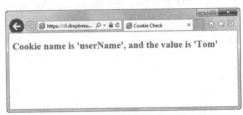. Listing 9.5 shows you how.

A If there are no cookies from the server your webpage is on, you'll see this result.

B If there are one or more cookies, then the script writes them into the document window.

To show all your cookies:

1. `var outMsg = "";`

   Start by initializing the variable **outMsg**, which will contain the message we want to display.

2. `if (document.cookie == "") {`
   `    outMsg = "There are no cookies`
   `→ here";`

   This conditional test is read, "If the **document.cookie** object is null (that is, empty), then set **outMsg** to 'There are no cookies here.'"

3. `var thisCookie = document.cookie.`
   `→ split("; ");`

   If the previous test failed (i.e., if there was at least one cookie present), then get the values of all of the cookies using **document.cookie.split("; ")** and stuff those values into an array called **thisCookie**. Remember that the **split("; ")** command creates an array of all of the cookies. Later, the script will be able to reference each of the values in that array.

Listing 9.5 This script steps through and displays all of the cookies on your machine that have been set by a particular website.

```
window.addEventListener("load",showCookies,
→ false);

function showCookies() {
    var outMsg = "";

    if (document.cookie == "") {
        outMsg = "There are no cookies here";
    }
    else {
        var thisCookie = document.cookie.
        → split("; ");

        for (var i=0; i<thisCookie.length;
        → i++) {
            outMsg += "Cookie name is '" +
            → thisCookie[i].split("=")[0];
            outMsg += "', and the value is
            → '" + thisCookie[i].split("=")
            → [1] + "'<br>";
        }
    }
    document.getElementById("cookieData").
    → innerHTML = outMsg;
}
```

4. `for (var i=0; i<thisCookie.length;`
   `→ i++) {`

This line starts a loop by first setting the value of **i**, the counter variable, to 0. Then, if **i** is less than the number of cookies in the **thisCookie** array, increment the value of **i** by 1.

5. `outMsg += "Cookie name is '" +`
   `→ thisCookie[i].split("=")[0]);`
   `outMsg += "', and the value is '"`
   `→ + thisCookie[i].split("=")`
   `→ [1] + "'<br>");`

As the script moves through the array, it puts the text string "**Cookie name is '**" into **outMsg**, followed by the name of the cookie. Then it concatenates the text string "**', and the value is '**" and the value of the cookie. And at the end of each line, we add an HTML break.

6. `document.getElementById.`
   `→ ("cookieData").innerHTML =`
   `→ outMsg;`

After setting the variable **outMsg**, it gets dumped out to the page via **innerHTML** when all the cookies have been gone through.

Using Cookies as Counters

Because cookies are persistent—that is, because they are available across multiple sessions between a web server and a browser—you can use cookies to store how many times a particular user has accessed a page. But this isn't the same thing as the page counters you see on older webpages. Because a cookie is specific to a user, you can only tell how many times *that* user has visited; you can't use cookies to tell all users how many times the page has been hit. Still, it's useful to know how to create such an individual counter, and you can adapt **Listing 9.6** for other purposes, too (see Tips).

To use a cookie as a counter:

1. `var expireDate = new Date();`
   `expireDate.setMonth(expireDate.`
   `→ getMonth()+6);`

   These two lines are the same as in steps 7 and 8 of the "Baking Your First Cookie" example. Refer there for an explanation.

2. `var hitCt = parseInt(cookieVal`
   `→ ("pageHit"));`

   The string **pageHit** is the name of the cookie. In a few steps, you'll see the function **cookieVal()**. This line sends the name of the cookie to **cookieVal()**, which returns the number of times visited as a string. This line then turns that into a number using the **parseInt()** method, and then stores the result in the variable **hitCt**. The **parseInt()** method changes a string (which is what is in the cookie) into a number (which is what the variable needs to use it as a counter).

Listing 9.6 This script counts your cookies.

```
window.addEventListener("load",initPage,
→ false);

function initPage() {
    var expireDate = new Date();
    expireDate.setMonth(expireDate.
    → getMonth()+6);

    var hitCt = parseInt(cookieVal
    → ("pageHit"));
    hitCt++;

    document.cookie = "pageHit=" + hitCt +
    → ";expires=" + expireDate.toGMTString();
    document.getElementById("pageHits").
    → innerHTML = "You have visited this
    → page " + hitCt + " times.";
}

function cookieVal(cookieName) {
    var thisCookie = document.cookie.
    → split("; ");

    for (var i=0; i<thisCookie.length; i++) {
        if (cookieName == thisCookie[i].
        → split("=")[0]) {
            return thisCookie[i].split("=")[1];
        }
    }
    return 0;
}
```

(A) Hard to believe we've visited this dull page this often.

3. `hitCt++;`

Now take the value of **hitCt** and add 1 to it, incrementing the counter.

4. `document.cookie = "pageHit=" +`
`→ hitCt + ";expires=" +`
`→ expireDate.toGMTString();`

This writes back the updated information to the cookie for future use. What's being written is a text string that combines the string "**pageHit=**" with the incremented value of **hitCt** and adds "**;expires=**" with the new expiration date, which was set to six months from today back in step 1.

5. `document.getElementById`
`→ ("pageHits").innerHTML =`
`→ "You have visited this page " +`
`→ hitCt + " times.";`

This line displays the user message in the document **(A)**. There are extra spaces after "page" and before "times" to make the line look right on screen.

6. `function cookieVal(cookieName) {`

This line begins a new function called **cookieVal()**. It is passed a string, which can then be referenced inside the function as the variable **cookieName**.

7. `var thisCookie = document.cookie.`
`→ split("; ");`

The variable **thisCookie** is set to the array generated by the **split("; ")** method.

8. `for (var i=0; i<thisCookie.length;`
`→ i++) {`

Here we're beginning a loop, just as in step 4 of the "Showing Your Cookies" example.

continues on next page

9. `if (cookieName == thisCookie[i].`
   `⇥ split("=")[0]) {`

   This conditional checks to see if **cookieName** is the same as that of the cookie in the **i**[th] element of the cookie array.

10. `return thisCookie[i].split("=")[1];`

    If the test in step 9 succeeded, then return the cookie's value.

11. `return 0;`

    If we've looked at all the items in the array and found no match, return a 0 value.

TIP When you load the HTML page that calls this script, press the Reload button in your browser to see the counter increment.

TIP As mentioned earlier, you can adapt Listing 9.6 for other purposes. One possibility would be to use a cookie to track when a particular user had last visited your site and display different pages depending on when that was. For example, some online magazines have a cover page with artwork and the names of the stories in the day's issue. If the user visits the site more than once in a 24-hour period, they only see the cover page the first time; subsequent visits jump the user directly to the site's Table of Contents page.

TIP If you want a true page-hit counter, one that tells how many times a page has been loaded by all users, you'll need to use a counter program that is installed on your web server. Check with your web hosting company to see if they have counters available, or put "webpage hit counter" into your favorite search engine.

Ⓐ It's good interface design to confirm with the user whenever you are going to erase or delete anything.

Listing 9.7 This script deletes cookies.

```
window.addEventListener("load",cookieDelete,
→ false);

function cookieDelete() {
    var cookieCt = 0;

    if (document.cookie != "" && confirm
→ ("Do you want to delete the
→ cookies?")) {
        var thisCookie = document.cookie.
→ split("; ");
        cookieCt = thisCookie.length;

        var expireDate = new Date();
        expireDate.setDate(expireDate.
→ getDate()-1);

        for (var i=0; i<cookieCt; i++) {
            var cookieName = thisCookie[i].
→ split("=")[0];
            document.cookie = cookieName +
→ ";expires=" + expireDate.
→ toGMTString();
        }
    }
    document.getElementById("cookieData").
→ innerHTML = "Number of cookies
→ deleted: " + cookieCt;
}
```

Deleting Cookies

At some point, you're going to want to delete a cookie, or many cookies, in a cookie record. It's fairly easy to do. One technique that works well is to simply set the cookie's expiration date to a date in the past, which causes the browser to delete it automatically. **Listing 9.7** shows how to force your cookies to become stale.

To delete cookies:

1. **`var cookieCt = 0;`**

   This script is going to keep track of how many cookies we've deleted, so we start off by creating the **cookieCt** variable and setting it to zero.

2. **`if (document.cookie != "" &&`**
   `→ confirm("Do you want to delete`
   `→ the cookies?")) {`

   This test first checks to make sure that the cookie contains something; that is, that there are some cookies. If the test shows that the cookie is empty, then the script does nothing. The second part of the test tells the browser to put up a confirmation dialog with the included text Ⓐ. If **confirm()** returns **true**, then we know the user wants to delete their cookies. If **false**, then we skip down to step 9.

3. **`var thisCookie = document.cookie.`**
   `→ split("; ");`

   This line splits the contents of the cookie into an array with the **split("; ")** method and assigns that array to the variable **thisCookie**.

continues on next page

4. `cookieCt = thisCookie.length;`

   We now know how many cookies we're going to be deleting, so that's stored in **cookieCt**.

5. `var expireDate = new Date();`
   `expireDate.setDate(expireDate.`
   `→ getDate()-1);`

   Here we create a new date object, **expireDate**, which is then set to the current date minus 1—in other words, to yesterday.

6. `for (var i=0; i<cookieCt; i++) {`

   Now begin a **for** loop so that we can delete all the cookies, not just one. First set the value of **i** to 0; then, as long as **i** is less than the number of cookies, increment **i** by 1.

7. `var cookieName = thisCookie[i].`
   `→ split("=")[0];`

   Use **split("=")[0]** to get the name of the **i**th cookie in the array, which is then stored in the variable **cookieName**.

8. `document.cookie = cookieName +`
   `→ "=;expires=" + expireDate.`
   `→ toGMTString();`

   Here's where the cookie with the changed expiration date gets written back out.

9. `document.getElementById`
   `→ ("cookieData").innerHTML =`
   `→ "Number of cookies deleted: " +`
   `→ cookieCt;`

   The script is out of the **for** loop now, and this line sets the number of cookies deleted in the HTML document 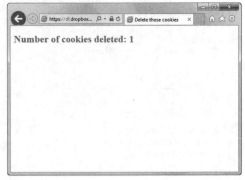.

B Users should also get feedback that events have occurred as expected.

```
window.addEventListener("load",initPage,
→ false);

function initPage() {
    var now = new Date();
    var expireDate = new Date();
    expireDate.setMonth(expireDate.
    → getMonth()+6);

    var hitCt = parseInt(cookieVal
    → ("pageHit"));
    hitCt++;

    var lastVisit = cookieVal("pageVisit");
    if (lastVisit == 0) {
        lastVisit = "";
    }

    document.cookie = "pageHit=" + hitCt +
    → ";expires=" + expireDate.toGMTString();
    document.cookie = "pageVisit=" + now +
    → ";expires=" + expireDate.toGMTString();

    var outMsg = "You have visited this
    → page " + hitCt + " times.";
    if (lastVisit != "") {
        outMsg += "<br>Your last visit
        → was " + lastVisit;
    }
    document.getElementById("cookieData").
    → innerHTML = outMsg;
}

function cookieVal(cookieName) {
    var thisCookie = document.cookie.
    → split("; ");

    for (var i=0; i<thisCookie.length; i++) {
        if (cookieName == thisCookie[i].
        → split("=")[0]) {
            return thisCookie[i].split("=")[1];
        }
    }
    return 0;
}
```

Handling Multiple Cookies

You will often want to deal with more than one cookie at a time, and **Listing 9.8** shows you how to read from more than one cookie and display the information. This example shares a fair amount of code with the "Using Cookies as Counters" example.

To handle multiple cookies:

1. `var lastVisit = cookieVal`
   `→ ("pageVisit");`

   We start off by looking for a cookie named **pageVisit** by passing that string to the **cookieVal()** function. It returns a value, which is then stored in **lastVisit**.

2. `if (lastVisit == 0) {`
   `    lastVisit = "";`
   `}`

   If the value of **lastVisit** is zero, then put a null value into **lastVisit**. We now know that the user has never been here before.

3. `document.cookie = "pageHit=" +`
   `→ hitCt + ";expires=" +`
   `→ expireDate.toGMTString();`
   `document.cookie = "pageVisit=" +`
   `→ now + ";expires=" +`
   `→ expireDate.toGMTString();`

   These two lines write the two cookies back to disk with an updated hit number and visit date.

   continues on next page

4.
```
var outMsg = "You have visited
→ this page " + hitCt + "
→ times. ";
if (lastVisit != "") {
   outMsg += "<br>Your last visit
   → was " + lastVisit;
}
```

The **outMsg** variable stores the outgoing message for our site's visitor and starts off by being set to tell them how many times they've been here. The next lines check if the user has been here before (in code: if **lastVisit** isn't null) and if they have, we remind them when.

5.
```
document.getElementById
→ ("cookieData").innerHTML =
→ outMsg;
```

And finally, **outMsg** is displayed on the screen, telling the user what they've done before. The result of this script is shown in Ⓐ.

Ⓐ The two cookies, written to the screen (along with some other text).

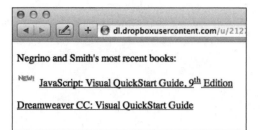

Negrino and Smith's most recent books:

New! JavaScript: Visual QuickStart Guide, 9th Edition

Dreamweaver CC: Visual QuickStart Guide

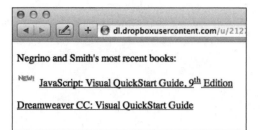 JavaScript can ask a cookie when you've last visited a site and flag new items for you.

Listing 9.9 The HTML of this page applies the next script's results to the page.

```
<!DOCTYPE html>
<html>
<head>
    <title>New for You</title>
    <link rel="stylesheet"
    → href="script07.css">
    <script src="script07.js"></script>
</head>
<body>
    <p>Negrino and Smith's most recent
    → books:</p>
    <p id="New-20140601"><a href="http://
    → www.javascriptworld.com">JavaScript:
    → Visual QuickStart Guide, 9<sup>th</sup>
    → Edition</a></p>
    <p id="New-20130812"><a href="http://
    → www.dreamweaverbook.com">Dreamweaver
    → CC: Visual QuickStart Guide</a></p>
</body>
</html>
```

Listing 9.10 The CSS combined with the JavaScript and HTML makes things personal.

```
body {
    background-color: #FFF;
}

p.newImg {
    padding-left: 35px;
    background-image: url(images/new.gif);
    background-repeat: no-repeat;
}
```

Displaying "New to You" Messages

You can use cookies and JavaScript to alert frequent visitors to your site to items that are new to them. This gives the user a more personalized experience when they visit, making your site a smarter and friendlier place. **Listings 9.9, 9.10,** and **9.11** add a little "New!" image to the beginning of lines when the cookie says that a line has been added since the last time the visitor was there 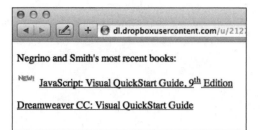. Again, you'll see familiar code from previous examples in this chapter.

To display a "New to You" message:

1. ```
   <p id="New-20140601"><a href=
   → "http://www.javascriptworld
   → .com">JavaScript: Visual
   → QuickStart Guide, 9<sup>th</sup>
   → Edition</a></p>
   <p id="New-20130812"><a href=
   → "http://www.dreamweaverbook
   → .com">Dreamweaver CC: Visual
   → QuickStart Guide</a></p>
   ```

   In Listing 9.9, the **id** attributes on these two paragraphs will signal to the JavaScript (as we'll see shortly) that they contain dates that get compared against the information set up in the following steps.

continues on page 237
   ```

Listing 9.11 This script can help you personalize your site by alerting the user to new content.

```
window.addEventListener("load",initPage,false);

function initPage() {
    var now = new Date();
    var lastVisit = new Date(cookieVal("pageVisit"));
    var expireDate = new Date();
    expireDate.setMonth(expireDate.getMonth()+6);

    document.cookie = "pageVisit=" + now + ";expires=" + expireDate.toGMTString();
    var allGrafs = document.getElementsByTagName("p");

    for (var i=0; i<allGrafs.length; i++) {
        if (allGrafs[i].id.indexOf("New-") != -1) {
            newCheck(allGrafs[i],allGrafs[i].id.substring(4));
        }
    }

    function newCheck(grafElement,dtString) {
        var yyyy = parseInt(dtString.substring(0,4),10);
        var mm = parseInt(dtString.substring(4,6),10);
        var dd = parseInt(dtString.substring(6,8),10);
        var lastChgd = new Date(yyyy,mm-1,dd);

        if (lastChgd.getTime() > lastVisit.getTime()) {
            grafElement.className += " newImg";
        }
    }
}

function cookieVal(cookieName) {
    var thisCookie = document.cookie.split("; ");

    for (var i=0; i<thisCookie.length; i++) {
        if (cookieName == thisCookie[i].split("=")[0]) {
            return thisCookie[i].split("=")[1];
        }
    }
    return "1 January 1970";
}
```

2.
```
p.newImg {
    padding-left: 35px;
    background-image: url(images/
    → new.gif);
    background-repeat: no-repeat;
}
```

In Listing 9.10, we use CSS to specify that anything on the page marked as a paragraph (within a **<p>** tag) which also has a class of **newImg** will have 35 pixels of padding added to the left and a "New!" image put in the background. However, since the padding ensures that nothing appears in front of the paragraph contents, the image won't look like a background pattern.

3.
```
var lastVisit = new Date
→ (cookieVal("pageVisit"));
var expireDate = new Date();
expireDate.setMonth(expireDate.
→ getMonth()+6);
```

In Listing 9.11, this section initializes the **lastVisit** and **expireDate** dates. The first is the saved date of the surfer's last visit to the site, and the second will be the expiration date of the cookie when it's rewritten.

4.
```
document.cookie = "pageVisit=" +
→ now + ";expires=" +
→ expireDate.toGMTString();
```

This line writes the cookie, putting the current date into the **pageVisit** value and the value of **expireDate** into **expires**.

5.
```
var allGrafs = document.
→ getElementsByTagName("p");
```

This line creates an array of all the **<p>** elements on the page, which allows us to go through each of them one by one looking for just the ones we care about.

continues on next page

6.
```
for (var i=0; i<allGrafs.length;
→ i++) {
```

Here, we start a loop to go through the array, looking at each paragraph element in turn.

7.
```
if (allGrafs[i].id.indexOf("New-")
→ != -1) {
```

If this paragraph has an **id** attribute that contains the text "**New-**", then we know that this is a paragraph we care about, so do the following.

8.
```
newCheck(allGrafs[i],
→ allGrafs[i].id.substring(4));
```

We want to check to see if this paragraph has something in it that will be new to the visitor. The **newCheck()** function will do that, and it's passed two parameters: the current paragraph element (**allGrafs[i]**) and the second part of the **id** attribute. The **substring()** grabs the part of the string from the fifth character on to the end, and as that's all we care about here, that's all we'll pass. (Remember that JavaScript strings are zero-relative, which is why the fifth character of the string is found at position 4.)

9.
```
function newCheck(grafElement,
→ dtString) {
```

This function is expecting two parameters to be passed in, which will be referred to internally as **grafElement** (that paragraph element) and **dtString** (the second part of the **id** attribute).

10.
```
var yyyy = parseInt(
→ dtString.substring(0,4),10);
var mm = parseInt(
→ dtString.substring(4,6),10);
var dd = parseInt(
→ dtString.substring(6,8),10);
```

Here, the date is parsed from a string; so, for example, "20140601" is 1 June 2014.

The **yyyy** variable gets the first 4 digits (starting at digit 0 and ending before digit 4), with the result of "2014". The **mm** variable gets the fourth and fifth digits, and the **dd** variable gets the sixth and seventh digits. In each case, we also do a **parseInt()** on the result, which forces the value returned by **substring()** into an integer.

11. ```
var lastChgd = new Date(yyyy,
→ mm-1, dd);
```

Finally, we can set **lastChgd**, because we've got a year, month, and day. But wait! JavaScript and its bizarre dates now hit us, and we have to subtract 1 from the month to get the correct result—just the month, mind you, not the year or day. Really. Months are zero-relative, years and days are one-relative. (See Chapter 11, "Making Your Pages Dynamic," for more on dates and their oddities.)

12. ```
if (lastChgd.getTime() >
→ lastVisit.getTime()) {
```

Now we can compare the two dates, and only do the following line if the date that the information last changed is after the date the surfer last visited.

13. ```
grafElement.className += " newImg";
```

Now, here's the slick part: we know that this is a paragraph that should display the "New!" image. So, if we add a class attribute of **newImg** to the **<p>** tag, that style (defined in the CSS file) automatically then applies to that paragraph, resulting in the display of the image.

*continues on next page*
```

That is, we can use JavaScript to add an attribute (and its associated value) to an element. In this case, the element is a **<p>**, the attribute is **class**, and the value of the attribute is "**newImg**". As the element may already have an existing class, this code takes care to add the value and not just overwrite what's currently there.

Once this attribute's new value has been added, it triggers the browser's rendering engine to immediately and automatically apply the style to the element, causing the image to appear.

14.
```
function cookieVal(cookieName) {
   var thisCookie = document.
→ cookie.split("; ");

   for (var i=0; i<thisCookie.
→ length; i++) {
     if (cookieName ==
     → thisCookie[i].split
     → ("=")[0]) {
        return thisCookie[i].
        → split("=")[1];
     }
   }
   return "1 January 1970";
}
```

This is the now-familiar **cookieVal()** function. The only difference here is that it has been changed to return "**1 January 1970**" instead of zero if no cookie with that name was found, which makes the code a bit simpler elsewhere. The oddity of that date is that JavaScript thinks that is when time began, so everything should be after that. That date won't appear to the user; it's just an internal reference date for JavaScript.

TIP You're probably more familiar with parseInt() being passed only a single parameter. Here, two are passed: the string to be converted, and 10. That last parameter tells parseInt() to always return a decimal number. Otherwise, when parseInt() is passed a string starting with 0, it may try to turn the result into octal (base 8 numbering), with incorrect results. In this case, a call to parseInt("09") doesn't return the same result as parseInt("09",10), and the latter is what we want. It's just a weird JavaScript thing that you need to be aware of.

TIP The command substring(to, from) returns the characters in a string, starting with the to position and ending with the character just before the from position, zero-relative. So, if the string contains "20140807", and you want characters 5 and 6, you want to use substring(4,6). Your result is the string "08".

The from parameter is optional; leaving it off means you'll get the string starting from the to position all the way to the end.

10

Objects and the DOM

Node manipulation is the W3C-recommended way for standards-compliant browsers to support webpages that act more like applications than like standard, static pages. For instance, you can create pages that change—without hitting the server—based on a user's entries. You can also update pages under script control. Although you can use techniques like `innerHTML`, as we've done elsewhere in this book, here we show the officially supported approach. True, this can be done on the server side, but it's only with JavaScript that you can provide this functionality without making the user go from page to page to page.

In this chapter, you'll learn a bit more about nodes and the Document Object Model (or DOM); add, delete, and work with specific nodes; and insert and replace nodes on your pages.

About Node Manipulation

This chapter takes you as deep as we will go into JavaScript and the DOM, so we'll first need to cover a little bit of history and terminology.

DOM 2 and the W3C

The W3C (as mentioned in Chapter 1) has released specifications for how browsers should handle the Document Object Model. The DOM Level 2 specification, which became an official recommendation in November 2000, goes into more depth as to how browsers should be able to refer to and manage the content on their pages. You can find more details about the specification at **www.w3.org/TR/DOM-Level-2-Core/**.

Although this specification has been around for years, there are still plenty of browsers in use that have incomplete or partial DOM 2 support. Before using any of these scripts, make sure that your intended audience is able to run them, or that you offer another way for older browsers to achieve the same results. Thankfully, the majority of surfers today use Internet Explorer 9+, Firefox, Chrome, or Safari, which should all work just fine with these scripts.

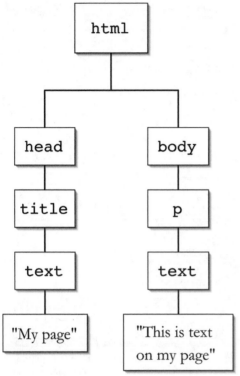

A The tree structure, showing nodes, is just another way of looking at how an HTML page is organized.

DOM 2 terminology

At the beginning of this book, we referred to JavaScript as "the snap-together language," because of the way that you can put objects, properties, and methods together to build JavaScript applications. There's a different way to look at HTML pages that we've only briefly mentioned before: as a tree structure with *nodes*. For example, this simple webpage

```
<html>
<head>
   <title>My page</title>
</head>
<body>
   <p>This is text on my page</p>
</body>
</html>
```

can be displayed as seen in **A**.

We can use JavaScript to modify any aspect of this tree, including the ability to add, access, change, and delete nodes on the tree. Each box on the tree is a node. If the node contains an HTML tag, it's referred to as an *element node*. Otherwise, it's referred to as a *text node*. Of course, element nodes can contain text nodes.

DOM 3

Level 3 of the DOM standard became an official recommendation in April 2004. That specification is at **www.w3.org/TR/DOM-Level-3-Core/**. As with so many other parts of the W3C process, we're still a long ways off from true support in shipping browsers, so this chapter sticks to discussing DOM 2. However, if you're interested in learning more about DOM 3, the best place to look is at ECMAScript bindings, which can be found at **www.w3.org/TR/DOM-Level-3-Core/ecma-script-binding.html**.

Adding Nodes

The easiest way to learn about nodes is to append an element node (which contains a text node) to the end of your document. Listings 10.1 (the HTML) and 10.2 allow the user to enter some data, click a button, and—voilà!—see a new paragraph added to the page **A**.

To add nodes:

1. `var newText = document.`
   `→ createTextNode(inText);`

   We start by creating a new text node (called **newText**) using the **createTextNode()** method. This will contain whatever text was found in **textArea**.

2. `var newGraf = document.`
   `→ createElement("p");`

   Next, we create a new element node using the **createElement()** method. While the node we're creating here is a paragraph tag, it could be any HTML container (**div**, **span**, etc.). The name of the new element is **newGraf**.

3. `newGraf.appendChild(newText);`

   In order to put the new text into the new paragraph, we have to call **appendChild()**. That's a method of **newGraf**, which, when passed **newText**, puts the text node into the paragraph.

4. `var docBody = document.`
   `→ getElementsByTagName("body")[0];`

   In order to add a new node into the body of our document, we need to figure out where the body is. The

A To add a node, enter the text in the field (top) and then click the button. The text appears on the page (bottom).

Listing 10.1 This HTML creates the text area and submit button that allow the user to add a text node.

```
<!DOCTYPE html>
<html>
<head>
    <title>Adding Nodes</title>
    <script src="script01.js"></script>
</head>
<body>
    <form id="theForm">
        <p><textarea id="textArea" rows="5"
        → cols="30"></textarea></p>
        <input type="submit" value="Add some
        → text to the page">
    </form>
</body>
</html>
```

Listing 10.2 With this script, the user can add any text they want to the page.

```
window.addEventListener("load",initAll,false);

function initAll() {
    document.getElementById("theForm").
    → addEventListener("submit",addNode,
    → false);
}

function addNode(evt) {
    var inText = document.getElementById
    → ("textArea").value;
    var newText = document.createTextNode
    → (inText);

    var newGraf = document.createElement
    → ("p");
    newGraf.appendChild(newText);

    var docBody = document.
    → getElementsByTagName("body")[0];
    docBody.appendChild(newGraf);

    evt.preventDefault();
}
```

`getElementsByTagName()` method gives us every **body** tag on our page. If our page is standards-compliant, there should only be one. The **[0]** property is that first **body** tag, and we store that in **docBody**.

5. `docBody.appendChild(newGraf);`

Appending **newGraf** onto **docBody** (using **appendChild()** again) puts the user's new text onto the page.

6. `evt.preventDefault();`

Now that we're using the advanced method of event handling (see Chapter 8), we have to do something to keep the form from being submitted. Unfortunately, simply returning false doesn't do the job. Instead, we tell the calling event not to run any default events.

TIP Why would you bother to go through all the hassle of creating a text node, creating an element node, and appending a child to each just to do what you could have done with a simple assignment to `innerHTML`? Here's one good reason: with this approach, you cannot make your page invalid. For example, every `<p>` or `<div>` tag that's added is automatically closed. With `innerHTML`, on the other hand, it's very easy (almost too easy) to create tag soup—and once you do, your page's DOM becomes difficult to work with. You can't read the contents of an element if it has a beginning but no ending tag, for instance.

TIP In case you're wondering: no, paragraphs cannot themselves contain other paragraphs. If you try pasting in multiple sentences broken up with blank lines, this code will turn them into a single giant paragraph. Instead, paste each paragraph separately.

Deleting Nodes

If you want to add content to your page, you're also likely to want to delete content from your page. **Listings 10.3** (HTML) and **10.4** delete the last paragraph on the page, as shown in .

To delete nodes:

1. `var allGrafs = document.`
   `→ getElementsByTagName("p");`

   This line uses the **getElementsByTagName** method to collect all the paragraph tags in our page and store them in the **allGrafs** array.

2. `if (allGrafs.length > 1) {`

   Before doing anything we regret, we have to check first that the **allGrafs** array has a **length** greater than one. We don't want to try to delete something that doesn't exist, and the **length** will always be at least one (as Listing 10.3's **textarea** form field is inside a **<p>** tag).

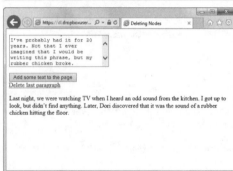

 The last paragraph on this page needed a little revision (top), so it's good that it can be deleted using the "Delete last paragraph" link (bottom).

Listing 10.3 This script adds a link, rather than a button, to delete a text node.

```
<!DOCTYPE html>
<html>
<head>
    <title>Deleting Nodes</title>
    <script src="script02.js"></script>
</head>
<body>
    <form id="theForm">
        <p><textarea id="textArea" rows="5"
        → cols="30"></textarea></p>
        <input type="submit" value="Add some
        → text to the page">
    </form>
    <a href="#" id="deleteNode">Delete last
    → paragraph</a>
</body>
</html>
```

Listing 10.4 Now the user can both add and delete text.

```
window.addEventListener("load",initAll,false);

function initAll() {
    document.getElementById("theForm").
    → addEventListener("submit",addNode,
    → false);
    document.getElementById("deleteNode").
    → addEventListener("click",delNode,
    → false);
}

function addNode(evt) {
    var inText = document.getElementById
    → ("textArea").value;
    var newText = document.createTextNode
    → (inText);

    var newGraf = document.createElement
    → ("p");
    newGraf.appendChild(newText);

    var docBody = document.
    → getElementsByTagName("body")[0];
    docBody.appendChild(newGraf);

    evt.preventDefault();
}

function delNode(evt) {
    var allGrafs = document.
    → getElementsByTagName("p");

    if (allGrafs.length > 1) {
        var lastGraf = allGrafs
        → [allGrafs.length-1];
        var docBody = document.
        → getElementsByTagName("body")[0];
        docBody.removeChild(lastGraf);
    }
    else {
        alert("Nothing to remove!");
    }

    evt.preventDefault();
}
```

3. `var lastGraf = allGrafs`
   `→ [allGrafs.length-1];`

If there are paragraphs, get the last one on the page by subtracting one from **length** and using that as our array index. Remember that **length** is one-relative while arrays are zero-relative, so subtracting one from the **length** gives us the last paragraph on the page.

4. `var docBody = document.`
   `→ getElementsByTagName("body")[0];`
   `docBody.removeChild(lastGraf);`

Just like the last task, in order to modify the document we need to get the contents of its **body**. Once we've got that, it's simply a matter of calling the **docBody.removeChild()** method and passing it **lastGraf**, which tells JavaScript which paragraph we want to delete. Our page should immediately show one less paragraph.

TIP Once again, remember that you can use JavaScript to delete element nodes other than paragraphs. To do this, you need to change the script so that `getElementsByTagName()` is passed something other than a p.

Deleting Specific Nodes

While always deleting the last paragraph might be interesting, you'll sometimes want to delete something that's not at the end of the page. **Listings 10.5** (HTML) and **10.6** make our code considerably more flexible, allowing the user to decide which paragraph should be history, as shown in and 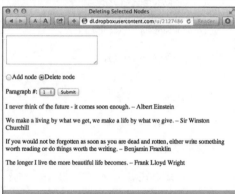.

To delete a particular node:

1. `nodeChgArea = document.`
   `→ getElementById("modifiable");`

   As our page now has multiple paragraphs, it could be confusing to keep track of which can and can't be deleted. Instead, we now set up an entirely new area: a **div** with the **id** of **modifiable**. Here, we set the global variable **nodeChgArea** to that element node.

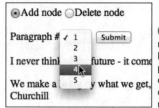

Ⓐ After adding nodes, the Paragraph # pop-up menu contains a list of paragraph numbers.

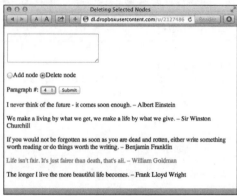

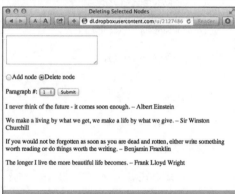

Ⓑ First, you click the "Delete node" radio button, and then you choose a paragraph to delete from the pop-up menu (top). Clicking the Submit button wipes out the selected paragraph (the William Goldman quote) and moves up the following paragraph (bottom).

Listing 10.5 We added radio buttons to this page to let you offer your visitors the choice to add or delete text.

```
<!DOCTYPE html>
<html>
<head>
        <title>Deleting Selected Nodes</title>
        <script src="script03.js"></script>
</head>
<body>
        <form id="theForm">
            <p><textarea id="textArea" rows="5"
            → cols="30"></textarea></p>
            <p>
                <label><input type="radio"
                → name="nodeAction">Add node
                → </label>
                <label><input type="radio"
                → name="nodeAction">Delete node
                → </label>
            </p>
            Paragraph #: <select id="grafCount">
            → </select>
            <input type="submit" value="Submit">
        </form>
        <div id="modifiable"> </div>
</body>
</html>
```

2. ```
var grafChoice = document.
→ getElementById("grafCount").
→ selectedIndex;
var allGrafs = nodeChgArea.
→ getElementsByTagName("p");
var oldGraf = allGrafs.
→ item(grafChoice);
```

When users choose to delete a paragraph, they must also pick which paragraph to delete. We read that number from the **grafCount** field and store it in **grafChoice**. The **allGrafs** variable is then set to be all the paragraphs within **nodeChangingArea**, and the paragraph to be deleted is then stored in **oldGraf**.

3. **nodeChgArea.removeChild(oldGraf);**

This step is just like that in the previous task, except that when it's run we'll see paragraphs disappear from the middle of our page.

**Listing 10.6** This script allows users to choose which paragraph they want to delete.

```
window.addEventListener("load",initAll,false);
var nodeChgArea;

function initAll() {
    document.getElementById("theForm").addEventListener("submit",nodeChanger,false);
    nodeChgArea = document.getElementById("modifiable");
}

function addNode() {
    var inText = document.getElementById("textArea").value;
    var newText = document.createTextNode(inText);

    var newGraf = document.createElement("p");
    newGraf.appendChild(newText);

    nodeChgArea.appendChild(newGraf);
}
```

listing continues on next page
```

TIP Having trouble figuring out some of the other code? The `nodeChanger()` function combines (in order of appearance) functionality from Listings 2.15, 6.5, and 6.13. It's very common in programming to have a library of simple routines, which, when put together, can create a single, much more complex whole.

TIP Note that in the code above we're using `nodeChgArea` where we previously used `docBody`—when you're working with nodes, it's straightforward to swap out code that works with one element node for another. Here, we're looking at just one part of the page instead of the whole, but the overall way to accomplish our task is identical.

TIP Instead of declaring `nodeChgArea` as a global variable and initializing it in `initAll()`, we could have created and initialized it locally inside every function in which it's used. Each choice has its pros and cons; here, we went with the global so that we didn't have to initialize it over and over again.

Listing 10.6 *continued*

```
function delNode() {
    var grafChoice = document.getElementById
    → ("grafCount").selectedIndex;
    var allGrafs = nodeChgArea.
    → getElementsByTagName("p");
    var oldGraf = allGrafs.item(grafChoice);

    nodeChgArea.removeChild(oldGraf);
}

function nodeChanger(evt)  {
    var actionType = -1;
    var pGrafCt = nodeChgArea.
    → getElementsByTagName("p").length;
    var radioButtonSet = document.
    → getElementById("theForm").nodeAction;

    for (var i=0; i<radioButtonSet.length;
    → i++) {
        if (radioButtonSet[i].checked) {
            actionType = i;
        }
    }

    switch(actionType) {
        case 0:
            addNode();
            break;
        case 1:
            if (pGrafCt > 0) {
                delNode();
                break;
            }
        default:
            alert("No valid action was
            → chosen");
    }

    document.getElementById("grafCount").
    → options.length = 0;

    for (i=0; i<nodeChgArea.
    → getElementsByTagName("p").length;
    → i++) {
        document.getElementById("grafCount").
        → options[i] = new Option(i+1);
    }

    evt.preventDefault();
}
```

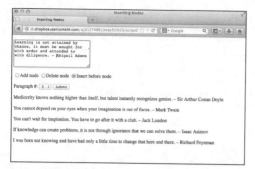

A To insert a paragraph, click the "Insert before node" radio button, select the desired paragraph you want for the insertion point (top), enter your text, and then click Submit (bottom).

Inserting Nodes

Along with wanting to delete nodes other than at the end of the document, you're likely to want to add nodes somewhere other than the end. With **Listings 10.7** (the HTML) and **10.8**, you'll be able to choose where you want your new nodes to appear. In **A**, you can see how the new node gets inserted.

To insert a node:

1. `var grafChoice = document.`
   `→ getElementById("grafCount").`
   `→ selectedIndex;`
   `var inText = document.`
   `→ getElementById("textArea").`
   `→ value;`

   In order to insert a paragraph, we need to know two things: where users want it inserted (**grafChoice**) and what text they want to insert (**inText**).

continues on page 253

Listing 10.7 Another radio button and some script changes allow a third option: inserting text before another paragraph.

```
<!DOCTYPE html>
<html>
<head>
    <title>Inserting Nodes</title>
    <script src="script04.js"></script>
</head>
<body>
    <form id="theForm">
        <p><textarea id="textArea" rows="5" cols="30"></textarea></p>
        <p>
            <label><input type="radio" name="nodeAction">Add node</label>
            <label><input type="radio" name="nodeAction">Delete node</label>
            <label><input type="radio" name="nodeAction">Insert before node</label>
        </p>
        Paragraph #: <select id="grafCount"></select>
        <input type="submit" value="Submit">
    </form>
    <div id="modifiable"> </div>
</body>
</html>
```

Listing 10.8 The user can now add text anywhere on the page.

```
window.addEventListener("load",initAll,false);
var nodeChgArea;

function initAll() {
    document.getElementById("theForm").addEventListener("submit",nodeChanger,false);
    nodeChgArea = document.getElementById("modifiable");
}

function addNode() {
    var inText = document.getElementById("textArea").value;
    var newText = document.createTextNode(inText);

    var newGraf = document.createElement("p");
    newGraf.appendChild(newText);

    nodeChgArea.appendChild(newGraf);
}

function delNode() {
    var grafChoice = document.getElementById("grafCount").selectedIndex;
    var allGrafs = nodeChgArea.getElementsByTagName("p");
    var oldGraf = allGrafs.item(grafChoice);

    nodeChgArea.removeChild(oldGraf);
}

function insertNode() {
    var grafChoice = document.getElementById("grafCount").selectedIndex;
    var inText = document.getElementById("textArea").value;

    var newText = document.createTextNode(inText);
    var newGraf = document.createElement("p");
    newGraf.appendChild(newText);

    var allGrafs = nodeChgArea.getElementsByTagName("p");
    var oldGraf = allGrafs.item(grafChoice);

    nodeChgArea.insertBefore(newGraf,oldGraf);
}

function nodeChanger(evt)  {
    var actionType = -1;
    var pGrafCt = nodeChgArea.getElementsByTagName("p").length;
    var radioButtonSet = document.getElementById("theForm").nodeAction;
```

listing continues on next page

Listing 10.8 *continued*

```
for (var i=0; i<radioButtonSet.length; i++) {
    if (radioButtonSet[i].checked) {
        actionType = i;
    }
}

switch(actionType) {
    case 0:
        addNode();
        break;
    case 1:
        if (pGrafCt > 0) {
            delNode();
            break;
        }
    case 2:
        if (pGrafCt > 0) {
            insertNode();
            break;
        }
    default:
        alert("No valid action was
        → chosen");
}

document.getElementById("grafCount").
→ options.length = 0;

for (i=0; i<nodeChgArea.
→ getElementsByTagName("p").length;
→ i++) {
    document.getElementById("grafCount").
    → options[i] = new Option(i+1);
}

evt.preventDefault();
}
```

2. `var newText = document.`
`→ createTextNode(inText);`
`var newGraf = document.`
`→ createElement("p");`
`newGraf.appendChild(newText);`

Here's our by-now-standard way of creating a new paragraph node and filling it with the user's text.

3. `var allGrafs = nodeChgArea.`
`→ getElementsByTagName("p");`
`var oldGraf = allGrafs.`
`→ item(grafChoice);`

Once again, we get all the **p** tags in our region, and then we store the target paragraph (the one we'll be inserting our new paragraph in front of) in **oldGraf**.

4. `nodeChgArea.insertBefore`
`→ (newGraf,oldGraf);`

To insert the new paragraph, we call **insertBefore()** with two parameters: the new node and the existing node that we want the new node to be inserted before (hence the name).

TIP You might think that if there's an insertBefore() there ought to be an insertAfter(), but that's not the case. If you want to add something to the end of the page, you need to use appendChild().

Replacing Nodes

While you can always delete existing nodes and insert new nodes, it's simpler to just replace nodes. **Listings 10.9** (the HTML) and **10.10** show how you can replace one node with another.  shows the replacement process.

To replace nodes:

- **nodeChgArea.replaceChild**
  → (newGraf,oldGraf);

  The only line in this script that should be new to you is this one (see other parts of this chapter for explanations about the rest of the script). Much like the last task, all we need to do is call **replaceChild()** with two parameters: the paragraph we want to swap in and the paragraph we want to swap out.

A Here, we've replaced the third paragraph (top) with new text (bottom).

Listing 10.9 Adding the "Replace node" radio button to the HTML rounds out our node manipulation examples.

```
<!DOCTYPE html>
<html>
<head>
    <title>Replacing Nodes</title>
    <script src="script05.js"></script>
</head>
<body>
    <form id="theForm">
        <p><textarea id="textArea" rows="5" cols="30"></textarea></p>
        <p>
            <label><input type="radio" name="nodeAction">Add node</label>
            <label><input type="radio" name="nodeAction">Delete node</label>
            <label><input type="radio" name="nodeAction">Insert before node</label>
            <label><input type="radio" name="nodeAction">Replace node</label>
        </p>
        Paragraph #: <select id="grafCount"></select>
        <input type="submit" value="Submit">
    </form>
    <div id="modifiable"> </div>
</body>
</html>
```

Listing 10.10 And now, the user can add, delete, and replace any text on the page.

```
window.addEventListener("load",initAll,false);
var nodeChgArea;

function initAll() {
    document.getElementById("theForm").addEventListener("submit",nodeChanger,false);
    nodeChgArea = document.getElementById("modifiable");
}

function addNode() {
    var inText = document.getElementById("textArea").value;
    var newText = document.createTextNode(inText);

    var newGraf = document.createElement("p");
    newGraf.appendChild(newText);

    nodeChgArea.appendChild(newGraf);
}

function delNode() {
    var grafChoice = document.getElementById("grafCount").selectedIndex;
    var allGrafs = nodeChgArea.getElementsByTagName("p");
    var oldGraf = allGrafs.item(grafChoice);

    nodeChgArea.removeChild(oldGraf);
}

function insertNode() {
    var grafChoice = document.getElementById("grafCount").selectedIndex;
    var inText = document.getElementById("textArea").value;

    var newText = document.createTextNode(inText);
    var newGraf = document.createElement("p");
    newGraf.appendChild(newText);

    var allGrafs = nodeChgArea.getElementsByTagName("p");
    var oldGraf = allGrafs.item(grafChoice);

    nodeChgArea.insertBefore(newGraf,oldGraf);
}

function replaceNode() {
    var grafChoice = document.getElementById("grafCount").selectedIndex;
    var inText = document.getElementById("textArea").value;

    var newText = document.createTextNode(inText);
    var newGraf = document.createElement("p");
    newGraf.appendChild(newText);
```

listing continues on next page

Listing 10.10 *continued*

```
      var allGrafs = nodeChgArea.getElementsByTagName("p");
      var oldGraf = allGrafs.item(grafChoice);

      nodeChgArea.replaceChild(newGraf,oldGraf);
}

function nodeChanger(evt) {
    var actionType = -1;
    var pGrafCt = nodeChgArea.getElementsByTagName("p").length;
    var radioButtonSet = document.getElementById("theForm").nodeAction;

    for (var i=0; i<radioButtonSet.length; i++) {
        if (radioButtonSet[i].checked) {
            actionType = i;
        }
    }

    switch(actionType) {
        case 0:
            addNode();
            break;
        case 1:
            if (pGrafCt > 0) {
                delNode();
                break;
            }
        case 2:
            if (pGrafCt > 0) {
                insertNode();
                break;
            }
        case 3:
            if (pGrafCt > 0) {
                replaceNode();
                break
            }
        default:
            alert("No valid action was chosen");
    }

    document.getElementById("grafCount").options.length = 0;

    for (i=0; i<nodeChgArea.getElementsByTagName("p").length; i++) {
        document.getElementById("grafCount").options[i] = new Option(i+1);
    }

    evt.preventDefault();
}
```

Writing Code with Object Literals

As covered in the sidebar "About Object Literals," there's more than one way to write any given JavaScript. **Listing 10.11** is an example of how Listing 10.10 can be rewritten to use object literals.

About Object Literals

Standard procedural JavaScript, like what you've seen so far, has been in the dot notation format:

```
var myCat = new Object;
myCat.name = "Pixel";
myCat.breed = "Tuxedo";
myCat.website = "www.pixel.mu";

function allAboutMyCat() {
      alert("Can I tell you about my cat?");
      tellMeMore = true;
}
```

Whereas in object literal format, that same code would be something like this:

```
var myCat = {
      name: "Pixel",
      breed: "Tuxedo",
      website: "www.pixel.mu",
      allAbout: function() {
            alert("Can I tell you about my cat?");
            tellMeMore = true;
      }
}
```

With either format, you can refer to a property of **myCat** as **myCat.name** (for instance). However, with object literal format, the function becomes **myCat.allAbout()** instead of **allAboutMyCat()**.

If at this point you're thinking that this looks sort of familiar, pat yourself on the back—it's very similar, in many ways, to CSS. At its most basic level, it's a list of property and value pairs, with the colon in between and a separator around each pair.

Some differences to remember when using object literals:

- Properties are set using **:** not **=**.
- Lines end with **,** instead of **;**.
- No comma is needed on the last statement inside the object.

To use an object literal:

1. `document.`
   `→ getElementById("theForm").`
   `→ addEventListener("submit",`
   `→ nodeChanger,false);`
   `chgNodes.init();`

   Just as with code you've seen before, we have to start off by doing our initializations. The first line is the same as what you've seen previously, but the second is a little different: it calls the **init()** function that's inside the **chgNodes** object.

2. `function nodeChanger(evt) {`
   `    return chgNodes.doAction(evt);`
   `}`

   The **nodeChanger()** function here doesn't do much at all—all it does is call **chgNodes.doAction()** and pass it an event. Why that function couldn't have been called directly will be covered shortly.

3. `var chgNodes = {`

   Here's the beginning of the **chgNodes** object. All we had to do to create it is start the line off as if we're setting a simple variable, but then end with a set of statements between braces.

4. `actionType: function() {`
   `    var radioButtonSet =`
   `    → document.getElementById`
   `    → ("theForm").nodeAction;`
   `    for (var i=0; i<radioButtonSet.`
   `    → length; i++) {`
   `      if (radioButtonSet[i].`
   `      → checked) {`
   `        return i;`
   `      }`
   `    }`
   `    return -1;`
   `},`

   In the previous version of the script, the first part of the **nodeChanger()** function was spent setting the **actionType**

listing continues on next page

Listing 10.11 *continued*

```
        myNewGraf.appendChild
        → (this.newText());
        return myNewGraf;
    },

    oldGraf: function () {
        return this.allGrafs().item
        → (this.grafChoice());
    },

    doAction: function(evt) {
        switch(this.actionType()) {
            case 0:
                this.nodeChgArea.append
                → Child(this.newGraf());
                break;
            case 1:
                if (this.pGrafCt() > 0) {
                    this.nodeChgArea.remove
                    → Child(this.oldGraf());
                    break;
                }
            case 2:
                if (this.pGrafCt() > 0) {
                    this.nodeChgArea.insert
                    → Before(this.newGraf(),
                    → this.oldGraf());
                    break;
                }
            case 3:
                if (this.pGrafCt() > 0) {
                    this.nodeChgArea.replace
                    → Child(this.newGraf(),
                    → this.oldGraf());
                    break;
                }
            default:
                alert("No valid action was
                → chosen");
        }

        document.getElementById("grafCount").
        → options.length = 0;

        for (var i=0; i<this.pGrafCt(); i++) {
            document.getElementById("grafCount").
            → options[i] = new Option(i+1);
        }
        evt.preventDefault();
    },

    init: function() {
        this.nodeChgArea = document.
        → getElementById("modifiable");
    }
}
```

variable. Here, **actionType()** is a method of **chgNodes**. While the style of the code is different, the end result should be identical.

5. ```
   allGrafs: function() {
       return this.nodeChgArea.
       → getElementsByTagName("p");
   },

   pGrafCt: function() {
       return this.allGrafs().length;
   },
   ```

   Here's an example of two simple functions inside **chgNodes**: **allGrafs()** and **pGrafCt()**. Because they return values, they can be used anywhere they're needed for adding, replacing, or deleting nodes.

6. ```
   doAction: function(evt) {
       switch(this.actionType()) {
           case 0:
               this.nodeChgArea.
               → appendChild(this.
               → newGraf());
               break;
   ```

   The **doAction()** function handles most of the heavy lifting needed in **chgNodes**—this small bit is just the start. Just as with the prior version, we look at the radio button to see which action we want to do, and that action is done by means of a **switch** statement.

7. ```
   init: function() {
       this.nodeChgArea = document.
       → getElementById("modifiable");
   }
   ```

   And finally, we end up with our **init()** function, and all it does is initialize **nodeChgArea** for later use. What's most important is that we do *not* have a comma at the end of this routine—every statement except the last should end with a comma (and yes, a function is basically an extended statement).
   ```

TIP In steps 1 and 2, you may have been wondering why we couldn't just write:

```
document.getElementById("theForm").
↪ addEventListener("submit",chgNodes.
↪ doAction(),false);
```

Or maybe you're wondering why we've used this so often in the code? Here's the trick: it's the same answer for both.

Inside an object literal, you can reference every other property and method of the object just by referring to this. If we use a var command, as in the case of myNewGraf or radioButtonSet, it's a normal variable that can't be accessed outside the parent object. By not using var, and instead always referring to it as this.whatever, those properties become part of the object itself.

However, this for object literals has to abide by the same rules that this does everywhere in JavaScript—what it evaluates to depends on from where it was called. If chgNodes.doAction() is called directly from the form, then this refers to the form object—which isn't what we want. Calling chgNodes.doAction() from nodeChanger() lets us work around this.

TIP If you are considering switching from procedural JavaScript but haven't made a firm decision, here's one more reason to think about using object literals instead: note that Listing 10.11 does the exact same thing as Listing 10.10—but it's about 20 percent shorter.

TIP This chapter is not by any means a thorough discussion of node manipulation—it's just a sample to get you started. If you want more documentation of all the available properties and methods, check out the W3C specification mentioned at the beginning of the chapter.

Why Object Literals?

By this point in the book, you've more than likely been looking through other people's code. And if you're looking at code that's longer than a page, or code from a company where many people work together on a site, it's very likely that you've noticed that theirs looks a tad... shall we say, different? That's very likely because they use the *object literal*, a different (although equally valid) way of writing JavaScript.

There are several reasons why a programmer might want to use the object literal versus procedural approach to JavaScript:

- Because each object (including methods and properties) is contained within one parent object, you never run into a problem with overwriting other people's code. If you and your co-worker both have a variable called **myText** in your respective **.js** files, and some page brings in both files, then whichever page loads last takes precedence—one is going to write directly over the other, and it will be as if that code never loaded. The solution: make sure you don't use global variables, and the simplest way to do that is to tuck all of yours away neatly inside an object literal.

- A subset of the object literal has been dubbed *JavaScript Object Notation*, better known as JSON (pronounced like the name "Jason"). JSON is one of the most common data formats for Ajax, and as such, you're likely to see a lot of it when you start working with Ajax.

- And finally, like everything else, programming languages have styles that go in and out of fashion. JavaScript itself is in its second or third upswing, and as part of the renewed interest in scripting, the current trend is towards increased use of object literals—so it helps to get used to seeing them.

Making Your
Pages Dynamic

Effective webpages are a result of many different factors, including compelling content, good design, and attention to detail, such as how fast the page loads. One of the ways to speed up page loads, while still providing the user with an interesting and interactive experience, is to use JavaScript to make individual page elements update within the user's browser. In other words, instead of your web server pushing the page experience to the user, the server pushes the script over the Internet. The script then uses the power of the user's computer to make the page come alive. Pages with scripts like these can be called *dynamic pages*.

By moving the processing from the server side to the client (user) side, you get better performance and, to some extent, you can personalize the user experience.

In this chapter, you'll learn how to use JavaScript to display the local date and time on your webpages; customize a greeting by the time of day where your user is; convert between different time formats; and move an object across the user's page under script control.

Putting the Current Date into a Webpage

JavaScript can determine the current date and time (which it gets as a number) from your computer, and then manipulate that figure in many ways. Your script has to handle the conversion from a computer-friendly number into a user-friendly textual date. **Listing 11.1** shows how to get the current date, convert it from a number into a standard date, and then write the result to a document window.

To put the current date into a webpage:

1. **window.addEventListener**
   →("load",initDate,false);

   When the document loads, call **initDate()**.

2. **var dayName = new Array("Sunday",**
   →"Monday", "Tuesday", "Wednesday",
   →"Thursday", "Friday", "Saturday");

   First, we need to create a new array that contains the days of the week. Make sure to use commas to separate the items in the array; and because they are text strings, each item must be enclosed in quotes. The array gets assigned to the variable **dayName**.

3. **var monName = new Array("January",**
   →"February", "March", "April",
   →"May", "June", "July", "August",
   →"September", "October",
   →"November", "December");

   In this step, we're doing the same thing with month names and assigning them to the brilliantly named **monName** variable.

Listing 11.1 This script writes the current date to the document window.

```
window.addEventListener("load",initDate,
→ false);

function initDate() {
    var dayName = new Array("Sunday",
    → "Monday", "Tuesday", "Wednesday",
    → "Thursday", "Friday", "Saturday");
    var monName = new Array("January",
    → "February", "March", "April", "May",
    → "June", "July", "August", "September",
    → "October", "November", "December");

    var now = new Date();
    var dtString = dayName[now.getDay()] +
    → ", " + monName[now.getMonth()] + " " +
    → now.getDate();

    document.getElementById("dtField").
    → innerHTML = dtString;
}
```

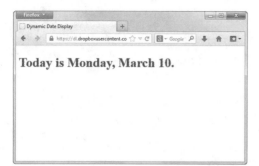

Today is Monday, March 10.

A JavaScript dynamically displays the current date in the window.

JavaScript's Inconsistent Handling of Time

As mentioned earlier in this book, JavaScript begins numbering at zero in most cases, so numbering begins with 0, 1, 2, 3, and so on. But this isn't consistent with dates, which begin with the number 1. So, if you have an array that deals with the days of the week, you'll have this:

Sunday = 0

Monday = 1

Tuesday = 2

Wednesday = 3

Thursday = 4

Friday = 5

Saturday = 6

In much the same way, the 12 months of the year are numbered from 0 through 11.

On the other hand, when you're dealing with the day of the month, it makes no sense to start at zero (personally, I've never heard of April 0), so JavaScript starts at 1.

Hours are dealt with from 0 (midnight) to 23 (11 P.M.), using a 24-hour clock. Later in this chapter we'll show you how to convert from a 24-hour clock to a 12-hour clock.

4. `var now = new Date();`

   Next, we tell JavaScript to create a new **Date** object, call it **now**, and fill it with the current date.

5. `var dtString = dayName[now.getDay()]`
   `→ + ", " + monName[now.getMonth()]`
   `→ + " " + now.getDate();`

   The object **dayName[now.getDay()]** is read from right to left: **getDay()** is the JavaScript method that gets the day of the week, and asking **now** for it gets today's day of the week. The numerical result references one of the entries in the array, **dayName**.

   Next, we concatenate a comma and a space to the text string that we're building. Then, we concatenate the month name, expressed by the object **monName[now.getMonth()]**. This gets the month name in much the same fashion as we did the day name, and references one of the entries in the array **monName**.

   A space is concatenated next, and we end with the object **now.getDate()**, which returns the day of the month. All of this is assigned to the **dtString** variable.

6. `document.getElementById("dtField").`
   `→ innerHTML = dtString;`

   The **id dtField** is in the HTML page (the HTML is trivial, so we haven't included it here); it's within a **<span>** tag, like so:

   `<h1>Today is <span id="dtField">`
   `→ </span>.</h1>`

   The JavaScript sets the **innerHTML** property of **dtField** to the value of **dtString**. The result is shown in **A**.

Working with Days

You might want to display a different message to your users if it's a weekend. Listing 11.2 tells you how to do it.

To figure out if it is a weekend:

1. `var now = new Date();`

Fill the variable **now** with the current date.

2. `if (now.getDay() > 0 &&`
`→ now.getDay() < 6) {`

This extracts the numerical day of the week from the **now** variable and asks if it is greater than 0 (remember that Sunday is 0). Next the line uses the **&&** operator, which is a logical *and* (i.e., both parts have to be true), and asks if **now** is less than 6, which is the number for Saturday.

3. `var dtString = "Sorry, it's a`
`→ weekday.";`

If the result of the last expression is greater than 0 and less than 6, it has to be between 1 and 5, which is to say, from Monday to Friday, so the script puts a string to that effect into **dtString**.

4. `else {`
`    var dtString = "Hooray, it's a`
`→ weekend!";`

If we failed the test in the step 2, it must be a weekend, and we put a string with the happy news in **dtString**.

5. `document.getElementById`
`→ ("dtField").innerHTML = dtString;`

Finally, we set the **innerHTML** property of **dtField** to the value of **dtString**, just as in the previous example .

A The happy news gets written to the window.

Listing 11.2 This script figures out if it is a weekday or weekend.

```
window.addEventListener("load",initDate,
→ false);

function initDate() {
    var now = new Date();

    if (now.getDay() > 0 && now.getDay()
    → < 6) {
        var dtString = "Sorry, it's a
        → weekday.";
    }
    else {
        var dtString = "Hooray, it's a
        → weekend!";
    }

    document.getElementById("dtField").
    → innerHTML = dtString;
}
```

A It was definitely too late at night when we wrote this.

Listing 11.3 Scripts can be used to check what time of day it is and react appropriately.

```
window.addEventListener("load",initDate,
→ false);

function initDate() {
    var now = new Date();
    document.getElementById("dtField").
    → innerHTML = timeString
    → (now.getHours());

    function timeString(theHour) {
        if (theHour < 5) {
            return "What are you doing up so
            → late?";
        }
        if (theHour < 9) {
            return "Good Morning!";
        }
        if (theHour < 17) {
            return "No surfing during working
            → hours!";
        }
        return "Good Evening!";
    }
}
```

Customizing a Message for the Time of Day

You can take the technique used in the last example and use it again to customize a message for the user, depending on the time of day. This could be used, for instance, as a friendly greeting when a user enters a site. **Listing 11.3** shows how it is done, and **A** shows how we were up writing way past our usual bedtime.

To customize messages for the time of day:

- ```
  if (theHour < 5) {
      return "What are you doing up
      → so late?";
  ```

  We begin the new code in this script by starting a conditional test. Earlier in this script, the **getHours()** method extracted **theHour** from the **now** variable, and here we test to see if that number is less than 5 (which corresponds to 5 A.M., since numbering in JavaScript starts at midnight).

  If it is before 5 A.M., the script scolds the user by writing this message to the document window, as shown in **A**.

  The rest of the script repeats the above line, adjusting it for the time of day and writing out a different message. If it is between 5 A.M. and 9 A.M., the script says "Good Morning!"; between 9 A.M. and 5 P.M., it says "No surfing during working hours!"; and after 5 P.M., it says "Good Evening!"
  ```

Displaying Dates by Time Zone

By default, the dates and times that are displayed are those on the user's machine (assuming that they are set correctly). If you want to display a date somewhere else, you need to calculate it based on UTC, Coordinated Universal Time. UTC is essentially a different name for Greenwich Mean Time (GMT); UTC also goes under the names "universal time" (UT) and "world time." **Listing 11.4** shows the HTML for the page; **Listing 11.5**, with the JavaScript, shows you how to calculate dates in other time zones.

To display dates by time zone:

1. `var spanTags = document.`
   `→ getElementsByTagName("span");`

   Inside the **initDate()** function, create the **spanTags** variable. The command **document.getElementsByTagName("span")** is a handy trick—that "**span**" tells JavaScript to return an array containing every **<span>** tag on the page. Then, we can just loop through it looking for things of interest.

continues on page 268

Listing 11.4 The HTML for the time zone script uses classes to tag the different offices with the time zone for that office.

```
<!DOCTYPE html>
<html>
<head>
    <title>Time Zones</title>
    <script src="script04.js"></script>
</head>
<body>
    <h3>Our office hours are 9:00 am to
    → 5:00 pm, Monday through Friday, at
    → each of our locations. It is now
    → </h3><ul>
    <li><span class="tz-8"> </span> in
    → San Francisco</li>
    <li><span class="tz-5"> </span> in
    → New York</li>
    <li><span class="tz-0"> </span> in
    → London</li>
    <li><span class="tz+7"> </span> in
    → Hong Kong</li></ul>
</body>
</html>
```

Listing 11.5 You can adapt this script to display any time zone you wish.

```
window.addEventListener("load",initDate,false);

function initDate() {
    var spanTags = document.getElementsByTagName("span");

    for (var i=0; i<spanTags.length; i++) {
        if (spanTags[i].className.indexOf("tz") == 0) {
            showTheTime(spanTags[i],spanTags[i].className.substring(2));
        }
    }
}

function showTheTime(currElem,tzOffset) {
    var dayName = new Array("Sunday","Monday","Tuesday","Wednesday","Thursday","Friday",
    → "Saturday");

    var thatTZ = new Date();
    var dateStr = thatTZ.toUTCString();

    dateStr = dateStr.substr(0,dateStr.length - 3);
    thatTZ.setTime(Date.parse(dateStr));
    thatTZ.setHours(thatTZ.getHours() + parseInt(tzOffset));

    currElem.innerHTML = showTheHours(thatTZ.getHours()) + showZeroFilled(thatTZ.getMinutes()) +
    → showAmPm(thatTZ.getHours()) + dayName[thatTZ.getDay()];

    function showTheHours(theHour) {
        if (theHour == 0) {
            return 12;
        }
        if (theHour < 13) {
            return theHour;
        }
        return theHour-12;
    }

    function showZeroFilled(inValue) {
        if (inValue > 9) {
            return ":" + inValue;
        }
        return ":0" + inValue;
    }

    function showAmPm(thatTime) {
        if (thatTime < 12) {
            return " AM ";
        }
        return " PM ";
    }
}
```

2.
```
for (var i=0; i<spanTags.length;
→ i++) {
  if (spanTags[i].className.
  → indexOf("tz") == 0) {
    showTheTime(spanTags[i],
    → spanTags[i].className.
    → substring(2));
  }
}
```

We begin a loop so we can walk through the **<span>** elements, represented by **spanTags**. The **spanTags[i]. className.indexOf("tz") == 0** bit just means, "does the *i*th **<span>** tag have an attribute **class** that starts with "tz"— if so, call **showTheTime()**."

The **showTheTime()** function is passed two parameters: first, the *i*th **<span>** tag element, and second, the part of the **class** attribute (seen in Listing 11.4) that is *after* the "tz", represented by **substring(2)**. Yes, we could figure out the second part from the first, but why bother? It makes the **showTheTime()** function much simpler, as that second parameter turns into the time zone offset.

3.
```
function showTheTime(currElem,
→ tzOffset) {
```

This function takes in the two parameters that were passed to **showTheTime()** in the previous step. Inside the function, they'll be called **currElem** and **tzOffset**, respectively.

4.
```
var thatTZ = new Date();
var dateStr = thatTZ.toUTCString();
```

We create a new date variable, **thatTZ**. The next line turns that date and time (based on UT) into a string (see **Table 11.1** at the end of the chapter), saving the result in **dateStr**.

5. `dateStr = dateStr.substr(0,`
   `↪dateStr.length - 3);`

What we're trying to do in this section is reset **thatTZ** to be based on UT instead of local time, so that we can then add the passed offset for the desired result. Unfortunately, JavaScript doesn't make this simple. We now have the universal time in string format, but if we just try to reset the time based on it, it'll outsmart us, believing that what we *really* want is local time. What we need to do is take the string version of the date and time and strip off the last three characters, which are **UTC**.

6. `thatTZ.setTime(Date.parse`
   `↪(dateStr));`

Once we've stripped off the last three characters, we can use the **parse()** method to turn the date into milliseconds and then the **setTime()** method to set **thatTZ** to our desired time.

7. `thatTZ.setHours(thatTZ.getHours()`
   `↪+ parseInt(tzOffset));`

Now that we've finally got the UT date stored, we need to add the passed number of hours that our desired time is off UT. As the time zone can be anywhere from +12 to −12, the time zone that was passed in can be anything from **"-12"** to **"+12"**. We use **parseInt()** to turn that string into a number from −12 to 12, and we then add it to the current UT time. The result gives us our desired value: the correct date and time in that time zone.

continues on next page

8. ```
currElem.innerHTML =
→ showTheHours(thatTZ.getHours())
→ + showZeroFilled(
→ thatTZ.getMinutes())
→ + showAmPm(thatTZ.getHours())
→ + dayName[thatTZ.getDay()];
```

This looks scary, but all it is doing is building the time value that goes into the document by concatenating the result from all of the other functions and then setting the **innerHTML** property of **currElem**, thereby putting the result of the calculation into the document 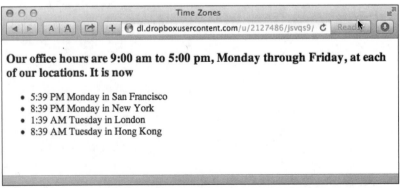.

The next three functions, **showTheHours()**, **showZeroFilled()**, and **showAmPm()**, are within the **showTheTime()** function so that they can share variables. As it turns out, they don't in this task, but they will in the next.

9. ```
function showTheHours(theHour) {
    if (theHour == 0) {
        return 12;
    }
```

First, set up a function called **showTheHours()**, which is passed the variable **theHour**. Then, if **theHour** is zero, return the result 12 (meaning the hour is 12 A.M.); otherwise, continue with the function.

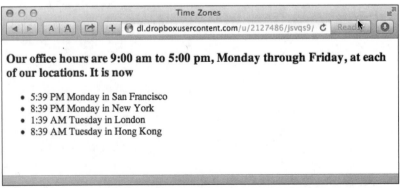

Ⓐ The script calculates the time in each office, based on its time zone.

10.
```
if (theHour < 13) {
    return theHour;
}
return theHour-12;
```

If the result of the hour portion of the time is less than 13, then simply return the variable **theHour**. Otherwise, return **theHour** minus 12 (which converts hours 13 and higher to their 12-hour-clock counterparts).

11.
```
function showZeroFilled(inValue) {
    if (inValue > 9) {
        return ":" + inValue;
    }
    return ":0" + inValue;
}
```

This function is used to pretty up the output; when the minutes or seconds figure is 9 or under, it pads the figure with a leading zero.

12.
```
function showAmPm(thatTime) {
    if (thatTime < 12) {
        return " AM ";
    }
    return " PM ";
}
```

This function adds AM or PM to the time. If the passed variable **thatTime** is less than 12, then the returned value of the function is " AM "; otherwise, it is " PM ". Note that the text strings each have a leading and a trailing space so things look nice.

TIP There's no simple and straightforward way to deal with daylight saving time. Some browsers just don't handle it correctly. And unfortunately, you're also at the mercy of computer users knowing how to set up their computers to be aware when it's happening. Luckily, both Windows and OS X have the ability to automatically set the time based on an Internet time server, which does take daylight saving time into account, so it's less of a problem than it used to be. The bad news: JavaScript doesn't have a way to get at that information from the OS, so it can't tell if you're in a time and place for it to apply.

TIP It's easy to add another city to the HTML without touching a single line of JavaScript—and it will all just work.

Converting 24-Hour Time to 12-Hour Time

JavaScript provides the time in 24-hour format, also known as military time. Many people are unfamiliar or uncomfortable with this format, so you'll want to know how to convert it to 12-hour format. In the next two scripts, you see one way to go about the task, which needs a bit of explanation. Our page (**Listings 11.6** for the HTML, **11.7** for the CSS) has two important elements: an **h2** tag and a pair of radio buttons. The script will write the time into the former, and the latter lets us switch the time from 24-hour format into 12-hour format **A**. The JavaScript behind this is in **Listing 11.8**.

To convert 24-hour to 12-hour time:

1. `document.getElementById`
   `→ ("showTime").innerHTML =`
   `→ showTheHours(now.getHours()) +`
   `→ showZeroFilled(now.getMinutes())`
   `→ + showZeroFilled(now.`
   `→ getSeconds()) + showAmPm();`

   As in the previous task, this may look daunting, but all it is doing is building the time value displayed on the page by concatenating the result of the other functions (covered below). The result gets put into the **innerHTML** property of **showTime**.

2. `setTimeout(showTheTime,1000);`

   This bit of code tells the display to update every second.

3. `function showTheHours(theHour) {`

   Next, set up a function called **showTheHours**, which is passed the variable **theHour**.

A The script in action.

Listing 11.6 This HTML uses **ids** to identify each radio button.

```
<!DOCTYPE html>
<html>
<head>
    <title>JavaScript Clock</title>
    <link href="script05.css"
    → rel="stylesheet">
    <script src="script05.js"></script>
</head>
<body>
<div class="centered">
    <h2 id="showTime"> </h2>
    Display 24-hour Clock?
    <input type="radio" name="timeClock"
    → id="show24" checked><label for=
    → "show24">Yes</label>
    <input type="radio" name="timeClock"
    → id="show12"><label for="show12">
    → No</label>
</div>
</body>
</html>
```

Listing 11.7 A little bit of style makes the page look better.

```
body {
    background-color: #FFF;
}

.centered {
    text-align: center;
}

label {
    padding-right: 10px;
}
```

Listing 11.8 This script converts between 24-hour and 12-hour time.

```
window.addEventListener("load",showTheTime,
→ false);

function showTheTime() {
    var now = new Date();

    document.getElementById("showTime").
    → innerHTML =
    → showTheHours(now.getHours())
    → + showZeroFilled(now.getMinutes())
    → + showZeroFilled(now.getSeconds())
    → + showAmPm();
    setTimeout(showTheTime,1000);

    function showTheHours(theHour) {
        if (show24Hour() || (theHour > 0 &&
        → theHour < 13)) {
            return theHour;
        }
        if (theHour == 0) {
            return 12;
        }
        return theHour-12;
    }

    function showZeroFilled(inValue) {
        if (inValue > 9) {
            return ":" + inValue;
        }
        return ":0" + inValue;
    }

    function show24Hour() {
        return (document.getElementById
        → ("show24").checked);
    }

    function showAmPm() {
        if (show24Hour()) {
            return "";
        }
        if (now.getHours() < 12) {
            return " AM";
        }
        return " PM";
    }
}
```

4. ```
   if (show24Hour() || (theHour >
   → 0 && theHour < 13)) {
       return theHour;
   }
   if (theHour == 0) {
       return 12;
   }
   return theHour-12;
   ```

   These conditionals say that if the user wants to show 24-hour time, or if the result of the hour portion of the time is greater than zero but less than 13, then simply return the variable **theHour**. Remember that the **||** operator means a logical *or*, as you first saw in Chapter 1. Otherwise, if **theHour** is zero, then return with the result 12 (when the hour is 12 A.M.); otherwise, return **theHour** minus 12 (which converts hours 13 and higher to their 12-hour counterparts).

5. ```
   function show24Hour() {
       return document.getElementById
       → ("show24").checked;
   ```

   This function returns a value based on which radio button the user has selected. If it's **show24**, then it should return true; otherwise it returns false.

6. ```
   if (show24Hour()) {
       return "";
   }
   if (now.getHours() < 12) {
       return " AM";
   }
   return " PM";
   ```

   The **showAmPm()** function adds the AM or PM to the 12-hour time. If the function **show24Hour** is true, it returns nothing and goes to the next function. If the hours portion of the **now** variable is less than 12, then the value of the function is AM; otherwise, it's PM. Again, there is a leading space in the AM or PM text string so things look nice.
   ```

Creating a Countdown

Sooner or later, you'll want to put a countdown on your pages that tells the user how many days or hours until a particular event. **Listings 11.9** (HTML) and **11.10** (JavaScript) let one of the authors know his responsibilities, in no uncertain terms .

To create a countdown:

1. `var spanTags = document.`
   `→ getElementsByTagName("span");`

   Create a new **spanTags** array, and fill it with every **<span>** tag on the page.

2. `for (var i=0; i<spanTags.length;`
   `→ i++) {`
   `   if (spanTags[i].className.`
   `→ indexOf("daysTill") > -1) {`
   `     spanTags[i].innerHTML =`
   `→ showTheDaysTill`
   `→ (spanTags[i].id);`
   `}`

   This loop scans through **spanTags** to see if the string **daysTill** is found in the **class** attribute of any **<span>** tag on the page. Remember that a tag can have multiple **class** attributes (i.e., **class="firstClass daysTill somethingElse fourthThing"**).

   If we found **daysTill**, we call the **showTheDaysTill()** function, which is passed one parameter: the **<span>** tag's **id** (which stores what date to put up on the page). That function returns a value that is then put into **innerHTML**.

   continues on page 276

A Loading this page gives one of the authors his marching orders.

Listing 11.9 The HTML for the countdown script.

```
<!DOCTYPE html>
<html>
<head>
     <title>Dynamic Countdown</title>
     <script src="script06.js"></script>
</head>
<body>
     <p>Dori says:</p>
     <p>It's only <span class="daysTill"
→ id="bday"> </span> days until
→ my birthday and <span class="daysTill"
→ id="xmas"> </span> days until
→ Christmas, so you'd better start
→ shopping now!</p>
     <p>And it's only <span class="daysTill"
→ id="anniv"> </span> days until our
→ anniversary...</p>
</body>
</html>
```

Listing 11.10 This script counts down the number of days Tom stays out of the doghouse.

```
window.addEventListener("load",showDays,false);

function showDays() {
    var spanTags = document.getElementsByTagName("span");

    for (var i=0; i<spanTags.length; i++) {
        if (spanTags[i].className.indexOf("daysTill") > -1) {
            spanTags[i].innerHTML = showTheDaysTill(spanTags[i].id);
        }
    }

    function showTheDaysTill(thisDate) {
        var theDays;

        switch(thisDate) {
            case "anniv":
                theDays = daysTill(5,6);
                break;
            case "bday":
                theDays = daysTill(8,7);
                break;
            case "xmas":
                theDays = daysTill(12,25);
                break;
            default:
        }
        return theDays + " ";
    }

    function daysTill(mm,dd) {
        var now = new Date();
        var inDate = new Date(now.getFullYear(),mm-1,dd);

        if (inDate.getTime() < now.getTime()) {
            inDate.setYear(now.getFullYear()+1);
        }

        return Math.ceil(dayToDays(inDate) - dayToDays(now));
    }

    function dayToDays(inTime) {
        return inTime.getTime() / (1000 * 60 * 60 * 24);
    }
}
```

3.
```
switch(thisDate) {
    case "anniv":
        theDays = daysTill(5,6);
        break;
    case "bday":
        theDays = daysTill(8,7);
        break;
    case "xmas":
        theDays = daysTill(12,25);
        break;
    default:
```

   If you don't remember the **switch/case** multi-level conditionals, you can review the discussion in Chapter 2. Here, we are using the value of **thisDate** to test against the three **case** statements. For the **anniv case**, we're setting **theDays** to May 6 (5,6 is the numerical representation, much like you would write it in the real world); for **bday**, we're setting it to August 7; and for **xmas**, **theDays** gets set to December 25.

4.
```
return theDays + " ";
```

   The **showTheDays()** function ends by returning the number of days followed by a space. This is to work around a problem in IE: it eats the spaces in the HTML. If the script doesn't return a space at the end, the number runs into the word "days". If you just stuck the word "days" into this function, then there'd need to be a space after that, and so on.

5.
```
function daysTill(mm,dd) {
    var now = new Date();
    var inDate = new Date
    → (nowgetFullYear(),mm-1,dd);
```

More Weird Time Stuff

Month numbering in JavaScript begins with 0 and day numbering with 1, and JavaScript deals inconsistently with years prior to 1970, depending on your browser and the version of JavaScript it uses.

Netscape Navigator 2 (using JavaScript 1.0) couldn't deal with years before 1970 at all and had a Year 2000 Problem, as it returned the wrong answer for dates in or after 2000. Navigator 3 (which used JavaScript 1.1) supposedly changed the value returned by the **getYear()** method to be two digits if the year is in the 1900s and four digits if the year was before 1900 or after 2000. However, this is not true for all versions of Netscape; for example, Netscape Navigator 4 for Mac returned 100 for the year 2000. And to make things even worse, this still occurs in Firefox—the current version (27) still returns numbers in the hundreds (versus in the 2000s) for **getYear()**.

JavaScript 1.2 (in Navigator 4, and also in ECMAScript-compatible browsers such as Internet Explorer 4 and later) introduced a new method, **getFullYear()**, which always returns four-digit years. We recommend that you use **getFullYear()** unless you know you must support ancient browsers, so that's what we're using throughout this book.

The **getTime()** method in JavaScript, for reasons probably best left unexplored, returns a number that is the number of milliseconds since January 1, 1970. Luckily, we hardly ever have to look at that number, as there have been a whopping number of milliseconds in the past four+ decades.

This step shows the **daysTill()** function, which receives the dates from the **case** statements in step 3. Then, we create the **now** and **inDate** variables. The latter variable is filled with the current year, but with the month (with 1 subtracted from it to get it right; see the "More Weird Time Stuff" sidebar) and the day that were passed in.

6. ```
if (inDate.getTime() <
→ now.getTime()) {
   inDate.setYear(now.getFullYear()
   → +1);
}
```

We then check that date against today. If that date in this year has already passed, we increment the year, going for next year's instead.

7. ```
return Math.ceil(dayToDays(inDate)
→ - dayToDays(now));
```

Here, we're calculating the number of days between **inDate** and the current date. The **Math.ceil()** method makes sure that our result is a whole number.

8. ```
function dayToDays(inTime) {
   return inTime.getTime() /
   → (1000 * 60 * 60 * 24);
```

JavaScript stores dates in milliseconds since January 1, 1970. In order to compare two dates, we need to get the number of days since January 1, 1970 for each date. To do that, divide the result of **getTime()** by the number of milliseconds in a day. We get that number by multiplying 1000 (the number of milliseconds in a second) by 60 (number of seconds in a minute), by 60 again (number of minutes in an hour), and then by 24 (number of hours in a day). The result is the number of days since January 1, 1970.
```

Hiding and Displaying Layers

Although your HTML, CSS, and JavaScript combine to make a single document, it's sometimes useful to make it appear as if you actually have multiple documents— that is, using a combination of CSS and JavaScript, you can have something like a pop-up window display inside, or on top of, your current HTML page. No, this doesn't use the obsolete Netscape **layer** tag; it just appears to be a separate layer so far as the user is concerned.

This requires three documents: the HTML document (**Listing 11.11**), the CSS style sheet (**Listing 11.12**), and the JavaScript file (**Listing 11.13**). We're using JavaScript to manipulate an element using the **id** assigned in the HTML, and CSS to set the positioning for our annoying advertisement on the page: in particular, its *z-index*, which is an indicator of which object is shown on top of another object. The object with the higher-numbered z-index is shown when two objects occupy the same space.

Listing 11.11 The HTML for the advertisement example uses **ids** to tag the elements we want to manipulate.

```html
<!DOCTYPE html>
<html>
<head>
    <title>Layered Divs</title>
    <link href="script07.css" rel="stylesheet">
    <script src="script07.js"></script>
</head>
<body>
    <div id="annoyingAdvert">
        This is an incredibly annoying ad of the type you might find on some web sites.
        <div id="closeBox">&otimes;</div>
    </div>
    <p>Lorem ipsum dolor sit amet, consectetuer adipiscing elit. Aenean lacus elit, volutpat
→ vitae, egestas in, tristique ut, nibh. Donec congue lacinia magna. Duis tortor justo,
→ dapibus vel, vulputate sed, mattis sit amet, leo. Cras purus quam, semper quis, dignissim
→ id, hendrerit eget, ante. Nulla id lacus eget nulla bibendum venenatis. Duis faucibus
→ adipiscing mauris. Integer augue. In vulputate purus eget enim. Nam odio eros, porta vitae,
→ bibendum sit amet, iaculis nec, elit. Cras egestas scelerisque pede. Donec a tellus. Nullam
→ consectetuer fringilla nunc.</p>

    <p>Nam varius metus congue ligula. In hac habitasse platea dictumst. In ut ipsum a pede
→ rhoncus convallis. Sed at enim. Integer sed metus quis est egestas vestibulum. Quisque
→ mattis tortor a lorem. Nam diam. Integer consequat lectus. Donec molestie elementum nisl.
→ Donec ligula sapien, volutpat eget, dictum quis, mollis a, odio. Aliquam augue enim, gravida
→ nec, tempor ac, interdum in, urna. Aliquam mauris. Duis massa urna, ultricies id,
→ condimentum ac, gravida nec, dolor. Morbi et est quis enim gravida nonummy. Cum sociis
→ natoque penatibus et magnis dis parturient montes, nascetur ridiculus mus. Mauris nisl quam,
→ tincidunt ultrices, malesuada eget, posuere eu, lectus. Nulla a arcu. Sed consectetuer arcu
→ et velit. Quisque dignissim risus vel elit.</p>

    <p>Nunc massa mauris, dictum id, suscipit non, accumsan et, lorem. Suspendisse non lorem quis
→ dui rutrum vestibulum. Quisque mauris. Curabitur auctor nibh non enim. Praesent tempor
→ aliquam ligula. Fusce eu purus. Vivamus ac enim eget urna pulvinar bibendum. Integer
→ porttitor, augue et auctor volutpat, lectus dolor sagittis ipsum, sed posuere lacus pede
→ eget wisi. Proin vel arcu ac velit porttitor pellentesque. Maecenas mattis velit scelerisque
→ tellus. Cras eu tellus quis sapien malesuada porta. Nunc nulla. Nullam dapibus malesuada
→ lorem. Duis eleifend rutrum tellus. In tempor tristique neque. Mauris rhoncus. Aliquam
→ purus.</p>

    <p>Morbi felis quam, placerat sed, gravida a, bibendum a, mauris. Aliquam porta diam. Nam
→ consequat feugiat diam. Fusce luctus, felis ut gravida mattis, ante mi viverra sapien,
→ a vestibulum tellus lectus ut massa. Duis placerat. Aliquam molestie tellus. Suspendisse
→ potenti. Fusce aliquet tellus a lectus. Proin augue diam, sollicitudin eget, hendrerit
→ non, semper at, arcu. Sed suscipit tincidunt nibh. Donec ullamcorper. Nullam faucibus
→ euismod augue. Cras lacinia. Aenean scelerisque, lorem sed gravida varius, nunc tortor
→ gravida odio, sed sollicitudin pede augue ut metus. Maecenas condimentum ipsum et enim.
→ Sed nulla. Ut neque elit, varius a, blandit quis, facilisis sed, velit. Suspendisse aliquam
→ odio sed nibh.</p>
</body>
</html>
```

To display and hide an object:

1. ```
var adBox = "annoyingAdvert";
document.getElementById(adBox).
→ style.display = "block";
```

    If you look at Listing 11.11, you'll see that
    the layer that we want to show has an **id**
    of **annoyingAdvert**. Listing 11.12 tells that
    layer it should start off hidden, so that it's
    not seen. However, once the page loads,
    our script tells it to appear by setting the
    **display** property to **block**.

2. ```
document.getElementById
→ ("closeBox").addEventListener(
    "click",
    function() {
        document.getElementById
        → (adBox).style.display =
        → "none";
    },
    false
);
```

    There's a reason why **annoyingAdvert**
    has that name: you can't read what's
    underneath it 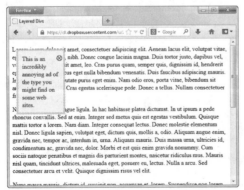! We'll be nice, though,
    and let the user close the layer (that is,
    hide it) by clicking what looks like a close
    widget. Setting the **display** property to
    none turns the layer back off again.

A The advertisement starts on the left, looking
like a layer that can be closed.

Listing 11.12 The CSS styles the layer to make it
look different from the rest of the document.

```
body {
    background-color: #FFF;
}

#annoyingAdvert {
    position: absolute;
    z-index: 2;
    display: none;
    width: 100px;
    background-color: #FFC;
    padding: 10px;
    margin: 10px;
    border: 5px solid yellow;
}

#closeBox {
    position: absolute;
    color: red;
    font-size: 1.5em;
    top: 0;
    right: 0;
}
```

Listing 11.13 The JavaScript shows the layer and
then (thankfully) lets you hide it again.

```
window.addEventListener("load",initAdvert,
→ false);

function initAdvert() {
    var adBox = "annoyingAdvert";

    document.getElementById(adBox).style.
    → display = "block";
    document.getElementById("closeBox").
    → addEventListener(
        "click",
        function() {
            document.getElementById(adBox).
            → style.display = "none";
        },
        false
    );
}
```

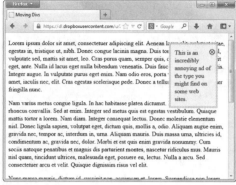

A In this version, it ends up on the right, where you can finally close it.

Moving an Object in the Document

JavaScript can move objects (images, text, or whatever) around your screen. In fact, you can make an object appear to move in three dimensions, so that it looks as though it passes behind other objects in the document. In this example, you'll see how that annoying ad in the previous task can be made even more annoying.

This again requires three documents; however, the HTML and CSS are identical to that in the previous version. Here, we'll just show the JavaScript file (**Listing 11.14**). Now, as soon as the user wants to close the advertisement layer, it starts to move away from them. Thankfully, it will stop before it goes off the screen **A**, allowing them to finally close it!

To move an object:

1. `document.getElementById(adBox).`
   `→ addEventListener("mouseover",`
   `→ slide, false);`

   In order to start the movement, we add a **mouseover** event handler to our advertisement, which tells it to trigger the **slide()** function.

2. `if (nextPos(adBox) <= (document.`
   `→ body.clientWidth-150)) {`

   Before we move the layer, we need to figure out if it's within the restrictions that we've placed on it—that's done by checking its current position (using the **nextPos()** function, which we'll describe below) and comparing it to the width of the document window. If it's equal to or less than that (minus another 150 pixels, to take the width of the layer itself into account), then we want to move it some more.

continues on next page

3. **`document.getElementById(adBox).`**
   `→ style.left = nextPos(adBox) +`
   `→ "px";`

   To move the layer (in a way that works cross-browser), we have to change its **`style.left`** property. Here, we change it by getting the object's next position and adding "**px**" to the end to put it in the correct format. Changing **`style.left`** is all that's needed to move it to its new location.

4. **`setTimeout(slide,100);`**

   Here's where we use JavaScript to keep on moving, by telling **`setTimeout()`** to call **`slide()`** again in one hundred milliseconds (one-tenth of a second).

5. **`function nextPos(elem) {`**

   Step 3 needed to get the current position of an element, and here's where we do it. All we need is the **`id`** of that element.

6. **`return document.getElementById`**
   `→ (elem).offsetLeft+1;`

   Given the **`id`** of the object, we can get the object. And given that, all we need is its **`offsetLeft`** property, which is the object's left position. The **`offsetLeft`** property contains a numeric value, so we can just return it, incremented by one.

   TIP You might be wondering: if **`offsetLeft`** is numeric, why jump through all those hoops to instead change the **`style.left`** property? We have to do that because **`offsetLeft`** is read-only; that is, you can read its value, but you can't change it. There aren't any cross-browser, writeable, numeric positioning elements.

Listing 11.14 The JavaScript gets the advertisement moving.

```
window.addEventListener("load",initAdvert,
→ false);

function initAdvert() {
    var adBox = "annoyingAdvert";

    document.getElementById(adBox).style.
    → display = "block";
    document.getElementById(adBox).
    → addEventListener("mouseover",slide,
    → false);
    document.getElementById("closeBox").
    → addEventListener(
        "click",
        function() {
            document.getElementById(adBox).
            → style.display = "none";
        },
        false
    );
}

function slide() {
    var adBox = "annoyingAdvert";

    if (nextPos(adBox) <= (document.body.
    → clientWidth-150)) {
        document.getElementById(adBox).style.
        → left = nextPos(adBox) + "px";
        setTimeout(slide,100);
    }

    function nextPos(elem) {
        return document.getElementById(elem).
        → offsetLeft+1;
    }
}
```

Date Methods

Because you'll often need to deal with dates, here's a table of all of the methods of the **Date** object. In **Table 11.1**, you'll see a reference to UTC, which stands for Coordinated Universal Time, which replaced Greenwich Mean Time (GMT) as the world standard for time in 1986. Any of the methods that contain UTC are available only in JavaScript 1.2 or later.

TABLE 11.1 Date Methods

Method	Description	Returned Values	JS Version
getDate() getUTCDate()	The day of the month	1–31	1.0 1.2
getDay() getUTCDay()	The integer value of the day of the week	0–6	1.0 1.2
getFullYear() getUTCFullYear()	The full four-digit year	1900+	1.2
getHours() getUTCHours()	The integer hour of the day	0–23	1.0 1.2
getMilliseconds() getUTCMilliseconds()	The number of milliseconds since the last second	0–999	1.2
getMinutes() getUTCMinutes()	The number of minutes since the last hour	0–59	1.0 1.2
getMonth() getUTCMonth()	The month of the year	0–11	1.0 1.2
getSeconds() getUTCSeconds()	The number of seconds since the last minute	0–59	1.0 1.2
getTime()	The number of milliseconds since midnight 1 January 1970		1.0
getTimezoneOffset()	The difference between local time and GMT in minutes	0–1439	1.0
getYear()	The year field of the date	0–99 for the years 1900–1999, four-digit year thereafter	1.0
parse()	Given a date/time string, return the number of milliseconds since midnight 1 January 1970		1.0

continues on next page

TABLE 11.1 Date Methods *continued*

Method	Description	Returned Values	JS Version
setDate() setUTCDate()	Set the day, given a number from 1–31	Date in milliseconds (as of JavaScript 1.2)	1.0 1.2
setFullYear() setUTCFullYear()	Set the year, given a four-digit year	Date in milliseconds	1.2
setHours() setUTCHours()	Set the hour, given a number from 0–23	Date in milliseconds (as of 1.2)	1.0 1.2
setMilliseconds() setUTCMilliseconds()	Set the milliseconds, given a number from 0–999	Date in milliseconds	1.0 1.2
setMinutes() setUTCMinutes()	Set the minutes, given a number from 0–59	Date in milliseconds (as of 1.2)	1.0 1.2
setMonth() setUTCMonth()	Set the month, given a number from 0–11	Date in milliseconds (as of 1.2)	1.0 1.2
setSeconds() setUTCSeconds()	Set the seconds, given a number from 0–59	Date in milliseconds (as of 1.2)	1.0 1.2
setTime()	Set a date, given the number of milliseconds since 1 January 1970	Date in milliseconds	1.0
setYear()	Set the year, given either a two- or four-digit value	Date in milliseconds (as of 1.2)	1.0
toGMTString() toUTCString()	The GMT date and time in string format	day dd mm yyyy hh:mm:ss GMT	1.0 1.2
toLocaleString()	The local date and time in string format	Varies based on OS, locale, and browser	1.0
toString()	The local date and time in string format	Varies based on OS and browser	1.0
UTC()	Given a date in year, month, day (and optional hours, minutes, seconds, and milliseconds) format, return the number of milliseconds since 1 January 1970	Date in milliseconds	1.0
valueOf()	The number of milliseconds since midnight 1 January 1970	Date in milliseconds	1.2

Applied JavaScript

In earlier chapters of this book, you learned how to use dozens of JavaScript techniques to accomplish specific tasks. On many webpages that you build, you'll often need just one technique, and you'll be able to use a script from this book (usually with minor modifications).

But sometimes you'll need to use more than one technique to get the job done. That's where this chapter comes in. The tasks you'll find here require a variety of approaches and are similar (in spirit, if not in specifics) to what you'll need to do on your own websites.

In this chapter, you'll learn to improve your site's user interface with outline-style sliding and fly-out menus; create a slideshow; process text by crunching it with JavaScript; let JavaScript do the hard work of displaying data in an easy-to-understand graphical manner; and switch between different style sheets under script control.

Using Sliding Menus

A sliding menu is a simple user interface widget that lets you put a lot of information on a page without cluttering things up. The user can view just as much (or as little) of the extra information as they want to see at a time. **Listing 12.1** contains the HTML, **Listing 12.2** the CSS, and **Listing 12.3** the JavaScript, which follows.

To use sliding menus:

1. ```
var allLinks = document.
   → getElementsByTagName("a");
   ```

   When the page loads, the **initAll()** function is called, and it begins by creating an array of all the links on the page.

2. ```
for (var i=0; i<allLinks.length;
   → i++) {
     if (allLinks[i].className.
   → indexOf("menuLink") > -1) {
       allLinks[i].addEventListener
   → ("click",toggleMenu,false);
     }
   }
   ```

   Once we have all the links, we loop through them, looking for those links with a class of **menuLink** and adding a **click** handler to just those links. Here, that **click** handler is set to call the **toggleMenu()** function when a link is clicked.

Listing 12.1 Here's a straightforward HTML page with a lot of links.

```
<!DOCTYPE html>
<html>
<head>
    <title>Shakespeare's Plays</title>
    <link rel="stylesheet"
    → href="script01.css">
    <script src="script01.js"></script>
</head>
<body>
    <h1>Shakespeare's Plays</h1>
    <div>
      <a href="menu1.html"
      → class="menuLink">Comedies</a>
      <ul class="menu" id="menu1">
        <li><a href="pg1.html">All's Well
        → That Ends Well</a></li>
        <li><a href="pg2.html">As You
        → Like It</a></li>
        <li><a href="pg3.html">Love's
        → Labour's Lost</a></li>
        <li><a href="pg4.html">The Comedy
        → of Errors</a></li>
      </ul>
    </div>
    <div>
      <a href="menu2.html"
      → class="menuLink">Tragedies</a>
      <ul class="menu" id="menu2">
        <li><a href="pg5.html">Anthony
        → &amp; Cleopatra</a></li>
        <li><a href="pg6.html">Hamlet
        → </a></li>
        <li><a href="pg7.html">Romeo &amp;
        → Juliet</a></li>
      </ul>
    </div>
    <div>
      <a href="menu3.html"
      → class="menuLink">Histories</a>
      <ul class="menu" id="menu3">
        <li><a href="pg8.html">Henry IV,
        → Part 1</a></li>
        <li><a href="pg9.html">Henry IV,
        → Part 2</a></li>
      </ul>
    </div>
</body>
</html>
```

Listing 12.2 It doesn't take much CSS to pull off this effect.

```css
body {
    background-color: #FFF;
    color: #000;
}

div {
    margin-bottom: 10px;
}

ul.menu {
    display: none;
    list-style-type: none;
    margin-top: 5px;
}

a.menuLink {
    font-size: 1.2em;
    font-weight: bold;
}
```

3.
```
var startMenu = this.href.
→ lastIndexOf("/")+1;
var stopMenu = this.href.
→ lastIndexOf(".");
```

Inside **toggleMenu()**, JavaScript has given us **this**. Here, **this** is the link object that the user clicked, which means that **this.href** is the full link URL. But we only want the part between the last forward slash and the last period (that is, if the link was to **http://www. javascriptworld.com/index.html**, we'd only want "index"), so we create and set **startMenu** and **stopMenu** to be the locations in **this.href** where we want to start and stop finding the string that will end up being our menu name.

continues on next page

Listing 12.3 Text (and links) can appear and disappear with this script.

```javascript
window.addEventListener("load",initAll,false);

function initAll() {
    var allLinks = document.getElementsByTagName("a");

    for (var i=0; i<allLinks.length; i++) {
        if (allLinks[i].className.indexOf("menuLink") > -1) {
            allLinks[i].addEventListener("click",toggleMenu,false);
        }
    }
}

function toggleMenu(evt) {
    var startMenu = this.href.lastIndexOf("/")+1;
    var stopMenu = this.href.lastIndexOf(".");
    var thisMenuName = this.href.substring(startMenu,stopMenu);

    var thisMenuStyle = document.getElementById(thisMenuName).style;
    if (thisMenuStyle.display == "block") {
        thisMenuStyle.display = "none";
    }
    else {
        thisMenuStyle.display = "block";
    }

    evt.preventDefault();
}
```

4. `var thisMenuName = this.href.`
`→ substring(startMenu,stopMenu);`

The menu name we want begins and ends at these two positions, so here's where we set it.

5. `var thisMenuStyle =`
`→ document.getElementById`
`→ (thisMenuName).style;`

The variable **thisMenuStyle** is set to the **style** property of the desired menu using the **getElementById()** method.

6. `if (thisMenuStyle.display ==`
`→ "block") {`
`   thisMenuStyle.display = "none";`
`}`
`else {`
`   thisMenuStyle.display = "block";`
`}`

If the **display** property of **thisMenuStyle** is **block**, then this code changes it to **none**. Alternatively, if it's **none**, it's changed to **block**. This is what toggles the menu display, as shown in Ⓐ and Ⓑ.

7. `evt.preventDefault();`

All that's left to do in the function is prevent any further processing of the clicked link, and that's done here.

> **TIP** Here's some of what's going on inside these menus: if you take a close look at the HTML, the links are actually inside `<ul>` and `<li>` tags—that is, they're unordered lists and list items. If a user has a browser that doesn't support CSS, they'll just see a list of items on the page Ⓒ. If the browser is capable, though, we can use CSS to style how we want those lists to look, with a result that looks nothing like a plain list.

Ⓐ The initial view of the sliding menus.

Ⓑ After a click, the menu expands and the additional choices appear.

Ⓒ When you turn off the CSS display—as we have done here—the menus are revealed for what they really are: a simple unordered list.

Listing 12.4 A little more CSS and a little more
JavaScript give your menus a more traditional look.

```
body {
    background-color: #FFF;
    color: #000;
}

div {
    margin-bottom: 10px;
    width: 15em;
    background-color: #9CF;
}

ul.menu {
    display: none;
    list-style-type: none;
    margin: 0;
    padding: 0;
}

ul.menu li {
    font: 1em arial, helvetica, sans-serif;
    padding-left: 10px;
}

a.menuLink, li a {
    text-decoration: none;
    color: #006;
}

a.menuLink {
    font-size: 1.2em;
    font-weight: bold;
}

ul.menu li a:hover {
    background-color: #006;
    color: #FFF;
    padding-right: 10px;
}
```

Adding Pull-Down Menus

You may have looked at the sliding menus in the previous task and said to yourself, that's nice, but what I really want are those pull-down menus that make webpages look like applications. Here's the secret: there's not a lot of difference between the previous task and this one. In fact, the HTML is identical (just refer back to Listing 12.1); the CSS is in **Listing 12.4**, and the JavaScript is in **Listing 12.5**.

Listing 12.5 This script turns your everyday links into pull-down menus.

```
window.addEventListener("load",initAll,false);

function initAll() {
    var allLinks = document.getElementsByTagName("a");

    for (var i=0; i<allLinks.length; i++) {
        if (allLinks[i].className.indexOf("menuLink") > -1) {
            allLinks[i].addEventListener("mouseover",toggleMenu,false);
            allLinks[i].addEventListener("click",clickHandler,false);
        }
    }
}

function clickHandler(evt) {
    evt.preventDefault();
}

function toggleMenu() {
    var startMenu = this.href.lastIndexOf("/")+1;
    var stopMenu = this.href.lastIndexOf(".");
    var thisMenuName = this.href.substring(startMenu,stopMenu);

    var menuParent = document.getElementById(thisMenuName).parentNode;
    var thisMenuStyle = document.getElementById(thisMenuName).style;
    thisMenuStyle.display = "block";

    menuParent.addEventListener("mouseout",function() {thisMenuStyle.display = "none";},false);
    menuParent.addEventListener("mouseover",function() {thisMenuStyle.display = "block";},false);
}
```

To add a pull-down menu:

1. ```
   allLinks[i].addEventListener
   → ("mouseover",toggleMenu,false);
   allLinks[i].addEventListener
   → ("click",clickHandler,false);
   ```

   Instead of adding a **click** handler to call **toggleMenu()** as we did previously, here we set **click** to instead call **clickHandler()**. We'll have **mouseover** call **toggleMenu()**, which means that the menu will open up whenever we move the mouse over it 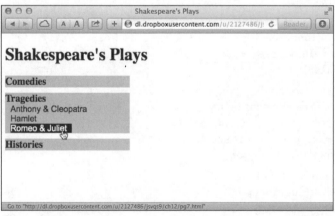.

2. ```
   function clickHandler(evt) {
       evt.preventDefault();
   }
   ```

   All the **clickHandler()** function needs to do is make sure that no further processing of the clicked link is done.

continues on next page

A The menus expand when you roll the mouse over them, highlighting the choice under the mouse pointer.

3.
```
var menuParent =
→ document.getElementById
→ (thisMenuName).parentNode;
var thisMenuStyle =
→ document.getElementById
→ (thisMenuName).style;
thisMenuStyle.display = "block";
```

After the menu displays, we have to figure out how to hide it again. The secret to a pull-down menu is that you don't want it to close when you move the mouse off the triggering link; you want it to close when you move the mouse off the entire **div**. That is, if you're anywhere on the menu, you want it to stay open. To do that, we need the parent of the menu name node, which we store in **menuParent**.

Lastly, we're not toggling quite the same way any more. Instead, we're now just going to set this menu to always display.

4.
```
menuParent.addEventListener
→ ("mouseout",function()
→ {thisMenuStyle.display =
→ "none";},false);
```

Here's the trick: if we got here, then by definition, the cursor is inside the **div**. And consequently, just setting the parent **div**'s **mouseover** event handler causes it to immediately trigger.

5.
```
menuParent.addEventListener
→ ("mouseover",function()
→ {thisMenuStyle.display =
→ "block";},false);
```

Here we tell the entire **div** to (again) display. Yes, we did it above in step 3, but we need to do it again here; otherwise, the moment we moved off the link, the menu would snap shut again.

Listing 12.6 Add one line of CSS, and you get an entirely new look to your menus.

```
body {
    background-color: #FFF;
    color: #000;
}

div {
    margin-bottom: 10px;
    width: 15em;
    background-color: #9CF;
    float: left;
}

ul.menu {
    display: none;
    list-style-type: none;
    margin: 0;
    padding: 0;
}

ul.menu li {
    font: 1em arial, helvetica, sans-serif;
    padding-left: 10px;
}
```

listing continues on next page

Enhancing Pull-Down Menus

Maybe you've looked at the previous example, and now you're saying, "I don't want a vertical menu; I want a horizontal menu!" That's straightforward (and doesn't even require any changes to the JavaScript!). Or maybe you want it to be a little more compatible for people who navigate using the keyboard? Here's how to do it. Once again, there's no change to the HTML, so you can refer back to Listing 12.1 if you need to see it.

To enhance pull-down menus:

1. `float: left;`

   Here's the sneaky trick: just add **float: left;** to the CSS for each menu **div**, as shown in **Listing 12.6** and Ⓐ. Yes, that's all it takes to turn a vertical menu into one that's horizontal—no JavaScript required.

continues on next page

Ⓐ A simple change to the CSS makes the menus appear across the page, rather than down the left side.

2. `allLinks[i].addEventListener`
`→ ("click",clickHandler,false);`

If you want to make your menus more accessible, however, you need to add a little more JavaScript, as you see in **Listing 12.7**. In particular, we'll need to add more code to the **click** event handler, so we're giving it a function of its own, **clickHandler**.

3. `function clickHandler(evt) {`

And here's that event handler, being passed the **evt** parameter. If you recall from earlier examples, some browsers pass an event object and some don't.

4. `if (evt) {`
`    evt.preventDefault();`

`    if (typeof evt.target ==`
`    → "string") {`
`       toggleMenu(evt,evt.target);`
`    }`
`    else {`
`       toggleMenu(evt,evt.target.`
`       → toString());`
`    }`
`}`
`else {`
`    toggleMenu(evt,window.event.`
`    → srcElement.href);`
`}`

Here's the code to handle those darn browsers that can pass in all kinds of different things. First off, we check to see if we have an event object—if we do, **evt** exists. Next, once we know we've got it, we tell the browser to stop processing this event. After that, we check to see if its **target** property is a string, because we're going to need it to be one. If it is, we pass both the event and its target to **toggleMenu()**.

Listing 12.6 *continued*

```
a.menuLink, li a {
    text-decoration: none;
    color: #006;
}

a.menuLink {
    font-size: 1.2em;
    font-weight: bold;
}

ul.menu li a:hover {
    background-color: #006;
    color: #FFF;
    padding-right: 10px;
}
```

Listing 12.7 A little more JavaScript lets the menu work without a mouse.

```
window.addEventListener("load",initAll,
→ false);

function initAll() {
    var allLinks = document.
    → getElementsByTagName("a");

    for (var i=0; i<allLinks.length; i++) {
        if (allLinks[i].className.
        → indexOf("menuLink") > -1) {
            allLinks[i].addEventListener
            → ("mouseover",toggleMenu,false);
            allLinks[i].addEventListener
            → ("click",clickHandler,false);
        }
    }
}

function clickHandler(evt) {
    if (evt) {
        evt.preventDefault();

        if (typeof evt.target == "string") {
            toggleMenu(evt,evt.target);
        }
```

listing continues on next page

Listing 12.7 *continued*

```
        else {
            toggleMenu(evt,evt.target.
            → toString());
        }
    }
    else {
        toggleMenu(evt,window.event.
        → srcElement.href);
    }
}

function toggleMenu(evt,currMenu) {
    if (toggleMenu.arguments.length < 2) {
        var currMenu = this.href;
    }

    var startMenu = currMenu.lastIndexOf
    → ("/")+1;
    var stopMenu = currMenu.lastIndexOf
    → (".");
    var thisMenuName = currMenu.substring
    → (startMenu,stopMenu);

    var menuParent = document.getElementById
    → (thisMenuName).parentNode;
    var thisMenuStyle = document.
    → getElementById(thisMenuName).style;
    thisMenuStyle.display = "block";

    menuParent.addEventListener("mouseout",
    → function() {thisMenuStyle.display =
    → "none";},false);
    menuParent.addEventListener("mouseover",
    → function() {thisMenuStyle.display =
    → "block";},false);
}
```

If **target** isn't a string, we force it to be one, by calling the **toString()** method, and use that (along with **evt**) as our parameters to **toggleMenu()**.

And finally, if there wasn't any event object, we'll send **toggleMenu()** a dummy **evt** object and **window.event.srcElement.href**—which is where IE stores the value we need.

5. ```
function toggleMenu(evt,currMenu) {
    if (toggleMenu.arguments.length
    → < 2) {
        var currMenu = this.href;
    }
```

Here's where the menu gets toggled, and because both a click and a mouse movement can trigger the display, **toggleMenu()** needs to be a little more complex to handle things. We start off the function with two parameters, but here's an important thing about JavaScript: just because a function is expecting to be passed two arguments, doesn't mean that it always *must* be passed both. In fact, the way we've written **toggleMenu()**, it can get:

▸ zero arguments, when the browser is IE and **toggleMenu()** was triggered via the mouse,

▸ one argument (the **event** object), when the browser isn't IE and **toggleMenu()** was triggered via the mouse, or

▸ two arguments (the **event** object and the menu name) when **toggleMenu()** was called by **clickHandler()**.

*continues on next page*
```

If we come in here with zero or one arguments (which we can check by looking at **toggleMenu.arguments. length**), we know that we can find the menu name by looking at **this.href**— in other words, it should work just the way it used to. But because we need the value in **currMenu**, that's where we'll store it.

6. ```
var startMenu = currMenu.
   →lastIndexOf("/")+1;
var stopMenu = currMenu.
   →lastIndexOf(".");
var thisMenuName = currMenu.
   →substring(startMenu,stopMenu);
```

Once again, we calculate **startMenu**, **stopMenu**, and **thisMenuName**, but now it's based off of **currMenu**.

**TIP** Blind users aren't the only ones who care about keyboard access to menu items. Some people prefer to use the keyboard in general, and some browsers (particularly mobile ones) don't handle mouseovers in the way that menus require. Accessibility is always a good idea. Never use JavaScript or fancy features as an excuse to not consider everyone's needs.

**TIP** In this example, clicking a menu item expands the menu, but a mouse is required to close it again.
```

A Slideshow with Captions

While a slideshow (like the one shown in Listings 4.18 and 4.19) can be handy, it's likely to be more useful if you can also show captions that change along with the images. **Listings 12.8** (HTML), **12.9** (CSS), and **12.10** (JavaScript) show an example of such a slideshow (with pictures of our summer vacation!). In this task, we'll show you how to blend together different techniques you've seen in earlier chapters into one script.

Listing 12.8 Our slideshow HTML page.

```
<!DOCTYPE html>
<html>
<head>
    <title>Our Summer Vacation!</title>
    <link rel="stylesheet" href="script04.css">
    <script src="script04.js"></script>
</head>
<body>
    <h1>Our Summer Vacation Slideshow</h1>
    <img src="images/slideImg0.jpg" alt="Our Vacation Pix" id="slideshow">
    <div id="imgText"> </div>
    <div id="chgImg">
        <input type="button" id="prevLink" value="&laquo; Previous">
        <input type="button" id="nextLink" value="Next &raquo;">
    </form>
</body>
</html>
```

To create a slideshow with captions:

1. ```
   document.getElementById
   → ("imgText").innerHTML =
   → captionText[currImg];
   ```

   Our **initAll()** function needs to set three things: the photo caption for the first slide (in the **imgText** area), and the **click** handlers for the forward and back buttons (in the following step).

2. ```
   document.getElementById
   → ("prevLink").addEventListener
   → ("click",function()
   → {newSlide(-1);},false);
   document.getElementById
   → ("nextLink").addEventListener
   → ("click",function()
   → {newSlide(1);},false);
   ```

   Yes, this really is all that these two lines need to do—well, mostly. We could rig up some convoluted code to know whether or not we want to go forward or backward based on which button was clicked, but instead, we just need to call **newSlide()**. The difference: one passes it a value of 1, and the other a value of –1, letting **newSlide()** know in which direction to move.

   continues on page 300

Listing 12.9 The external Cascading Style Sheet called by Listing 12.8.

```
body {
    background-color: #FFF;
    color: #000;
    font: 12px verdana, arial, helvetica,
    → geneva, sans-serif;
}

h1 {
    font: 24px "trebuchet ms", verdana,
    → arial, helvetica, geneva, sans-serif;
    margin-left: 100px;
}

#chgImg {
    margin-left: 100px;
    clear: both;
}

#slideshow {
    padding: 0 10px 10px 10px;
    float: left;
    height: 240px;
    width: 320px;
}

#imgText {
    padding: 10px 0 0 10px;
    float: left;
    width: 200px;
    height: 150px;
    border-top: 1px solid #000;
    border-left: 1px solid #000;
}
```

Listing 12.10 The slideshow script displays the photo and the caption.

```
window.addEventListener("load",initAll,false);

var currImg = 0;
var captionText = [
    "Our ship, leaving Vancouver.",
    "We took a helicopter ride at our first port, Juneau.",
    "The helicopter took us to Mendenhall Glacier.",
    "The happy (and chilly) couple, on the glacier.",
    "Here's what our second stop, Ketchikan, looked like from the ship.",
    "We got to cruise through Glacier Bay. It was absolutely breathtaking!",
    "In Skagway, we took a train up into the mountains, all the way to the Canadian Border.",
    "Looking back down at Skagway from the train.",
    "On a trip this romantic, I shouldn't have been surprised by a proposal, but I was
    → (obviously, I said yes).",
    "It's nice to go on vacation, but it's nice to be home again, too."
];

function initAll() {
    document.getElementById("imgText").innerHTML = captionText[currImg];
    document.getElementById("prevLink").addEventListener("click",function()
    → {newSlide(-1);},false);
    document.getElementById("nextLink").addEventListener("click",function() {newSlide(1);},false);
}

function newSlide(direction) {
    var imgCt = captionText.length;

    currImg = currImg + direction;
    if (currImg < 0) {
        currImg = imgCt-1;
    }
    if (currImg == imgCt) {
        currImg = 0;
    }
    document.getElementById("slideshow").src = "images/slideImg" + currImg + ".jpg"
    document.getElementById("imgText").innerHTML = captionText[currImg]
}
```

3. ```
document.getElementById
   → ("slideshow").src =
   → "images/slideImg" + currImg +
   → ".jpg";
document.getElementById
   → ("imgText").innerHTML =
   → captionText[currImg];
```

This step changes both the image and its corresponding caption at the same time .

**TIP** Wondering what's going on with captionText and its syntax? Just remember what we said early on: there's no one right way to do things. JavaScript gives you more than one way to declare a new array. There's no difference in the result if we say

```
var dice = new Array(1,2,3,4,5,6);
```

or

```
var dice = [1,2,3,4,5,6];
```

Both methods will produce an array containing the possible values of a six-sided die.

Ⓐ The script calculates which photo and caption to display.
```

A Silly Name Generator

You may have seen web-based toys that take your name and transform it into a new name, like "Your Superhero Name" or "Your Name if You Were a Character in *The Sopranos*." We've settled for simply being ridiculous, so **Listings 12.11** and **12.12** can show you how to get your own new, silly name. In the process, you can see how to combine string handling, arrays, error checking, and form field validation into one darned silly script.

Listing 12.11 The webpage where you can enter your real name and get your silly name.

```
<!DOCTYPE html>
<html>
<head>
    <title>Silly Name Generator</title>
    <script src="script05.js"></script>
</head>
<body>
<h1>What's your silly name?</h1>
<table>
    <tr>
        <td class="rtAlign">First Name:</td>
        <td><input type="text" id="fName" size="30"></td>
    </tr>
    <tr>
        <td class="rtAlign">Last Name:</td>
        <td><input type="text" id="lName" size="30"></td>
    </tr>
    <tr>
        <td> </td>
        <td><input type="submit" value="Submit" id="sillySubmit"></td>
    </tr>
</table>
<p id="msgField"> </p>
</body>
</html>
```

To combine JavaScript techniques:

1. `document.getElementById`
   `→ ("msgField").innerHTML =`
   `→ getSillyName();`
   `return false;`

   When the page first loads, the submit button's **click** handler is set to call a function, and this is its entire content. First, we call **getSillyName()**. That function returns a string value (either the silly name or an error message), which we then write out to the page. Then we return **false**, so that the **click** doesn't try to do anything else.

Listing 12.12 This script generates a silly name from three arrays, based on characters from the first and last names entered by the user.

```
window.addEventListener("load",initAll,false);

function initAll() {
    document.getElementById("sillySubmit").addEventListener(
        "click",
        function() {
            document.getElementById("msgField").innerHTML = getSillyName();
            return false;
        },
        false
    );
}

function getSillyName() {
    var firstName = ["Runny", "Buttercup", "Dinky", "Stinky", "Crusty", "Greasy", "Gidget",
    → "Cheesypoof", "Lumpy", "Wacky", "Tiny", "Flunky", "Fluffy", "Zippy", "Doofus", "Gobsmacked",
    → "Slimy", "Grimy", "Salamander", "Oily", "Burrito", "Bumpy", "Loopy", "Snotty", "Irving",
    → "Egbert"];
    var lastName1 = ["Snicker", "Buffalo", "Gross", "Bubble", "Sheep", "Corset", "Toilet",
    → "Lizard", "Waffle", "Kumquat", "Burger", "Chimp", "Liver", "Gorilla", "Rhino", "Emu",
    → "Pizza", "Toad", "Gerbil", "Pickle", "Tofu", "Chicken", "Potato", "Hamster", "Lemur",
    → "Vermin"];
    var lastName2 = ["face", "dip", "nose", "brain", "head", "breath", "pants", "shorts", "lips",
    → "mouth", "muffin", "butt", "bottom", "elbow", "honker", "toes", "buns", "spew", "kisser",
    → "fanny", "squirt", "chunks", "brains", "wit", "juice", "shower"];

    var firstNm = document.getElementById("fName").value.toUpperCase();
    var lastNm = document.getElementById("lName").value.toUpperCase();
    var validName = true;
```

listing continues on next page

Listing 12.12 *continued*

```
if (firstNm == "") {
    validName = false;
}
else {
    var firstNum = firstNm.charCodeAt(0)
    → - 65;
    if (firstNum < 0 || firstNum > 25) {
        validName = false;
    }
}

if (!validName) {
    document.getElementById("fName").
    → focus();
    document.getElementById("fName").
    → select();
    return "That's not a valid first
    → name";
}

if (lastNm == "") {
    validName = false;
}
else {
    var lastNum1 = lastNm.charCodeAt(0)
    → - 65;
    var lastNum2 = lastNm.charCodeAt
    → (lastNm.length-1) - 65;

    if (lastNum1 < 0 || lastNum1 > 25 ||
    → lastNum2 < 0 || lastNum2 > 25) {
        validName = false;
    }
}

if (!validName) {
    document.getElementById("lName").
    → focus();
    document.getElementById("lName").
    → select();
    return "That's not a valid last
    → name";
}

return "Your silly name is " +
→ firstName[firstNum] + " " +
→ lastName1[lastNum1] +
→ lastName2[lastNum2];
}
```

2. ```
var firstNm = document.
→ getElementById("fName").value.
→ toUpperCase();
var lastNm = document.
→ getElementById("lName").value.
→ toUpperCase();
```

Anyone visiting this page will be asked to enter their first and last names into text fields. When Submit is clicked, we start off the **getSillyName()** function by converting both names to all uppercase and storing the result in the variables **firstNm** and **lastNm**.

3. ```
if (firstNm == "") {
    validName = false;
}
```

It's required that a visitor enter at least one character for the first name, so that check is done here. Remember, the expression is read as "if **firstNm** is equal to nothing, then." If that's the case, we set **validName** to false.

4. ```
var firstNum =
→ firstNm.charCodeAt(0) - 65;
```

Otherwise, the **charCodeAt()** method takes a single character from a string. That single character in the string is based on the number passed to the method; in this case, it is the character in the 0th place, which means the first character in the string (remember, JavaScript starts counting at 0), and returns the ASCII value for that character. The uppercase alphabet starts with "A" having an ASCII value of 65 and ends with "Z" having a value of 90. We then subtract 65 to get a result between 0 and 25, and this result is saved as **firstNum**.

*continues on next page*
```

5. `if (firstNum < 0 || firstNum > 25) {`
  `validName = false;`
`}`

If the user enters a first name that doesn't start with a character between "A" and "Z", there won't be an equivalent silly name. Here, we make sure that it's within this range before checking the last name. If it isn't, we set `validName` to false.

6. `if (!validName) {`
  `document.getElementById`
  `→ ("fName").focus();`
  `document.getElementById`
  `→ ("fName").select();`
  `return "That's not a valid`
  `→ first name";`
`}`

At this point, we know that if `validName` is false, it means that the user didn't enter a valid first name. When this happens, we put the cursor in the field, select anything that's in that field, and return an error message.

7. `if (lastNm == "") {`
  `validName = false;`
`}`

Just as with the first name, they have to enter something in the last name field.

8. `var lastNum1 = lastNm.`
  `→ charCodeAt(0) - 65;`
  `var lastNum2 = lastNm.charCodeAt`
  `→ (lastNm.length-1) - 65;`

To figure out the visitor's new silly last name, we'll need to calculate the ASCII values of both the first and last characters of the last name. The first is found in the same fashion as in step 4. The last character in the string is found by taking the length of `lastNm`, subtracting 1, and then passing that number to `charCodeAt()`.

Ⓐ The resulting silly name.

Your Silly Name

Your silly name is found by taking the first letter of your first name, the first letter of your last name, and the last letter of your last name, and looking each up on the chart in **Table 12.1**. The first letter of your first name gives you your new first name, and the two letters from your last name give you the first and second parts of your new silly last name.

For example, the "T" in Tom gives a new first name of "Oily," and the "N" and "O" from Negrino produce a new last name of "Gorillahonker." The "D" in Dori turns into "Stinky," and the "S" and "H" from Smith turn into "Gerbilshorts." Consequently, the silly names of this book's authors are Oily Gorillahonker and Stinky Gerbilshorts.

TABLE 12.1 Chart of Silly Names

	First Letter of First Name	First Letter of Last Name	Last Letter of Last Name
A	Runny	Snicker	face
B	Buttercup	Buffalo	dip
C	Dinky	Gross	nose
D	Stinky	Bubble	brain
E	Crusty	Sheep	head
F	Greasy	Corset	breath
G	Gidget	Toilet	pants
H	Cheesypoof	Lizard	shorts
I	Lumpy	Waffle	lips
J	Wacky	Kumquat	mouth
K	Tiny	Burger	muffin
L	Flunky	Chimp	butt
M	Fluffy	Liver	bottom
N	Zippy	Gorilla	elbow
O	Doofus	Rhino	honker
P	Gobsmacked	Emu	toes
Q	Slimy	Pizza	buns
R	Grimy	Toad	spew
S	Salamander	Gerbil	kisser
T	Oily	Pickle	fanny
U	Burrito	Tofu	squirt
V	Bumpy	Chicken	chunks
W	Loopy	Potato	brains
X	Snotty	Hamster	wit
Y	Irving	Lemur	juice
Z	Egbert	Vermin	shower

9. ```
if (lastNum1 < 0 || lastNum1 > 25
→ || lastNum2 < 0 || lastNum2 >
→ 25) {
   validName = false;
}
```

As with the first name field, we have to make sure that both the first and last letter of the last name contain a character between "A" and "Z", so once again, we set **validName** to false if there's a problem.

10. ```
if (!validName) {
   document.getElementById
   → ("lName").focus();
   document.getElementById
   → ("lName").select();
   return "That's not a valid last
   → name";
}
```

Just as we did in step 6, if the name isn't valid, we want to let the user know.

11. ```
return "Your silly name is " +
→ firstName[firstNum] + " " +
→ lastName1[lastNum1] +
→ lastName2[lastNum2];
```

If we've passed all the tests, it's time to calculate the new silly name. Because we turned the characters into numbers between 0 and 25, we can use the results as indices into the name arrays **firstName**, **lastName1**, and **lastName2**. The result of each array lookup is concatenated to the next, with a blank space between the first name and the last name. Notice that the two parts of the last name are concatenated without a space. When we're done, that name is returned and put into the document, as shown in Ⓐ.
```

A Bar Graph Generator

Graphs are excellent ways to display visual information. You can create bar graphs by drawing them in Adobe Photoshop or by calculating them in Microsoft Excel, but for dynamic data that might need to change on a regular basis, why not have JavaScript do it instead on the fly? While we've said throughout this book that JavaScript is object-oriented (and therefore buzzword-compliant), and we've used objects throughout the book, we've only briefly shown you how to create your own custom objects. Here's a more in-depth example of how objects work, as seen in **Listings 12.13** (HTML), **12.14** (CSS), and **12.15** (JavaScript).

To generate a bar graph:

1. ```
   var radioButtons = document.
   → getElementsByTagName("input");

   for (var i=0; i<radioButtons.
   → length; i++) {
     if (radioButtons[i].type ==
   → "radio") {
       radioButtons[i].
       → addEventListener("click",
       → chgChart,false);
     }
   }
   chgChart();
   ```

   As we've done so many times, the **initAll()** function starts the ball rolling. Here, we get all the radio buttons and loop through them, setting each to call **chgChart()** when they're clicked. When that's done, we call **chgChart()** manually to display the default view of the page.

Listing 12.13 The HTML page for the bar chart generator.

```
<!DOCTYPE html>
<html>
<head>
    <title>Bar Chart Display</title>
    <link rel="stylesheet"
    → href="script06.css">
    <script src="script06.js"></script>
</head>
<body>
<div id="chartType">
    Choose a chart:<br>
    <input type="radio" name="type"
    → value="browser" checked> Browser
    → Usage<br>
    <input type="radio" name="type"
    → value="platform"> Mobile Device
    → Vendors<br>
    <p><br></p>
    Choose a color:<br>
    <input type="radio" name="color"
    → value="lilRed.gif" checked> Red<br>
    <input type="radio" name="color"
    → value="lilGreen.gif"> Green<br>
    <input type="radio" name="color"
    → value="lilBlue.gif"> Blue<br>
    <p><br></p>
    Choose a direction:<br>
    <input type="radio" name="direction"
    → value="horizontal" checked>
    → Horizontal<br>
    <input type="radio" name="direction"
    → value="vertical"> Vertical
</div>
<div id="chartArea"> </div>
</body>
</html>
```
```

Listing 12.14 This script contains the styles for the bar chart example.

```css
body {
    background-color: #FFF;
    color: #000;
    font-size: 12px;
}

#chartType {
    float: left;
    width: 200px;
}

th {
    font-size: 16px;
    padding-left: 20px;
    padding-right: 15px;
}

.horiz th {
    border-right: 1px #000 solid;
}

.horiz img {
    height: 15px;
    vertical-align: bottom;
    margin-right: 10px;
}

.vert {
    text-align: center;
    vertical-align: bottom;
}

.vert th {
    border-left: 1px #000 solid;
    border-bottom: 1px #000 solid;
}

.vert img {
    width: 15px;
    padding-left: 10px;
    padding-right: 10px;
    margin-top: 10px;
}
```

2. `var bChart = {`

Here inside **chgChart()** is where we start to create our first custom object, **bChart** (short for "browser chart"). Yep, that's all there is to it.

3.
```
name: "Desktop browser usage by
→ year",
years: [2010,2011,2012,2013,2014],
fieldnames: ["MS IE","Firefox",
→ "Chrome"],
fields: [
    [51.45,42.93,33.74,29.25,24.5],
    [31.27,28.2,24.15,20.82,20.53],
    [10.25,21.08,33.23,42.63,46.6]
]
```

The properties for a custom object are created and initialized simply by assigning values to them. Here, we set up the **name**, **years**, **fieldnames**, and **fields** properties of **bChart**. Those fields are, respectively, the name of the chart, the years covered by the chart, the labels for the chart values, and the sets of values for each year and each label (in this case, each browser).

Note that we're not using the **var** keyword before each of these; that's because they aren't new variables. Instead, they're new properties that we're adding to an existing variable (albeit one we just created).

Our new **fields** property uses two levels of square brackets because it's a two-dimensional array. We can then refer to the first row as **bChart.fields[0][n]**, the second as **bChart.fields[1][n]**, and the third as **bChart.fields[2][n]**.

continues on next page

4. }

The closing curly brace signifies that we've finished creating our new **bChart** object.

5.
```
var mobiChart = {
    name: "Mobile device vendors by
    → year",
    years: [2010,2011,2012,2013,2014],
    fieldnames: ["Nokia","Apple",
    → "Samsung","RIM"],
    fields: [
        [36.93,38.44,29.27,21.4,17.6],
        [28.88,27.51,24.39,24.01,23.23],
        [4.5,11,18.96,25.47,29.39],
        [19.78,14.38,5.22,3.65,2.87]
    ]
}
```

In the same way that we created the **bChart** object, we now create the **mobiChart** ("Mobile device chart") object and assign its properties. For the mobile device chart, we again have the years, but this time we're displaying what percentage of market share was held by each of the vendors.

Listing 12.15 And here's the code that draws the bar chart.

```
window.addEventListener("load",initAll,
→ false);

function initAll() {
    var radioButtons = document.
    → getElementsByTagName("input");

    for (var i=0; i<radioButtons.length;
    → i++) {
        if (radioButtons[i].type == "radio") {
            radioButtons[i].addEventListener
            → ("click",chgChart,false);
        }
    }
    chgChart();
}

function chgChart() {
    var bChart = {
        name: "Desktop browser usage by
        → year",
        years: [2010,2011,2012,2013,2014],
        fieldnames: ["MS IE","Firefox",
        → "Chrome"],
        fields: [
            [51.45,42.93,33.74,29.25,24.5],
            [31.27,28.2,24.15,20.82,20.53],
            [10.25,21.08,33.23,42.63,46.6]
        ]
    }

    var mobiChart = {
        name: "Mobile device vendors by
        → year",
        years: [2010,2011,2012,2013,2014],
        fieldnames: ["Nokia","Apple",
        → "Samsung","RIM"],
        fields: [
            [36.93,38.44,29.27,21.4,17.6],
            [28.88,27.51,24.39,24.01,23.23],
            [4.5,11,18.96,25.47,29.39],
            [19.78,14.38,5.22,3.65,2.87]
        ]
    }
```

listing continues on next page

Listing 12.15 *continued*

```
      var radioButtons = document.
      → getElementsByTagName("input");
      var currDirection =
      → getButton("direction");
      var imgSrc = "images/" +
      → getButton("color");

      if (getButton("type")=="browser") {
         var thisChart = bChart;
      }
      else {
         var thisChart = mobiChart;
      }

      var chartBody = "<h2>"+thisChart.name
      → +"</h2><table>";

      for (var i=0; i<thisChart.years.length;
      → i++) {
         if (currDirection == "horizontal") {
            chartBody += "<tr class=
            → 'horiz'><th rowspan="+
            → (thisChart.fieldnames.
            → length+1);
            chartBody += ">"+thisChart.
            → years[i]+"</th><td colspan=2>
            → </td></tr>";
            for (var j=0; j<thisChart.
            → fieldnames.length; j++) {
               chartBody += "<tr class=
               → 'horiz'><td>"+thisChart.
               → fieldnames[j];
               chartBody += "</td><td>
               → <img alt='horiz bar'
               → src='"+imgSrc;
               chartBody += "' width="
               → +thisChart.fields[j]
               → [i]*3+">";
               chartBody += thisChart.
               → fields[j][i]+"</td></tr>";
            }
         }
         else {
```

listing continues on next page

6. ```
   var radioButtons = document.
   → getElementsByTagName("input");
   var currDirection =
   → getButton("direction");
   var imgSrc = "images/" +
   → getButton("color");
   ```

   Before we draw our chart, we need to know which radio buttons have been selected. The **radioButtons** array contains all the input elements on the page, and once we've got that, we can call the **getButton()** function. The **getButton()** function is passed a string (the name of the radio set), and it returns a string (the current value of that set).

   We could have written **getButton()** to set up **radioButtons** instead of doing it here, but this way means that it's only initialized once instead of three times (once for every time **getButton()** is called).

   continues on next page
   ```

7.
```
if (getButton("type")=="browser") {
   var thisChart = bChart;
}
else {
   var thisChart = mobiChart;
}
```

When the user clicks any of the radio buttons to change the chart, the **chgChart()** function is called. When that happens, if the browser chart is the one that's wanted, the entire **bChart** object gets stored in **thisChart**. Otherwise, it's the mobile device chart for us, so **thisChart** is assigned the **mobiChart** object.

8.
```
var chartBody = "<h2>"+
→ thisChart.name+"</h2><table>";
```

Here's the start of the actual drawing code. First, we write out the name of the chart (stored in **thisChart.name** and displayed inside an **<h2>** tag), and then we open up a **<table>** tag. From here on out, we're adding to the **chartBody** variable, and when we're done, we'll write it out to the page.

9.
```
for (var i=0;
→ i<thisChart.years.length; i++) {
```

Here's the first of two loops that we'll be going through (remember that two-dimensional array from step 3?). This external loop uses **i** as the index variable, and how many times it loops around is based on the number of years covered by the chart.

Listing **12.15** *continued*

```
         chartBody += "<tr class='vert'>
→ <th rowspan=2>"
→ +thisChart.years[i]+"</th>";
         for (var j=0; j<thisChart.
→ fieldnames.length; j++) {
            chartBody += "<td><img alt=
→ 'vert bar' src='"+imgSrc;
            chartBody += "' height=
→ "+thisChart.fields[j]
→ [i]*3+"></td>";
         }
         chartBody += "</tr><tr
→ class='vert'>";
         for (j=0; j<thisChart.fieldnames.
→ length; j++) {
            chartBody += "<td>"+thisChart.
→ fields[j][i]+"<br>";
            chartBody += thisChart.
→ fieldnames[j]+"</td>";
         }
         chartBody += "</tr>";
      }
   }

   chartBody += "</table>";
   document.getElementById("chartArea").
→ innerHTML = chartBody;

   function getButton(buttonSet) {
      for (var i=0; i<radioButtons.length;
→ i++) {
         if (radioButtons[i].name ==
→ buttonSet &&
→ radioButtons[i].checked) {
            return radioButtons[i].value;
         }
      }
      return -1;
   }
}
```

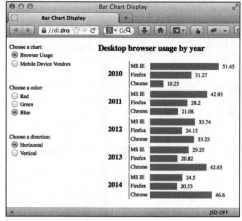

Ⓐ The initial, horizontal version of the bar graph.

10. `if (currDirection=="horizontal") {`

If the user wants to see the horizontal version of the chart **Ⓐ**, run the following code.

11. `chartBody += "<tr class='horiz'>`
`⋯ <th rowspan="+(thisChart.`
`⋯ fieldnames.length+1);`
`chartBody +=">"+thisChart.years[i]`
`⋯ +"</th><td colspan=2></td>`
`⋯ </tr>";`

The first row of each horizontal chart contains the **i**th year label. Because the two charts may not have the same number of fields, we need to calculate the **rowspan** on the fly.

12. `for (var j=0; j<thisChart.`
`⋯ fieldnames.length; j++) {`

Here's the horizontal version of the second of the two loops. This internal loop uses **j** as its index, and how many times it loops around is based on the number of fieldnames that we stored.

13. `chartBody += "<tr class='horiz'>`
`⋯ <td>"+thisChart.fieldnames[j];`

The detail row of the table is started here, and we first write out the value label (either the browser type or the JavaScript version), which is stored in the **j**th element of **fieldnames**.

continues on next page

14. `chartBody += "</td><td><img`
→ `alt='horiz bar' src='"+imgSrc;`
`chartBody += "' width="+`
→ `thisChart.fields[j][i]*3+">";`

Next, we close the previous cell and calculate the bar image. The color of the bar is based on **imgSrc**, and the width is the value of the **j**th by **i**th index in the array, multiplied by 3. For example, if **imgSrc** is **lilBlue.gif** and **thisChart.fields[3][4]** is 30, this would write out an image tag to draw a blue rectangle 90 pixels wide.

15. `chartBody += thisChart.fields[j][i]+`
→ `"</td></tr>";`

Now the actual data value is written out to the right of the bar to finish off this row. This is the end of the interior loop for the horizontal section of the code.

16. `chartBody += "<tr class='vert'>`
→ `<th rowspan=2>"+`
→ `thisChart.years[i]+"</th>";`

If the user wants to see the chart drawn vertically **B**, we start by writing the initial row of the chart. The vertical version of the chart is somewhat more complex and requires two internal (but separate) **j** loops. Here we write out the label for the chart.

17. `for (var j=0; j<thisChart.`
→ `fieldnames.length; j++) {`

Here's the first internal loop. This one writes out each vertical bar on the graph in a row.

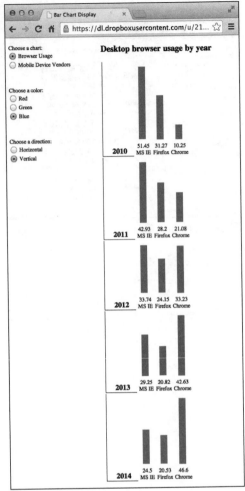

B The vertical version of the bar graph.

18. `chartBody += "<td><img`
`→ alt='vert bar' src='"+imgSrc;`
`chartBody += "' height="+`
`→ thisChart.fields[j][i]*3`
`→ +"></td>";`

And here's the image tag being written on the fly. This time, the height varies based on the value found in the two-dimensional array. For example, if **imgSrc** is **lilGreen.gif** and **thisChart.fields[3][4]** is 30, this would write out an image tag to draw a green rectangle 90 pixels high.

19. `chartBody += "</tr><tr`
`→ class='vert'>";`

When all the bars on the graph have been written out, close that table row and start the next row.

20. `for (j=0; j<thisChart.fieldnames.`
`→ length; j++) {`

Here's the second internal loop. This one writes the value of each data point, under its corresponding bar, followed by the y-axis label.

21. `chartBody += "<td>"+`
`→ thisChart.fields[j][i]+"<br>";`
`chartBody += thisChart.fieldnames[j]`
`→ +"</td>";`

Here's the information being written out for each bar. The variable **thisChart.fields[j][i]** is the value of that bar, and **thisChart.fieldnames[j]** is the data label for that bar.

22. `chartBody += "</tr>";`

After the last internal loop is complete, we need to write out a final end row tag.

continues on next page

23. `chartBody += "</table>";`
`document.getElementById`
`→("chartArea").innerHTML =`
`→chartBody;`

At this point, both the horizontal and vertical sections are done, and the external loop has completed, so we write out the final table tag to end our script and then put the entire thing into the `innerHTML` property of the `chartArea` section of the page.

TIP This code uses three images: `lilRed.gif`, `lilBlue.gif`, and `lilGreen.gif`. Each of these is a single-pixel GIF in its corresponding color. HTML allows you to set the height and width regardless of the image's actual physical dimensions, so a single pixel allows us to create bars of any size and shape.

TIP In case you were wondering, the horizontal bar's height and the vertical bar's width are both set in the CSS file, Listing 12.14. Because those values are static (i.e., they don't change), there's no reason to use JavaScript to set them on the fly.

TIP This chart can be changed to graph almost anything simply by changing the array values in steps 3 and 5. No matter what you set the arrays to, you shouldn't have to change the loops that create the graphs.

TIP The statistics on these charts are based on those found at StatCounter's Global Statistics, at `gs.statcounter.com`.

TIP If the code for the arrays in steps 3 and 5 looks unfamiliar, take a look at Listing 12.10.

TIP If the code for creating new objects looks unfamiliar, you might want to review Listing 10.11.

A Some visitors prefer to read smaller, sans-serif text because more of it can squeeze on the page.

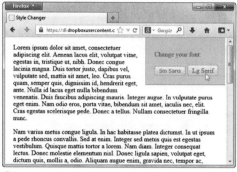

B Other visitors will be glad to choose larger, serif text that they find more readable.

Style Sheet Switcher

One of the most powerful uses of JavaScript is the ability to modify, on the fly, which style sheet is being used. For example, you can offer your site's visitors the ability to choose the style and size of the text on your site. Some people like to read tiny, sans-serif text that packs lots of words on the screen **A**, while others prefer larger, serif text that's a bit more readable **B**. Now you can make both kinds of visitors happy. This script also uses cookies to store the user's choice for future visits.

To allow the user to switch between style sheets:

1. `<link href="sansStyle.css"`
   `→ rel="stylesheet" title="default">`

   Listing 12.16 shows a standard `link` to bring in an external style sheet, with one new twist: it has a `title` attribute with a value of "default". That comes into play later.

continues on page 317

Listing 12.16 This page has the content for the page and the user controls, and it calls the external style sheets that the user can choose.

```
<!DOCTYPE html>
<html>
<head>
    <title>Style Changer</title>
    <link href="script07.css" rel="stylesheet">
    <link href="sansStyle.css" rel="stylesheet" title="default">
    <link href="serifStyle.css" rel="alternate stylesheet" title="serif">
    <script src="script07.js"></script>
</head>
<body>
    <div class="navBar"><p>Change your font:</p>
        <input type="button" id="default" class="sansBtn" value="Sm Sans">
        <input type="button" id="serif" class="serifBtn" value="Lg Serif">
    </div>
    <p>Lorem ipsum dolor sit amet, consectetuer adipiscing elit. Aenean lacus elit, volutpat
    → vitae, egestas in, tristique ut, nibh. Donec congue lacinia magna. Duis tortor justo,
    → dapibus vel, vulputate sed, mattis sit amet, leo. Cras purus quam, semper quis, dignissim
    → id, hendrerit eget, ante. Nulla id lacus eget nulla bibendum venenatis. Duis faucibus
    → adipiscing mauris. Integer augue. In vulputate purus eget enim. Nam odio eros, porta vitae,
    → bibendum sit amet, iaculis nec, elit. Cras egestas scelerisque pede. Donec a tellus. Nullam
    → consectetuer fringilla nunc.</p>

    <p>Nam varius metus congue ligula. In hac habitasse platea dictumst. In ut ipsum a pede
    → rhoncus convallis. Sed at enim. Integer sed metus quis est egestas vestibulum. Quisque
    → mattis tortor a lorem. Nam diam. Integer consequat lectus. Donec molestie elementum nisl.
    → Donec ligula sapien, volutpat eget, dictum quis, mollis a, odio. Aliquam augue enim, gravida
    → nec, tempor ac, interdum in, urna. Aliquam mauris. Duis massa urna, ultricies id,
    → condimentum ac, gravida nec, dolor. Morbi et est quis enim gravida nonummy. Cum sociis
    → natoque penatibus et magnis dis parturient montes, nascetur ridiculus mus. Mauris nisl quam,
    → tincidunt ultrices, malesuada eget, posuere eu, lectus. Nulla a arcu. Sed consectetuer arcu
    → et velit. Quisque dignissim risus vel elit.</p>

    <p>Nunc massa mauris, dictum id, suscipit non, accumsan et, lorem. Suspendisse non lorem quis
    → dui rutrum vestibulum. Quisque mauris. Curabitur auctor nibh non enim. Praesent tempor
    → aliquam ligula. Fusce eu purus. Vivamus ac enim eget urna pulvinar bibendum. Integer
    → porttitor, augue et auctor volutpat, lectus dolor sagittis ipsum, sed posuere lacus pede
    → eget wisi. Proin vel arcu ac velit porttitor pellentesque. Maecenas mattis velit scelerisque
    → tellus. Cras eu tellus quis sapien malesuada porta. Nunc nulla. Nullam dapibus malesuada
    → lorem. Duis eleifend rutrum tellus. In tempor tristique neque. Mauris rhoncus. Aliquam
    → purus.</p>

    <p>Morbi felis quam, placerat sed, gravida a, bibendum a, mauris. Aliquam porta diam. Nam
    → consequat feugiat diam. Fusce luctus, felis ut gravida mattis, ante mi viverra sapien,
    → a vestibulum tellus lectus ut massa. Duis placerat. Aliquam molestie tellus. Suspendisse
    → potenti. Fusce aliquet tellus a lectus. Proin augue diam, sollicitudin eget, hendrerit
    → non, semper at, arcu. Sed suscipit tincidunt nibh. Donec ullamcorper. Nullam faucibus
    → euismod augue. Cras lacinia. Aenean scelerisque, lorem sed gravida varius, nunc tortor
    → gravida odio, sed sollicitudin pede augue ut metus. Maecenas condimentum ipsum et enim.
    → Sed nulla. Ut neque elit, varius a, blandit quis, facilisis sed, velit. Suspendisse aliquam
    → odio sed nibh.</p>
</body>
</html>
```

Listing 12.17 This Cascading Style Sheet contains the styles that always load, no matter which font style you've picked.

```css
body {
    margin: 0 20px;
    padding: 0;
    background-color: #FFF;
    color: #000;
}

div.navBar {
    background-color: #CCC;
    width: 175px;
    position: relative;
    top: -20px;
    right: -20px;
    float: right;
    padding: 20px 0 20px 20px;
    border-left: 2px groove #999;
    border-bottom: 2px groove #999;
}

.sansBtn {
    font: 12px/13px verdana, geneva, arial,
    ⇥ helvetica, sans-serif;
}

.serifBtn {
    font: 16px/17px "Times New Roman",
    ⇥ Times, serif;
}
```

2. ```html
<link href="serifStyle.css"
⇥ rel="alternate stylesheet"
⇥ title="serif">
```

Here's another style sheet, again using the **link** tag. However, the **rel** attribute isn't set to the usual **stylesheet**; instead, it's set to **alternate stylesheet**. This is because this style sheet isn't actually in use—instead, it'll only be used if the user chooses it.

3. ```html
<input type="button" id="default"
⇥ class="sansBtn" value="Sm Sans">
<input type="button" id="serif"
⇥ class="serifBtn"
⇥ value="Lg Serif">
```

There are two buttons: Sm Sans and Lg Serif. Clicking the former puts all the text on the page into a small sans-serif font, while clicking the latter puts all the text on the page into a larger, serif font. If supported by the browser, the styles in **Listing 12.17** cause the buttons to themselves appear in the destination font, giving the user a signal as to what they will see if they choose that button.

continues on next page

4. ```
   body, p, td, ol, ul, select, span,
   → div, input {
       font: 12px/13px verdana, geneva,
       → arial, helvetica, sans-serif;
   }
   ```

   Listing 12.18 (better known as **sansStyle.css**), just tells the browser that when it's loaded, every tag that it covers should be displayed in **12px Verdana** (or one of the other sans-serif fonts on the user's computer).

5. ```
   body, p, td, ol, ul, select, span,
   → div, input {
       font: 16px/17px "Times New
       → Roman", Times, serif;
   }
   ```

   In a complementary way, **Listing 12.19** (also better known as **serifStyle.css**) tells the browser that every tag that *it* covers should be displayed in **16px Times New Roman** (or again, any other serif font the browser can find).

Listing 12.18 This style sheet, **sansStyle.css**, changes all the text to a smaller, sans-serif font.

```
body, p, td, ol, ul, select, span, div,
→ input {
    font: 12px/13px verdana, geneva, arial,
    → helvetica, sans-serif;
}
```

Listing 12.19 This style sheet, **serifStyle.css**, changes the page text to a larger, serif font.

```
body, p, td, ol, ul, select, span, div,
→ input {
    font: 16px/17px "Times New Roman",
    → Times, serif;
}
```

Listing 12.20 This script handles setting the active style sheet.

```
window.addEventListener("load",initStyle,
→ false);
window.addEventListener("unload",
→ unloadStyle,false);

function initStyle() {
    var thisCookie = cookieVal("style");
    if (thisCookie) {
        var title = thisCookie;
    }
    else {
        var title = getPreferredStylesheet();
    }
    setActiveStylesheet(title);

    var allButtons = document.
    → getElementsByTagName("input");
    for (var i=0; i<allButtons.length; i++) {
        if (allButtons[i].type == "button") {
            allButtons[i].addEventListener
            → ("click",setActiveStylesheet,
            → false);
        }
    }
}

function unloadStyle() {
    var expireDate = new Date();
    expireDate.setYear(expireDate.
    → getFullYear()+1);
    document.cookie = "style=" +
    → getActiveStylesheet() + ";expires=" +
    → expireDate.toGMTString() + ";path=/";
}

function getPreferredStylesheet() {
    var thisLink, relAttribute;
    var linksFound = document.
    → getElementsByTagName("link");

    for (var i=0; i<linksFound.length; i++) {
```

listing continues on next page

6.
```
   var thisCookie =
   → cookieVal("style");
   if (thisCookie) {
      var title = thisCookie;
   }
   else {
      var title =
      → getPreferredStylesheet();
   }
   setActiveStylesheet(title);
```

The **initStyle()** function in **Listing 12.20** is loaded when the page runs, and its goal is to initialize everything that the page needs. Here, we're checking to see if the user has a cookie already set that saved their preferred style. Our old buddy the **cookieVal()** function comes back from Chapter 9 to read the cookies and see if there's one called "style". If there is, its value is the style sheet we want; if not, **getPreferredStylesheet()** is called. Once the desired style sheet is known, **setActiveStylesheet()** is called to set the wanted appearance.

continues on next page

7. ```
var allButtons = document.
→ getElementsByTagName("input");
for (var i=0; i<allButtons.length;
→ i++) {
   if (allButtons[i].type ==
   → "button") {
      allButtons[i].
      → addEventListener("click",
      → setActiveStylesheet,false);
   }
}
```

The **initStyle()** function also needs to add event handlers to our buttons. Here, we tell them both to call **setActiveStylesheet()** when they're clicked.

8. ```
function unloadStyle() {
   var expireDate = new Date();
   expireDate.setYear(expireDate.
   → getFullYear()+1);
   document.cookie = "style=" +
   → getActiveStylesheet() +
   → ";expires=" + expireDate.
   → toGMTString() + ";path=/";
}
```

When the page is unloaded, we need to set the cookie for the future. The cookie's expiration date is set to one year from today, **getActiveStylesheet()** is called to establish what the user currently has, and the cookie is written out for future use.

9. ```
function getPreferredStylesheet() {
   var thisLink, relAttribute;
   var linksFound = document.
   → getElementsByTagName("link");
```

If, when the page is loaded, there's no cookie saying which style the user has previously chosen, our script needs to be able to figure out what is the preferred style sheet. That's the goal of the **getPreferredStylesheet()** function in this step and the next.

*Listing 12.20 continued*

```
      thisLink = linksFound[i];
      relAttribute = thisLink.getAttribute
      → ("rel");
      if (relAttribute.indexOf("style") >
      → -1 && relAttribute.indexOf
      → ("alternate") == -1 && thisLink.
      → getAttribute("title")) {
         return thisLink.getAttribute
         → ("title");
      }
   }
   return "";
}

function getActiveStylesheet() {
   var thisLink, relAttribute;
   var linksFound = document.
   → getElementsByTagName("link");

   for (var i=0; i<linksFound.length; i++) {
      thisLink = linksFound[i];
      relAttribute = thisLink.getAttribute
      → ("rel");
      if (relAttribute.indexOf("style") >
      → -1 && thisLink.getAttribute("title")
      → && !thisLink.disabled) {
         return thisLink.getAttribute
         → ("title");
      }
   }
   return "";
}

function setActiveStylesheet(inVal) {
   var thisLink, relAttribute;
   var linksFound = document.
   → getElementsByTagName("link");

   if (inVal) {
      if (typeof inVal == "string") {
         var title = inVal;
      }
      else {
         var title = inVal.target.id;
      }
   }
```

listing continues on next page
```

Listing 12.20 *continued*

```
    else {
        var title = window.event.
        ⇢ srcElement.id;
    }

    for (var i=0; i<linksFound.length; i++) {
        thisLink = linksFound[i];
        relAttribute = thisLink.getAttribute
        ⇢ ("rel");
        if (relAttribute.indexOf("style") >
        ⇢ -1 && thisLink.getAttribute
        ⇢ ("title")) {
            if (thisLink.getAttribute("title")
            ⇢ == title) {
                thisLink.disabled = false;
            }
            else {
                thisLink.disabled = true;
            }
        }
    }
}

function cookieVal(cookieName) {
    var thisCookie = document.cookie.
    ⇢ split("; ");
    for (var i=0; i<thisCookie.length; i++) {
        if (cookieName == thisCookie[i].
        ⇢ split("=")[0]) {
            return thisCookie[i].split("=")
            ⇢ [1];
        }
    }
    return "";
}
```

listing continues on next page

10. ```
for (var i=0; i<linksFound.length;
⇢ i++) {
    thisLink = linksFound[i];
    relAttribute = thisLink.
    ⇢ getAttribute("rel");
    if (relAttribute.
    ⇢ indexOf("style") > -1 &&
    ⇢ relAttribute.indexOf
    ⇢ ("alternate") == -1 &&
    ⇢ thisLink.getAttribute
    ⇢ ("title")) {
        return thisLink.getAttribute
        ⇢ ("title");
    }
}
}
```

This function loops through each **link** tag, looking to see if each has a **rel** attribute, if that attribute has a value that contains "style", if that attribute has a value that does *not* contain "alternate", and if the tag has a **title** attribute. If one is found that matches all these criteria, that's the preferred style sheet, and its **title** attribute is returned.

To see which of the actual tags in our code is the preferred style sheet, look at the **link** tags in our HTML file. While there are three **link** tags, only two of them have **title** attributes. And of those two, one has a **rel** attribute of "stylesheet", while the other is "alternate stylesheet". Consequently, the preferred style sheet has to be **default**.

*continues on next page*
```

```
11. for (var i=0; i<linksFound.length;
    → i++) {
    thisLink = linksFound[i];
    relAttribute = thisLink.
    → getAttribute("rel");
    if (relAttribute.indexOf
    → ("style") > -1 && thisLink.
    → getAttribute("title") &&
    → !thisLink.disabled) {
        return thisLink.getAttribute
        → ("title");
    }
}
```

As mentioned above, we're going to want to use a cookie to store the user's chosen style sheet when they leave this site so that they'll be greeted with their favorite font when they return. While we could write out a cookie every time they click the style button, it's a better idea to only write it out once when they leave the site. Here, the **getActiveStylesheet()** function (which is called when the page is unloaded, as we saw above) looks through all the **link** tags, chooses the one that's currently enabled, and returns the **title** of that style.

```
12. var thisLink, relAttribute;
    var linksFound = document.
    → getElementsByTagName("link");

    if (inVal) {
        if (typeof inVal == "string") {
            var title = inVal;
        }
        else {
            var title = inVal.target.id;
        }
    }
    else {
        var title = window.event.
        → srcElement.id;
    }
```

As seen above, when the user loads this page, the **setActiveStylesheet()** function is called and passed a parameter that's referred to inside the function as **inVal**. When **setActiveStylesheet()** is called after a button is clicked, however, there may or may not be a parameter passed, depending on which browser is being used and how it handles events. Here's where we do a little checking to figure out how we got here and what the user wants to do. There are three possibilities:

▸ **initStyle()** called this function and passed it a string containing the preferred stylesheet. In this case, **inVal** exists and it's a string, so **title** is set to **inVal**.

▸ A style button was clicked in a browser that supports W3C-style events. In this case, **inVal** is automatically set to the event that triggered the function, so **inVal** will exist but it won't be a string. When that happens, we know that the **target** of the event (what caused the event to trigger) is the button that was clicked, and the **id** of that button stores the style desired.

▸ A style button was clicked in a browser that doesn't support W3C standards but does support the IE event model. If that's the case, the **inVal** variable won't exist, so we instead grab the style desired from **window.event.srcElement.id**.

continues on next page

13.
```
thisLink = linksFound[i];
relAttribute = thisLink.
→ getAttribute("rel");
if (relAttribute.indexOf
→ ("style") > -1 && thisLink.
→ getAttribute("title")) {
  if (thisLink.getAttribute
  → ("title") == title) {
    thisLink.disabled = false;
  }
  else {
    thisLink.disabled = true;
  }
}
```

The **setActiveStylesheet()** function loops through all the link tags in the document, checking each one to make sure that it has both a **rel** attribute that contains "style" and an existing **title** attribute. If both of these are true, the link is enabled if the **title** attribute is set to the **title** value and disabled if it is not.

So, if the current style sheet being used has the **title** attribute of "default", and the user clicks the Lg Serif button, JavaScript sees that it should load the **serif** style sheet. There's one **link** tag with a **title** of "serif", so all others (i.e., the **default** style sheet, in this case) are disabled, and only the **serif** style sheet is turned on.

Introducing Ajax

The web is always changing, and for web and JavaScript developers the ground shifted under their feet beginning in early 2005. New and immediately popular web applications appeared, some of them from Google, such as Gmail and Google Maps, and some from others, such as Flickr. The common denominator of all of these sites was that they acted more like desktop applications, with fast, responsive user interfaces. Instead of the traditional web application—where the user clicked, waited some number of seconds for the server to respond and refresh the page, and then repeated the process—these new sites were more reactive, updating pages right away, providing superior interaction, and making for a better user experience.

In This Chapter

There was something new (actually not so new, as we'll see) powering these sites: *Ajax*. You can use Ajax techniques to make your sites more responsive and attractive, which makes your site's users happier in the process. Best of all, you don't have to learn a completely new technology, because Ajax is made from building blocks you already know (and we've covered earlier in this book).

In this chapter, you'll learn how to request information from the server in the background and turn it into a form your Ajax application can use; automatically refresh the information from the server; build a cool previewing effect for objects on your page; and build an Ajax application that auto-completes form fields, just like a desktop application. Let's get to it.

Ajax: Pinning It Down

A This is the article that launched a zillion Ajax sites.

One of the interesting things about Ajax is that there is some confusion and even a little disagreement as to what Ajax really is. We know it's important and very popular; heck, we even changed the name of this book in previous editions to hitch onto Ajax's popularity. So here's our take on what Ajax is and isn't, and what we mean when we use the term.

First, a little history: In February 2005, Jesse James Garrett, a founder of Adaptive Path (a web interface and design shop in San Francisco), coined the term Ajax in an article on their site. He said Ajax was shorthand (but *not* an acronym) for "Asynchronous JavaScript and XML." You can read the article for yourself at **adaptivepath.com/ideas/ajax-new-approach-web-applications/ A**.

According to Garrett, Ajax was not in itself a new technology, but rather a technique combining several long-standing web technologies:

- Using HTML and CSS for structure and presentation
- Displaying and manipulating pages using the Document Object Model
- Using the browser's **XMLHttpRequest** object to transfer data between the client and the server
- Using XML as the format for the data flowing between the client and server
- And finally, using JavaScript to dynamically display and interact with all of the above

An Ajax application places an intermediary between the user and the server. This *Ajax engine* (also known as the JavaScript part of a webpage) provides an interface to the user (in concert, of course, with HTML and CSS), and if a user action doesn't require a request to the server (for example, displaying data that is already local), the Ajax engine responds. This allows the browser to react immediately to many user actions and makes the webpage act with the snappiness we've come to expect from our desktop programs. If the user action does require a server call, the Ajax engine performs it *asynchronously*—that is, without making the user wait for the server response; the user can continue to interact with the application, and the engine updates the page when the requested data arrives. The important part is that the user's actions don't come to a screeching halt while waiting for the server.

As the technique evolved, not all of the pieces had to be in place to call something an Ajax application, and this is where the confusion and disagreements set in. In fact, even the authors disagree about this:

Tom says, "I'm fine with just manipulating the page with the DOM, HTML and CSS, and JavaScript and calling it Ajax. There are tons of effects that people are referring to as Ajax, and the whole look of modern sites has changed because of this approach. The change from the static web to the dynamic webpage (sometimes called 'Web 2.0') owes its look and feel to the Ajax approach, whether or not there's a server call behind the scenes. Maybe calling it Ajax won't please the purists, but it's good enough for me."

Dori, who's the real JavaScript programmer in the family, says, "To call it Ajax, you need to transfer some data between the client and server. Otherwise, what's so new about it?"

Dori's writing the code, so for the most part in this chapter we're sticking to her sensibilities as to what an Ajax application is and what it should do. But elsewhere, we'll show you how to add some great (but still useful, not just flashy) eye candy to your sites.

Now, let's talk a little about what's not Ajax. Because you can do some cool visual effects on webpages using Ajax, some people think Ajax is *anything* you can do that looks good on a page, leading them to refer to things like interfaces made in Flash as "Ajax." But just saying it doesn't make it so. Ajax is not about loading up your sites with cute user interface widgets and adding user interface tweaks that are cool but change or break behaviors that people are used to with webpages.

That leads us to problems with Ajax, and they can be significant. For example, to work correctly, an Ajax site needs to be running in a reasonably modern browser. It also requires JavaScript. So what do you do about people using older browsers or who have turned JavaScript off? Or what about disabled users, or people who may be browsing your site with limited-capability handheld devices such as mobile phones or pads? The answer is that you must write your sites to degrade gracefully, meaning that users with less-capable browsers get a subset of your site's functionality or, at the minimum, get a meaningful error message explaining why they can't use your site.

Another potential problem with Ajax applications is that they may break the expected behavior of the browser's back button. With a static page, users expect that clicking the back button will move the browser to the last page it loaded. But because Ajax-enabled pages are dynamically updated, that might not be a valid expectation. There are solutions for the "back button problem," and before you dive wholeheartedly into Ajax, you should take the problem and its solutions into account.

Additionally, Ajax isn't dependent on specific server-side technologies. A number of companies tried to use the Ajax boom to sell their own server-side solutions—and that's what they're in business to do—but there's no reason why their products are required. So long as what's on the back end is something your JavaScript can read (i.e., XML), you're fine. Just because the guys in the snappy suits (*cough* IBM *cough*) wanted to hitch their buzzword-compliant products to Ajax's success in order to get you to buy doesn't mean you have to fall for it.

Listing 13.1 The HTML for the text and XML file request example.

```
<!DOCTYPE html>
<html>
<head>
     <title>My First Ajax Script</title>
     <script src="script01.js"></script>
</head>
<body>
     <p>
          <a id="makeTextRequest"
          ↪ href="gAddress.txt">Request a text
          ↪ file</a><br>
          <a id="makeXMLRequest"
          ↪ href="us-states.xml">Request an XML
          ↪ file</a>
     </p>
     <div id="updateArea"> </div>
</body>
</html>
```

Listing 13.2 This JavaScript gets the files from the server.

```
window.addEventListener("load",initAll,
↪ false);
var xhr = false;

function initAll() {
     document.getElementById
     ↪ ("makeTextRequest").addEventListener
     ↪ ("click",getNewFile,false);
     document.getElementById
     ↪ ("makeXMLRequest").addEventListener
     ↪ ("click",getNewFile,false);
}

function getNewFile(evt) {
     makeRequest(this.href);
     evt.preventDefault();
}

function makeRequest(url) {
     if (window.XMLHttpRequest) {
          xhr = new XMLHttpRequest();
     }
     else {
          if (window.ActiveXObject) {
               try {
                    xhr = new ActiveXObject
                    ↪ ("Microsoft.XMLHTTP");
```

listing continues on next page

Reading Server Data

We begin our exploration of Ajax with the basics: using the **XMLHttpRequest** object to retrieve and display information from a server.

To get the job done, we'll use **Listings 13.1** (HTML) and **13.2** (JavaScript). There are two possible files that can be read: the plain text file shown in **Listing 13.3** and the XML file that is **Listing 13.4**.

To request server data:

1. `var xhr = false;`

   In Listing 13.2, the **xhr** variable is one you'll be seeing a lot of in this chapter. It's an **XMLHttpRequest** object (or it will be later, after it's initialized). At this point, we just need to create it outside any functions in order to make it globally available.

2. `function initAll() {`
   `    document.getElementById`
   `    ↪ ("makeTextRequest").`
   `    ↪ addEventListener`
   `    ↪ ("click",getNewFile,false);`
   `    document.getElementById`
   `    ↪ ("makeXMLRequest").`
   `    ↪ addEventListener`
   `    ↪ ("click",getNewFile,false);`
   `}`

   When the page is first loaded, it knows to call the **initAll()** function. Here, we set two **click** handlers so that when a user clicks either of the links, the **getNewFile** function is triggered.

   continues on next page

3.
```
function getNewFile(evt) {
    makeRequest(this.href);
    evt.preventDefault();
}
```

Someone's clicked a link, so it's time to do something. Here, that something is to call **makeRequest()**—but that function needs to know which file was requested. Thankfully, we know that information is tucked away in **this.href**, so we can pass it along. When we come back we're done, so we tell the event to stop any further processing.

4.
```
if (window.XMLHttpRequest) {
    xhr = new XMLHttpRequest();
}
```

Now, we're inside **makeRequest()**, and it's here that things get interesting. Modern browsers support a native **XMLHttpRequest** object (see **Table 13.1**) as a property of **window**. So, we check to see if that property exists, and if it does, we create a new **XMLHttpRequest** object.

5.
```
if (window.ActiveXObject) {
    try {
        xhr = new ActiveXObject
        → ("Microsoft.XMLHTTP");
    }
    catch (e) {
    }
}
```

However, there's a browser that supports **XMLHttpRequest** that doesn't have a native version of the object, and that's Microsoft Internet Explorer (versions 5.5 and 6). In that case, we have to check to see if the browser supports ActiveX. If it does, we then check (using a **try**/**catch** error check) to see if we can create an **XMLHttpRequest** object based on ActiveX. If we can, great.

Listing 13.2 *continued*

```
        }
        catch (e) {
        }
    }
}

if (xhr) {
    xhr.addEventListener
    → ("readystatechange",showContents,
    → false);
    xhr.open("GET", url, true);
    xhr.send(null);
}
else {
    document.getElementById
    → ("updateArea").innerHTML = "Sorry,
    → but I couldn't create an
    → XMLHttpRequest";
}
}

function showContents() {
    if (xhr.readyState == 4) {
        if (xhr.status == 200) {
            if (xhr.responseXML &&
            → xhr.responseXML.childNodes.
            → length > 0) {
                var outMsg = getText
                → (xhr.responseXML.
                → getElementsByTagName
                → ("choices")[0]);
            }
            else {
                var outMsg = xhr.responseText;
            }
        }
        else {
            var outMsg = "There was a problem
            → with the request " + xhr.status;
        }
        document.getElementById
        → ("updateArea").innerHTML = outMsg;
    }
}

function getText(inVal) {
    if (inVal.textContent) {
        return inVal.textContent;
    }
    return inVal.text;
}
}
```

6. `if (xhr) {`
    `xhr.addEventListener`
    `→ ("readystatechange",`
    `→ showContents,false);`
    `xhr.open("GET", url, true);`
    `xhr.send(null);`
`}`

Either way, we should have a new **xhr** object, and if we do, we need to do the following three things with it:

▸ Set the **xhr**'s **readystatechange** event handler. Anytime the **xhr.readyState** property changes its value, this handler is triggered.

▸ We call **open()** and pass in three parameters: an HTTP request method (e.g., **"GET"**, **"POST"**, or **"HEAD"**), a URL to a file on the server, and a Boolean telling the server if the request is *asynchronous* (that is, if the script can go on as normal until the results come back, or if we need to sit around waiting for it).

▸ And finally, we **send()** the request we just created. If we were requesting a **POST**, the parameters would be passed here.

continues on next page

TABLE 13.1 The XMLHttpRequest Object

Properties	Methods	Event Handlers
readyState	abort	onload
response	addEventListener	onloadend
responseText	getAllResponseHeaders	onloadstart
responseXML	getResponseHeader	onreadystatechange
status	open	ontimeout
statusText	overrideMimeType	
timeout	send	
upload	setRequestHeader	
withCredentials		

7. ```
else {
    document.getElementById
    → ("updateArea").innerHTML =
    → "Sorry, but I couldn't create
    → an XMLHttpRequest";
}
```

If we end up here, we couldn't create an **XMLHttpRequest** for some reason, and there's nothing else that can be done.

8. ```
if (xhr.readyState == 4) {
    if (xhr.status == 200) {
```

Now we're down in the **showContents()** function. The **readyState** property can have one of several values (see **Table 13.2**), and every time the server changes its value, the **showContents()** function is triggered. However, we don't actually want to do anything (at least not here) until the request is finished, so we start off by checking to see if **readyState** is 4. If it is, we're good to go, and we can check to see what the request returned.

The first thing to check is the request's **status**, which will be a result code returned by the web server (servers routinely return these codes behind the scenes for every file served, although browsers only show them to you if there's an error). A status code of 200 means everything's fine. The status here is the same status returned by any web server call; for instance, if you ask for a file that doesn't exist you'll get a 404 error from the web server.

TABLE 13.2 readyState Property Values

Value	What It Means
0	Uninitialized; object contains no data
1	The object has been opened and is currently loading its data
2	The requested headers have been received
3	Loading; user may interact with the object even though it is not fully loaded
4	Complete; object has finished initializing

Listing 13.3 The requested text file.

```
Four score and seven years ago our fathers
→ brought forth on this continent, a new
→ nation, conceived in Liberty, and
→ dedicated to the proposition that all men
→ are created equal.

Now we are engaged in a great civil war,
→ testing whether that nation, or any nation
→ so conceived and so dedicated, can long
→ endure. We are met on a great battle-
→ field of that war. We have come to
→ dedicate a portion of that field, as a
→ final resting place for those who here
→ gave their lives that that nation might
→ live. It is altogether fitting and proper
→ that we should do this.

But, in a larger sense, we can not dedicate
→ -- we can not consecrate -- we can not
→ hallow -- this ground. The brave men,
→ living and dead, who struggled here, have
→ consecrated it, far above our poor power
→ to add or detract. The world will little
→ note, nor long remember what we say here,
→ but it can never forget what they did
→ here. It is for us the living, rather,
→ to be dedicated here to the unfinished
→ work which they who fought here have thus
→ far so nobly advanced. It is rather for
→ us to be here dedicated to the great
→ task remaining before us -- that from
→ these honored dead we take increased
→ devotion to that cause for which they gave
→ the last full measure of devotion -- that
→ we here highly resolve that these dead
→ shall not have died in vain -- that this
→ nation, under God, shall have a new birth
→ of freedom -- and that government of the
→ people, by the people, for the people,
→ shall not perish from the earth.
```

9. ```
   if (xhr.responseXML &&
   → xhr.responseXML.childNodes.
   → length > 0) {
     var outMsg = getText
     → (xhr.responseXML.
     → getElementsByTagName
     → ("choices")[0]);
   }
   else {
     var outMsg = xhr.responseText;
   }
   ```

If we're here, everything is fine, and we want to look at what the server actually gave us. There were two different types of files we could be reading, so we need to check what type of data we got back. The **responseXML** property contains the data if it's XML. However, it sometimes contains a value even when the data isn't XML. If **responseXML.childNodes.length** is greater than zero (that is, it contains more than just a dummy object), then we know we've got a properly formatted DOM object back, and we can use commands we've seen before (such as **getElementsByTagName()**) to traverse its nodes. In fact, we'll use just that approach here, and pass its result to the **getText()** function. The value it returns gets saved in **outMsg**.

If what we got back isn't valid XML, then it's our text file. In that case, we want to put **xhr**'s **responseText** property into **outMsg**.

continues on next page
   ```

10.
```
else {
    var outMsg = "There was a
    → problem with the request " +
    → xhr.status;
}
```

If what we got back had a **status** other than 200, we've got a problem, so we set **outMsg** to say that and append the status error so we can try to figure out what the problem is.

11.
```
document.getElementById
→ ("updateArea").innerHTML =
→ outMsg;
```

And finally, we take **outMsg** and write it to the document, as shown in .

12.
```
if (inVal.textContent) {
    return inVal.textContent;
}
return inVal.text;
```

Here's **getText()**; all it does is look to see if whatever came in has a **textContent** property. If it does, it gets returned; if not, we return its **text** property instead.

 By clicking the appropriate link, you can fetch either a text file of the Gettysburg Address (top) or an XML file of U.S. states and their abbreviations (bottom).

Listing 13.4 And this is the requested XML file.

```xml
<?xml version="1.0"?>
<choices xml:lang="EN">
  <item><label>Alabama</label><value>AL</value></item>
  <item><label>Alaska</label><value>AK</value></item>
  <item><label>Arizona</label><value>AZ</value></item>
  <item><label>Arkansas</label><value>AR</value></item>
  <item><label>California</label><value>CA</value></item>
  <item><label>Colorado</label><value>CO</value></item>
  <item><label>Connecticut</label><value>CT</value></item>
  <item><label>Delaware</label><value>DE</value></item>
  <item><label>Florida</label><value>FL</value></item>
  <item><label>Georgia</label><value>GA</value></item>
  <item><label>Hawaii</label><value>HI</value></item>
  <item><label>Idaho</label><value>ID</value></item>
  <item><label>Illinois</label><value>IL</value></item>
  <item><label>Indiana</label><value>IN</value></item>
  <item><label>Iowa</label><value>IA</value></item>
  <item><label>Kansas</label><value>KS</value></item>
  <item><label>Kentucky</label><value>KY</value></item>
  <item><label>Louisiana</label><value>LA</value></item>
  <item><label>Maine</label><value>ME</value></item>
  <item><label>Maryland</label><value>MD</value></item>
  <item><label>Massachusetts</label><value>MA</value></item>
  <item><label>Michigan</label><value>MI</value></item>
  <item><label>Minnesota</label><value>MN</value></item>
  <item><label>Mississippi</label><value>MS</value></item>
  <item><label>Missouri</label><value>MO</value></item>
  <item><label>Montana</label><value>MT</value></item>
  <item><label>Nebraska</label><value>NE</value></item>
  <item><label>Nevada</label><value>NV</value></item>
  <item><label>New Hampshire</label><value>NH</value></item>
  <item><label>New Jersey</label><value>NJ</value></item>
  <item><label>New Mexico</label><value>NM</value></item>
  <item><label>New York</label><value>NY</value></item>
  <item><label>North Carolina</label><value>NC</value></item>
  <item><label>North Dakota</label><value>ND</value></item>
  <item><label>Ohio</label><value>OH</value></item>
  <item><label>Oklahoma</label><value>OK</value></item>
  <item><label>Oregon</label><value>OR</value></item>
  <item><label>Pennsylvania</label><value>PA</value></item>
  <item><label>Rhode Island</label><value>RI</value></item>
  <item><label>South Carolina</label><value>SC</value></item>
  <item><label>South Dakota</label><value>SD</value></item>
  <item><label>Tennessee</label><value>TN</value></item>
  <item><label>Texas</label><value>TX</value></item>
  <item><label>Utah</label><value>UT</value></item>
  <item><label>Vermont</label><value>VT</value></item>
  <item><label>Virginia</label><value>VA</value></item>
  <item><label>Washington</label><value>WA</value></item>
  <item><label>West Virginia</label><value>WV</value></item>
  <item><label>Wisconsin</label><value>WI</value></item>
  <item><label>Wyoming</label><value>WY</value></item>
</choices>
```

TIP Because of the way Ajax works, when you are doing your development and testing, the files you're reading must reside on a server; they can't just be local files.

TIP Back in step 5, we said IE 5.5 and 6 used an ActiveX control to create the XMLHttpRequest object. Thankfully, IE versions 7 and up have a native object, so that's no longer required. However, this means you always have to check for the existence of a native object first—if you check for window.ActiveXObject first, that will be true for IE7+, and then you'll be going down the wrong path. A considerable amount of older, pre-IE7 Ajax code has this problem.

TIP If it matters deeply to your code which version of Microsoft's ActiveX object you actually get, here's a code snippet for you to use instead:

```
if (window.ActiveXObject) {
    try {
        xhr = new ActiveXObject
        → ("Msxml2.XMLHTTP");
    }
    catch (e) {
        try {
            xhr = new ActiveXObject
            → ("Microsoft.XMLHTTP");
        }
        catch (e) { }
    }
}
```

This approach attempts to use the IE6 version (Msxml2.XMLHTTP) of the XMLHttpRequest object first and only falls back to the older version if it can't find it. However, the Microsoft.XMLHTTP version should always give you the latest version available on the PC, so we'll just be using that in this chapter—because eventually, the older code will be going away.

TIP One drawback of Ajax calls is that they can be cached; that is, it looks like your application is contacting the server and getting new data, but it's really just looking at stuff it read previously. If that's the case, setting the headers of the request can help. Adding one or more of these can help force recalcitrant servers to fork over the goods:

```
xhr.setRequestHeader("If-Modified-
→ Since","Wed, 15 Jan 1995 01:00:00
→ GMT");
xhr.setRequestHeader("Cache-Control",
→ "no-cache");
xhr.setRequestHeader("Cache-Control",
→ "must-revalidate");
xhr.setRequestHeader("Cache-Control",
→ "no-store");
xhr.setRequestHeader("Pragma",
→ "no-cache");
xhr.setRequestHeader("Expires","0");
```

TIP You can force the call to return XML data by overriding the MIME type:

```
xhr.overrideMimeType("text/xml");
```

However, this may cause problems with certain browsers and configurations, so use it with care.

Listing 13.5 This simple HTML page will be much more impressive with the addition of some JavaScript.

```html
<!DOCTYPE html>
<html>
<head>
    <title>My Second Ajax Script</title>
    <link rel="stylesheet"
    → href="script02.css">
    <script src="script02.js"></script>
</head>
<body>
    <div id="pictureBar"> </div>
</body>
</html>
```

Listing 13.6 Only a little bit of CSS, but it's needed to make the page look good.

```css
img {
    border-width: 0;
    margin: 5px;
}
```

Parsing Server Data

Once we have data from the server, we have to find the exact information we need and make sure it is in a format that our Ajax application can use. To do that, we'll first examine the information. Because the data is a nicely structured XML document, our script walks the XML document tree to find and extract the particular data we need and store it in variables. Then, if needed, the script can reformat the data for later use.

The HTML and CSS in **Listings 13.5** and **13.6** couldn't be much simpler, so we're only going to look at the code in the JavaScript file, **Listing 13.7**. For this task, the XML file is data about photographs stored on Flickr; a portion of the XML can be seen in **Listing 13.8**.

To parse information from the server:

1. ```
   xhr.addEventListener
   → ("readystatechange",
   → showPictures,false);
   xhr.open("GET", "flickrfeed.xml",
   → true);
   ```

   Every time **readyState** changes, we want to call the **showPictures()** function. The file name we want to read off the server is **flickrfeed.xml**. Both those values are set here.

2. ```
   var tempText =
   → document.createElement("div");
   var theText;
   ```

   Down in **showPictures()** is where the real work is done. We start by creating variables to store two elements: **tempText** and **theText**, the former of which is a temporary **div** placeholder.

   continues on next page

3. `var allImages = xhr.responseXML.`
   `→ getElementsByTagName("content");`

   The response back from the server contained XML, so we're taking that response and looking for every **content** node. If you take a look at the XML in Listing 13.8, you'll see there's a lot of stuff there we don't care about at all—in fact, all we want is what's in the **<a>** tags (and really, only half of those). Here, we've started to narrow down to just what we want.

4. `for (var i=0; i<allImages.length;`
   `→ i++) {`

   Now we need to loop through all the nodes we found to get the actual data we want.

5. `tempText.innerHTML =`
   `getPixVal(allImages[i]);`

   Calling **getPixVal()** (described later) gives us the text of the **i**th **<content>** node.

continues on page 342

Getting Your Data

One of the things people want to do when they first hear about Ajax is write JavaScript that reads in all kinds of XML files (including RSS and Atom feeds), mash them up, and then put the results on their own webpage.

The bad news: it doesn't quite work that way—a script can only read a file that comes from the same server as the one the script itself is on. If you think about it for a while, you'll start to figure out why; after all, if a script could read anything, then that would open up all kinds of possible security scams and fake sites.

The sort-of good news: you can have a program on your web server go out periodically, grab an XML file, and store it locally. Once you've done that, your Ajax application will have no problems reading it. In this example and the next, it's assumed you've got something running that grabs the Flickr data file of your choice periodically and saves it on your server. How to do that, though, is beyond the scope of this book.

The better news, though, is that you can (in some cases) use a script that's hosted by the destination server itself—which can then read its own files and report the results back to you. We'll see an example of that shortly.

Listing 13.7 The additional JavaScript in this script allows you to parse the data you previously requested.

```
window.addEventListener("load",initAll,false);
var xhr = false;

function initAll() {
    if (window.XMLHttpRequest) {
        xhr = new XMLHttpRequest();
    }
    else {
        if (window.ActiveXObject) {
            try {
                xhr = new ActiveXObject("Microsoft.XMLHTTP");
            }
            catch (e) {
            }
        }
    }

    if (xhr) {
        xhr.addEventListener("readystatechange",showPictures,false);
        xhr.open("GET", "flickrfeed.xml", true);
        xhr.send(null);
    }
    else {
        alert("Sorry, but I couldn't create an XMLHttpRequest");
    }
}

function showPictures() {
    var tempText = document.createElement("div");
    var theText;

    if (xhr.readyState == 4) {
        if (xhr.status == 200) {
            var allImages = xhr.responseXML.getElementsByTagName("content");

            for (var i=0; i<allImages.length; i++) {
                tempText.innerHTML = getPixVal(allImages[i]);

                theText = tempText.getElementsByTagName("p")[1].innerHTML;
                theText = theText.replace(/240/g,"75");
                theText = theText.replace(/180/g,"75");
                theText = theText.replace(/_m/g,"_s");
                document.getElementById("pictureBar").innerHTML += theText;
            }
        }
        else {
            alert("There was a problem with the request " + xhr.status);
        }
    }

    function getPixVal(inVal) {
        return (inVal.textContent) ? inVal.textContent : inVal.text;
    }
}
```

6. `theText = tempText.`
`→ getElementsByTagName("p")[1].`
`→ innerHTML;`
`theText = theText.replace`
`→ (/240/g,"75");`
`theText = theText.replace`
`→ (/180/g,"75");`
`theText = theText.replace`
`→ (/_m/g,"_s");`

As previously mentioned, we only want half the `<a>` nodes, so we winnow out the ones we don't want. In a file with information about 20 photos, there will be 20 `<content>` nodes, each of which contains two paragraphs. Each `<content>` node contains the photographer's name (linked to their Flickr page), followed by an image that links to the Flickr-hosted version. We want just the latter, so we can just take the **innerHTML** from the second paragraph of **theText**, which gives us the `<a>` inside the paragraph (and the `<img>` tag it contains, as well).

Next, we're using regular expressions to tweak the results. Flickr has sent us the tags for the medium-sized version of the image, but we only want the thumbnail version. Because our images are either 240 wide by 180 tall or 180 wide by 240 tall (that is, they're either horizontal or vertical), and we know the thumbnails are always 75 x 75, we just find any use of the numbers 240 or 180 in the text and change them to 75. We finish up by changing the image name itself; Flickr gives the medium-sized version a name that ends with _m, while the small version ends with _s, so we can just swap one for the other.

A These thumbnail images were read from Flickr.

7. `document.getElementById`
`→ ("pictureBar").innerHTML +=`
`→ theText;`

Inside the loop, we take the now-modified node we want and then append it onto the HTML page's **pictureBar**. The end result is as we see it in Ⓐ, where every thumbnail image on the page is a link back to the full-sized version.

8. `return (inVal.textContent) ?`
`→ inVal.textContent : inVal.text;`

Because we've got XML data, we can use its **textContent** (or **text**, as the case may be) property to get the text of the node. Here's the entire contents of the **getPixVal()** function—fundamentally, it's identical to the **getText()** function seen in Listing 13.2, except that it uses an alternate syntax (covered back in Chapter 2's "There's No One Right Way" sidebar).

TIP While you can't read a data file that's stored on another server (see the "Getting Your Data" sidebar for more about why that's the case), you can always have your HTML file load information from another server. Here, your webpage, no matter where it is, is able to display images from Flickr's servers.

TIP One of the best things about newer web-based companies is that they understand that people want access to data—and not just their own data, but other people's data (when they've agreed to make it public) as well. For instance, it's possible to search Flickr for all the photographs containing the tags "Hawaii" and "sunset," and then get the result as an XML file. Combine that with this script or the next, and you'll always have new and lovely photos on your page.

Listing 13.8 This is an edited and shortened version of the XML file Flickr provides. The original was approximately 500 lines long!

```
<?xml version="1.0" encoding="utf-8" standalone="yes"?>
<feed xmlns="http://www.w3.org/2005/Atom"
      xmlns:dc="http://purl.org/dc/elements/1.1/"  xmlns:flickr="urn:flickr:" xmlns:media=
   ➝ "http://search.yahoo.com/mrss/">

    <title>Content from Paradise Ridge Sculpture Grove</title>
    <link rel="self" href="http://api.flickr.com/services/feeds/photoset.gne?set=
   ➝ 72157600976524175&amp;nsid=23922109@N00&amp;lang=en-us" />
    <link rel="alternate" type="text/html" href="http://www.flickr.com/photos/dorismith/
   ➝ sets/72157600976524175"/>
    <id>tag:flickr.com,2005:http://www.flickr.com/photos/23922109@N00/sets/72157600976524175</id>
    <icon>http://farm2.static.flickr.com/1335/882568164_72eee9b41f_s.jpg</icon>
    <subtitle>The &lt;a href=&quot;http://www.paradiseridgewinery.com/&quot;&gt;Paradise Ridge
   ➝ Winery&lt;/a&gt; not only has great wines, but they also have a sculpture garden. We visited
   ➝ on 22 July 2007.</subtitle>
    <updated>2007-07-24T05:19:08Z</updated>
    <generator uri="http://www.flickr.com/">Flickr</generator>

    <entry>
      <title>IMG_0045.JPG</title>
      <link rel="alternate" type="text/html" href="http://www.flickr.com/photos/dorismith/
   ➝ 882590644/in/set-72157600976524175/"/>
      <id>tag:flickr.com,2005:/photo/882590644/in/set-72157600976524175</id>
      <published>2007-07-24T05:19:08Z</published>
      <updated>2007-07-24T05:19:08Z</updated>
      <dc:date.Taken>2007-07-22T13:42:49-08:00</dc:date.Taken>
      <content type="html">&lt;p&gt;&lt;a href=&quot;http://www.flickr.com/people/dorismith/
   ➝ &quot;&gt;Dori Smith&lt;/a&gt; posted a photo:&lt;/p&gt;&lt;p&gt;&lt;a
   ➝ href=&quot;http://www.flickr.com/photos/dorismith/882590644/&quot; title=&quot;
   ➝ IMG_0045.JPG&quot;&gt;&lt;img src=&quot;http://farm2.static.flickr.com/1063/
   ➝ 882590644_5a4a0d89f3_m.jpg&quot; width=&quot;240&quot; height=&quot;180&quot;
   ➝ alt=&quot;IMG_0045.JPG&quot; /&gt;&lt;/a&gt;&lt;/p&gt;

      </content>
      <author>
         <name>Dori Smith</name>
         <uri>http://www.flickr.com/people/dorismith/</uri>
      </author>
      <link rel="enclosure" type="image/jpeg" href="http://farm2.static.flickr.com/1063/
   ➝ 882590644_5a4a0d89f3_m.jpg" />

      <category term="winery" scheme="http://www.flickr.com/photos/tags/" />
      <category term="sonomacounty" scheme="http://www.flickr.com/photos/tags/" />
      <category term="sculptures" scheme="http://www.flickr.com/photos/tags/" />
      <category term="dorismith" scheme="http://www.flickr.com/photos/tags/" />
      <category term="paradiseridge" scheme="http://www.flickr.com/photos/tags/" />
      <category term="paradiseridgesculptures" scheme="http://www.flickr.com/photos/tags/" />
    </entry>
```

listing continues on next page

Listing 13.8 *continued*

```
<entry>
    <title>IMG_0032.JPG</title>
    <link rel="alternate" type="text/html" href="http://www.flickr.com/photos/dorismith/
→ 882568164/in/set-72157600976524175/"/>
    <id>tag:flickr.com,2005:/photo/882568164/in/set-72157600976524175</id>
    <published>2007-07-24T05:15:14Z</published>
    <updated>2007-07-24T05:15:14Z</updated>
    <dc:date.Taken>2007-07-22T13:35:09-08:00</dc:date.Taken>
    <content type="html">&lt;p&gt;&lt;a href=&quot;http://www.flickr.com/people/dorismith/
→ &quot;&gt;Dori Smith&lt;/a&gt; posted a photo:&lt;/p&gt;&lt;p&gt;&lt;a
→ href=&quot;http://www.flickr.com/photos/dorismith/882568164/&quot; title=&quot;
→ IMG_0032.JPG&quot;&gt;&lt;img src=&quot;http://farm2.static.flickr.com/1335/
→ 882568164_72eee9b41f_m.jpg&quot; width=&quot;240&quot; height=&quot;180&quot;
→ alt=&quot;IMG_0032.JPG&quot; /&gt;&lt;/a&gt;&lt;/p&gt;

    </content>
    <author>
        <name>Dori Smith</name>
        <uri>http://www.flickr.com/people/dorismith/</uri>
    </author>
    <link rel="enclosure" type="image/jpeg" href="http://farm2.static.flickr.com/1335/
→ 882568164_72eee9b41f_m.jpg" />

    <category term="winery" scheme="http://www.flickr.com/photos/tags/" />
    <category term="sonomacounty" scheme="http://www.flickr.com/photos/tags/" />
    <category term="sculptures" scheme="http://www.flickr.com/photos/tags/" />
    <category term="dorismith" scheme="http://www.flickr.com/photos/tags/" />
    <category term="paradiseridge" scheme="http://www.flickr.com/photos/tags/" />
    <category term="paradiseridgesculptures" scheme="http://www.flickr.com/photos/tags/" />
</entry>

</feed>
```

Refreshing Server Data

Our Ajax application fetched information from the server and then parsed and acted upon the data. Now we'll show you how to make the application retrieve a new version of the data from the server, which automatically refreshes the page. Listing 13.9 contains the necessary JavaScript.

To refresh server information:

1. ```
   function getPix() {
       xhr.open("GET", "flickrfeed.
       → xml", true);
       xhr.addEventListener
       → ("readystatechange",
       → showPictures,false);
       xhr.send(null);

       setTimeout(getPix,5 * 1000);
   }
   ```

   Where the previous script did its **xhr** call inside **initAll()**, this script pushes it down into its own function, **getPix()**. There's one addition: the **setTimeout()** afterwards. Five seconds after the script has grabbed a random image, it goes and gets another.

Listing 13.9 Use this script to automatically refresh server information.

```
window.addEventListener("load",initAll,
→ false);
var xhr = false;

function initAll() {
    if (window.XMLHttpRequest) {
        xhr = new XMLHttpRequest();
    }
    else {
        if (window.ActiveXObject) {
            try {
                xhr = new ActiveXObject
                → ("Microsoft.XMLHTTP");
            }
            catch (e) {
            }
        }
    }

    if (xhr) {
        getPix();
    }
    else {
        alert("Sorry, but I couldn't create
        → an XMLHttpRequest");
    }
}

function getPix() {
    xhr.open("GET", "flickrfeed.xml", true);
    xhr.addEventListener("readystatechange",
    → showPictures,false);
    xhr.send(null);

    setTimeout(getPix, 5 * 1000);
}

function showPictures() {
    var tempText = document.createElement
    → ("div");

    if (xhr.readyState == 4) {
        if (xhr.status == 200) {
```

listing continues on next page
```

Listing 13.9 *continued*

```
            var allImages = xhr.responseXML.
            → getElementsByTagName
            → ("content");
            var randomImg = Math.floor
            → (Math.random() * allImages.
            → length);

            tempText.innerHTML = getPixVal
            → (allImages[randomImg]);
            var thisImg = tempText.
            → getElementsByTagName("p")[1];
            document.getElementById
            → ("pictureBar").innerHTML =
            → thisImg.innerHTML;
        }
        else {
            alert("There was a problem with
            → the request " + xhr.status);
        }
    }

    function getPixVal(inVal) {
        return (inVal.textContent) ?
        → inVal.textContent : inVal.text;
    }
}
```

2. ```
   var randomImg = Math.floor
   → (Math.random() * allImages.
   → length);

   tempText.innerHTML = getPixVal
   → (allImages[randomImg]);
   var thisImg = tempText.
   → getElementsByTagName("p")[1];
   ```

Instead of looping as we did in the previous task, this time we only want a single, random image. We start by calculating a random number between zero and one less than the number of images, using **Math.random()** and **Math.floor()** as we did back in Chapter 4 in "Displaying a Random Image." We use that random number as an index into the **allImages** array, getting our precise node from the **getPixVal()** function.

continues on next page
   ```

3. `document.getElementById`
→ `("pictureBar").innerHTML =`
→ `thisImg.innerHTML;`

Now that we've got our single image, we put it into our webpage .

TIP You might wonder why this script bothers to read from the same XML file every time—after all, if the file isn't changing, why not just keep the data in variables after the first time through? If you keep in mind the technique referred to in the previous sidebar ("Getting Your Data"), you'll then realize the XML file could be changing at any point. Say your server-side program grabs a new version of the XML file every few minutes—why should anyone have to wait to see the latest pictures? This way, your site's visitors always get the most recent version.

TIP If you take the approach just mentioned, you're likely to run into the Ajax drawback covered earlier in this chapter: caching. Different browsers (and different versions, and different platforms) all have their own unique caching peculiarities, most of which are solved by modifying the headers as discussed earlier. Another solution many recommend is to change the GET to a POST. But here's what we've found works: instead of the order in which they're seen in Listing 13.2, we've swapped the order of `open()` and `addEventListener()` in Listing 13.9, as shown in step 1.

A The script fetches one image after another.

```
<!DOCTYPE html>
<html>
<head>
    <title>Using JSON Data</title>
    <link rel="stylesheet"
    → href="script02.css">
    <script src="script04.js"></script>
    <script src="http://api.flickr.com/
    → services/feeds/photoset.gne?nsid=
    → 23922109@N00&set=72157600976524175&
    → format=json"></script>
</head>
<body>
    <div id="pictureBar"> </div>
</body>
</html>
```

Listing 13.11 Our JavaScript file can be short
because most of the work is being done by the
remote server.

```
window.addEventListener("load",initAll,
→ false);
var imgDiv = "";

function initAll() {
    document.getElementById("pictureBar").
    → innerHTML = imgDiv;
}

function jsonFlickrFeed(flickrData) {
    for (var i=0; i<flickrData.items.length;
    → i++) {
        imgDiv += "<img src='";
        imgDiv += flickrData.items[i].
        → media.m.replace(/_m/g,"_s");
        imgDiv += "' alt='" + flickrData.
        → items[i].title + "'>";
    }
}
```

Getting Data From a Server

As mentioned in the earlier sidebar "Getting Your Data," Ajax limits where you can read data from. After all, you don't want everyone in the world reading any file you have, right? But there are cases in which a company may want people to read files and then be able to create their own content on their own sites. For instance, Flickr (as seen in the previous examples) lets your server get their XML files, and what you do next is only up to your imagination.

But sometimes you don't have that kind of access to a server—so Flickr has also made files available in another format: JavaScript Object Notation, known as JSON (pronounced like the name Jason). The neat trick here is in the HTML file, **Listing 13.10**; the JavaScript file (**Listing 13.11**) just takes advantage of it.

To read and parse server data:

1. **`<script src="http://api.flickr.com/`**
   `→ services/feeds/photoset.`
   `→ gne?nsid=23922109@N00&set=`
   `→ 72157600976524175&format=json">`
   `→ </script>`

   Remember how we said earlier that a script can only read files from the same server on which it resides? That's still true—but there's nothing that says you can't call a script file that itself is on another server. In this case, the script is on the **api.flickr.com** machine, and therefore, it can read in data from that server.

   continues on next page

2. `document.getElementById`
   → `("pictureBar").innerHTML =`
   → `imgDiv;`

   Back over in the JavaScript file, this single line of code puts all the images onto the page when it loads, as seen in 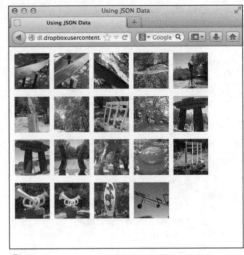 **Ⓐ**.

3. `function jsonFlickrFeed`
   → `(flickrData) {`

   By now, you're surely wondering where all the code is that sets up the images, and here's the other part of the slick functionality: it's mostly in the data file itself (**Listing 13.12**). What JSON gets you is a data file containing code that JavaScript recognizes. In this case, the data file says it's expecting to find a function named **jsonFlickrFeed()**, so here we've created one. Whatever name we give the parameter coming in is where the data itself is stored.

Ⓐ Not only do the images come from Flickr's servers, but so does the data used to create the page.

4. ```
for (var i=0; i<flickrData.items.
→ length; i++) {
  imgDiv += "<img src='";
  imgDiv += flickrData.items[i].
  → media.m.replace(/_m/g,"_s");
  imgDiv += "' alt='" +
  → flickrData.items[i].title +
  → "'>";
}
```

   Because we have the data in a format JavaScript already understands, we don't have much work to do. Here, we loop through all the images in the **items** array, building one large text string that will (in step 2, above) be displayed on the screen. Each element in **items** has a variety of information about an image, but all we want is the URL, which is stored in **media.m**. And once again, a little bit of regular expression magic turns our medium-sized image into a thumbnail.
```

Listing 13.12 An excerpt of the JSON file—note that it's about half the size of the XML file, while including all the same data.

```
jsonFlickrFeed({
    "title": "Content from Paradise Ridge Sculpture Grove",
    "link": "http://www.flickr.com/photos/dorismith/sets/72157600976524175",
    "description": "The &lt;a href=&quot;http://www.paradiseridgewinery.com/&quot;&gt;Paradise
→ Ridge Winery&lt;/a&gt; not only has great wines, but they also have a sculpture garden.
→ We visited on 22 July 2007.",
    "modified": "2007-07-24T05:19:08Z",
    "generator": "http://www.flickr.com/",
    "items": [
        {
            "title": "IMG_0045.JPG",
            "link": "http://www.flickr.com/photos/dorismith/882590644/in/set-72157600976524175/",
            "media": {"m":"http://farm2.static.flickr.com/1063/882590644_5a4a0d89f3_m.jpg"},
            "date_taken": "2007-07-22T13:42:49-08:00",
            "description": "&lt;p&gt;&lt;a href=&quot;http://www.flickr.com/people/dorismith/
→ &quot;&gt;Dori Smith&lt;/a&gt; posted a photo:&lt;/p&gt; &lt;p&gt;&lt;a href=&quot;
→ http://www.flickr.com/photos/dorismith/882590644/&quot; title=&quot;IMG_0045.JPG&quot;
→ &gt;&lt;img src=&quot;http://farm2.static.flickr.com/1063/882590644_5a4a0d89f3_m.
→ jpg&quot; width=&quot;240&quot; height=&quot;180&quot; alt=&quot;IMG_0045.JPG&quot;
→ /&gt;&lt;/a&gt;&lt;/p&gt; ",
            "published": "2007-07-24T05:19:08Z",
            "author": "nobody@flickr.com (Dori Smith)",
            "author_id": "23922109@N00",
            "tags": "winery sonomacounty sculptures dorismith paradiseridge paradiseridgesculptures"
        },
        {
            "title": "IMG_0032.JPG",
            "link": "http://www.flickr.com/photos/dorismith/882568164/in/set-72157600976524175/",
            "media": {"m":"http://farm2.static.flickr.com/1335/882568164_72eee9b41f_m.jpg"},
            "date_taken": "2007-07-22T13:35:09-08:00",
            "description": "&lt;p&gt;&lt;a href=&quot;http://www.flickr.com/people/dorismith/
→ &quot;&gt;Dori Smith&lt;/a&gt; posted a photo:&lt;/p&gt; &lt;p&gt;&lt;a href=&quot;
→ http://www.flickr.com/photos/dorismith/882568164/&quot; title=&quot;IMG_0032.JPG&quot;
→ &gt;&lt;img src=&quot;http://farm2.static.flickr.com/1335/882568164_72eee9b41f_m.
→ jpg&quot; width=&quot;240&quot; height=&quot;180&quot; alt=&quot;IMG_0032.JPG&quot;
→ /&gt;&lt;/a&gt;&lt;/p&gt; ",
            "published": "2007-07-24T05:15:14Z",
            "author": "nobody@flickr.com (Dori Smith)",
            "author_id": "23922109@N00",
            "tags": "winery sonomacounty sculptures dorismith paradiseridge paradiseridgesculptures"
        }
    ]
})
```

TIP If you're wondering why JSON sounds slightly familiar, we introduced it when covering Object Literals in Chapter 10. The JSON format itself is a subset of the object literal. And if JSON doesn't sound familiar, you might want to go back and review that section to learn more.

TIP You won't always use exactly the URL that's in step 1; in fact, if you do, you'll just get the same results shown on this page. Flickr allows you to put in many combinations of tags, sets, and groups so that you'll get personalized results. Go to Flickr, find the webpage matching what you want in your images file, and find the feed directions on that page. Once you've got that, just add `&format=json` to the end of the URL, and you should be set.

TIP Another name for the function in step 3 is *callback*. So long as you put your code into a correctly named callback function, it will run—but give it a name that's even slightly off and nothing at all will happen.

A When you hover over a link, this script reads the HTML file on the server and gives you an overlay containing a preview of the first few lines of the file.

Listing 13.13 This HTML builds the page for the preview example.

```
<!DOCTYPE html>
<html>
<head>
    <title>Previewing Links</title>
    <link rel="stylesheet"
    → href="script05.css">
    <script src="script05.js"></script>
</head>
<body>
    <h2>A Gentle Introduction to
    → JavaScript</h2>
    <ul>
        <li><a href="jsintro/2000-08.html">
        → August column</a></li>
        <li><a href="jsintro/2000-09.html">
        → September column</a></li>
        <li><a href="jsintro/2000-10.html">
        → October column</a></li>
        <li><a href="jsintro/2000-11.html">
        → November column</a></li>
    </ul>
    <div id="previewWin"> </div>
</body>
</html>
```

Previewing Links with Ajax

There's a handy and great-looking visual effect that many sites use in which, when you hover the mouse pointer over a link, the first few lines of the page that is the link's destination appear in a floating window under the cursor **A**. This turns out to be a fairly easy-to-create Ajax application. You'll find the HTML in **Listing 13.13**, the CSS in **Listing 13.14**, and the JavaScript in **Listing 13.15**.

To use Ajax to preview links:

1. `var allLinks = document.`
   `→ getElementsByTagName("a");`
   `for (var i=0; i< allLinks.length;`
   `→ i++) {`
   `    allLinks[i].addEventListener`
   `    → ("mouseover",getPreview,false);`
   `}`

   Here's our **initAll()** function, which simply plows through all the links on the page and adds a **mouseover** event handler to each. This (as you'll see, below) will read the destination page and display a preview for the (possible) visitor.

   continues on next page

2.
```
if (evt) {
   var url = evt.target;
}
else {
   evt = window.event;
   var url = evt.srcElement;
}
xPos = parseInt(evt.clientX);
yPos = parseInt(evt.clientY);
```

Here in **getPreview()**, the first thing we need to do is figure out what file we want to read, and that's done by looking at the event's properties. Depending on which browser your visitor is using, the URL is in either **evt.target** or **window.event.srcElement**. Once we've got that, we grab the **x** and **y** positions of the mouse for later use.

3.
```
var prevWin = document.
→ getElementById("previewWin");

if (xhr.readyState == 4) {
```

Having used Ajax to read the file, we're now down in the **showContents()** function. We store the **previewWin** element for later use in **prevWin**, and when **xhr.readyState** is 4, it's time to show off.

4.
```
if (xhr.status == 200) {
   prevWin.innerHTML =
   → xhr.responseText;
}
else {
   prevWin.innerHTML = "There was
   → a problem with the request "
   → + xhr.status;
}
prevWin.style.top = yPos+2 + "px";
prevWin.style.left = xPos+2 +
"px";
prevWin.style.visibility =
→ "visible";
```

Listing 13.14 This CSS styles the preview pop-up.

```
#previewWin {
    background-color: #FF9;
    width: 400px;
    height: 100px;
    font: .8em arial, helvetica, sans-serif;
    padding: 5px;
    position: absolute;
    visibility: hidden;
    top: 10px;
    left: 10px;
    border: 1px #CC0 solid;
    clip: auto;
    overflow: hidden;
}

#previewWin h1, #previewWin h2 {
    font-size: 1.0em;
}
```

Listing 13.15 The JavaScript that allows the server request and the appearance of the pop-up.

```
window.addEventListener("load",initAll,
→ false);
var xhr = false;
var xPos, yPos;

function initAll() {
    var allLinks = document.
    → getElementsByTagName("a");

    for (var i=0; i< allLinks.length; i++) {
        allLinks[i].addEventListener
        → ("mouseover",getPreview,false);
    }
}

function getPreview(evt) {
    if (evt) {
        var url = evt.target;
    }
    else {
        evt = window.event;
        var url = evt.srcElement;
    }
    xPos = parseInt(evt.clientX);
    yPos = parseInt(evt.clientY);
```

listing continues on next page

Listing 13.15 *continued*

```
        if (window.XMLHttpRequest) {
            xhr = new XMLHttpRequest();
        }
        else {
            if (window.ActiveXObject) {
                try {
                    xhr = new ActiveXObject
                    ➝ ("Microsoft.XMLHTTP");
                }
                catch (e) {
                }
            }
        }

        if (xhr) {
            xhr.addEventListener
            ➝ ("readystatechange",showContents,
            ➝ false);
            xhr.open("GET", url, true);
            xhr.send(null);
        }
        else {
            alert("Sorry, but I couldn't create
            ➝ an XMLHttpRequest");
        }
}

function showContents() {
    var prevWin = document.getElementById
    ➝ ("previewWin");

    if (xhr.readyState == 4) {
        if (xhr.status == 200) {
            prevWin.innerHTML =
            ➝ xhr.responseText;
        }
        else {
            prevWin.innerHTML = "There was a
            ➝ problem with the request " +
            ➝ xhr.status;
        }
        prevWin.style.top = yPos+2 + "px";
        prevWin.style.left = xPos+2 + "px";
        prevWin.style.visibility = "visible";

        prevWin.addEventListener("mouseout",
        ➝ function() {prevWin.style.
        ➝ visibility = "hidden";}, false);
    }
}
```

```
prevWin.addEventListener
➝ ("mouseout", function()
➝ {prevWin.style.visibility =
➝ "hidden";}, false);
```

If everything's fine, then **xhr.status** is 200 and the data we want to put into **prevWin.innerHTML** is in **xhr.responseText**. If not, we put the error message there instead.

Once that's done, it's simply a matter of figuring out where to place the preview window, and that's where those **x** and **y** mouse coordinates come in handy. It's a pop-up, so we put it just below and to the right (2 pixels over and 2 down) of the cursor position that triggered this call.

To finish up, we set **prevWin** to be visible and let JavaScript know **prevWin** should be hidden when the cursor moves off the preview.

TIP The data being read is in HTML format. Putting **xhr.responseText** into **innerHTML** tells the browser that when the preview window displays, it should interpret the HTML as, well, HTML. If you wanted something else to display (say, for instance, you wanted to see the actual source of the page), you could modify what's in **innerHTML** before displaying the preview.

TIP Ajax requires that the file being read reside on the same server—but it doesn't require that it be in the same directory. If the page you're reading in is in a different directory, and the page contains relative links, then those links will not work. If your pages refer to a particular CSS file, or images, or JavaScript, you won't be able to preview those particular parts of the file. The same solution applies here as well: modify **prevWin.innerHTML** before displaying it.

Auto-Completing Form Fields

A first-rate way to help your site's visitors is to lessen the drudgery of data entry into fields. Helping them fill out forms that have a large number of choices saves them time and effort, and additionally helps provide your site with valid data.

For this example, **Listing 13.16** (HTML), **Listing 13.17** (CSS), and **Listing 13.18** (JavaScript) automatically show a list of U.S. states matching the letters the user types into a form field **A**. As the user continues typing, the list shrinks until there is only one state left; this is then automatically put into the entry field, and the list goes away.

Listing 13.16 This simple HTML provides the form field that will be auto-completed.

```
<!DOCTYPE html>
<html>
<head>
    <title>Auto-fill Form Fields</title>
    <link rel="stylesheet"
    → href="script06.css">
    <script src="script06.js"></script>
</head>
<body>
    <form action="#">
        Please enter your state:<br>
        <input type="text" id="searchField"
        → autocomplete="off"><br>
        <div id="popups"> </div>
    </form>
</body>
</html>
```

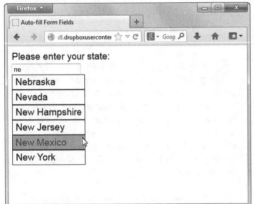 

A As you type, the number of possible choices narrows.

Listing 13.17 The CSS here styles the search field and the pop-up menu.

```css
body, #searchfield {
    font: 1.2em arial, helvetica,
    → sans-serif;
}

.suggestions {
    background-color: #FFF;
    padding: 2px 6px;
    border: 1px solid #000;
}

.suggestions:hover {
    background-color: #69F;
}

#popups {
    position: absolute;
}

#searchField.error {
    background-color: #FFC;
}
```

To build auto-completing form fields:

1. ```
   Please enter your state:<br>
   <input type="text"
   → id="searchField"
   → autocomplete="off"><br>
   <div id="popups"> </div>
   ```

   Here's the bit of HTML we care about. It's the one tricky part: that **autocomplete** attribute. It tells browsers not to do any auto-completion on this field, as we'll be handling it with the script.

2. ```
   document.getElementById
   → ("searchField").addEventListener
   → ("keyup",searchSuggest,false);
   ```

   In order to grab and process each keystroke, we need an event handler, and here's ours, set in **initAll()**.

3. ```
   xhr.addEventListener
   → ("readystatechange",
   → setStatesArray,false);
   xhr.open("GET", "us-states.xml",
   → true);
   xhr.send(null);
   ```

   Unlike those photographs earlier in this chapter, the names of the United States aren't likely to change. We can read the XML file (Listing 13.4) in once, initialize our array, and safely assume our list will still be valid at the end of this session.

   continues on next page
   ```

4.
```
if (xhr.responseXML) {
   var allStates = xhr.responseXML.
   → getElementsByTagName("item");
   for (var i=0; i<allStates.
   → length; i++) {
     statesArray[i] = allStates[i].
       → getElementsByTagName
       → ("label")[0].firstChild;
   }
}
```

Here we read that file in, look at each **item** node to find the **label** node inside, and then store **label**'s **firstChild**—the name of the state itself. Each goes into a slot in the **statesArray** array.

5.
```
var str = document.getElementById
   → ("searchField").value;
document.getElementById
   → ("searchField").className = "";
```

When you start typing in the field, you end up in the **searchSuggest()** event handler. We start off by getting the value of **searchField**, which is whatever has been typed so far. Next, we clear that field's **class** attribute.

6.
```
if (str != "") {
   document.getElementById
   → ("popups").innerHTML = "";
```

If nothing's been entered, we don't want to do anything, so there's a check here to make sure the user's entry has a value before we start popping up possibilities. If there's something there, we then blank out the previous list of possibilities.

7.
```
for (var i=0; i<statesArray.
   → length; i++) {
   var thisState = statesArray[i].
   → nodeValue;
```

Listing 13.18 This JavaScript handles the server request and the pop-up display.

```
window.addEventListener("load",initAll,
→ false);
var xhr = false;
var statesArray = new Array();

function initAll() {
    document.getElementById("searchField").
    → addEventListener("keyup",
    → searchSuggest,false);

    if (window.XMLHttpRequest) {
        xhr = new XMLHttpRequest();
    }
    else {
        if (window.ActiveXObject) {
            try {
                xhr = new ActiveXObject
                → ("Microsoft.XMLHTTP");
            }
            catch (e) {
            }
        }
    }

    if (xhr) {
        xhr.addEventListener
        → ("readystatechange",
        → setStatesArray,false);
        xhr.open("GET", "us-states.xml",
        → true);
        xhr.send(null);
    }
    else {
        alert("Sorry, but I couldn't create
        → an XMLHttpRequest");
    }
}

function setStatesArray() {
    if (xhr.readyState == 4) {
        if (xhr.status == 200) {
            if (xhr.responseXML) {
                var allStates =
                → xhr.responseXML.
                → getElementsByTagName("item");
                for (var i=0; i<allStates.
                → length; i++) {
```

listing continues on next page

Listing 13.18 *continued*

```
            statesArray[i] =
            ↪ allStates[i].
            ↪ getElementsByTagName
            ↪ ("label")[0].firstChild;
         }
      }
   }
   else {
      alert("There was a problem with
      ↪ the request " + xhr.status);
   }
 }
}

function searchSuggest() {
   var str = document.getElementById
   ↪ ("searchField").value;
   document.getElementById("searchField").
   ↪ className = "";
   if (str != "") {
      document.getElementById("popups").
      ↪ innerHTML = "";

      for (var i=0; i<statesArray.length;
      ↪ i++) {
         var thisState = statesArray[i].
         ↪ nodeValue;

         if (thisState.toLowerCase().
         ↪ indexOf(str.toLowerCase())
         ↪ == 0) {
            var tempDiv = document.
            ↪ createElement("div");
            tempDiv.innerHTML = thisState;
            tempDiv.addEventListener
            ↪ ("click",makeChoice,false);
            tempDiv.className =
            ↪ "suggestions";
            document.getElementById
            ↪ ("popups").appendChild
            ↪ (tempDiv);
         }
      }
      var foundCt = document.getElementById
      ↪ ("popups").childNodes.length;
```

listing continues on next page

Now, we loop through the list of states, storing the current state we're looking at in **thisState**.

8. **if (thisState.toLowerCase().**
   ↪ indexOf(str.toLowerCase())
   ↪ == 0) {

   We want to see if what they've entered so far is part of a state name—but that alone isn't sufficient; we also have to make sure what they've entered is at the beginning of the name. If you type in **Kansas**, you don't want to see a drop-down box asking if you want **Arkansas** or **Kansas**, after all. And so long as we're doing that check, we'll also force the comparison to be lowercase on both sides before checking **indexOf()**.

   If **indexOf()** returns 0—that is, the entered string was found starting at position 1 of **thisState**—then we know we have a hit.

9. **var tempDiv = document.**
   ↪ createElement("div");
   tempDiv.innerHTML = thisState;
   tempDiv.addEventListener("click",
   ↪ makeChoice,false);
   tempDiv.className = "suggestions";
   document.getElementById("popups").
   ↪ appendChild(tempDiv);

   Because this state is a possibility, we want to add it to the list that will display. That's done by creating a temporary **div**, setting its **innerHTML** to the name of the state, adding a **click** handler and **className**, and then appending the whole to the **popups div**. Adding each state as a separate **div** allows us to manipulate each using JavaScript and CSS.

continues on next page

10. `var foundCt = document.`
    ` getElementById("popups").`
    ` childNodes.length;`

   When we've looped through all the states, we're done setting up the **popups**—but how many do we have? We calculate that, the **foundCt**, here.

11. `if (foundCt == 0) {`
       `document.getElementById`
       ` ("searchField").className =`
       ` "error";`
    `}`

   If **foundCt** is 0, they've entered something unexpected. We let them know that by setting the **className** to "**error**", which causes the entry field to display with a pale yellow background (based on a CSS style rule in Listing 13.17).

12. `if (foundCt == 1) {`
       `document.getElementById`
       ` ("searchField").value =`
       ` document.getElementById`
       ` ("popups").firstChild.`
       ` innerHTML;`
       `document.getElementById`
       ` ("popups").innerHTML = "";`
    `}`

   If **foundCt** is 1, however, we know they've got a unique hit, so we can then put that state into the entry field. If they've typed in **ca**, they shouldn't have to type in **lifornia** also; we already know which state they want. We give them the full state by using the single **div** in **popups** to fill in the entry field, and then we blank out the **popups div**.

Listing 13.18 *continued*

```
            if (foundCt == 0) {
                document.getElementById
                 ("searchField").className =
                 "error";
            }
            if (foundCt == 1) {
                document.getElementById
                 ("searchField").value =
                 document.getElementById
                 ("popups").firstChild.
                 innerHTML;
                document.getElementById("popups").
                 innerHTML = "";
            }
        }
    }

    function makeChoice(evt) {
        if (evt) {
            var thisDiv = evt.target;
        }
        else {
            var thisDiv = window.event.
             srcElement;
        }
        document.getElementById("searchField").
         value = thisDiv.innerHTML;
        document.getElementById("popups").
         innerHTML = "";
    }
```

```
13. function makeChoice(evt) {
       if (evt) {
          var thisDiv = evt.target;
       }
       else {
          var thisDiv = window.event.
          → srcElement;
       }
       document.getElementById
       → ("searchField").value =
       → thisDiv.innerHTML;
       document.getElementById
       → ("popups").innerHTML = "";
    }
```

Another way the user can enter a state name is to click one from the pop-up list. In that case, the **makeChoice()** event handler function is called. First, we figure out which state the user clicked by looking at the target of the event, and that gives us a particular **div**. Looking at the **innerHTML** for that **div** gives us the state name, and we put that into the entry field. And finally, we clear out the pop-up list of possibilities.

TIP You can see an example of this technique when you're using Google Instant. As you type into the usual Google search field, a pop-up list appears with suggested search ideas. As you type, the search suggestions are continually filtered in the list.

TIP You may have noticed that this task and the last spent a lot more time and effort making things look good than actually demonstrating Ajax, XML, and server-side technologies. That's because much of what has come to be known (or at least thought of by some) as Ajax involves not just the underlying technology but also the way the technology works. How to make that all much simpler is covered in the next few chapters.

Checking Whether a File Exists

By now, you've seen this book's image rollover examples many times. But did you ever stop to wonder what would happen if the "_on" version of the image didn't exist? That sad result can be seen in . In this task, **Listing 13.19** uses Ajax to see whether the alternate version of the image exists before setting up a rollover.

To check whether a file exists:

1. ```
   window.addEventListener("load",
   → rolloverInit,false);
   var rolloverFound;
   ```

   We need a global variable to flag when a valid rollover "_on" image is found, and that variable—**rolloverFound**—is created here at the top.

A If the rollover version of the image doesn't exist, you could get a nasty broken image icon.

Listing 13.19 The really final version of our ongoing image rollover script example.

```
window.addEventListener("load",rolloverInit,
→ false);
var rolloverFound;

function rolloverInit() {
    for (var i=0; i<document.images.length;
    → i++) {
        if (document.images[i].parentNode.
        → tagName.toLowerCase() == "a") {
            setupRollover(document.images[i]);
        }
    }
}

function setupRollover(theImage) {
    var re = /\s*_off\s*/;

    rolloverFound = false;
    if (theImage.src.indexOf("_off")) {
        findImage(theImage.src.replace
        → (re,"_on"));
    }

    if (!rolloverFound) {
        return;
    }
```

listing continues on next page
```

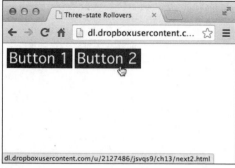

B But with a quick Ajax lookup, we avoid that UI problem.

Listing 13.19 *continued*

```
theImage.outImage = new Image();
theImage.outImage.src = theImage.src;
theImage.addEventListener("mouseout",
→ function() {this.src = this.outImage.
→ src;}, false);

theImage.overImage = new Image();
theImage.overImage.src = theImage.src.
→ replace(re,"_on");
theImage.addEventListener("mouseover",
→ function() {this.src = this.overImage.
→ src;}, false);

theImage.clickImage = new Image();
theImage.clickImage.src = theImage.src.
→ replace(re,"_click");
theImage.addEventListener("click",
→ function() {this.src = this.clickImage.
→ src;}, false);

theImage.parentNode.childImg = theImage;
theImage.parentNode.addEventListener
→ ("blur", function() {this.childImg.src
→ = this.childImg.outImage.src;},
→ false);
```

listing continues on next page

2. ```
   rolloverFound = false;
   if (theImage.src.indexOf("_off")) {
       findImage(theImage.src.replace
       → (re,"_on"));
   }
   if (!rolloverFound) {
       return;
   }
   ```

Here are all the changes necessary to the **setupRollover()** function. We start off by saying that the default value for **rolloverFound** is false. Next, we check to see whether the image's URL contains "**_off**"; if it doesn't, we can already tell that it isn't a valid rollover. If the URL does contain "**_off**", then we want to see if the "**_on**" version exists, and that check is done in **findImage()** below.

When we come back, if **rolloverFound** is still false, then we return immediately and skip the rest of the function. Consequently, the rollover is never created, causing the "**_off**" image to always display **B**.

continues on next page
   ```

3. ```
if (xhr) {
    xhr.addEventListener
    → ("readystatechange",picExists,
    → false);
    xhr.open("GET", url, false);
    xhr.send(null);
}
```

This code, in **findImage()**, is a pretty standard **xhr** request, with one difference: the last parameter passed to **xhr.open()** is **false**. That tells the server that the request is *synchronous*; that is, we can't continue on until we get the results back. Thankfully, the check shouldn't take too long.

4. ```
function picExists() {
    if (xhr.readyState == 4) {
        if (xhr.status == 200) {
            rolloverFound = true;
        }
    }
}
```

Finally, we check to see whether the image actually exists. If it does, **xhr.readyState** will be 4 and **xhr.status** will be 200—so we set **rolloverFound** to **true**.

Listing 13.19 *continued*

```
        theImage.parentNode.addEventListener
        → ("focus", function() {this.childImg.
        → src = this.childImg.overImage.src;},
        → false);
}

function findImage(url) {
    if (window.XMLHttpRequest) {
        xhr = new XMLHttpRequest();
    }
    else {
        if (window.ActiveXObject) {
            try {
                xhr = new ActiveXObject
                → ("Microsoft.XMLHTTP");
            }
            catch (e) {
            }
        }
    }

    if (xhr) {
        xhr.addEventListener
        → ("readystatechange",picExists,
        → false);
        xhr.open("GET", url, false);
        xhr.send(null);
    }
}

function picExists() {
    if (xhr.readyState == 4) {
        if (xhr.status == 200) {
            rolloverFound = true;
        }
    }
}
```

Toolkits, Frameworks, and Libraries

Here's what we didn't tell you earlier: writing JavaScript applications can be difficult. They often require a great deal of knowledge of working with the DOM, CSS, JavaScript, and server resources. Since this is a book for beginning scripters, we've shown you how to do some easy things so you can see that learning these techniques is well within your reach. But many books have been written that are completely devoted to showing intermediate-to-advanced scripters how to create JavaScript applications, and our chapters are no substitute for that kind of in-depth exploration.

Does that mean that you can't make good use of JavaScript on your sites, even though you're not yet a total scripting wizard? Not at all! This chapter shows you how to take advantage of JavaScript *toolkits*: prewritten, already-programmed *libraries* and *frameworks* of functions that make it easy for you to bring the power of scripting to your projects.

There are many toolkits available for download, and most of them are free. For this book, we're using jQuery (**jquery.com**), a freely downloadable, open-source set of utilities and controls that help you build interactive web applications. We think it's one of the best. In the next few chapters, we'll show you how to use jQuery to enable a user to drag and drop page elements; add menus and calendars; create overlays and sort table data; and in general, add cool (and useful!) effects to your pages.

Why jQuery?

Whatever your personal programming preferences, there's probably a JavaScript framework to match. In other words, while there are large variations in libraries, including some that aren't quite as good as others, there are many libraries that are top-notch but that have different strengths and weaknesses.

Some of jQuery's strengths are:

- **Lightweight:** jQuery is considerably smaller than many of its competitors, which means sites using it load more quickly.

- **Active development community:** Ask a question in the jQuery forums and you'll get a fast response. You can also search the archives to see if your question is included in the FAQ.

- **Plugin architecture:** If you need a feature that isn't in jQuery, there's a good chance that someone's written it as a plugin. An additional benefit of plugins is that you're only adding them to your site when they're needed—that is, you don't have their added weight on every page.

- **Support for older browsers:** If you need to support IE versions 6–8, you can use jQuery 1 (rather than jQuery 2), which is still supported.

- **Speed:** jQuery compares well to its competition (see **jsperf.com** for examples).

- **Ease of use for non-geeks:** Because its selection queries are based on CSS, people who aren't full-time professional programmers can easily drop into jQuery, add some functionality to their sites, and have everything work the way they expect.

For all these reasons, jQuery has become one of the—if not *the*—most popular JavaScript frameworks available.

(A) Here's your welcome to the wonderful world of jQuery.

Listing 14.1 This line of HTML introduces the jQuery library to our page.

```
<!DOCTYPE html>
<html>
<head>
    <title>Welcome to jQuery!</title>
    <script src="http://code.jquery.com/
    → jquery-2.1.0.js"></script>
    <script src="script01.js"></script>
</head>
<body>
    <h1 id="welcome"> </h1>
</body>
</html>
```

Listing 14.2 This is a very small amount of jQuery code, and it's just a start.

```
$(document).ready(function() {
    alert("Welcome to jQuery!");
});
```

Adding jQuery

In order for your site to use any JavaScript framework, you'll need to make some changes. With jQuery, there are only a few modifications that you'll need to make.

To add jQuery to your page:

1. `<script src="http://code.jquery.com/` `→ jquery-2.1.0.js"></script>`

   Listing 14.1 includes the one line of HTML needed to bring in the jQuery library.

2. `$(document).ready(function() {` `    alert("Welcome to jQuery!");` `});`

   The JavaScript file, **Listing 14.2**, is where you'll notice that things have changed a little. No need to panic; there's really no difference between that code and

   ```
   window.addEventListener("load",
       function() {
           alert("Welcome to jQuery!");
       },
       false
   );
   ```

   which you've seen many times before **(A)**. Here's what's changed:

   ▸ **$()** The dollar sign is what people often notice first about jQuery-based code. That's partly because it's not commonly used in vanilla JavaScript, and partly because it's ubiquitous in jQuery. Most lines of jQuery-enabled code start with a **$**, and this one's no exception. The **$** is simply a function name—one that's valid, although uncommon—that jQuery uses to access, well, *everything*.

continues on next page

- **document** Because we need to get to everything through **$**, we shouldn't be surprised that **document** itself (usually the top-most element) is the first thing we get.

- **ready()** Where previously we checked **onload** to see if the page was completely loaded, we can now depend on jQuery's **ready()** function to handle the job. The only difference is that whereas **onload** is an event handler (and so must be assigned a function), **ready()** is a function that's passed a parameter.

TIP If you're wondering where that line of HTML came from, read the "Serving jQuery" sidebar.

TIP Although jQuery is one of the lightest-weight frameworks available, there's a way to make it even lighter: change step 1 to download `jquery-2.1.0.min.js` instead. That's a version of the code that's compressed for maximum speed.

Serving jQuery

It used to be that if you wanted to use a JavaScript framework (framework being another word for library), you'd have to serve the files from your own server. A surfer who regularly goes to several high-end websites could end up downloading large parts of various libraries (or multiple copies of them) in a day.

There's now a solution to this: jQuery, like many frameworks, is available via what's known as a *Content Delivery Network* (usually just referred to as a *CDN*). A CDN hosts stable versions of libraries, and you're encouraged to link to them directly. This means that if someone visiting your site has already been to one of many other jQuery-using sites that day, they may already have some of these files cached, making your site appear to be amazingly fast. And even if they haven't, it's almost guaranteed that the CDN has better Internet connectivity than you do, so it can serve these files faster.

For your part, all you have to do is make a slight modification to your pages: where you normally would have your HTML pages refer to

```
<script src="directory/script.js">
```

they should instead have

```
<script src="http://code.jquery.com/script.js">
```

You might now be wondering about versions—and this is where things get even better. As we go to print, the most recent version of jQuery is 2.1.0. If you want that version, the URL above becomes

```
<script src="http://code.jquery.com/jquery-2.1.0.js">
```

Want the version before that?

```
<script src="http://code.jquery.com/jquery-2.0.3.js">
```

If you want jQuery 1—for example, to support Internet Explorer versions 6–8—you can always get the most recent version by loading

```
<script src="http://code.jquery.com/jquery.js">
```

(Be careful, though: this method can cause support nightmares for the websites using it, so it wasn't continued for jQuery 2.)

Updating a Page with jQuery

Much of what you've learned in this book so far is how to update your pages dynamically—and of course, jQuery can do that, too. This example is similar to the previous task, but here we'll update the page itself instead of just popping up an alert .

To update a page using jQuery:

- `$("#welcome").append("Welcome to → jQuery!");`

  The HTML for this task is similar enough to the previous that it's not worth showing, so all that matters is this one line in **Listing 14.3**.

  Here again, just as with **document**, we use **$** to get an element from our page; now, it's the **#welcome** element. And all we want to do with that element is set its **innerHTML**, which we do with jQuery's **append()** function.

  TIP If you're thinking that #welcome looks CSS-like, you're right. One of the reasons for jQuery's popularity is that its selectors are very much like those in CSS, which makes it easy for designer-types to get up to speed.

A By now, you should be feeling properly welcomed by jQuery.

Listing 14.3 This line of jQuery code lets us modify the DOM of our page.

```
$(document).ready(function() {
    $("#welcome").append("Welcome to
    → jQuery!");
});
```

Listing 14.4 This HTML page lets the user choose what color to make the header.

```
<!DOCTYPE html>
<html>
<head>
    <title>Welcome to jQuery #3!</title>
    <link rel="stylesheet"
    ⇥ href="script03.css">
    <script src="http://code.jquery.com/
    ⇥ jquery-2.1.0.js"></script>
    <script src="script03.js"></script>
</head>
<body>
    <h1 id="colorMe">Pick a color</h1>
    <p>
        <a id="red">Red</a>
        <a id="green">Green</a>
        <a id="blue">Blue</a>
    </p>
</body>
</html>
```

Listing 14.5 Some of the work is being done by the CSS.

```
a {
    display: block;
    float: left;
    padding: 10px;
    margin: 10px;
    font-weight: bold;
    color: white;
    background-color: gray;
}

a:hover {
    color: black;
    background-color: silver;
}
```

Interacting with jQuery

Now that you've seen the basics, it's time to start showing off some of jQuery's real strengths. **Listing 14.4** (HTML), **Listing 14.5** (CSS), and **Listing 14.6** (JavaScript) demonstrate how easy it is to add a little user interaction.

The page shows three button-like links: red, green, and blue. When the user clicks one, the "Pick a color" page header turns the selected color **A**.

To add user interaction:

1. `$("a").click(function(evt) {`

   This line uses jQuery to say that, for every link (that is, anchor element) in the document, do the following when the link is clicked by the user.

2. `$("#colorMe").css({`

   As you might expect by now, this gets the element with the **id colorMe**. Because the attribute we want to change is CSS-related, we can use the **css()** function. It needs a list of object literals: that is, a series of name and value pairs inside a pair of braces **{}** and separated by commas. Each name and value are separated by a colon.

   continues on next page

3. `"color": $(this).attr("id")`

The element **$(this)** is just like the **this** element that we're used to seeing, where its value depends on the context in which it's being used. Here, because the context is a **click** handler, we know we've got the link that was clicked.

Given that element, we want its **id**, which will be **red**, **green**, or **blue**. We get that by passing **attr()** just one parameter: the attribute name. That value is then stored as the new color for the header.

A Click the Red button to see the red header.

Listing 14.6 But the real changes are done in a few lines of jQuery code.

```
$(document).ready(function() {
    $("a").click(function(evt) {
        $("#colorMe").css({
            "color": $(this).attr("id")
        });
        evt.preventDefault();
    });
});
```

Other Toolkits

Back in the late 1990s, when Dynamic HTML was the latest rage, people wrote and made available a variety of DHTML toolkits. Some of the best were (in effect) written by a couple of guys in a garage somewhere. When the dot-com boom dot-bombed, the toolkits' authors had to get day jobs, and the packages were abandoned and not maintained. So when we first looked for JavaScript toolkits, we were a bit wary.

We've chosen to discuss jQuery in this book because it is documented, high quality, open source, and actively supported by a large developer community, which makes it more likely to stay available for the lifetime of this book. But there are many other good toolkits available. There are even sites that rate the different toolkits; our favorite is Wikipedia's, at **en.wikipedia.org/wiki/ Comparison_of_JavaScript_frameworks**.

We think that the most important thing you should look for in a toolkit is that it does a great job of supporting web standards. That means that it should fully support the most popular browsers and work across different platforms. To us, that list includes Firefox, Safari, and Chrome for Windows and Mac, and Internet Explorer 9 and up for Windows. It's also important that the toolkit be thoroughly debugged and that it have good documentation.

We suggest that you also take a look at these other toolkits, all of which are popular, well supported, and well documented. They all have great demos on their sites so you can see if one meets your needs:

- Dojo (**dojotoolkit.org**)
- YUI (**developer.yahoo.com/yui/**)
- Prototype (**prototypejs.org**)
- Modernizr (**modernizr.com**)
- MooTools (**mootools.net**)

Interacting and Updating

If the previous example didn't have enough updating and interaction for you, here's a little more. Now the text of the buttons will also change color 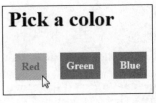, letting your users know just what they're letting themselves in for.

As you might guess, the HTML is sufficiently similar to the previous example that we don't need to duplicate it; **Listing 14.7** (CSS) and **Listing 14.8** (JavaScript) contain everything that matters.

To add further interaction and updates:

1. **$("a").hover(function() {**

   We can't update our buttons with just CSS, so we need jQuery to do the work. Its **hover()** function does the equivalent of a **mouseover**.

2. **$(this).css({**

   When we're over the object in question, we know we want to change some of its attributes. Again, as the attributes we want to change are all CSS-related, we can use the **css()** function.

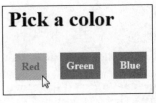
A When users hover over the button, they now get a hint as to what will happen.

Listing 14.7 With more of the work being done by jQuery, we don't need as much CSS.

```
a {
    display: block;
    float: left;
    padding: 10px;
    margin: 10px;
    font-weight: bold;
    color: white;
    background-color: gray;
}
```

Listing 14.8 But it still doesn't take much jQuery to handle this task.

```
$(document).ready(function() {
    $("a").hover(function() {
        $(this).css({
            "color": $(this).attr("id"),
            "background-color": "silver"
        });
    });

    $("a").mouseout(function() {
        $(this).css({
            "color": "white",
            "background-color": "gray"
        });
    });

    $("a").click(function(evt) {
        $("#colorMe").css({
            "color": $(this).attr("id")
        });
        evt.preventDefault();
    });
});
```

3. `"color": $(this).attr("id"),`
`"background-color": "silver"`

We're modifying more than one attribute this time, so we need to pass a list of multiple object literals. When this list is passed to **css()**, the element's color and background-color styles are reset to the passed values.

4. `$("a").mouseout(function() {`

Here's the other half of the **hover()**: the **mouseout()**. When the user moves the cursor off the button, we want them to return to their normal colors.

5. `"color": "white",`
`"background-color": "gray"`

And here's our normal white-on-gray button color scheme again.

TIP If you need a refresher on object literals, they were originally introduced in Chapter 10.

TIP You might be wondering if the **mouseout()** section is really needed—after all, if the values being reset are static, can't it just be done in CSS? Sadly, the answer is no—once **hover()** modifies the buttons, they stay those colors until they're reset via jQuery.

Striping Tables

If your site has a lot of tabular data, you should add stripes to your tables—without them, the information can be difficult to read and understand. Unfortunately, there's still no way to use CSS to stripe table rows in a way that works in all commonly-used browsers. It used to be the case that using JavaScript to stripe table rows was so difficult that most people didn't bother. With jQuery, it's nice and simple, as seen in .

To create zebra-striped tables:

1. ```
   $("tr").mouseover(function() {
       $(this).addClass("over");
   });
   ```

   Listing 14.9 (our HTML file) and Listing 14.10 (our CSS file) don't have anything new or original. The only thing that might be a little curious is that the CSS file sets rules for table rows with the class set to "**over**" and "**even**", but nowhere in the HTML is either of those ever set up. That's because it's all done in the JavaScript file, **Listing 14.11**.

continues on page 379

Beatles Discography

Album	Year	Label
Please Please Me	1963	Parlophone
With The Beatles	1963	Parlophone
A Hard Day's Night	1964	Parlophone
Beatles for Sale	1964	Parlophone
Help!	1965	Parlophone
Rubber Soul	1965	Parlophone
Revolver	1966	Parlophone
Sgt. Pepper's Lonely Hearts Club Band	1967	Parlophone
Magical Mystery Tour	1967	Capitol
The Beatles	1968	Apple
Yellow Submarine	1969	Apple
Abbey Road	1969	Apple
Let It Be	1970	Apple

A This list of albums, with its alternating stripes, is easy to read.
   ```

Listing 14.9 The HTML for a very standard table, with no inline scripts or styles.

```html
<!DOCTYPE html>
<html>
<head>
    <title>Striped Tables</title>
    <link rel="stylesheet" href="script05.css">
    <script src="http://code.jquery.com/jquery-2.1.0.js"></script>
    <script src="script05.js"></script>
</head>
<body>
    <h1>Beatles Discography</h1>
    <table>
        <thead>
            <tr>
                <th>Album</th>
                <th>Year</th>
                <th>Label</th>
            </tr>
        </thead>
        <tr>
            <td>Please Please Me</td>
            <td>1963</td>
            <td>Parlophone</td>
        </tr>
        <tr>
            <td>With The Beatles</td>
            <td>1963</td>
            <td>Parlophone</td>
        </tr>
        <tr>
            <td>A Hard Day's Night</td>
            <td>1964</td>
            <td>Parlophone</td>
        </tr>
        <tr>
            <td>Beatles for Sale</td>
            <td>1964</td>
            <td>Parlophone</td>
        </tr>
        <tr>
            <td>Help!</td>
            <td>1965</td>
            <td>Parlophone</td>
        </tr>
```

listing continues on next page

Listing 14.9 *continued*

```
            <tr>
                <td>Rubber Soul</td>
                <td>1965</td>
                <td>Parlophone</td>
            </tr>
            <tr>
                <td>Revolver</td>
                <td>1966</td>
                <td>Parlophone</td>
            </tr>
            <tr>
                <td>Sgt. Pepper's Lonely Hearts
                → Club Band</td>
                <td>1967</td>
                <td>Parlophone</td>
            </tr>
            <tr>
                <td>Magical Mystery Tour</td>
                <td>1967</td>
                <td>Capitol</td>
            </tr>
            <tr>
                <td>The Beatles</td>
                <td>1968</td>
                <td>Apple</td>
            </tr>
            <tr>
                <td>Yellow Submarine</td>
                <td>1969</td>
                <td>Apple</td>
            </tr>
            <tr>
                <td>Abbey Road</td>
                <td>1969</td>
                <td>Apple</td>
            </tr>
            <tr>
                <td>Let It Be</td>
                <td>1970</td>
                <td>Apple</td>
            </tr>
        </table>
    </body>
</html>
```

Listing 14.10 A small bit of CSS, which will be enabled via jQuery.

```
table {
    border-collapse: collapse;
}

tr.even {
    background-color: #C2C8D4;
}

tr.over {
    background-color: #8797B7;
}

td {
    border-bottom: 1px solid #C2C8D4;
    padding: 5px;
}

th {
    border-right: 2px solid #FFF;
    color: #FFF;
    padding-right: 40px;
    padding-left: 20px;
    background-color: #626975;
}

th.sortUp {
    background: #626975 url(jquery/images/
    → asc.png) no-repeat right center;
}

th.sortDown {
    background: #626975 url(jquery/images/
    → desc.png) no-repeat right center;
}
```

Beatles Discography

Album	Year	Label
Please Please Me	1963	Parlophone
With The Beatles	1963	Parlophone
A Hard Day's Night	1964	Parlophone
Beatles for Sale	1964	Parlophone
Help!	1965	Parlophone
Rubber Soul	1965	Parlophone
Revolver	1966	Parlophone
Sgt. Pepper's Lonely Hearts Club Band	1967	Parlophone
Magical Mystery Tour	1967	Capitol
The Beatles	1968	Apple
Yellow Submarine	1969	Apple
Abbey Road	1969	Apple
Let It Be	1970	Apple

B Hovering over any row highlights that row.

Listing 14.11 Here's all the code necessary to add striping to your tables.

```
$(document).ready(function() {
    $("tr").mouseover(function() {
        $(this).addClass("over");
    });

    $("tr").mouseout(function() {
        $(this).removeClass("over");
    });

    $("tr:even").addClass("even");
});
```

This section of code acts as a rollover: whenever the mouse is over a row, the **mouseover** for that **tr** is triggered. That tells jQuery to add a class of "**over**" to that row, and our CSS tells the browser that it should now display that row in a different color (as shown in **B**).

2. $("tr").mouseout(function() {
       $(this).removeClass("over");
   });

   Here's where that's turned off again: when the mouse pointer moves off the row, its **mouseout** is triggered, and the class attribute of "**over**" is removed.

3. $("tr:even").addClass("even");

   Yes, this is really all there is to adding zebra stripes. Because jQuery understands the concept of odd and even rows, we can tell it to just set all even rows to have a class attribute of "**even**". And because our CSS has a rule that applies to **tr.even**, every other row is automatically colored, without ever having to touch a bit of HTML.

Sorting Tables

While it's nice enough to have a table that's striped, sometimes you want a site that allows user interaction. Maybe the user wants to be able to sort the columns in a different order—instead of having the years increase, they want them to decrease. Or maybe they want to sort by name, or by name in reverse order. Or... you get the idea.

Here's the one example where jQuery doesn't contain this functionality out of the box. Instead, we'll have to use a plugin. This one's called, meaningfully enough, `tablesorter`.

To create sortable tables:

1. `<script src="jquery/jquery.` → `tablesorter.js"></script>`

   Listing 14.12, our HTML file, is virtually identical to Listing 14.9. There are only two changes: we added this line to bring in the new **jquery.tablesorter.js** routine, and we've added an **id** of "**theTable**" to the table itself.

2. `th.sortUp {`
   `    background: #626975`
   `    → url(jquery/images/asc.png)`
   `    → no-repeat right center;`
   `}`

   `th.sortDown {`
   `    background: #626975`
   `    → url(jquery/images/desc.png)`
   `    → no-repeat right center;`
   `}`

Listing 14.12 You need to add very little to your HTML to add sorting to your tables.

```
<!DOCTYPE html>
<html>
<head>
    <title>Sorted Tables</title>
    <link rel="stylesheet"
    → href="script05.css">
    <script src="http://code.jquery.com/
    → jquery-2.1.0.js"></script>
    <script src="jquery/jquery.tablesorter.
    → js"></script>
    <script src="script06.js"></script>
</head>
<body>
    <h1>Beatles Discography</h1>
    <table id="theTable">
        <thead>
            <tr>
                <th>Album</th>
                <th>Year</th>
                <th>Label</th>
            </tr>
        </thead>
        <tr>
            <td>Please Please Me</td>
            <td>1963</td>
            <td>Parlophone</td>
        </tr>
        <tr>
            <td>With The Beatles</td>
            <td>1963</td>
            <td>Parlophone</td>
        </tr>
        <tr>
            <td>A Hard Day's Night</td>
            <td>1964</td>
            <td>Parlophone</td>
        </tr>
        <tr>
            <td>Beatles for Sale</td>
            <td>1964</td>
            <td>Parlophone</td>
        </tr>
        <tr>
            <td>Help!</td>
            <td>1965</td>
            <td>Parlophone</td>
        </tr>
```

listing continues on next page

Listing 14.12 *continued*

```
        <tr>
            <td>Rubber Soul</td>
            <td>1965</td>
            <td>Parlophone</td>
        </tr>
        <tr>
            <td>Revolver</td>
            <td>1966</td>
            <td>Parlophone</td>
        </tr>
        <tr>
            <td>Sgt. Pepper's Lonely Hearts
            ↪ Club Band</td>
            <td>1967</td>
            <td>Parlophone</td>
        </tr>
        <tr>
            <td>Magical Mystery Tour</td>
            <td>1967</td>
            <td>Capitol</td>
        </tr>
        <tr>
            <td>The Beatles</td>
            <td>1968</td>
            <td>Apple</td>
        </tr>
        <tr>
            <td>Yellow Submarine</td>
            <td>1969</td>
            <td>Apple</td>
        </tr>
        <tr>
            <td>Abbey Road</td>
            <td>1969</td>
            <td>Apple</td>
        </tr>
        <tr>
            <td>Let It Be</td>
            <td>1970</td>
            <td>Apple</td>
        </tr>
    </table>
</body>
</html>
```

Let's take a quick look back at Listing 14.10, where we previously skipped covering these two rules. Here, they're put to work, telling the browser that when the user wants to sort up or down, the table header should display an appropriately pointed arrow.

3. **$("#theTable").tablesorter({**

Here's our big change to the JavaScript code, in **Listing 14.13**: telling jQuery that we want users to be able to sort the contents of the table. That's done with the code in this step and the next. We select the element with the **id** of **theTable** (as mentioned in step 1) and run the **tablesorter()** method on it.

continues on next page

Listing 14.13 And just a few lines of code, and our jQuery-enabled table is sortable and striped.

```
$(document).ready(function() {
    $("tr").mouseover(function() {
        $(this).addClass("over");
    });

    $("tr").mouseout(function() {
        $(this).removeClass("over");
    });

    $("#theTable").tablesorter({
        sortList:[[1,0]],
        cssAsc: "sortUp",
        cssDesc: "sortDown",
        widgets: ["zebra"]
    });
});
```

4. `sortList:[[1,0]],`
`   cssAsc: "sortUp",`
`   cssDesc: "sortDown",`
`   widgets: ["zebra"]`

This is jQuery, so there are several possible options for how we want our table to display. The ones we're using here are:

▸ `sortList:[[1,0]]`: We want the table to be sorted in a particular way when the page first loads (as in **A**), and here's where that's defined. Count your columns starting with zero; the column you want is the first parameter. Here we want our table to be sorted by the second column, so we pass a 1 (remember, JavaScript is zero-relative!). The second parameter is which way we want to sort: 0 is up, 1 is down.

▸ `cssAsc: "sortUp"`: When the user chooses to sort up, we want a new CSS rule to apply to this **th** cell. This will automatically assign a class of **"sortUp"** when that's what the user wants, which will then show an upward-pointing arrow to the right of the label.

Beatles Discography

Album	Year ▼	Label
Please Please Me	1963	Parlophone
With The Beatles	1963	Parlophone
A Hard Day's Night	1964	Parlophone
Beatles for Sale	1964	Parlophone
Help!	1965	Parlophone
Rubber Soul	1965	Parlophone
Revolver	1966	Parlophone
Sgt. Pepper's Lonely Hearts Club Band	1967	Parlophone
Magical Mystery Tour	1967	Capitol
The Beatles	1968	Apple
Yellow Submarine	1969	Apple
Abbey Road	1969	Apple
Let It Be	1970	Apple

A When the sortable table initially loads, it's sorted by year—and you know that because of the downward arrow to the right of the Year header.

Beatles Discography

Album	Year ▲	Label
Let It Be	1970	Apple
Yellow Submarine	1969	Apple
Abbey Road	1969	Apple
The Beatles	1968	Apple
Sgt. Pepper's Lonely Hearts Club Band	1967	Parlophone
Magical Mystery Tour	1967	Capitol
Revolver	1966	Parlophone
Help!	1965	Parlophone
Rubber Soul	1965	Parlophone
A Hard Day's Night	1964	Parlophone
Beatles for Sale	1964	Parlophone
Please Please Me	1963	Parlophone
With The Beatles	1963	Parlophone

Ⓑ Click the Year label, and the table re-sorts itself and changes the arrow to point up.

Beatles Discography

Album ▼	Year	Label
A Hard Day's Night	1964	Parlophone
Abbey Road	1969	Apple
Beatles for Sale	1964	Parlophone
Help!	1965	Parlophone
Let It Be	1970	Apple
Magical Mystery Tour	1967	Capitol
Please Please Me	1963	Parlophone
Revolver	1966	Parlophone
Rubber Soul	1965	Parlophone
Sgt. Pepper's Lonely Hearts Club Band	1967	Parlophone
The Beatles	1968	Apple
With The Beatles	1963	Parlophone
Yellow Submarine	1969	Apple

Ⓒ Click any other label (such as Album, shown here), and that column becomes the sort field.

▸ **cssDesc: "sortDown"**: We want the user to know when they're sorting downward instead, and clicking the **th** cell again changes the class to **"sortDown"**, which displays a downward-pointing arrow to the right of the label Ⓑ. Because you might want to sort on any column, not just the one the web developer decided to make the default, all a user has to do is click a different **th** cell, and the results immediately change Ⓒ without you having to add any more code.

▸ **widgets: ["zebra"]**: With **tablesorter()**, zebra-striping is a thrown-in freebie widget. Just say that you want to add the zebra widget, and you've got stripes.

TIP You can get the **tablesorter** plugin (along with documentation and examples) at **tablesorter.com**.

TIP When you use a jQuery plugin, the code needs to be hosted on your own server. Here, we've put it into a directory named "jquery". Plugins will be covered in more depth in Chapter 16.

Learning More About jQuery

If this brief coverage whets your appetite to learn more about jQuery, here are some resources:

- The main jQuery site is at **jquery.com**.
- To download jQuery (in any of a number of formats), go to **jquery.com/download**.
- You can find jQuery documentation at **learn.jquery.com**. If you feel that anything's missing, they invite you to add it.
- The jQuery discussion forums can be found at **forum.jquery.com**.
- There are a number of tutorials at **try.jquery.com**.
- On its own, jQuery is mostly about adding functionality. If what you want to do primarily affects the appearance of your page, you'll want to check out jQuery UI, at **jqueryui.com**.
- If you want help building websites that work on both desktop computers and mobile devices, check out jQuery Mobile, at **jquerymobile.com**.
- If what you want doesn't appear to be included in jQuery, chances are there's a plugin, and those can be found at **plugins.jquery.com**.
- And last but not least, the jQuery blog is located at **blog.jquery.com**.

And it wouldn't be proper to discuss jQuery and not give some credit to its creator and lead developer, John Resig. His site is at **ejohn.org**.

Designing
with jQuery

Web development began to require the use of JavaScript frameworks around the same time that web design began to frequently feature certain user interface elements (such as elements that slide their way on and off screen and the ubiquitous "yellow fade"). That's not entirely coincidental, and one of the main reasons for jQuery's success is its sidekick, jQuery UI. As you might guess from the name, jQuery uses jQuery UI to handle common user interface elements.

In this chapter, we'll be talking about that "Web 2.0" look and feel: both how it's created and why it's used. While demonstrating these elements, we'll give a further introduction to the advantages and uses of jQuery and jQuery UI. You'll learn how to highlight elements, create accordion-like menus, and display modal dialogs (with accompanying visual effects). We'll also cover smarter calendar pickers, including both single and double month displays, and finish off by showing you how to create your own custom themes.

In This Chapter

Highlighting New Elements

The "yellow fade" has become almost a cliché of web design: when something new materializes on the page, viewers expect to see it appear with a yellow background, which then slowly fades to white (or whatever the site's usual background color is). It's a handy way to let visitors know that something has changed without the overhead of having to keep track of what's new versus newer versus newest.

It's also a good introduction to jQuery UI, as you'll be able to see how much can be done with only a few lines of code.

To highlight an element's display:

1. ```
   <script src="http://code.jquery.
   → com/jquery-2.1.0.js"></script>
   <script src="http://code.jquery.
   → com/ui/1.10.4/jquery-ui.js">
   → </script>
   <script src="script01.js"></script>
   ```

   In order for **Listing 15.1** (our HTML page) to be jQuery UI-savvy, it needs to have access to two files: **jQuery-*version*.js** and **jquery-ui.js**. The third file included is our own local script file, **script01.js**.

2. `$(document).ready(function() {`

   In **Listing 15.2**, we start our JavaScript routines. As mentioned in the previous chapter, we're passing in an anonymous function here, which is shown in the following steps.

Listing 15.1 Adding jQuery and jQuery UI to a page starts with adding a couple of `<script>` tags.

```
<!DOCTYPE html>
<html>
<head>
    <title>Show/Hide Text</title>
    <script src="http://code.jquery.com/
    → jquery-2.1.0.js"></script>
    <script src="http://code.jquery.com/
    → ui/1.10.4/jquery-ui.js"></script>
    <script src="script01.js"></script>
</head>
<body>
    <a href="#" id="textToggle">show/hide
    → text</a><br>
    <div id="bodyText">Lorem ipsum dolor sit
    → amet, consectetuer adipiscing elit.
    → Nulla viverra aliquet mi. Cras
    → urna. Curabitur diam. Curabitur eros
    → nibh, condimentum eu, tincidunt at,
    → commodo vitae, nisi. Duis nulla
    → lectus, feugiat et, tincidunt nec,
    → iaculis vehicula, tortor. Sed tortor
    → felis, viverra vitae, posuere et,
    → ullamcorper a, leo. Suspendisse
    → euismod libero at orci. Pellentesque
    → odio massa, condimentum at,
    → pellentesque sed, lacinia quis,
    → mauris. Proin ultricies risus cursus
    → mi. Cras nibh quam, adipiscing vel,
    → tincidunt a, consequat ut, mi. Aenean
    → neque arcu, pretium posuere, tincidunt
    → non, consequat sit amet, enim. Duis
    → fermentum. Donec eu augue. Mauris sit
    → amet ligula.</div>
</body>
</html>
```
```

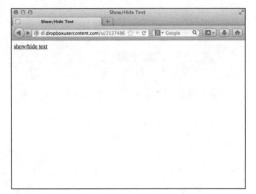

A Not much is going on here when this page first loads.

Listing 15.2 This script (using jQuery and jQuery UI) makes highlighting a new page element easy.

```
$(document).ready(function() {
    $("#bodyText").hide();

    $("#textToggle").click(
        function() {
            $("#bodyText").toggle("highlight",
            → {}, 2000);
            return false;
        }
    );
});
```

3. **$("#bodyText").hide();**

   One of jQuery's most useful features is the way you tell it what object you want to do something with—it's virtually just like CSS. With CSS, if we want a rule to hide an element with an **id** of **bodyText**, we might write something like this:

   #bodyText { display:none; }

   And as you can see, that CSS is much shorter than the equivalent JavaScript command:

   document.getElementById
   → ("bodyText").style.display =
   → "none";

   The line of code in this step does the same thing as both the standard JavaScript and the CSS rule above: it tells the browser not to display this particular element, as seen in **A**. It uses jQuery's built-in **hide()** method, which needs no parameters.

4. **$("#textToggle").click(**

   Here, we want to call another method built into jQuery: **click()**. Unlike the code in the previous step (which is run when the document loads), this line is triggered by a particular event—it runs whenever the element with the **id** of **textToggle** is clicked.

   The **click()** method is passed a function as a parameter that contains the code to trigger when clicked.

   continues on next page

5.
```
function() {
    $("#bodyText").toggle
    → ("highlight", {}, 2000);
    return false;
}
```

Here's the function passed to **click()**. We start by letting jQuery find the element with the **id** of **bodyText**; that's what's going to be displayed when **toggle()** is called. It needs three parameters:

- ▸ **"highlight"**: the effect we want.

- ▸ **{}**: the options desired on that effect. The yellow fade technique is so prevalent that yellow is the default color, so we don't need to modify any options here.

- ▸ **2000**: the speed at which we want the effect to display. This is set in milliseconds, so we're saying that we want the fade-out to last two seconds.

And finally, we return a value of **false** so that the browser doesn't try to follow the link. **B** shows the brief fade, and **C** shows the final result.

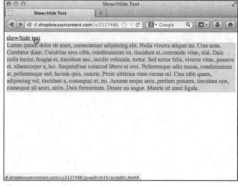

B But click the link, and text appears with a brief yellow highlight that then fades out.

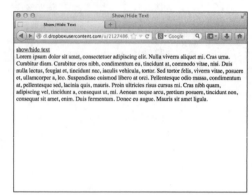

C Here's the final display of the page.

TIP Did you notice the one place above where jQuery UI is used? If not, well, that's one of jQuery's best features: the two work together so smoothly that you can miss what's part of what. In this example, only the **toggle()** method is part of jQuery UI.

TIP If you're now wondering why jQuery doesn't automatically include its UI elements, keep in mind that much of what it does is behind the scenes—and there's no reason to always have the overhead of including the UI effects if they're not going to be used.

Creating Accordion Menus

One way to choose a framework is to pick a common thing you want to add to a site, and then see how much that framework helps you to accomplish that task. Here, we want an accordion menu—a type of menu where, when one section is opened, any others automatically close. Similar to a tabbed interface, it's a common design element.

To create accordion menus:

1. ```
<link rel="stylesheet"
→ href="http://code.jquery.com/
→ ui/1.10.4/themes/cupertino/
→ jquery-ui.css">
<link rel="stylesheet"
→ href="script02.css">
```

   Listing 15.3 needs two CSS files: Cupertino (one of jQuery UI's built-in themes) and ours (**script02.css**, seen in **Listing 15.4**) that adds on the little bit of CSS needed to make things look just the way we want.

2. ```
$(document).ready(function() {
```

   Here we are now in **Listing 15.5**. As before, if we want something to run when the page loads, it needs to be inside this function.

3. ```
$("#theMenu").accordion({
```

   In Listing 15.3, our menu is structured as an outline, using unordered list items as the contents of each menu. Here's an example of the simplicity of jQuery: all Listing 15.5 needs to do is take the **id** from the top-level **ul** (in this case, **theMenu**) and then apply the built-in **accordion()** method to it.

*continues on page 391*
```

Listing 15.3 The links in this outline will, via jQuery, be seen in a browser as an accordion menu.

```html
<!DOCTYPE html>
<html>
<head>
    <title>Accordion Menus</title>
    <link rel="stylesheet" href="http://code.jquery.com/ui/1.10.4/themes/cupertino/jquery-ui.css">
    <link rel="stylesheet" href="script02.css">
    <script src="http://code.jquery.com/jquery-2.1.0.js"></script>
    <script src="http://code.jquery.com/ui/1.10.4/jquery-ui.js"></script>
    <script src="script02.js"></script>
</head>
<body>
    <h1>Shakespeare's Plays</h1>
    <ul id="theMenu">
        <li><a href="menu1.html" class="menuLink">Comedies</a>
            <ul>
                <li><a href="pg1.html">All's Well That Ends Well</a></li>
                <li><a href="pg2.html">As You Like It</a></li>
                <li><a href="pg3.html">Love's Labour's Lost</a></li>
                <li><a href="pg4.html">The Comedy of Errors</a></li>
            </ul>
        </li>
        <li><a href="menu2.html" class="menuLink">Tragedies</a>
            <ul>
                <li><a href="pg5.html">Anthony &amp; Cleopatra</a></li>
                <li><a href="pg6.html">Hamlet</a></li>
                <li><a href="pg7.html">Romeo &amp; Juliet</a></li>
            </ul>
        </li>
        <li><a href="menu3.html" class="menuLink">Histories</a>
            <ul>
                <li><a href="pg8.html">Henry IV, Part 1</a></li>
                <li><a href="pg9.html">Henry IV, Part 2</a></li>
            </ul>
        </li>
    </ul>
</body>
</html>
```

Listing 15.4 While we've done similar menus previously, using jQuery means a lot less CSS.

```css
#theMenu {
    width: 400px;
}
```

Listing 15.5 And with jQuery, it needs even less JavaScript.

```javascript
$(document).ready(function() {
    $("#theMenu").accordion({
        animate: false,
        collapsible: true,
        header: ".menuLink",
        heightStyle: "content"
    });
});
```

A You can set whether the user can or cannot collapse the entire menu.

A When clicked, the accordion menu closes one sub-menu and opens another.

4. `animate: false,`
   `collapsible: true,`
   `header: ".menuLink",`
   `heightStyle: "content"`

   We need to set a few options, and that's done right inside `accordion()`. They are:

   - **animate**: if you want menu items to display with an animated effect, set this to the name of the desired effect (e.g., **"slide"**, **"easeslide"**).

   - **collapsible**: allows the user to collapse all the menu items **A** versus requiring one to always display.

   - **header**: how jQuery can identify the headers for each menu. Here, they all have the class "**menuLink**", and clicking one of the headers gives a page that looks like **B**.

   - **heightStyle**: when set to **"content"**, the accordion area will always have a fixed height based on the largest area needed.

TIP There are additional options for `accordion()` besides the ones above—those are only where we wanted to override the default. If, for instance, we wanted the accordion to open when the user hovered the mouse over a menu label (versus only when the user clicks a menu label), all we'd do is add this to the last step: `event: "mouseover"`.

TIP If you want your accordion to start off completely collapsed, add `active: false` to the list of options. If you want the page to load with the accordion open to something other than the first menu item, use `active: 2` (or 3, or whatever the case might be).

TIP Don't like the Cupertino theme, and wondering what other options might be available? Be sure to check out the "Pick a Theme, Any Theme" sidebar.

Creating Smarter Dialogs

Another common design element in modern sites is dialogs that don't look like the usual **prompt()**, **alert()**, or **confirm()** ones we learned about back in Chapter 2. Instead, they look more like the dialogs you see in applications, such as modal dialogs; that is, dialogs that force you to respond to them before you can go back to the webpage. Once again, jQuery makes it straightforward to accomplish a task.

To create smarter dialogs:

1. ```
<link rel="stylesheet"
→ href="http://code.jquery.com/
→ ui/1.10.4/themes/redmond/
→ jquery-ui.css">
<link rel="stylesheet"
→ href="script03.css">
```

We're using another one of jQuery UI's built-in themes here, Redmond. Here's where **Listing 15.6** loads it into our page. In addition, we're also loading in our specific CSS page, shown in **Listing 15.7**.

**Listing 15.6** Again, we only need a few **`<script>`** tags added here to start off our jQuery changes.

```
<!DOCTYPE html>
<html>
<head>
    <title>Modal Dialog</title>
    <link rel="stylesheet"
    → href="http://code.jquery.com/
    → ui/1.10.4/themes/redmond/
    → jquery-ui.css">
    <link rel="stylesheet"
    → href="script03.css">
    <script src="http://code.jquery.com/
    → jquery-2.1.0.js"></script>
    <script src="http://code.jquery.com/
    → ui/1.10.4/jquery-ui.js"></script>
    <script src="script03.js"></script>
</head>
<body>
    <div id="example" title="This is a modal
    → dialog">
        So long as you can see this dialog,
        → you can't touch the page below
    </div>
    <h1>Welcome to my page</h1>
    <div id="bodyText">Lorem ipsum dolor sit
    → amet, consectetuer adipiscing elit.
    → Nulla viverra aliquet mi. Cras urna.
    → Curabitur diam. Curabitur eros nibh,
    → condimentum eu, tincidunt at, commodo
    → vitae, nisi. Duis nulla lectus,
    → feugiat et, tincidunt nec, iaculis
    → vehicula, tortor. Sed tortor felis,
    → viverra vitae, posuere et, ullamcorper
    → a, leo. Suspendisse euismod libero at
    → orci. Pellentesque odio massa,
    → condimentum at, pellentesque sed,
    → lacinia quis, mauris. Proin ultricies
    → risus cursus mi. Cras nibh quam,
    → adipiscing vel, tincidunt a, consequat
    → ut, mi. Aenean neque arcu, pretium
    → posuere, tincidunt non, consequat sit
    → amet, enim. Duis fermentum. Donec eu
    → augue. Mauris sit amet ligula.</div>
</body>
</html>
```
```

A This modal dialog box can be dragged around the browser window, but you can't get to what's below it until it's closed.

Listing 15.7 This little bit of CSS creates the solid dark background behind the dialog.

```
.ui-widget-overlay {
    background: #000 none;
}
```

Listing 15.8 This tiny bit of jQuery code handles the modal dialog.

```
$(document).ready(function() {
    $("#example").dialog({
        modal: true,
        resizable: false,
        buttons: [{
            text: "OK",
            click: function() {
                $(this).dialog("close");
            }
        }]
    });
});
```

2. ```
$("#example").dialog({
    modal: true,
    resizable: false,
```
We want a draggable modal dialog on the page, and the little bit of custom code we need is shown in **Listing 15.8**. This code runs when the page first loads, finding the **example** element and using it as the basis of a dialog. That dialog is modal (because of the line **modal: true**) and is not resizable (because of the line **resizable: false**), as seen in **A**.

3. ```
buttons: [{
    text: "OK",
    click: function() {
        $(this).dialog("close");
    }
}]
```
This dialog has a single button that says "OK," and when it's clicked, the dialog closes. If you want more buttons or more actions to take place when the dialog is clicked, they would go here.

TIP By default, dialogs are both resizable and draggable. If you want yours to be resizable as well, all you have to do is remove the **resizable: false** line in step 2.

Pick a Theme, Any Theme

By this point in the book, you've no doubt noticed that we aren't professional web designers. If you're in the same situation, you'll appreciate the number of professional themes jQuery UI makes freely available Ⓐ.

Chapter 14 covered how you can use jQuery's CDN to serve its JavaScript files. Happily, you can do the same thing with jQuery UI's CSS files.

Instead of using **/jquery-version#** files, though, you'll find the CSS in **/ui/version#/themes/themeName/jQuery-ui.css**, where:

- **version#** is the version of jQuery UI (*not* jQuery) you want to use
- **themeName** is any of the increasing number of available themes (current count: 24). You can find a list of the current names and locations at **blog.jqueryui.com**.

If you compare Listings 15.3 and 15.6, all we needed to do to change the page's style was edit the theme name in the **<link>** tag. It's easy to switch from one theme to another, so try them all out and see which ones work for you.

Dark Hive

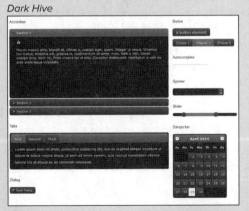

Hot Sneaks

Ⓐ Some of the many themes available: Dark Hive, Hot Sneaks, Humanity, Le Frog, Overcast, South Street, Swanky Purse, and Vader. Not to mention the several others shown elsewhere in this chapter. And of course, they all look even better in color!

Humanity

Le Frog

Overcast

South Street

Swanky Purse

Vader

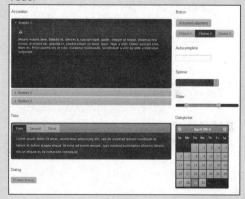

Auto-Completing Fields

At the end of Chapter 13, you may recall that we needed a great deal of code to keep users from entering invalid state names. Here, you'll see how jQuery turns lengthy code into one-liners. **Listing 15.9** has the HTML, and **Listing 15.10** our JavaScript.

To use jQuery to handle auto-completing fields:

1. ```
   var stateList = "Alabama*Alaska
   →*Arizona*Arkansas*California
   →*Colorado*Connecticut*Delaware
   →*Florida*Georgia*Hawaii*Idaho
   →*Illinois*Indiana*Iowa*Kansas
   →*Kentucky*Louisiana*Maine
   →*Maryland*Massachusetts
   →*Michigan*Minnesota*Mississippi
   →*Missouri*Montana*Nebraska
   →*Nevada*New Hampshire*New Jersey
   →*New Mexico*New York
   →*North Carolina*North Dakota
   →*Ohio*Oklahoma*Oregon
   →*Pennsylvania*Rhode Island
   →*South Carolina*South Dakota
   →*Tennessee*Texas*Utah*Vermont
   →*Virginia*Washington
   →*West Virginia*Wisconsin
   →*Wyoming";
   ```

   We need a list of states, and this time, we'll just hard-code it into a variable, **stateList**. Here are all 50 states, separated by asterisks.

Listing 15.9 This HTML page brings in the big guns to do its work.

```
<!DOCTYPE html>
<html>
<head>
    <title>Auto-fill Form Fields</title>
    <link rel="stylesheet"
    → href="http://code.jquery.com/
    → ui/1.10.4/themes/smoothness/
    → jquery-ui.css">
    <script src="http://code.jquery.com/
    → jquery-2.1.0.js"></script>
    <script src="http://code.jquery.com/
    → ui/1.10.4/jquery-ui.js"></script>
    <script src="script04.js"></script>
</head>
<body>
    <div class="ui-widget">
        <label for="searchField">Please enter
        → your state:</label>
        <input id="searchField">
    </div>
</body>
</html>
```

Listing 15.10 Here, jQuery makes short work out of what used to be a lengthy task.

```
$(function(){
    var stateList = "Alabama*Alaska*Arizona
    →*Arkansas*California*Colorado
    →*Connecticut*Delaware*Florida*Georgia
    →*Hawaii*Idaho*Illinois*Indiana*Iowa
    →*Kansas*Kentucky*Louisiana*Maine
    →*Maryland*Massachusetts*Michigan
    →*Minnesota*Mississippi*Missouri
    →*Montana*Nebraska*Nevada*New Hampshire
    →*New Jersey*New Mexico*New York
    →*North Carolina*North Dakota*Ohio
    →*Oklahoma*Oregon*Pennsylvania
    →*Rhode Island*South Carolina
    →*South Dakota*Tennessee*Texas*Utah
    →*Vermont*Virginia*Washington
    →*West Virginia*Wisconsin*Wyoming";

    $("#searchField").autocomplete({
        source: stateList.split("*")
    });
});
```
```

A This menu lets users choose a state by typing, by clicking, or by using the arrow keys to move up and down the list.

2. **$("#searchField").autocomplete({**

   Whenever the user types into the **searchField** input field, do the following.

3. **source: stateList.split("*")**

   The **autocomplete()** function has one element that needs a value, **source**. The **source** element needs to be passed an array, and all we have to do to provide that is **split()** our **stateList** on every asterisk. Given that array, jQuery does all the work for us **A**.

> **TIP** There are a few things this example doesn't do that the earlier one did. For instance, this one doesn't limit its matches to the beginnings of state names. On the other hand, this one does something big that the earlier one didn't: it lets users select a state from the drop-down menu by using the arrow keys.

Adding Sortable Tabs

By now, you should be used to seeing unordered lists turned into all kinds of menus, accordion or otherwise. In this example, we're using an unordered list of links for the menu names, combined with **div**s that contain the contents. **Listing 15.11** shows the HTML, **Listing 15.12** the CSS, and **Listing 15.13** the small amount of code required. Thanks to jQuery, you need to add very little to make the menu items re-sortable.

Listing 15.11 In this HTML page, note that the link destinations match the **id**s of the contents you want to see.

```
<!DOCTYPE html>
<html>
<head>
    <title>Sortable Tabs</title>
    <link rel="stylesheet" href="//code.jquery.com/ui/1.10.4/themes/pepper-grinder/jquery-ui.css">
    <link rel="stylesheet" href="script05.css">
    <script src="http://code.jquery.com/jquery-2.1.0.js"></script>
    <script src="http://code.jquery.com/ui/1.10.4/jquery-ui.js"></script>
    <script src="script05.js"></script>
</head>
<body>
    <h2>Compact Stars</h2>
    <div id="tabs">
        <ul>
            <li><a href="#tabs-1">Neutron Star</a></li>
            <li><a href="#tabs-2">Pulsar</a></li>
            <li><a href="#tabs-3">Black Hole</a></li>
        </ul>
        <div id="tabs-1">
            <p><span><img src="images/Neutron_star.png" alt="neutron star"><br>Wikimedia Commons
            → </span>A <b>neutron star</b> is a type of stellar remnant that can result from the
            → gravitational collapse of a massive star during some kinds of supernova events.
            → Neutron stars are the densest and tiniest stars known to exist in the universe;
            → although having only the diameter of about 10 km (6 mi), they may have a mass of
            → several times that of the Sun. Neutron stars probably appear white to the naked eye.
            </p>
        </div>
        <div id="tabs-2">
```

listing continues on next page

Listing 15.11 *continued*

```
                 <p><span><img src="images/pulsar.jpg" alt="pulsar"><br>NASA's Marshall Space Flight
              → Center</span>A <b>pulsar</b> is a highly magnetized, rotating neutron star that emits
              → a beam of electromagnetic radiation. This radiation can only be observed when the
              → beam of emission is pointing toward the Earth, much the way a lighthouse can only be
              → seen when the light is pointed in the direction of an observer, and is responsible for
              → the pulsed appearance of emission.
                 </p>
          </div>
          <div id="tabs-3">
                 <p><span><img src="images/blackhole.jpg" alt="black hole"><br>NASA's Marshall Space
              → Flight Center</span>A <b>black hole</b> is defined as a region of spacetime from
              → which gravity prevents anything, including light, from escaping. The theory of general
              → relativity predicts that a sufficiently compact mass will deform spacetime to form
              → a black hole. The hole is called "black" because it absorbs all the light that hits
              → its event horizon, reflecting nothing, just like a perfect black body in
              → thermodynamics. The discovery of neutron stars sparked interest in gravitationally
              → collapsed compact objects as a possible astrophysical reality. Black holes of stellar
              → mass are expected to form when very massive stars collapse at the end of their
              → life cycle. After a black hole has formed it can continue to grow by absorbing mass
              → from its surroundings. By absorbing other stars and merging with other black holes,
              → supermassive black holes of millions of solar masses may form. There is general
              → consensus that supermassive black holes exist in the centers of most galaxies.
                 </p>
          </div>
      </div>
</body>
</html>
```

Listing 15.12 The CSS in this example is solely there to make the images look good—if you don't have images in your content, you can skip including the CSS altogether.

```css
span {
    float: right;
    margin-left: 1em;
    font-size: .75em;
    text-align: center;
}

img {
    width: 300px;
}

p::after {
    clear: both;
    content: "";
    display: block;
}
```

To add sortable tabs:

1. `var tabs = $("#tabs").tabs();`

   In this line, we create a new variable, **tabs**, which will contain all the tabbed menu items along with their contents, by getting everything within the **tabs div**. This is all that's necessary to make the tabbed interface work, as seen in Ⓐ and Ⓑ.

2. ```
tabs.find(".ui-tabs-nav").
  → sortable({
    axis: "x",
    stop: function() {
      tabs.tabs("refresh");
    }
  });
```

   Here's the code that handles the sorting. The **ui-tabs-nav** class was applied to the tabs by jQuery in the previous step, and we use its **sortable()** method to define how the user can re-arrange the tabs. In this case, we're saying that sorting can occur only along the x-axis Ⓒ, and that the display should refresh when the user has stopped moving things around.

Listing 15.13 Here's the jQuery that handles the tabbed UI and the ability to sort.

```
$(function() {
    var tabs = $("#tabs").tabs();
    tabs.find(".ui-tabs-nav").sortable({
        axis: "x",
        stop: function() {
            tabs.tabs("refresh");
        }
    });
});
```

Ⓐ When the page loads, the first tabbed item is displayed.

Ⓑ Clicking the second tab changes the content to that of the second item.

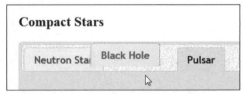

Ⓒ Because the menu is re-sortable, users can put the tabs into the order they prefer.
```

Using Check Boxes as Buttons

Unordered lists aren't the only HTML tags that can be turned into snazzy UI elements. Here, we turn boring check boxes into elegant buttons—all with a single line of jQuery.

To use check boxes as buttons:

1. ```
<div id="stylemenu">
    <input type="checkbox"
    → id="check1">
    <label for="check1">B</label>
    <input type="checkbox"
    → id="check2">
    <label for="check2">I</label>
    <input type="checkbox"
    → id="check3">
    <label for="check3">U</label>
    <input type="checkbox"
    → id="check4">
    <label for="check4">Code</label>
    <input type="checkbox"
    → id="check5">
    <label for="check5">ABC</label>
    <input type="checkbox"
    → id="check6">
    <label for="check6">Abc</label>
</div>
```

    This snippet of HTML (from **Listing 15.14**) would normally display as a line of check boxes and labels. The CSS in **Listing 15.15** styles the labels to match their intended functionality.

*continues on page 403*
```

Listing 15.14 The HTML sets up the content for the page.

```
<!DOCTYPE html>
<html>
<head>
    <title>Checkbox Buttons</title>
    <link rel="stylesheet" href="http://code.jquery.com/ui/1.10.4/themes/blitzer/jquery-ui.css">
    <link rel="stylesheet" href="script06.css">
    <script src="http://code.jquery.com/jquery-2.1.0.js"></script>
    <script src="http://code.jquery.com/ui/1.10.4/jquery-ui.js"></script>
    <script src="script06.js"></script>
</head>
<body>
    <div id="stylemenu">
        <input type="checkbox" id="check1"><label for="check1">B</label>
        <input type="checkbox" id="check2"><label for="check2">I</label>
        <input type="checkbox" id="check3"><label for="check3">U</label>
        <input type="checkbox" id="check4"><label for="check4">Code</label>
        <input type="checkbox" id="check5"><label for="check5">ABC</label>
        <input type="checkbox" id="check6"><label for="check6">Abc</label>
    </div>
    <textarea cols="45" rows="10">
    </textarea>
</body>
</html>
```

Listing 15.15 The CSS contains styles to match the use of each check box/button.

```
#stylemenu {
    padding: 2em 0;
}

#stylemenu input + label {
    font-weight: normal;
}

#stylemenu #check1 + label {
    font-weight: bold;
}

#stylemenu #check2 + label {
    font-style: italic;
}

#stylemenu #check3 + label {
    text-decoration: underline;
}

#stylemenu #check4 + label {
    font-family: monospace;
    font-size: 1.4em;
}

#stylemenu #check5 + label {
    text-decoration: line-through;
}

#stylemenu #check6 + label {
    font-variant: small-caps;
}
```

Listing 15.16 And jQuery easily turns the HTML and CSS into an attractive UI element.

```
$(function() {
    $("#stylemenu").buttonset();
});
```

2. **$("#stylemenu").buttonset();**

   This single line of jQuery code in **Listing 15.16** tells the browser to find the contents of the element with the **id** of **stylemenu** and turn it into the standard text formatting buttons seen in Ⓐ.

   TIP Note that while the buttons do toggle off and on in this example, they aren't actually set up to modify the text entered in the **textarea** field.

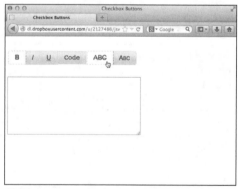

Ⓐ Here, a user has chosen bold and strike-through options for the text.

Adding a Calendar to Your Page

Many web applications need a calendar that the user can refer to and interact with. Reservation forms, to-do lists, navigation for posts on blogs—the list goes on and on. The jQuery library has a good calendar widget that is easy to implement . Best of all, it's very flexible; you can change its look and abilities by adding simple bits of code. Here's an example of an interactive one-up calendar (where only one month appears).

Ⓐ When you first bring up the page, the **datepicker** widget appears in the theme you've selected.

To add a one-up calendar:

1. `<h2>Date: <span id="datepicked">`
   `→ </span></h2>`
   `<div id="datepicker"></div>`

   Here's all that **Listing 15.17**, our HTML page, needs to support a jQuery calendar.

Listing 15.17 The HTML page for our calendar example. Note that we're pointing at a jQuery-hosted copy of jQuery.

```
<!DOCTYPE html>
<html>
<head>
    <title>1-up Date Picker</title>
    <link rel="stylesheet" href="//code.jquery.com/ui/1.10.4/themes/ui-darkness/jquery-ui.css">
    <script src="http://code.jquery.com/jquery-2.1.0.js"></script>
    <script src="http://code.jquery.com/ui/1.10.4/jquery-ui.js"></script>
    <script src="script07.js"></script>
</head>
<body>
    <h2>Date: <span id="datepicked"></span></h2>
    <div id="datepicker"></div>
</body>
</html>
```

Date: Monday, October 27, 2014

◀		October 2014				▶
Su	Mo	Tu	We	Th	Fr	Sa
			1	2	3	4
5	6	7	8	9	10	11
12	13	14	15	16	17	18
19	20	21	22	23	24	25
26	27	28	29	30	31	

B Once you make a date selection with your mouse, the selection highlights in the calendar. In this instance, we've also added code to display the date above the calendar.

Listing 15.18 This JavaScript file calls jQuery and sets the parameters used to display the date after the user clicks the calendar.

```
$(function() {
    $("#datepicker").datepicker({
        dateFormat: "DD, MM dd, yy",
        onSelect: function(selectedDate) {
            $("#datepicked").empty().append
            ↵ (selectedDate);
        }
    });
});
```

2. **`$("#datepicker").datepicker({`**

   Our HTML has a **datepicker div**, and in this line of JavaScript from **Listing 15.18**, we attach the jQuery UI **datepicker** widget to it.

3. **`dateFormat: "DD, MM dd, yy",`**

   We know that we're going to want to display the date on our page in a certain fashion, and this is where we tell jQuery just what fashion that is: the day of the week, followed by the full month name, the day of the month, and the four-digit year.

4. **`onSelect: function(selectedDate) {`**

   The date widget automatically pops up on the page, and when any date is selected, the **onSelect** jQuery event handler is triggered.

5. **`$("#datepicked").empty().append`**
   `→ (selectedDate);`

   When a date is chosen, we want to update the display on the page. That's done here. We update the **datepicked span**, first by emptying its current value (if any) and then by appending selectedDate **B**.

> **TIP** It may look odd, but yes, yy gives us a four-digit year. If you want a two-digit year instead, use y.

Adding a two-up calendar to your page

Sometimes you only need one calendar that includes appointments, restaurant reservations, or what have you. But two-up calendars are also common; they're used for events that begin and end on different dates. You'll often see them when making hotel reservations and purchasing plane tickets, for instance.

To add a two-up calendar:

1. ```
   <label for="from">From</label>
   → <input type="text" id="from"
   → name="from">
   <label for="to">to</label>
   → <input type="text" id="to"
   → name="to">
   ```

   Here's the minimal amount of HTML that needs to be added to **Listing 15.19**, our webpage ⓒ. **Listing 15.20**, our CSS file, is even shorter.

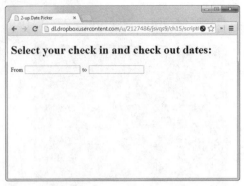

ⓒ In the two-up variant of the **datepicker** widget, we begin with two date fields. When you tab to the first field or click in it with your mouse, the two-calendar **datepicker** appears.

Listing 15.19 In this HTML page, we've added a two-up calendar, including the two date fields.

```
<!DOCTYPE html>
<html>
<head>
    <title>2-up Date Picker</title>
    <link rel="stylesheet" href="//code.jquery.com/ui/1.10.4/themes/start/jquery-ui.css">
    <link rel="stylesheet" href="script08.css">
    <script src="http://code.jquery.com/jquery-2.1.0.js"></script>
    <script src="http://code.jquery.com/ui/1.10.4/jquery-ui.js"></script>
    <script src="script08.js"></script>
</head>
<body>
<h1>Select your check in and check out dates:</h1>
    <label for="from">From</label> <input type="text" id="from" name="from">
    <label for="to">to</label> <input type="text" id="to" name="to">
</body>
</html>
```
```

Listing 15.20 The CSS shown here just moves the two-up date picker down a little ways.

```
div#ui-datepicker-div {
    margin-top: 10px;
}
```

2. **var dates = $("#from, #to).**
   → datepicker({

   Our JavaScript page, **Listing 15.21**, starts off similarly to Listing 15.18, but not identically. Instead of attaching **datepicker** to one element on the page, we're now attaching it to two: **from** and **to**. Additionally, we're returning the result of **datepicker** and storing it in the **dates** variable for future use.

3. **defaultDate: "+1w",**

   We can tell the **datepicker** widget to have a default start date, and here we set that to always be one week from today.

4. **numberOfMonths: 2,**

   One of the reasons we're using jQuery is its flexibility, and one of the ways in which the **datepicker** widget is flexible is that it's easy to modify how many months to show. We tell it here to show two months at a time.

   continues on next page

Listing 15.21 This jQuery function attaches the **datepicker** object to the two date fields on the page, and stores the results in a variable.

```
$(function() {
    var dates = $("#from, #to").datepicker({
        defaultDate: "+1w",
        numberOfMonths: 2,
        onSelect: function(selectedDate) {
            var option = (this.id == "from") ? "minDate" : "maxDate";
            date = $.datepicker.parseDate($.datepicker._defaults.dateFormat, selectedDate);
            dates.not(this).datepicker("option", option, date);
        }
    });
});
```

5. **onSelect: function(selectedDate) {**

Again, there are things we want to accomplish when a date is selected, and that happens here .

6. **var option = (this.id == "from") ?**
   → "minDate" : "maxDate";

Here, we figure out which calendar we're in, and store that in **option**. If **this.id** is **from**, **option** is set to **minDate**. Otherwise (if **this.id** is **to**), **option** is set to **maxDate**.

7. **date = $.datepicker.parseDate**
   → ($.datepicker._defaults.
   → dateFormat, selectedDate);

We automatically get **selectedDate**, but that's not the format we want. Here, we use **datepicker**'s **parseDate()** routine to set **date**.

8. **dates.not(this).datepicker**
   → ("option", option, date);

And finally, we use our just-set values for **option** and **date** to help set the beginning (**minDate**) and ending (**maxDate**) days of our selected range .

D You can click the round arrow buttons at the left and right edges of the bar with the month names to change the months display. To pick the first date, simply click a date in the left-hand calendar.

E Note that once a date is picked in the left-hand calendar, all prior dates are dimmed. The first date that you picked is also entered into the first date field above the date picker. Now you can choose the second date (which is highlighted) in the right-hand calendar. That date will be placed into the second date field.

A It's usually best to begin customizing a theme in ThemeRoller by picking one of the existing themes from the Gallery tab.

B Clicking the Roll Your Own tab shows you the wide range of customization options that are available.

Using ThemeRoller to Customize Your Look

As a web developer, you need to work with designers to create a unified look across your site. Happily, the creators of jQuery understand that simply adding functionality to your site isn't enough; that functionality must also work within the look and feel of your site. That's why they created ThemeRoller, a tool that allows you to design custom jQuery user interface themes for your projects. You can create a completely custom theme or modify one of the many predesigned themes. To get started with ThemeRoller, go to **jqueryui.com/themeroller**.

To create a custom theme:

1. The simplest way to make your own theme is to use one of the many existing jQuery themes as your starting point. To view your choices, click "Gallery" in the left sidebar **A**.

2. Scroll through the available themes, and find the one that's closest to your desired look. Click the Edit button just underneath and to the right of the theme. The left sidebar will then switch to the Roll Your Own panel **B**.

continues on next page

3. At this point, you can pick any of the accordion menu options on the panel, and that option's settings appear **C**.

4. As you edit the values in the sidebar, the body of the page updates to match, allowing you to immediately see (and judge!) the difference.

5. When you're happy with the result, click the Download Theme button at the top of the panel and you'll be taken to the Download Builder page **D**.

6. On this page, you can choose how light or heavy you want your CSS to be—if you select all the components, your pages will take longer to download and render than if you pick the minimum. That is, if you know that your site is never going to use the Shake or Pulsate effects, just deselect their check boxes and their overhead won't be included.

7. When you know just what you want, click the Download button at the bottom of the page. You should end up with a downloaded folder of jQuery goodness, with an index.html file at its root level. Open that page in a browser, and it should tell you exactly what you've downloaded and give you directions on how to add your new theme to your pages.

TIP If you use a custom theme, make sure your pages reference the files you just downloaded and not jQuery's CDN. And of course, remember to upload them to your server!

C As you make changes to categories in the Roll Your Own tab, ThemeRoller gives you a live preview on the right side of the screen. In this case, we've bumped up the font weight to Bold, increased the font size from 1.1em to 1.5em, and added a more visible diagonal crosshatch pattern to the Header/Toolbar section, which you can see most clearly in the Tabs and Datepicker widgets.

D Clicking the Download Theme button in ThemeRoller brings you to the Download Builder page, where you can further customize the components you want to build and download. When you have just the options you want, click the Download button at the bottom of the page.

Building on jQuery

In the last couple of chapters, you've seen how jQuery can be used to add complex functions to websites with a minimum of coding, and in ways that leverage your existing knowledge of HTML and CSS. It's usually easier to add JavaScript functions to your sites with jQuery than to code them individually.

The previous chapter covered jQuery's user interface toolkit, which allows you to easily add the features—such as menus, buttons, dialogs, and progress bars—that OS X and Windows users are used to. Besides user interface enhancements, the jQuery library works well as a foundation on which to add almost unlimited functionality to a site. As just two examples: you can use jQuery to access remote data from servers using Ajax, JSON, or both; and with jQuery plugins, you can add entirely new abilities to jQuery and, therefore, to your sites. Let's start building!

In This Chapter

Using jQuery as a Foundation

One of the most important things you'll gain from using jQuery is freedom from worrying about browser compatibility. Because no two browsers use JavaScript in quite the same way, hand-coding JavaScript often requires you to write code that works around the idiosyncrasies of different browsers. When you use jQuery, that problem simply goes away because jQuery gives you a common set of functions that work across all browsers. Behind the scenes, jQuery worries about browser quirks, so you don't have to.

Using jQuery, you can access and manipulate any of the elements on a page, using familiar CSS selectors, including classes and IDs. You get even more control over your page because jQuery gives you the ability to create or delete HTML elements at any time.

Because jQuery loads before any of the other elements on your page (it's called from the **head** section of the page; the rest of the page elements will be in the **body**), the library can run code as soon as the elements you want to manipulate are ready. This is better than using the browser's **onload** function, which gets called only after all of the page elements, including images, have loaded. The benefit to your user is that the page will appear to be more responsive to their actions.

Ajax, JSON, and jQuery

The jQuery library has a rich set of Ajax functions that let your page talk to the server behind the scenes, fetching more data without needing to refresh the page.

This is great because it allows web-based applications to be as responsive as desktop applications. Once the updated data has been received from the server, jQuery lets you update page elements without a noticeable flicker while the page refreshes.

As you've seen in prior chapters, it's certainly possible to code Ajax requests with your own JavaScript, using the **XMLHttpRequest** object. You have to load any data that you want to send to the server into that object, and then set up another function to receive the server's response. You also need error checking code to make sure that the server's response makes sense. Instead of writing all that code, you can simply use the jQuery function **$.ajax()** to handle the entire process.

Similarly, jQuery provides **$.getJSON()**, which lets you easily access and then manipulate data received in JSON format.

jQuery plugins

The main jQuery library has a lot of built-in functionality, but it's easy for developers to add new features as plugins, which add a virtually unlimited feature set to your sites. There are hundreds of plugins that extend jQuery in many different areas and are freely available for downloading. You'll find plugins that add animation effects, let you drag and drop page elements, change the page layout, deal with different media types, work with page navigation, add useful widgets, as well as many more.

A simple search in your favorite search engine will lead you to a bountiful selection of jQuery plugins, or you can begin your search at **plugins.jquery.com**.

Dragging and Dropping Elements

One of the nicest UI features is the ability to drag and drop page elements to suit your preferences. In this example, we've created a virtual light-table page for a web-based slideshow **A**. You can drag and drop the images into a particular order on the page **B**. If this were a complete web application, you could then click the "Build it!" button to create and play the slideshow in the order you chose **C**. The HTML for the page is in **Listing 16.1**, the CSS is in **Listing 16.2**, and the JavaScript is in **Listing 16.3**.

A When you first load the slideshow page, the photos appear in a preset order.

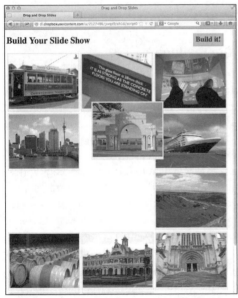

B Clicking and dragging an image makes the other images move out of its way.

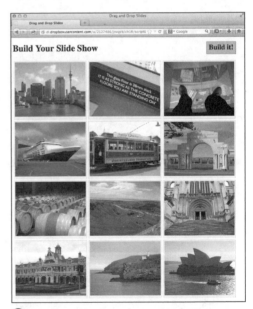

C The rearranged images are ready to be built into a slide show once you click the "Build it!" button (but that step involves another plugin).

To enable drag and drop for page elements:

1.
```
<ul id="sortable">
    <li class="ui-state-default">
    → <img src="images/img_0001.jpg"
    → alt="slide #1"></li>
    <li class="ui-state-default">
    → <img src="images/img_0002.jpg"
    → alt="slide #2"></li>
```

   Here are the first two (of twelve) list items on our HTML page. If you want more or fewer images in your slideshow, all you have to do is add or delete list elements.

continues on next page

Listing 16.1 The HTML page for the virtual light table has an unordered list that contains all the images.

```
<!DOCTYPE html>
<html>
<head>
    <title>Drag and Drop Slides</title>
    <link rel="stylesheet" href="//code.jquery.com/ui/1.10.4/themes/flick/jquery-ui.css">
    <link rel="stylesheet" href="script01.css">
    <script src="http://code.jquery.com/jquery-2.1.0.js"></script>
    <script src="http://code.jquery.com/ui/1.10.4/jquery-ui.js"></script>
    <script src="script01.js"></script>
</head>
<body>
    <h1>Build Your Slide Show <a href="#">Build it!</a></h1>
    <ul id="sortable">
        <li class="ui-state-default"><img src="images/img_0001.jpg" alt="slide #1"></li>
        <li class="ui-state-default"><img src="images/img_0002.jpg" alt="slide #2"></li>
        <li class="ui-state-default"><img src="images/img_0003.jpg" alt="slide #3"></li>
        <li class="ui-state-default"><img src="images/img_0004.jpg" alt="slide #4"></li>
        <li class="ui-state-default"><img src="images/img_0005.jpg" alt="slide #5"></li>
        <li class="ui-state-default"><img src="images/img_0006.jpg" alt="slide #6"></li>
        <li class="ui-state-default"><img src="images/img_0007.jpg" alt="slide #7"></li>
        <li class="ui-state-default"><img src="images/img_0008.jpg" alt="slide #8"></li>
        <li class="ui-state-default"><img src="images/img_0009.jpg" alt="slide #9"></li>
        <li class="ui-state-default"><img src="images/img_0010.jpg" alt="slide #10"></li>
        <li class="ui-state-default"><img src="images/img_0011.jpg" alt="slide #11"></li>
        <li class="ui-state-default"><img src="images/img_0012.jpg" alt="slide #12"></li>
    </ul>
</body>
</html>
```

2. ```css
#sortable {
    list-style-type: none;
    margin: 0;
    padding: 0;
    width: 820px;
}
```

In our CSS, all the list items we want to sort are inside the **sortable** div, and here's where we lay out the bulk of the page.

3. ```css
#sortable li {
    margin: 3px;
    padding: 3px;
    float: left;
}
```

Each individual list item gets a little bit of margin and padding and is floated left to fit snugly next to its neighbors.

4. ```css
#sortable li img {
    width: 256px;
    height: 192px;
}
```

Here's where we tell the browser what size we want for our images.

5. ```
$("#sortable").sortable().
↪ disableSelection();
```

And finally, the jQuery code... that's it? Yes, really. All of the above gets handled by a single line of jQuery, in which we tell the **sortable** div that we want to be able to sort whatever it contains—but by the way, we don't want anyone actually selecting any of our items.

Listing 16.2 The CSS file for the virtual light table defines the physical appearance of the page.

```css
#sortable {
    list-style-type: none;
    margin: 0;
    padding: 0;
    width: 820px;
}

#sortable li {
    margin: 3px;
    padding: 3px;
    float: left;
}

#sortable li img {
    width: 256px;
    height: 192px;
}

h1 a {
    float: right;
    display: inline-block;
    font-size: .8em;
    padding: 8px;
    text-decoration: none;
    background-color: silver;
    border: 1px solid gray;
    margin: -5px 25px 0 0;
}
```

Listing 16.3 This simple jQuery function is all you need to allow the user to drag and drop the images on the page.

```javascript
$(function() {
    $("#sortable").sortable().
↪ disableSelection();
});
```

Using jQuery with External Data

Conceptually, the idea of using external (that is, XML or JSON) data on your web-page is simple. The users have a page on their screen; there's more data somewhere out there on a server; you want to load that data onto the page without a page refresh.

The data out on the server can be almost anything: text, images, music, video, and more. In this example, we'll combine the drag-and-drop functionality of the previous task with jQuery loading in the same Flickr feed we used in Chapter 13. The HTML is in **Listing 16.4**, the CSS in **Listing 16.5**, and the JavaScript (described next) in **Listing 16.6**.

Listing 16.4 When you want to grab and display an external data feed (in this case a Flickr feed), you need to first create the HTML page.

```
<!DOCTYPE html>
<html>
<head>
    <title>Drag and Drop External Data</title>
    <link rel="stylesheet" href="//code.jquery.com/ui/1.10.4/themes/eggplant/jquery-ui.css">
    <link rel="stylesheet" href="script02.css">
    <script src="http://code.jquery.com/jquery-2.1.0.js"></script>
    <script src="http://code.jquery.com/ui/1.10.4/jquery-ui.js"></script>
    <script src="script02.js"></script>
</head>
<body>
    <h2 id="head"></h2>
    <h4 id="subhead"></h4>
    <ul id="sortable"></ul>
</body>
</html>
```

To use jQuery to access a data feed:

1.
```
$.getJSON(
    "http://api.flickr.com/services/
    → feeds/photoset.gne?nsid=
    → 23922109@N00&set=
    → 72157600976524175&format=
    → json&jsoncallback=?",
    function(data) {
        createPage(data);
    }
);
```

This may look complex at first, but it really isn't. There are just two parameters being passed to **$.getJSON**:

▸ A string containing the URL of the data we want; in this case, it's the Flickr feed we saw back in Listing 13.12.

▸ An anonymous function that will be called when we get that data. Here,

Listing 16.5 This CSS file styles the different elements once they've been parsed out of the feed.

```
#sortable {
    list-style-type: none;
    padding: 0;
}

#sortable li {
    margin: 3px;
    padding: 3px;
    float: left;
}
```

Listing 16.6 The jQuery in this JavaScript file starts off by getting us the feed in JSON format.

```
$.getJSON(
    "http://api.flickr.com/services/feeds/photoset.gne?nsid=23922109@N00&set=72157600976524175
    → &format=json&jsoncallback=?",
    function(data) {
        createPage(data);
    }
);

function createPage(imgData) {
    var imgs = "";
    $("#head").html(imgData.title);
    $("#subhead").html(imgData.description);

    $.each(imgData.items, function(i, item) {
        imgs += "<li class='ui-state-default'><a href='" + item.link + "'><img src='";
        imgs += item.media.m.replace(/_m/g,"_q") + "' alt='" + item.title + "'></a></li>";
    });

    $("#sortable").append(imgs);
    $("#sortable").sortable().disableSelection();
}
```

A The jQuery code grabs a JSON data feed (in this case, one of the authors' Flickr stream), parses it, and displays the result on the page.

that function does one thing: call another function, **createPage()**.

2. ```
var imgs = "";
$("#head").html(imgData.title);
$("#subhead").html(
→ imgData.description);
```

Here we are inside **createPage()**, where we want to start parsing our input (now an array of data called **imgData**) so we can add elements to our page. First off, we initialize a new variable, **imgs**, which we'll be seeing a lot more of later.

Next, we get general information about the images themselves and put it into our head and subhead elements.

3. ```
$.each(imgData.items,
→ function(i, item) {
```

Next up: we need to loop through each individual image. The built-in **$.each()** function knows how to get the data out of each line and put it into **item**.

4. ```
imgs += "<li class=
→ 'ui-state-default'><a href='"
→ + item.link + "'><img src='";
imgs += item.media.m.replace
→ (/_m/g,"_q") + "' alt='" +
→ item.title + "'></a></li>";
```

Here's where the work really happens: for each image in the feed, we add text onto the **imgs** variable. Each image is turned into an image tag, which is inside a link tag (**a**), which is inside a list element (**li**). The image link, the image source, and the image's alt text all come from the feed.

5. ```
$("#sortable").append(imgs);
$("#sortable").sortable().
→ disableSelection();
```

The completed **imgs** variable is added to the page, and finally, we again make the images sortable **A**.

Using jQuery Plugins

As noted earlier, developers have created jQuery plugins to extend jQuery's core functionality in many different directions. There are far too many plugins for us to discuss all of them in this book, so we'll use just a couple of examples to show off their power.

In this task, we'll use a plugin, "SlidesJS," to display a professional-looking image slideshow . SlidesJS is a free download that, just as with custom themes, you then need to integrate into your site. That same download includes the CSS needed to style the slideshow.

A Here's how our slideshow page starts off.

Listing **16.7** This HTML page includes files from the SlidesJS plugin.

```
<!DOCTYPE html>
<html>
<head>
    <title>jQuery Plugin Slideshow</title>
    <link rel="stylesheet" href="SlidesJS/css/example.css">
    <link rel="stylesheet" href="SlidesJS/css/font-awesome.min.css">
    <link rel="stylesheet" href="script03.css">
    <script src="http://code.jquery.com/jquery-2.1.0.js"></script>
    <script src="SlidesJS/source/jquery.slides.min.js"></script>
    <script src="script03.js"></script>
</head>
<body>
    <div id="slides">
        <img src="images/01estock_commonswiki.jpg" alt="01estock_commonswiki.jpg">
        <img src="images/02estock_commonswiki.jpg" alt="02estock_commonswiki.jpg">
        <img src="images/03estock_commonswiki.jpg" alt="03estock_commonswiki.jpg">
        <img src="images/04estock_commonswiki.jpg" alt="04estock_commonswiki.jpg">
        <img src="images/05estock_commonswiki.jpg" alt="05estock_commonswiki.jpg">
        <img src="images/06estock_commonswiki.jpg" alt="06estock_commonswiki.jpg">
        <a href="#" class="slidesjs-navigation slidesjs-previous"><i class="icon-chevron-left
        → icon-large"></i></a>
        <a href="#" class="slidesjs-navigation slidesjs-next"><i class="icon-chevron-right
        → icon-large"></i></a>
    </div>
</body>
</html>
```

Listing 16.8 This CSS file adds on the little bit of
CSS we still want.

```css
body {
    padding: 20px;
}

#slides {
    display: none;
}

#slides a {
    color: #333;
}

#slides a:hover,
#slides a:active {
    color: #9e2020;
}

div.slidesjs-container {
    margin-bottom: 10px;
}

.slidesjs-pagination {
    float: right;
    list-style: none;
    margin: 0;
}

.slidesjs-pagination li {
    float: left;
}

.slidesjs-pagination li a {
    display: block;
    width: 13px;
    height: 0;
    padding-top: 13px;
    background-image: url(SlidesJS/images/
    ↪ pagination.png);
    overflow: hidden;
}

.slidesjs-pagination li a.active,
.slidesjs-pagination li a:hover.active {
    background-position: 0 -13px
}

.slidesjs-pagination li a:hover {
    background-position: 0 -26px
}
```

To use a jQuery plugin:

1. ```html
   <link rel="stylesheet"
   ↪ href="SlidesJS/css/example.css">
   <link rel="stylesheet"
   ↪ href="SlidesJS/css/font-awesome.
   ↪ min.css">
   ```

   The plugin comes with recommended
   style sheets, and we can use them just
   as they were packaged, as shown in
   Listing 16.7. Similarly, the script
   jquery.slides.min.js will be loaded
   in later. **Listing 16.8** contains the minimal CSS that we still need locally.

   continues on next page
   ```

2. `$("#slides").slidesjs({`

   Because we brought in the files for SlidesJS, we now have access to the **slidesjs** function in **Listing 16.9**. Here's where we set it up.

3. `navigation: {`
   `    active: false,`
   `    effect: "fade"`
   `},`

   We want custom navigation on our slideshow page, so **active** is set to **false** . We want the images to fade in when appearing and fade out when leaving, so **effect** is set to **"fade"** (versus the default, **"slide"**).

4. `pagination: {`
   `    effect: "fade"`
   `},`

   We want the same effect when we jump from page to page as when we move forward through pages, so we set **pagination**'s **effect** to also be **"fade"** .

5. `effect: {`
   `    fade: {`
   `        speed: 800`
   `    }`
   `}`

   We're using the fade effect in this example, and we really want to show it off—so here, we tell the script to take 800 milliseconds to animate the fade.

   TIP SlidesJS was written by Nathan Searles. Find information about the plugin at `slidesjs.com`. Download it from `github.com/nathansearles/Slides`, and find support at `groups.google.com/forum/#!forum/slidesjs`.

   TIP Unlike jQuery and jQuery UI, plugins must be downloaded from the author's site and uploaded to your server—there's no fixed CDN for plugins.

B We can move from one slide to the next using the navigation arrows at the bottom left.

C Or, we can jump from page to page by clicking one of the circles in the bottom right.

Listing 16.9 The jQuery in this JavaScript file sets up the slideshow.

```
$(function(){
    $("#slides").slidesjs({
        navigation: {
            active: false,
            effect: "fade"
        },
        pagination: {
            effect: "fade"
        },
        effect: {
            fade: {
                speed: 800
            }
        }
    });
});
```

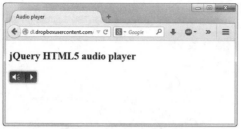

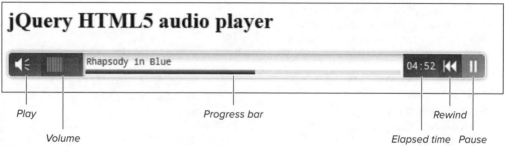

Adding a jQuery Audio Plugin

In this example, you'll see how to use a jQuery plugin to implement a full-featured audio player that takes advantage of the HTML5 **audio** tag, with a Flash fallback for browsers that don't support HTML5. When the page loads, there are just a couple of small buttons **Ⓐ**, but press Play and it expands to show all its features **Ⓑ**.

Ⓐ This jQuery plugin creates an HTML5 audio player. When loaded, the controls are minimized.

Play

Volume

Progress bar

Rewind

Elapsed time *Pause*

Ⓑ Once you click the Play button and start playing the file, you get the familiar range of playback controls.

To add an audio player:

1. `<script src="mbPlayer/inc/jquery.`
   `→ mb.miniPlayer.js"></script>`
   `<script src="mbPlayer/inc/jquery.`
   `→ jplayer.min.js"></script>`

   In **Listing 16.10**, these script tags bring in the two parts of the audio plugin.

2. `<a class="audio {ogg:'mbPlayer/`
   `→ Rhapsody_in_Blue.ogg'}"`
   `→ href="mbPlayer/Rhapsody_in_`
   `→ Blue.mp3">Rhapsody in Blue</a>`

   Following the directions (included with the download) produces this link, which, when loaded, plays either the MP3 or Ogg version of one of our favorite pieces.

3. `$(".audio").mb_miniPlayer({`
   `    width: 360,`
   `    inLine: false,`
   `    showRew: true,`
   `    showTime: true`
   `});`

   Listing 16.11 contains all the jQuery code we have to add—everything else is handled for us by the plugin scripts. In this step, we set the player's **width** to 360 pixels, we set **inLine** to **false** (that is, it's not part of the regular document flow), and we set the player to show both the Rewind button and the elapsed time.

> **TIP** This plugin was written by Matteo "Pupunzi" Bicocchi. The plugin's site is pupunzi.com/#mb.components/ mb.miniAudioPlayer/miniAudioPlayer. html. Download it from github.com/ pupunzi/jquery.mb.miniAudioPlayer.

> **TIP** Need help with the plugin? Its author has a support website at jquery.pupunzi.com.

Listing 16.10 On this HTML page, we've added a jQuery plugin that provides an HTML5 audio player.

```
<!DOCTYPE html>
<html>
<head>
    <title>Audio player</title>
    <link rel="stylesheet" href="mbPlayer/
    → css/miniplayer.css"/>
    <script src="http://code.jquery.com/
    → jquery-2.1.0.js"></script>
    <script src="mbPlayer/inc/jquery.
    → mb.miniPlayer.js"></script>
    <script src="mbPlayer/inc/jquery.
    → jplayer.min.js"></script>
    <script src="script04.js"></script>
</head>
<body>
    <h2>jQuery HTML5 audio player</h2>
    <div>
    <a class="audio {ogg:'mbPlayer/
    → Rhapsody_in_Blue.ogg'}" href=
    → "mbPlayer/Rhapsody_in_Blue.
    → mp3">Rhapsody in Blue</a>
    </div>
</body>
</html>
```

Listing 16.11 The JavaScript file with the jQuery call to the audio player plugin is almost anticlimactic.

```
$(function(){
    $(".audio").mb_miniPlayer({
        width: 360,
        inLine: false,
        showRew: true,
        showTime: true
    });
});
```

Scripting
Mobile Devices

The newest big opportunities and
challenges in web development have
all come from the same event: the
growth in popularity of mobile devices.
A significant percentage of web surfing
(and more importantly, online purchasing)
now happens on phones and tablets. It's
time to face mobile devices head on. In
this chapter, you'll learn how to handle
device rotation and location, launch other
applications from the browser, and target
particular devices.

In This Chapter

Changing Your Orientation

One of the biggest differences in coding for mobile devices versus desktop computers is that a device's orientation can change—that is, users can flip their phones from horizontal to vertical or vice versa. You never need to check orientation when you're creating websites viewed on a desktop, but you will frequently when working with mobile sites.

For instance, we didn't take mobile devices into account when we originally designed this site. When we check how it appears in a mobile device, it looks like  (portrait) and Ⓑ (landscape). The former is OK, but to save us some scrolling the font could be a tiny bit smaller Ⓒ. In landscape, the font is way too large, so we need to shrink it even more Ⓓ. Here's how that's done.

Ⓐ The before version of our page, in portrait mode.

Ⓑ The before version of our page, now rotated to landscape.

C The portrait version of our site, after tweaking the font size.

D The landscape version now displays considerably more text.

To handle orientation changes:

1.
```css
@media only screen and
→ (max-device-width:1024px) {
   main {
      width: 100%;
   }
   nav {
      font-weight: normal;
   }
   h1, h2, h3, h4, h5, h6 {
      font-family: Albany, Georgia,
      → "Times New Roman", serif;
   }
   .landscape {
      font-size: .5em;
   }
   .portrait {
      font-size: .8em;
   }
}
```

The HTML (**Listing 17.1**) and the CSS (**Listing 17.2**) are pretty normal, until you get down to this section of the CSS. What we care about are the last two rules, which set the **font-size** differently depending on whether the **.landscape** or **.portrait** class is applied. You'll notice, though, that neither class is used in the HTML; instead, that's all up to JavaScript.

continues on page 430

Listing 17.1 A fairly ordinary company page.

```
<!DOCTYPE html>
<html>
<head>
    <title>Welcome to Alpaca Repo</title>
    <meta name="viewport" content="width=560">
    <link rel="stylesheet" href="script01.css">
    <script src="script01.js"></script>
</head>
<body>
    <main>
        <header>
            <img src="images/header.jpg" alt="header">
        </header>
        <article>
            <h2>When They Don't Pay, We Tow 'Em Away</h2>
            <p class="photo"><img src="images/3alpacas.jpg" alt="alpacas">Some of the alpacas we've
            → recovered.</p>
            <ul>
                <li><p>Are you a bank in need of someone to repossess an Alpaca from a breeder with
                → an outstanding loan?</p></li>
                <li><p>Are you a breeder looking to pick up an inexpensive bank-foreclosed Alpaca?
                → </p></li>
            </ul>
            <p>If you answered yes to either of these questions, you've come to the right place!
            → Contact us now to see what we can do for you.</p>
            <p>Lorem ipsum dolor sit amet, consectetuer adipiscing elit. Praesent aliquam,  justo
            → convallis luctus rutrum, erat nulla fermentum diam, at nonummy quam  ante ac quam.
            → Maecenas urna purus, fermentum id, molestie in, commodo  porttitor, felis. Nam blandit
            → quam ut lacus. Quisque ornare risus quis  ligula. Phasellus tristique purus a augue
            → condimentum adipiscing. Aenean  sagittis. Etiam leo pede, rhoncus venenatis, tristique
            → in, vulputate at,  odio. Donec et ipsum et sapien vehicula nonummy. Suspendisse
            → potenti. Fusce  varius urna id quam. Sed neque mi, varius eget, tincidunt nec,
            → suscipit id,  libero. In eget purus. Vestibulum ut nisl. Donec eu mi sed turpis
            → feugiat  feugiat. Integer turpis arcu, pellentesque eget, cursus et, fermentum ut,
            → sapien. Fusce metus mi, eleifend sollicitudin, molestie id, varius et, nibh.  Donec
            → nec libero.</p>
            <h2>H2 level heading</h2>
            <p>Lorem ipsum dolor sit amet, consectetuer adipiscing elit. Praesent aliquam,  justo
            → convallis luctus rutrum, erat nulla fermentum diam, at nonummy quam  ante ac quam.
            → Maecenas urna purus, fermentum id, molestie in, commodo  porttitor, felis. Nam blandit
            → quam ut lacus. Quisque ornare risus quis  ligula. Phasellus tristique purus a
            → augue condimentum adipiscing. Aenean  sagittis. Etiam leo pede, rhoncus venenatis,
            → tristique in, vulputate at, odio.</p>
        </article>
        <footer>
            <p>Copyright &copy; 2009-2014 Alpaca Repo. All rights reserved.</p>
        </footer>
    </main>
</body>
</html>
```

Listing 17.2 Add a little bit of custom CSS.

```css
body {
    font-family: Verdana, Helvetica, Arial,
    → sans-serif;
    background-color: #666;
    color: #000;
    margin: 0;
    padding: 0;
    text-align: center;
}

h1, h2, h3, h4, h5, h6 {
    font-family: Cambria, "Palatino
    → Linotype", "Book Antiqua",
    → "URW Palladio L", serif;
}

main {
    width: 80%;
    margin: 0 auto;
    padding: 0;
    text-align: left;
}

header {
    background-color: #91A43D;
    text-align: center;
    margin: 0;
    padding: 0;
    overflow: hidden;
}

header img {
    width: 100%;
    max-width: 800px;
    height: 110px;
}

article {
    background-color: #FFF;
    padding: 10px 20px 0 1em;
}

article::after {
    clear: both;
    content: "";
    display: table;
}
```

listing continues

Listing 17.2 *continued*

```css
.photo {
    float: right;
    margin-left: .8em;
    width: 200px;
    font-size: .8em;
    font-style: italic;
    line-height: 1em;
}

footer p {
    margin: 0;
    padding: 10px 0;
    background-color: #DDD;
    text-align: center;
    font-size: .8em;
}

@media only screen and (max-device-width:
→ 1024px) {
    main {
        width: 100%;
    }

    nav {
        font-weight: normal;
    }

    h1, h2, h3, h4, h5, h6 {
        font-family: Albany, Georgia,
        → "Times New Roman", serif;
    }

    .landscape {
        font-size: .5em;
    }

    .portrait {
        font-size: .8em;
    }
}

@media only screen and (min-resolution:
→ 192dpi), only screen and (
→ -webkit-min-device-pixel-ratio:2),
→ only screen and (min-device-width:768px)
→ and (min-device-height:768px) and
→ (max-device-width:1024px) {
    header img {
        width: 640px;
    }
}
```

2. `addEventListener("load",resetPage,`
   `→ false);`
   `addEventListener("orientation`
   `→ change",resetPage,false);`

   In the JavaScript code (**Listing 17.3**), we start off by adding a couple of event handlers: **load** (which we've seen many times before) and **orientationchange**. When triggered, both call the **resetPage()** function.

3. `if (Math.abs(window.orientation)`
   `→ == 90) {`
   `   classVal = "landscape";`
   `}`
   `else {`
   `   classVal = "portrait";`
   `}`

   The **orientation** property of **window** has one of four values: 0 (portrait, right-side-up), 90 (landscape, rotated left), 180 (portrait, upside-down), and −90 (landscape, rotated right).

   Here inside **resetPage()**, if the absolute value of **window.orientation** is 90, we know we're in landscape mode, regardless of direction. Otherwise, we're in portrait mode, and either way, we set **classVal** to our current situation.

4. `document.getElementsByTagName`
   `→ ("main")[0].setAttribute("class",`
   `→ classVal);`

   And finally, we apply the stored value of **classVal** as a **class** attribute of the **main** tag.

Listing 17.3 Add a little bit of JavaScript as well and you get a more attractive page via responsive design.

```
addEventListener("load",resetPage,false);
addEventListener("orientationchange",
→ resetPage,false);

function resetPage() {
    if (Math.abs(window.orientation) == 90) {
        classVal = "landscape";
    }
    else {
        classVal = "portrait";
    }
    document.getElementsByTagName("main")
    → [0].setAttribute("class", classVal);
}
```

TIP The @media query in step 1 makes the CSS apply only when it runs on a mobile device. The last @media query in Listing 17.2 limits the CSS to when it's running on a high-resolution mobile device.

TIP In general, @media queries are outside the realm of this book; if you want further information, check your favorite HTML or CSS book (ours is *HTML and CSS: Visual Quick-Start Guide, 8th Edition* [Peachpit Press, 2014], by Elizabeth Castro and Bruce Hyslop).

Debugging Mobile Devices

When it's time for debugging your site, it's unlikely that you have every iOS and Android device easily at hand. Thankfully, Apple and Google have spared you the expense of purchasing a multitude of phones and tablets by providing an Android emulator and an iOS simulator. You will find each when you download their respective SDK (Software Development Kit).

- **Android emulator:** Download the cross-platform Android SDK from **developer.android.com/sdk/**. You'll find detailed information about how the emulator works at **developer.android.com/tools/devices/emulator.html**.

- **iOS simulator:** Apple bundles its simulator with the Xcode developer tools. Download these from **developer.apple.com/xcode/downloads/**. Using the simulator is pretty much self-explanatory; unfortunately, it's Mac only.

Both these tools are free.

TIP If you're debugging webpages on iOS, here's a cool trick: run Safari while you're looking at your webpage in the emulator. Swap over to Safari, look at the Develop menu, and you'll see a new option: iPhone (or iPad) Simulator **A**. This will let you use Safari's development tools (such as the Web Inspector) on the page loaded into the simulator.

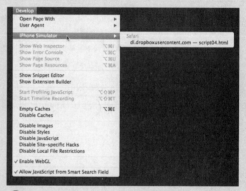

A This handy little menu item helps you debug mobile pages with the full set of tools you have on your desktop.

TABLE 17.1 Mobile Events

Event	Triggered By
gesturestart	Two or more fingers touching the surface
gesturechange	Fingers moving during a gesture
gestureend	End of the gesture
orientationChange	Device is rotated
touchstart	A finger touching the surface
touchmove	Finger moving during a touch
touchend	End of a touch
touchcancel	The browser itself canceling touch tracking

TABLE 17.2 Touch Properties

Properties	Meaning
clientX clientY	Touch location relative to the window's viewport
identifier	Unique identifier for this touch
pageX pageY	Touch location in page coordinates
screenX screenY	Touch location in screen coordinates
target	Target of the touch

TABLE 17.4 TouchEvent Object

Properties	Methods
altKey ctrlKey metaKey rotation scale shiftKey targetTouches changedTouches touches	initTouchEvent

TABLE 17.3 GestureEvent Object

Properties	Methods
altKey ctrlKey metaKey rotation scale shiftKey target	initGestureEvent

TABLE 17.5 DeviceMotionEvent Object

Properties	Methods
acceleration accelerationIncludingGravity interval rotationRate	initDeviceMotionEvent

TABLE 17.6 DeviceOrientationEvent Object

Properties	Methods
alpha beta gamma webkitCompassAccuracy webkitCompassHeading	initDeviceOrientationEvent

Listing 17.4 This HTML page is pretty dull.

```
<!DOCTYPE html>
<html>
<head>
    <title>Drag n' drop touch demo</title>
    <meta name="viewport"
    ➝ content="width=device-width">
    <link rel="stylesheet" href="script02.css">
    <script src="script02.js"></script>
</head>
<body>
    <div id="draggable">
        Drag me!
        <p id="boxLocation"></p>
    </div>
</body>
</html>
```

Handling Touch Events

Working with mobile devices, as you'll soon find out, comes with tradeoffs. An obvious one is that you give up hover events, but in return you get touch events. This small example makes it possible to move an element around your page via touch. The HTML is in **Listing 17.4**, the CSS in **Listing 17.5**, and the JavaScript, discussed here, in **Listing 17.6**.

Listing 17.5 A bit of styling makes it more interesting.

```
#draggable {
    position: absolute;
    background-color: #FFC;
    border: 5px solid yellow;
    width: 100px;
    height: 100px;
    padding: 50px;
    text-align: center;
    font-family: Albany, Georgia, "Times New Roman", serif;
}
```

Listing 17.6 But it really comes to life after it starts to move.

```
window.addEventListener(
    "load",
    function() {
        document.getElementById("draggable").addEventListener("touchmove",moved,false);
    },
    false
);

function moved(evt) {
    evt.preventDefault();
    var dragBox = document.getElementById("draggable");

    dragBox.style.left = (evt.changedTouches[0].pageX - 100) + "px";
    dragBox.style.top = (evt.changedTouches[0].pageY - 100) + "px";

    document.getElementById("boxLocation").innerHTML = "Top: " + dragBox.style.top +
    ➝ "<br>Left: " + dragBox.style.left;
}
```

To handle touch events:

1.
```
window.addEventListener(
    "load",
    function() {
        document.getElementById
        ⇥("draggable").
        ⇥addEventListener(
        ⇥"touchmove",moved,
        ⇥false);
    },
    false
);
```

When the page first loads , we want to add an event handler to the element with the **id draggable**. That new event, **touchmove**, will call **moved()** whenever it's triggered; that is, every time a user touches and then moves the element.

Ⓐ Here's our page (shown on an Android device) when it first loads.

2.
```
evt.preventDefault();
var dragBox = document.
⇥getElementById("draggable");
```

Normally, touching the screen and moving your finger will trigger a selection. We don't want that, so the **moved()** function starts off by preventing the default behavior. We next create a new variable, **dragBox**, which keeps us from having to type **document.getElementById** over and over again.

B And here's what it looks like after we've pushed it around a little.

3. ```
dragBox.style.left = (evt.changed
→Touches[0].pageX - 100) + "px";
dragBox.style.top = (evt.changed
→Touches[0].pageY - 100) + "px";
```

Here's where we actually move the box by resetting its **top** and **left** properties. This may look a little confusing at first glance, so we'll take it slowly.

Resetting the top and left corners moves the element's top-left corner—but chances are, that's not where your finger or stylus actually touches the display. If we reset the element's top-left corner to where your finger is, the element would appear to be jumping around.

It's more likely your finger is toward the center of the element. To move the top-left corner based on the movement of the element's center, we need to subtract 100 pixels each from both the left and top locations (i.e., the X and Y axes). Those are found in **evt.changedTouches[0].pageX** and **evt.changedTouches[0].pageY**, respectively.

4. ```
document.getElementById
→("boxLocation").innerHTML =
→"Top: " + dragBox.style.top +
→"<br>Left: " +
→dragBox.style.left;
```

Lastly, just to make it obvious that we're actually moving the element, we display the current location of its top-left corner **B**.

TIP If this method of resetting an element's location isn't familiar to you, you'll want to review Listings 8.9 and 11.14.

Differentiating Devices

Because different devices come from different makers and run different operating systems and different browsers, they will sometimes act... differently. As a result, there will be times when you want to specifically target certain devices. In this example, we'll target devices running on Android.

Listing 17.7 A little bit of JavaScript lets us specifically target Android devices.

```
window.addEventListener(
    "load",
    function() {
        document.getElementById("draggable").addEventListener("touchmove",moved,false);
        androidSS();
    },
    false
);

function androidSS() {
    if (navigator.userAgent.match(/android/i)) {
        var fileref = document.createElement("link");
        fileref.setAttribute("rel","stylesheet");
        fileref.setAttribute("href","script03.css");
        document.getElementsByTagName("head")[0].appendChild(fileref);
    }
}

function moved(evt) {
    evt.preventDefault();
    var dragBox = document.getElementById("draggable");

    dragBox.style.left = (evt.changedTouches[0].pageX - 100) + "px";
    dragBox.style.top = (evt.changedTouches[0].pageY - 100) + "px";

    document.getElementById("boxLocation").innerHTML = "Top: " + dragBox.style.top +
    → "<br>Left: " + dragBox.style.left;
}
```

A The same page, now with a new style.

Listing 17.8 This style sheet will be loaded only on Android devices.

```css
#draggable {
    font-family: "Droid Sans", sans-serif;
}
```

TIP This technique isn't limited to just bringing in additional style sheets; it can also or alternatively be used for targeted scripting as well.

TIP At press time, there are (sadly) no fonts that are available on all mobile devices. To see what fonts are available, we recommend checking out the compatibility list at `jordanm.co.uk/tinytype`, which covers iOS, Android, Windows Phone, and BlackBerry devices. For instance, Android devices ship with only four fonts: Droid Sans, Droid Serif, Droid Sans Mono, and Roboto.

To differentiate between devices:

1. ```js
   window.addEventListener(
       "load",
       function() {
           document.getElementById
           → ("draggable").
           → addEventListener(
           → "touchmove",moved,false);
           androidSS();
       },
       false
   );
   ```

   This task's HTML and CSS are the same as in the previous example, but now, we want to include another style sheet *only* if the user has an Android device. The **androidSS()** function handles that, so it's called here when the page initially loads in **Listing 17.7**.

2. ```js
   function androidSS() {
       if (navigator.userAgent.match
       → (/android/i)) {
           var fileref = document.
           → createElement("link");
           fileref.setAttribute("rel",
           → "stylesheet");
           fileref.setAttribute
           → ("href","scripto3.css");
           document.getElementsByTagName
           → ("head")[0].appendChild
           → (fileref);
       }
   }
   ```

   The **navigator** object has a property named **userAgent**, which contains a string describing the device. If **userAgent** contains the string "**android**" (disregarding case), we add a link to another style sheet, **Listing 17.8**. As a result, Android users will now see the text in our draggable box in a sans serif font **A**.

Locating Your Device

One of the handiest things you can do with a mobile device is use it to target your current location—and you can even do it for websites (with a little bit of JavaScript). What's important here isn't just that we can figure out where we are; we can also launch other apps as well—that is, the map that's launched is outside the browser, not inside.

To use geolocation:

1. `<a href="http://maps.apple.com?z=`
   `→ 16&amp;ll=" id="mapQuery">`
   `→ View address on map</a>`

   Listing 17.9 contains the HTML that's needed to set up the link **A**. Clicking this link automatically launches the device's map app (in this case, Apple's Maps app) **B**.

Listing 17.9 This simple HTML page contains a new power on mobile devices: the ability to launch another application.

```
<!DOCTYPE html>
<html>
<head>
    <title>Form example</title>
    <meta name="viewport" content=
    → "width=device-width">
    <script src="script04.js"></script>
</head>
<body>
    <p>
        <input type="text" pattern="[0-9]*"
        → placeholder="Zip code"><br>
        <input type="email" placeholder=
        → "Enter your email address"
        → size="40">
    </p>
    <p>
        Lat: <input type="text"
        → id="lat_field" name="latitude"><br>
        Lng: <input type="text"
        → id="lng_field" name="longitude">
    </p>
    <a href="http://maps.apple.com?z=
    → 16&amp;ll=" id="mapQuery">View address
    → on map</a>
</body>
</html>
```

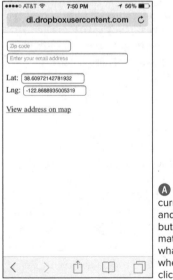

A Here's our current latitude and longitude—but what really matters is what happens when the link is clicked.

B Apple's Map app on an iPhone does a good job of showing my current location.

2. **if (navigator.geolocation) {**
   navigator.geolocation.
   → getCurrentPosition(

   In **Listing 17.10**, the **getLocation()**
   function is called when the page loads.
   That function starts off by checking to
   see if the **navigator** object contains
   the **geolocation** property; if it does,
   its **getCurrentPosition()** function
   is called.

3. **function(position) {**
   document.getElementById
   → ("lat_field").value =
   → position.coords.latitude;
   document.getElementById
   → ("lng_field").value =
   → position.coords.longitude;

   The **getCurrentPosition()** function is
   passed an anonymous function with the
   parameter **position**. Using **position**,
   the script retrieves our longitude and
   latitude, which are then displayed on
   the page Ⓐ.

continues on next page

Listing 17.10 This JavaScript fills the latitude and longitude fields and then sets up the map link.

```
window.addEventListener("load",getLocation,false);

function getLocation() {
    if (navigator.geolocation) {
        navigator.geolocation.getCurrentPosition(
            function(position) {
                document.getElementById("lat_field").value = position.coords.latitude;
                document.getElementById("lng_field").value = position.coords.longitude;

                document.getElementById("mapQuery").href += position.coords.latitude + "," +
                → position.coords.longitude;
            }
        );
    }
}
```

4. `document.getElementById`
   `→ ("mapQuery").href +=`
   `→ position.coords.latitude + "," +`
   `→ position.coords.longitude;`

The script finishes off by appending the latitude and longitude to the map query link, precisely targeting our current location.

TIP In step 1, the `ll` pretty obviously stands for latitude and longitude. The `z` stands for "zoom"—that is, how far you want to zoom into or out of the map. The larger the number, the more detailed the map.

TIP The good news: both Apple and Google's map services use the same `z` and `ll` attributes.

TIP Sadly, there's no single map URL that works on all devices. The one shown in step 1 (`maps.apple.com`) works on iOS-based devices such as iPhones and iPads. On Android devices, you'll want to use the process shown in the previous task to load `maps.google.com` instead. That's not to say that `maps.google.com` won't work if you're on an iOS device; it might—but only if you've previously installed the Google Maps app. You can't depend on that, so your code will need to handle both situations.

TIP When the page first loads, a prompt appears asking if it's OK for the site to access its current location data. Users must agree for this functionality to work.

TIP Table 17.7 gives some other examples of apps that can be launched by using different link targets.

TABLE 17.7 Launching Mobile Apps

Value of `href`	Result
`mailto:me@example.com`	Launches Mail app
`facetime:me@example.com`	Launches FaceTime app and starts a chat (iOS only)
`tel:555-1212`	Switches to a phone app and dials a number
`sms:555-1212`	Launches SMS app (e.g., Messages on iOS)
`http://www.youtube.com`	Launches YouTube app (if available)

18

Bookmarklets

You know that JavaScript can be used to control web browsers from inside your webpages. However, you can also use JavaScript to control your browser without using webpages, by using what are called *bookmarklets*. Bookmarklets are bookmarks that contain a call to the browser's JavaScript interpreter instead of to an external URL (if you are more accustomed to the term *favorites* rather than bookmarks, bookmarklets can also be called *favelets*). The JavaScript in your bookmarklets can do anything from getting details about images, to giving you the definition of a word, to resizing your browser window. And because you know JavaScript, harnessing this functionality is an easy way to make your browser a smarter, better tool.

Bookmarklets differ from other JavaScript code that you'll write because they have a significant and interesting formatting limitation: they must be written all in one line. You'll use semicolons to string commands together.

In this chapter, you'll be introduced to a variety of useful bookmarklets, and with a bit of effort, you'll be able to go forth and write your own.

In This Chapter

Your First Bookmarklet

OK, **Listing 18.1** isn't the most thrilling script you'll ever see. It's a variation on our old friend the "Hello World" script. But what's important is that you're getting something to happen in a web browser without ever loading a webpage. This example also demonstrates how to create and use a bookmarklet in various browsers.

To create a bookmarklet (Firefox):

1. From the Bookmarks menu, choose Show All Bookmarks **A**. The Library window opens.

2. In the left column, choose Bookmarks Toolbar. From the toolbar above, choose the Action menu (Mac, **B**) or the Organize menu (Windows, **C**), and select New Bookmark.

3. In the Name field, type the name you want to appear on the toolbar. In this case, type **Hello**.

4. In the Location field **D**, type `javascript:alert('Hello World');` and then click Add.

   We'll return to the Library window.

5. Close the Library window. Our new button should appear on the Bookmarks Toolbar. Clicking the button activates the command and makes the alert box appear with the text "Hello World."

> **TIP** If you can't see the Bookmarks Toolbar in Firefox, choose View > Toolbars > Bookmarks Toolbar to display it.

Listing 18.1 Yikes! It's the return of "Hello World."

```
javascript:alert('Hello World');
```

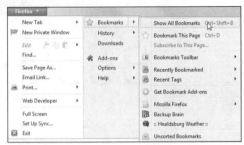

A Firefox (for Windows, in this case, but the Mac version is similar) allows you to enter bookmarklets in the Library by choosing Show All Bookmarks.

B Firefox for Mac has the New Bookmark menu item in the Action menu.

C Firefox for Windows has the New Bookmark menu item in the Organize menu.

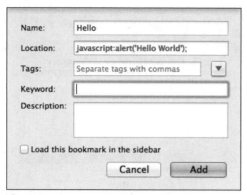

D In Firefox, add the bookmarklet code to the Location field in the New Bookmark dialog.

javascript:alert('Hello%20V

E After entering the bookmarklet code in the Address Bar and dragging it to the Favorites Bar, Safari lets you enter a name for the bookmarklet.

The Origin of Bookmarklets

The original idea came from the Netscape JavaScript Guide, which told how to add JavaScripts to the Personal Toolbar. Steve Kangas, who now runs the site Bookmarklets.com, coined the term "bookmarklet." His website at **www.bookmarklets.com** hasn't been changed in several years, but it still contains hundreds of useful bookmarklets; this chapter just touches on the possibilities. Some of the examples in this chapter are loosely based on scripts on his site and are used by permission.

To create a bookmarklet (Safari):

1. Make sure the Favorites Bar is visible by making sure that an item in the View menu displays "Hide Favorites Bar" and not "Show Favorites Bar."

2. In the Address Bar, type `javascript:alert('Hello World');`

3. Drag the globe icon (to the left of the text you typed) from the Address Bar to the Favorites Bar, and release the mouse button. A text field appears, asking you to name the new bookmark **E**.

4. Enter the bookmarklet's name.

   The new bookmarklet appears in the Favorites Bar as a button. Click the button to activate the command.

TIP You can use Bookmarks > Edit Bookmarks to reposition the bookmarklet from the Favorites Bar to the Bookmarks menu, if you prefer.

TIP To remove a bookmarklet from the Favorites Bar, drag it off the bar and into the browser window. It disappears in a puff of animated smoke. If you accidentally delete the wrong bookmark, undo the mistake by pressing Cmd-Z.

To create a bookmarklet (Chrome):

1. Right-click on the Bookmarks menu bar, and choose Add Page . The Add Page dialog appears.

2. Verify that Bookmarks Bar is highlighted on the bottom. Then, in the Name field, type **Hello**.

3. In the URL field, type **javascript:alert('Hello World');**  and click "Save." The new bookmarklet appears in the Bookmarks Bar as a button. Click the button to activate the command.

TIP Chrome has a particular odd behavior: in order for bookmarklets to run, you must be on a webpage. That is, bookmarklets don't work on the usual New Tab page; instead, you need to load a webpage (any webpage) first.

F In Chrome, you add a bookmarklet by adding a page from the Bookmarks bar.

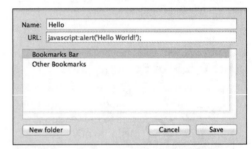

G Add your bookmarklet's code to the URL field in this Chrome dialog.

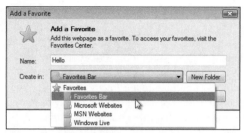

H Here's IE's Add a Favorite dialog.

I Modify the properties to add the JavaScript code to your bookmarklet.

To create a bookmarklet (Internet Explorer):

1. From the Favorites menu, choose Add to Favorites. The Add a Favorite dialog appears **H**.

2. In the Name field, type **Hello**.

3. In the "Create in" section of the dialog, choose the Favorites Bar folder to ensure that the new bookmark appears in the Favorites Toolbar, and click Add.

4. Right-click the new "Hello" bookmarklet in the Links Toolbar, and choose Properties. The Properties dialog appears. In the URL field, type `javascript:alert('Hello World');` **I** and, if you're fine with the icon IE assigns to the button (it's usually the icon of the current webpage you're on), click OK.

5. (Optional) If you want to change the icon, click Change Icon in the Properties dialog. The Change Icon dialog appears; choose the icon you want, click OK, and then click OK again to dismiss the Properties dialog.

6. If IE's security settings are appropriately set, you'll see the Problem with Shortcut dialog appear. This is to help prevent malicious scripts from being added to your browser. We're not malicious (at least not to our own computers!), so everything is OK. Click Yes.

7. Click the "Hello" button in the Links Toolbar to activate the command.

> **TIP** By default, IE hides its Favorites Bar. To show it, right-click the toolbar at the top of the window and choose Favorites Bar from the resulting shortcut menu.

Bookmarklets vs. IE Security

It's no secret that Microsoft Internet Explorer has had many security problems that Microsoft has addressed in various ways. The problems first came to light with Windows XP, and its Service Pack 2 was heavily devoted to beefing up security, including changes to IE6 (by the way, if you're still using IE6, we recommend you upgrade immediately). IE7, incorporating more security features, was initially scheduled to ship with Vista but shipped earlier after Vista was repeatedly delayed. More security was added with Vista, and then even more with later versions of IE and Windows.

We've discovered that the behavior of bookmarklets between IE versions is, in our tests, inconsistent. Some bookmarklets can only be run on some pages, and some bookmarklets can't be run at all, depending on a complex combination of which security settings you have enabled in IE. These settings include whether or not you have the pop-up blocker turned on and the many settings in the Security tab of Tools > Internet Options. In short, by adding successive layers of security to IE, Microsoft has made it harder for bookmarklets to work in Internet Explorer. It's possible to get more bookmarklets to work in IE by changing security settings, but because IE has such a history of security problems, we don't recommend that course of action.

Here's our advice: if you have to make a choice between lowering your security levels in IE or not running bookmarklets, we recommend using Firefox, Safari, or Chrome instead. This pretty much solves your browser security problems, and you'll get consistent bookmarklet functionality.

Listing 18.2 This script, which changes the background color to white, improves many a design-impaired page.

```
javascript:void(document.body.style.
→background='#FFF');
```

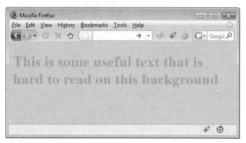

A It's difficult to read the text on the page's original background color.

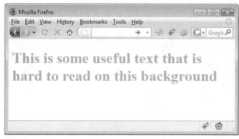

B Against white, the text is much more legible.

Resetting a Webpage's Background

Listing 18.2 is simple but powerful. Have you ever visited a site that you knew had lots of useful information, but the background color was so close to the text color that the information was unreadable? Or worse, the page's author used violently clashing colors that made your eyes water? This little bookmarklet solves those problems. Note that at this point, using the bookmarklet changes the way that you're viewing someone else's page—that's part of the power of bookmarklets. Of course, it doesn't change the actual page, just the way that your browser displays it.

To reset the background of a page:

- ```
  javascript:void(document.body.
  →style.background='#FFF');
  ```

  This script uses the object **document.body.style.background** and resets it to white. Now, we can see what's actually written, as shown in **A** and **B**.

TIP Note that the bookmarklet uses the form **javascript:void(command);**. This is because a bookmarklet must return some value, which would normally be used to overwrite the contents of the current page. Using the **void()** method, nothing is returned and nothing is overwritten.

TIP Bookmarklets use single quotes, not double quotes. This is because, behind the scenes, each bookmarklet is inside an **<a href="">** tag. Using double quotes would end the bookmarklet prematurely.
  ```

Changing a Page's Styles

The previous example works fine if the background color of an offensive page is set in the page's HTML. But it's ineffective if the page uses style sheets to change the background color or to apply a background image to a page element. This next bookmarklet (**Listing 18.3**) replaces the CSS styles for a page's background color, text color, and link colors. The background color changes to white and the text color to black, links will be blue, and visited links will be purple. You can see these sorts of changes in the example shown in Ⓐ and Ⓑ.

Listing 18.3 Don't be thrown off by the gray arrows; they're only there because of the limited size of this book's pages. Remember that the actual bookmarklet is all on one line. This script changes the styles on a page to make it more readable.

```
javascript:(function(){var styles=
 '*{background:#FFF !important;color:#000
 !important}:link,:link *{color:#00F
 !important}:visited,:visited *{color:#93C
 !important}';var newSS=document.
 createElement('link');newSS.rel=
 'stylesheet';newSS.href='data:text/css,
 '+escape(styles);document.
 getElementsByTagName('head')[0].
 appendChild(newSS);})();
```

Ⓐ The original page can be a bit difficult to read, so we want to swap out the CSS styles to make it more readable.

Ⓑ By changing the background and link colors, we've made the page easier to read.

If you have trouble reading webpages that use white text on a black background, or you get annoyed at sites that use too-similar colors for links and body text, this is the perfect bookmarklet for you. We use this one more than any other bookmarklet in our day-to-day web browsing. Once again, we remind you that the bookmarklet just changes the look of the page in your browser, not the page itself. In fact, if you reload the page, it reappears in its original, hard-to-read glory. But with this bookmarklet, visual relief is just a button click away.

To change a page's styles:

1. `javascript:(function(){`

    We're changing things up here again a little bit: now, instead of using **void()** to return a null value to the browser, we're instead putting the entire bookmarklet itself into an anonymous function.

2. `var styles = '* {background:#FFF`
    `→ !important; color:#000`
    `→ !important} :link, :link *`
    `→ {color:#00F !important}`
    `→ :visited, :visited * {color:#93C`
    `→ !important}';`

    This line creates a variable that contains the styles that we want to add to the page: the background will be white, the text color black, the links blue, and visited links purple. The **!important** forces these styles to override all other styles, and the * says that these new styles apply to all elements on the page.

continues on next page

3. `var newSS = document.`
   `→ createElement('link');`
   `newSS.rel = 'stylesheet';`

   The first line creates a new **link** element on the page and then stores that element in the new variable **newSS**. The second creates a new **rel** attribute for the newly created link and then sets its value to **stylesheet**. Here, the **rel** attribute tells the browser that we're linking to a style sheet.

4. `newSS.href = 'data:text/css,' +`
   `→ escape(styles);`

   This line adds a new **href** attribute to the newly created **link** element and then sets it to the style we created previously.

5. `document.getElementsByTagName`
   `→ ('head')[0].appendChild(newSS);`

   This line inserts the new link element into the webpage, causing the new styles to take effect and make the page readable.

6. `})();`

   Here we end the anonymous function we started up above (the **}**) and then end the function wrapper (the **)**). The **()** next just says, "You know that function you just created? Run it now."—which the browser then does.

TIP Does that seem like a lot of trouble to go to just to avoid the void()? Here's why it's particularly useful: JavaScript sees bookmarklets as running inside the current page you're on, and with the old way, there's no way to be sure that the variables you're using in the bookmarklet aren't already in use by the page itself. When you wrap the entire bookmarklet inside a function, the variables stay within the scope (covered back in Chapter 2) of the function, and you're guaranteed to be safe.

TIP As mentioned in this chapter's introduction, a bookmarklet must be a single line of code. Putting the semicolons between statements allows you to put all the commands on a single line.

Listing 18.4 **Listing 18.4** This bookmarklet performs a dictionary lookup.

```
javascript:(function(){var inText=window.
→ getSelection()+'';if(!inText){inText=
→ prompt('Word:','');}if(inText){window.open
→ ('http://www.answers.com/topic/'+escape
→ (inText)+'#American_Heritage_Dictionary_ds',
→ 'dictWin','width=800,height=500,left=75,
→ top=175,scrollbars=yes');}})();
```

Listing 18.5 This bookmarklet performs a thesaurus lookup.

```
javascript:(function(){var inText=window.
→ getSelection()+'';if(!inText){inText=
→ prompt('Word:','');}if(inText){window.open
→ ('http://www.answers.com/topic/'+escape
→ (inText)+'#Roget\'s_Thesaurus_ds','thesWin',
→ 'width=800,height=500,left=75,top=175,
→ scrollbars=yes');}})();
```

Word Lookups

If you use your web browser for writing (email in particular), you'll find that you wish you had the dictionary and thesaurus tools that are available in most word processors. With **Listings 18.4** and **18.5**, you'll be able to have this functionality in all your writing. You do it using a bookmarklet to query an online dictionary or thesaurus. Because the scripts are so similar, we've presented them all in one task. Listing 18.4 shows how to do a dictionary lookup, and Listing 18.5 does a thesaurus lookup.

To look up a word:

1. `var inText = window.getSelection()` `→ + '';`

   This line creates a new variable, **inText**, which is set to the value of the selected text in the browser.

   Note that that very last bit is two single quotes, not one double-quote. That's done because the browser may return something that isn't a string, and this forces the result to be a string.

2. `if (!inText) {`
   `    inText = prompt('Word:','');`
   `}`

   If we didn't select any text, then we ask for a word to be entered.

3. `if (inText) {`

   The user has had two chances, so they should have entered something to look up by now. Even so, we check before doing the lookup.

   continues on next page

4.
```
window.open('http://www.answers.
→ com/topic/' + escape(inText) +
→ '#American_Heritage_Dictionary_
→ ds','dictWin','width=800,
→ height=500,left=75,top=175,
→ scrollbars=yes');
```

or

```
window.open('http://www.answers.
→ com/topic/' + escape(inText) +
→ '#Roget\'s_Thesaurus_ds','thesWin',
→ 'width=800,height=500,left=75,
→ top=175,scrollbars=yes');
```

We pick one of these two, depending on whether we want to do a dictionary or thesaurus lookup, as shown in **A** and **B**. Either opens a new window, with the information that we requested. You can change the window dimensions to fit the size of your screen by changing the **height** and **width** attributes of the **window.open()** call.

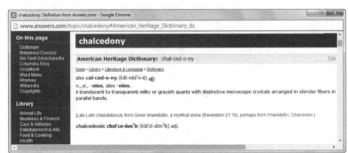

A Triggering the dictionary bookmarklet returns this window with the lookup's results.

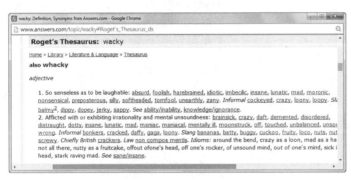

B The thesaurus lookup results.

I could tell she was flummoxed, as her line fine

he lib
ally,
poli
seer

Dictionary
flummoxed | ˈfləməkst | adjective
bewildered or perplexed: *he became flummoxed and speechless.*

Thesaurus
flummox verb
informal at age ten, he created intricate math problems that flummoxed his teachers: BAFFLE, perplex, puzzle, bewilder, mystify, bemuse, …

c pol
on. A
pwd
calls

Under OS X, a dictionary and thesaurus are built in.

TIP This has nothing to do with JavaScript, but it's cool and worth mentioning: if you're on a Mac running OS X 10.4 or later, in Safari or many other programs, you can just place the cursor over a word and press Cmd-Ctrl-D, and the OS pops up a dictionary/thesaurus window, based on the Dictionary application **C**. This works in any Cocoa-based program (great), so if you use Firefox on the Mac, it doesn't work (bummer). If you don't know what a "Cocoa-based program" is, don't worry about it; just give it a try and see if it works for the program you're in.

Viewing Images

A useful tool for designers is the ability to view all the images on a page, apart from the layout of the page. **Listing 18.6** allows you to peek behind the scenes of someone else's page and see a list of the page's individual images, the height and width of the images (in modern browsers), and their URLs.

To view images:

1. ```
   var iWin,i,t = '',
     → di=document.images;
   ```

   The bookmarklet starts and initializes four variables: **iWin**; **i**; **t**, which will later contain all the output; and **di**, which contains the **document.images** object.

2. ```
   for (i=0;i<di.length;i++) {
   ```

   We now loop through each image in the document.

3. ```
   if (t.indexOf(di[i].src)<0) {
   ```

   In this step, we check to see if we've already put the image on the page. This line of code keeps that from happening more than once.

Listing 18.6 You can view a table of page images with this script.

```
javascript:(function(){var iWin,i,t='',di=document.images;for(i=0;i<di.length;i++){if(t.indexOf
→ (di[i].src)<0){t+='<tr><td><img src='+di[i].src+'></td><td>'+di[i].height+'</td><td>'+di[i].
→ width+'</td><td>'+di[i].src+'</td></tr>';}}if(t==''){alert('No images!');}else{iWin=window.open
→ ('','IW','width=800,height=600,scrollbars=yes');iWin.document.body.innerHTML='<table border=1
→ cellpadding=10 cellspacing=0><tr><th>Image</th><th>Height</th><th>Width</th><th>URL</th>
→ </tr>'+t+'</table>';}})();
```
```

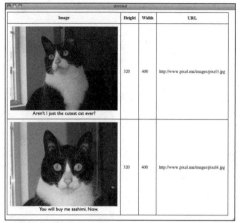

A The script formats the images and information into an attractive table.

4.
```
t += '<tr><td><img src=' +
→ di[i].src + ' /></td><td>' +
→ di[i].height + '</td><td>' +
→ di[i].width + '</td><td>' +
→ di[i].src + '</td></tr>';}}
```

All the information we want is written out here, in a nice table format. The first cell contains the image; the second contains the height; the third, the width; and the last contains the URL of the image.

5.
```
if (t=='') {
    alert('No images!');
}
```

When the loop completes, check to see if we've found any images. If not, an alert window that says "No images!" is displayed.

6.
```
else {
    iWin = window.open('','IW',
    → 'width=800,height=600,
    → scrollbars=yes');
```

If we found images, open up a new window for the image information.

7.
```
iWin.document.body.innerHTML =
→ '<table border=1 cellpadding=
→ 10 cellspacing=0><tr><th>Image
→ </th><th>Height</th><th>Width
→ </th><th>URL</th></tr>'+t+'
→ </table>';
```

Here is where the new window is created and displayed. The image information, with heading information for each column, is written out, as shown in **A**.

Displaying ISO Latin Characters

If you're authoring webpages by hand, it can be a hassle to remember codes for different characters like á and à. **Listing 18.7** shows you a list of common variations of the vowels.

To display ISO Latin characters:

1. ```
   var eWin,n,i,j,w,t =
   → '<table border=1 cellpadding=
   → 20 cellspacing=0>',l =
   → document.createElement('p'),
   ```

   Start off the bookmarklet by initializing several variables.

2. ```
   v = 'aAeEiIoOuUyY',
   ```

   Initialize a string, **v**, which contains all the vowels.

3. ```
   s = new Array('acute', 'circ',
   → 'elig', 'Elig', 'grave', 'ring',
   → 'slash', 'tilde', 'uml');
   ```

   Here's an array, **s**, which contains all the diacritical character codes.

Listing 18.7 Rather than look up an accented character in a book, let JavaScript generate a list whenever you need one.

```
javascript:(function(){var eWin,n,i,j,w,t='<table border=1 cellpadding=20 cellspacing=0>',
→ l=document.createElement('p'),v='aAeEiIoOuUyY',s=new Array('acute','circ','elig','Elig',
→ 'grave','ring','slash','tilde','uml');for(i=0;i<v.length;i++){for(j=0;j<s.length;j++)
→ {w=v.charAt(i)+s[j]+';';l.innerHTML='&'+w;n=l.innerHTML;if(n.length==1){t+='<tr><td>&'+w+'</td>
→ <td>&'+'amp;'+w+'</td><td>&'+'amp;#'+n.charCodeAt(0)+';</td></tr>';}}}eWin=window.open('','EW',
→ 'scrollbars=yes,width=300,height='+screen.height);eWin.document.body.innerHTML=t+'</table>';})();
```
```

4. `for (i=0;i<v.length;i++) {`

This line sets up **i** to loop through the characters in the **v** string.

5. `for (j=0;j<s.length;j++) {`

And this line sets up **j** to loop through the **s** array.

6. `w = v.charAt(i) + s[j] + ';';`

In this line, we set up the variable **w** to be the vowel concatenated with the code, followed by a semicolon.

7. `l.innerHTML = '&' + w;`
`n = l.innerHTML;`

For an upcoming step, we'll need not the string representation of the entity, but the entity itself—that is, we want ã, not **ã**. We can get that by taking our string **w** (set in the previous step) and putting it (with a leading ampersand) into the **innerHTML** of an already created element, **l**. That converts it from the string value to its displayed value. In order to use that value, we set the variable **n** to the contents of that same **innerHTML**.

8. `if (n.length==1) {`

In order to get every possible entity, our lists of vowels and diacritical characters have a few that don't combine to make up a valid result. We know when that's the case because the previous conversion step won't actually convert our string. That is, while **æ** converts to æ and **Á** to Á, **&Aelig;** (which looks like it should be Æ) doesn't—and so, the previous step leaves it as a seven-character string. Valid entities, though, will end up as one-character strings, and will do the next bit of code.

continues on next page

9. ```
t += '<tr><td>&' + w +
→'</td><td>&' + 'amp;' +
→w + '</td><td>&' + 'amp;#' +
→n.charCodeAt(0) + ';</td></tr>';
```

We've got a valid entity here, and so we want to put it into our table. In the first column we want the entity itself, the second its string representation, and in the third, its numeric representation. We get that last value by using the **charCodeAt()** method on our entity.

10. ```
eWin = window.open('','EW',
→'scrollbars=yes,width=300,
→height=' + screen.height);
eWin.document.body.innerHTML =
→t + '</table>';
```

When we're done, we open a new window and then write our table into it, as shown in **A**.

TIP Our table can be lengthy, so we've been a little tricky with the height of the window we're opening. Instead of giving it a fixed height, it's instead set based on the height of the user's display. If that's not what you want, you can set it to a fixed size instead.

TIP If you're wondering how to get an Æ in HTML, it's Æ—that is, it needs an upper-case E, not a lowercase e. Now you can see why we find bookmarklets like this so handy!

○ ○ ○	Untitled	⟋
🗋 about:blank		
á	&aacute;	&#225;
â	&acirc;	&#226;
æ	&aelig;	&#230;
à	&agrave;	&#224;
å	&aring;	&#229;
ã	&atilde;	&#227;
ä	&auml;	&#228;
Á	&Aacute;	&#193;
Â	&Acirc;	&#194;
Æ	&AElig;	&#198;
À	&Agrave;	&#192;

A The result of the script is a new window with all the possible variants of the vowels as HTML entities.

A The first part of the script prompts the user for the RGB values.

Converting RGB Values to Hex

Another useful little widget web developers frequently wish they had on hand is an RGB-to-hexadecimal converter. This is useful whenever you need to translate a color value from a graphics program like Adobe Photoshop or Fireworks into a browser color, for page backgrounds or text colors. **Listing 18.8** shows the conversion calculator done in JavaScript and turned into a bookmarklet.

To convert RGB values to hexadecimal:

1. `var s,i,n,h = '#',`

   Start off the bookmarklet by initializing four variables.

2. `x = '0123456789ABCDEF',`

   The variable **x** is set to the valid hexadecimal digits.

3. `c = prompt('R,G,B:','');`

   This line prompts the user for the requested RGB values, separated by commas, as shown in **A**.

4. `if (c) {`

   If the user entered anything, continue with the code. Otherwise, the value of **c** will be null, and the bookmarklet skips all the following steps.

continues on next page

Listing 18.8 This script takes RGB color values and turns them into their hexadecimal equivalents.

```
javascript:(function(){var s,i,n,h='#',x='0123456789ABCDEF',c=prompt('R,G,B:','');if(c)
→{s=c.split(',');for(i=0;i<3;i++){n=parseInt(s[i]);h+=x.charAt(n>>4)+x.charAt(n&15);}
→prompt('Hexcolor:',h);}})();
```

5. `s = c.split(',');`

Split the entry in **c**, separated by commas, and put the result into the **s** array.

6. `for (i=0;i<3;i++) {`

Loop around the following lines once for each of the three red, green, and blue color values.

7. `n = parseInt(s[i]);`

Turn the current element of **s** into a number, and save it as **n**.

8. `h += x.charAt(n>>4) +`
`→ x.charAt(n&15);`

This line converts **n** into 2 hexadecimal digits and adds the result to **h**.

9. `prompt('Hexcolor:',h);`

The result (ready to be copied into an HTML page) is displayed via a prompt command, as shown in Ⓑ. It's done this way instead of with an alert so that we can copy the code and paste it later.

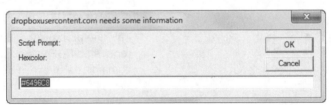

Ⓑ Another prompt box provides the calculated hex value.

A First, ask for the number to be converted.

Converting Values

The possibilities are endless for the types of values that can be converted from one form to another. **Listing 18.9** shows another example: how to convert kilometers to miles.

To convert kilometers to miles:

1. `var t,expr = prompt('Length in → kilometers:','');`

   The bookmarklet starts by prompting the user for a length in kilometers **A**.

2. `if (isNaN(parseFloat(expr))) {`

   Check to see if the user entered a numeric value.

3. `t = expr + ' is not a number';`

   If not, set **t** to be an error message.

continues on next page

Listing 18.9 You can create bookmarklets for almost any kind of unit conversion. This script converts kilometers to miles.

```
javascript:(function(){var t,expr=prompt('Length in kilometers:','');if(isNaN(parseFloat(expr)))
→ {t=expr+' is not a number';}else{t='Length in miles is '+Math.round(expr*6214)/10000;}
→ alert(t);})();
```

4. ```
else {
    t = 'Length in miles is ' +
    → Math.round(expr*6214)/10000;
}
```

   Otherwise, convert the value to miles and store it in **t**.

5. `alert(t);`

   Whether the input value is good or bad, we've stored the result in **t**. Here we display that result, as shown in 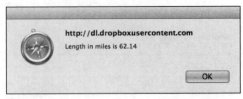.

**B** JavaScript returns the result of the conversion.

**TIP** It's a straightforward process to adapt this script into any kind of conversion you need. Just change the label in step 1, and replace the math expression in step 4 to the correct expression for the particular conversion you're looking for.

**TIP** You can make up a bunch of bookmarklets with different conversions and then organize them all into folders in your **Bookmarks** or **Favorites** menu. Conversions can be just a mouse click away.
```

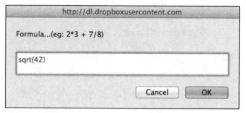

(A) The user must be prompted for a formula.

A Bookmarklet Calculator

If you think about it, it's really a bit too difficult to create a full-fledged calculator with buttons and a running value with just one long line of code. However, you can use a bookmarklet like **Listing 18.10** to do fairly complex calculations, using JavaScript's built-in Math functions.

To use a JavaScript calculator:

1. `var evl,expr = prompt('Formula...` `→ (eg: 2*3 + 7/8)','');`

   This line sets up a variable **evl** and then prompts the user for an expression or formula, as shown in **(A)**, which is stored in **expr**.

2. `with(Math) try {`

   The next few lines need to be evaluated using JavaScript's built-in Math routines. The **with(Math)** part tells the interpreter that when any of these functions are seen, to evaluate them as Math commands.

   The **try** block warns JavaScript that what we're doing may well fail, and if so, don't panic. In fact, don't even put up an error message if there's a problem, as we'll be handling the errors ourselves.

   continues on next page

Listing 18.10 Surprisingly complex equations can be evaluated with this bookmarklet.

```
javascript:(function(){var evl,expr=prompt('Formula...(eg: 2*3 + 7/8)','');with(Math)try{evl=
→ parseFloat(eval(expr));if(isNaN(evl)){throw Error('Not a number!');}prompt('Result of
→ '+expr+':',evl);}catch(evl){alert(evl);}})();
```

3. `evl = parseFloat(eval(expr));`

   Evaluate the expression, and turn it into a floating-point number, which is then stored in **evl**.

4. `if (isNaN(evl)) {`

   If the resulting value in **evl** is not a number (**NaN**), do the following line.

5. `throw Error('Not a number!');`

   If we're here, for some reason what the user entered didn't work out to a number. When that happens we want to force an error message of "Not a number!" to display. Here's where the message is set; it will be displayed in step 7.

6. `prompt('Result of ' +`
   `→ expr + ';', evl);`

   Otherwise, the expression was valid, so display the result, as shown in .

7. `catch(evl) {`
   `   alert(evl);`
   `}`

   Here's the end of that **try** block that started in step 2. To get here, one of two things happened: either we ran into the error in step 5, or some other error entirely occurred. Either way, we "catch" the error that was "thrown" and put it up on the screen in an alert.

B JavaScript returns the result of the calculation.

TIP Trying to remember where you've seen that `try`/`throw`/`catch` syntax before? It was originally covered back in the "Handling Errors" section of Chapter 2.

TIP if you're wondering what mathematical functions you can use, remember that the `Math` object and its methods were covered back in Chapter 3.

A There are a number of uses for shorter versions of URLs, and the bookmarklet makes it simple to get that short URL.

Shortening URLs

There are a number of reasons why you might want a short version of a URL— maybe you're using a Twitter-like service with few characters allowed, or maybe you're going to paste the result into an email and you don't want the URL to wrap. Either way, **Listing 18.11** makes shortening URLs simple.

To shorten URLs:

- ```
  window.open('http://tinyurl.com/
  →create.php?url=' + location.href,
  →'','width=750,height=500,
  →scrollbars=yes');
  ```

  Here we're opening a new window and using the TinyURL.com service to set our short URL. We pass the service our current page location (found in `location.href`), and that's all the information it needs. Because TinyURL.com immediately puts the new, shortened URL onto your clipboard for you, all you have to do (once you're on the right webpage) is click the bookmarklet, glance at the page that opens to make sure everything worked as it should **A**, close it, and paste your new URL wherever you want.

TIP There are a number of different URL-shortening services online. If you don't like TinyURL.com, check out `bit.ly`, `goo.gl`, or `is.gd`.

TIP If you're on Twitter, feel free to say "Hi!" to us at @negrino and @dori.

Listing 18.11 Shorten URLs with a single click of a mouse (and this script).

```
javascript:(function(){window.open('http://tinyurl.com/create.php?url='+location.href,'',
→'width=750,height=500,scrollbars=yes');})();
```
```

Validating Pages

When creating your pages, it's a great idea to make sure that you're making sites that adhere to web standards. Such pages load more quickly in modern browsers and are easier to maintain. The easiest way to check a page that you're working on for valid code is by running it against the page validator maintained by the World Wide Web Consortium (W3C), at **validator.w3.org**. This bookmarklet, **Listing 18.12**, checks the page currently shown in your browser for validity. It does this by taking the URL of the current page, passing it to the validator, and then opening a new window with the validator's results, as shown in 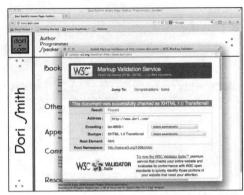.

A If you've written your code correctly, running your page against the W3C validator returns this happy result.

To validate your pages:

- ```
  window.open('http://validator.
  → w3.org/check?uri=' + location.
  → href,'','width=800,height=900,
  → resizable=yes,scrollbars=yes');
  ```

  This one, useful as it is, isn't exactly rocket science. First, we open a window and pass that window the URL to the validator. You'll note the validator has a parameter, **uri**, which accepts the URL of the current page, which we pass as **location.href**. The plus sign between the two concatenates the location object to the validator's URL. The rest of the line is just parameters for the window's size and other attributes.

Listing 18.12 Use this script to make sure your pages contain web-standard, valid markup.

```
javascript:(function(){window.open('http://validator.w3.org/check?uri='+location.href,'',
→'width=800,height=900,resizable=yes,scrollbars=yes');})();
```
```

(A) One click opens a new mail window, with the start of your message already begun.

Mailing Pages

Sometimes as you're surfing along, you'll find a page that's so useful that you need to share it with your co-workers. Or, maybe it's so funny you need to share it with your best friend. This bookmarklet, **Listing 18.13**, takes the page you're on, plus any highlighted text, and uses it to create a new outgoing email.

To mail a webpage:

- ```
  location.href = 'mailto:?SUBJECT='
  → + document.title + '&BODY=' +
  → escape(location.href) + '\r' +
  → window.getSelection();
  ```

  If you've ever put a **mailto** link on a webpage, you should recognize this syntax. All this does is act as if you had clicked on an **<a href='mailto:'></a>** link. The subject of the email is set to the title of the current document, and the body of the email is set to the URL of the page plus any text you have currently selected, as seen in (A).

  TIP No, you don't have to be using Gmail, or even web mail, for this to work. Whatever mail client you've set up as the default on your computer is what will open and create the mail.

Listing 18.13 If you want to mail all or part of a webpage to someone, you can't make it much simpler than using this bookmarklet.

```
javascript:(function(){location.href='mailto:?SUBJECT='+document.title+'&BODY='+escape
→(location.href)+' \r'+window.getSelection();})();
```
```

Resizing Pages

When you're working on a site, it's useful to be able to see how a page looks with a smaller display than the one you're using. This bookmarklet, **Listing 18.14**, resets your browser window to 640×480.

To resize your page:

- `resizeTo(640,480);`
  `moveTo(0,0);`

  The first command, `resizeTo()`, changes the dimensions of your browser window. The next, `moveTo()`, tells the browser where to put the upper-left corner **A**.

TIP By itself, this bookmarklet is only moderately useful. Where it shines is when you create a folder full of almost identical versions of this, with all the various window sizes that you could want. As you can see, it's straightforward to duplicate this for any size window.

TIP It's also useful (if your display is large enough) to be able to open windows side by side with identical dimensions. For instance, you can have one bookmarklet that resizes your window to be 700px wide by the max height of your display:

`resizeTo(700,screen.availHeight);`
`moveTo(0,0);`

And also this one:

`resizeTo(700,screen.availHeight);`
`moveTo(screen.availWidth-700,0);`

The latter resizes a page to the same 700px wide by the max height of your display, but positions the window such that it's against the right edge of your screen versus the left. If your display is 1400 or more pixels wide, you should see them perfectly aligned without overlapping, each flush against one side.

TIP If you find that this bookmarklet isn't working for you, make sure that the window you're trying to resize has only a single tab open.

Listing 18.14 If you want to see how your page looks at a different size, bookmarklets like this one come in handy.

```
javascript:(function(){resizeTo(640,480);
→ moveTo(0,0);})();
```

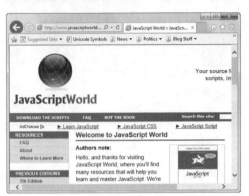

A We can see at a glance that the small-screen version of this site doesn't show much of the content.

JavaScript Genealogy and Reference

Over the course of close to two decades, JavaScript has undergone transformation after transformation since its introduction as part of Netscape Navigator 2.0. This appendix briefly discusses the different versions of JavaScript and which browsers include which version of JavaScript.

You'll also find a table listing most JavaScript objects up to and including ECMAScript Edition 3, along with their properties, methods, and event handlers.

JavaScript Versions

The scripting language that you think of as JavaScript has several different names (depending on whose product you have) and almost a dozen different versions. Besides JavaScript, there are also JScript and ECMAScript. Here's a guide to which version does what.

Netscape's JavaScript

The first version of JavaScript, originally called LiveScript, was released in Netscape Navigator 2.0. Netscape intended LiveScript to be a way to extend the capabilities of browsers and to allow web designers to add some interactivity to their sites. The JavaScript version in Navigator 2.0 was JavaScript 1.0.

Along with Navigator 3.0 came JavaScript 1.1, which added support for images, arrays, Java applets, and plug-ins, among many other changes.

With the release of Navigator 4.0 (also known as Netscape Communicator), JavaScript 1.2 was born, with more enhancements and refinements. Netscape 4.5 later shipped with JavaScript 1.3. JavaScript 1.4 was server-side only, and Netscape 6 introduced JavaScript 1.5.

Current versions of JavaScript are developed by the open-source Mozilla project, mainly for the benefit of its Firefox browser. Recent versions of Firefox fully support ECMAScript-262 Edition 5.

At press time for this book, the current version of JavaScript is 1.8.6, which initially shipped with Firefox 17 (as seen in **Table A.1**).

TABLE A.1 JavaScript Versions

Browser	JavaScript Version
Netscape 2	1.0
Netscape 3	1.1
Netscape 4.0–4.05	1.2
Netscape 4.06–4.7	1.3
Netscape 6.0, 7.0, Mozilla, Firefox 1.0–1.41	1.5
Firefox 1.5	1.6
Firefox 2	1.7
Firefox 3	1.8
Firefox 4	1.8.5
Firefox 17+	1.8.6

TABLE A.2 JScript Versions

Browser	JScript Version
MSIE 4	3.0
MSIE 5	5.0
MSIE 5.5	5.5
MSIE 6	5.6
MSIE 7	5.7
MSIE 8	5.8
MSIE 9+	9.0

Microsoft's JScript

As is so often the case, Microsoft implemented JavaScript in its own fashion, which is not always compatible with the Netscape version. Called JScript version 1, the Microsoft version of JavaScript was more-or-less compatible with JavaScript 1.0; there were some differences. Naturally, JScript appears only in Windows and versions of Microsoft Internet Explorer (MSIE).

On Windows, there was also a JScript version 2 (somewhat comparable to JavaScript 1.1) for Windows 95/NT that came with upgraded versions of MSIE 3.02 and later. Not all versions of MSIE 3.02 had JScript 2.0. If you happen to have one of these oldies, you can tell what version of JScript you have installed by searching your disk for **jscript.dll**. Get the file's properties, and click the Version tab. If the file version does not begin with at least 2, you've still got the original.

On the Macintosh, MSIE 3.0 had no JScript, but version 3.01 did. That included JScript 1.0, but not the identical version as on Windows; there were differences between the Mac and Windows versions of JScript (for example, the Mac version supported the Image object for mouse rollovers, while the Windows JScript 1.0 did not). In 2003, Microsoft discontinued MSIE for Mac, ending official support in 2005.

Confused yet? You're in good company. But wait, there's more: JScript 3.0 was roughly equivalent to JavaScript 1.2, and JScript 5.x was roughly equivalent to JavaScript 1.5. **Table A.2** helps you identify which version of JScript you have depending on which version of IE you're running.

ECMAScript

In 1996, web developers began to complain that Netscape was going in one direction with JavaScript, and Microsoft in a somewhat-compatible but different direction with JScript. Nobody likes to have to code pages to handle different dialects of JavaScript, or have their code work in one browser but not another. Developers wanted a standard. So Microsoft went to an international standards body called ECMA and submitted the JScript language specification to it, and Netscape threw in its own comments and suggestions. ECMA did whatever it is that standards bodies do and in June of 1997 produced a standard called ECMA-262 (also known as ECMAScript, a term that just dances off the tongue). This standard closely resembled JavaScript 1.1 but (sigh) was not exactly the same; subsequent versions rectified this problem. If you're interested in reading the official ECMAScript specification, you can download it from **ecma-international.org**. Look for the Standards link and then follow it to the ECMA-262 specification.

ECMAScript has also had several versions since 1997: Edition 3 (December 1999), Edition 5 (December 2009), and Edition 5.1 (June 2011). Edition 4 was never completed, and it was finally abandoned. The current crop of browsers have full support for Edition 3 (roughly comparable to JavaScript 1.5), and most are (or nearly are) in compliance with Edition 5. It's important to note that ECMAScript is now driving the standards process; all current browser makers have the goal of making their implementations ECMAScript-compliant.

So as long as you write ECMAScript-compatible code, it should run just fine under browsers as far back as MSIE 4 and Netscape Navigator 6. But you should always test your code with different browsers, platforms, and versions just to be sure.

Apple Safari (based on WebKit) and Google Chrome (based on Blink) are both recent enough to have always supported ECMAScript.

The Big Object Table

No JavaScript book is complete without the whopping big table of JavaScript objects, along with their associated properties, methods, and event handlers (check Chapter 1 for definitions of these terms). **Table A.3** covers most of the JavaScript objects in the language up through and including ECMAScript Edition 3. We've omitted a few very obscure objects, objects used solely by specific browsers, and some older objects from earlier versions that have been superseded by new or extended objects.

If you want information about all of the objects available to you in a given browser, check out that browser's developer tools. For instance, the Chrome developer tools are shown in **Ⓐ**, on the next page. While not everything is cross-browser, it will give you a number of places to start.

A With Chrome Developer Tools, you can see precisely how the browser sees your code. Other browsers have their own equivalents.

TABLE A.3 JavaScript Object Table

Object	Properties	Methods	Event Handlers
Anchor	name	none	none
anchors array	length	none	none
Applet	align code codeBase height hspace name vspace width	applet's methods blur focus	onblur onclick ondblclick onfocus onkeydown onkeypress onkeyup onmousedown onmousemove onmouseout onmouseover onmouseup onresize
applets array	length	none	none
Area	alt cords hash host hostname href noHref pathname port protocol search shape target	none	onblur onclick ondblclick onfocus onkeydown onkeypress onkeyup onmousedown onmousemove onmouseout onmouseover onmouseup onresize
Array	length	concat join reverse slice sort splice toLocaleString toString	none

Table continues on next page

TABLE A.3 JavaScript Object Table *(continued)*

Object	Properties	Methods	Event Handlers
Body	alink background bgColor link text vlink	none	onblur onclick ondblclick onfocus onkeydown onkeypress onkeyup onmousedown onmousemove onmouseout onmouseover onmouseup onresize
Button	form name type value	blur click focus	onblur onchange onclick ondblclick onfocus onkeydown onkeypress onkeyup onmousedown onmousemove onmouseout onmouseover onmouseup
Checkbox	checked defaultChecked form name type value	blur click focus	onblur onchange onclick ondblclick onfocus onkeydown onkeypress onkeyup onmousedown onmousemove onmouseout onmouseover onmouseup

Object	Properties	Methods	Event Handlers
Date	none	getDate	none
		getDay	
		getFullYear	
		getHours	
		getMilliseconds	
		getMinutes	
		getMonth	
		getSeconds	
		getTime	
		getTimezoneOffset	
		getUTCDate	
		getUTCDay	
		getUTCFullYear	
		getUTCHours	
		getUTCMilliseconds	
		getUTCMinutes	
		getUTCMonth	
		getUTCSeconds	
		getYear	
		parse	
		setDate	
		setFullYear	
		setHours	
		setMilliseconds	
		setMinutes	
		setMonth	
		setSeconds	
		setTime	
		setUTCDate	
		setUTCFullYear	
		setUTCHours	
		setUTCMilliseconds	
		setUTCMinutes	
		setUTCMonth	
		setUTCSeconds	
		setYear	
		toGMTString	
		toLocaleDateString	
		toLocaleString	
		toLocaleTimeString	
		toString	
		toUTCString	
		UTC	
		valueOf	

Table continues on next page

Object	Properties	Methods	Event Handlers
document	alinkColor	clear	onblur
	Anchor	close	onclick
	anchors	createElement	ondblclick
	Applet	createTextNode	onfocus
	applets	focus	onkeydown
	Area	getElementById	onkeypress
	attributes	getElementsByName	onkeyup
	bgColor	getElementsByTagName	onmousedown
	Body	open	onmousemove
	childNodes	write	onmouseout
	cookie	writeln	onmouseover
	documentElement		onmouseup
	domain		onresize
	embed		
	embeds		
	fgColor		
	firstChild		
	Form		
	forms		
	Image		
	images		
	lastChild		
	lastModified		
	linkColor		
	Link		
	links		
	location		
	namespaceURI		
	nextSibling		
	nodeName		
	nodeType		
	parentNode		
	plugins		
	previousSibling		
	referrer		
	Script		
	StyleSheet		
	styleSheets		
	title		
	URL		
	vlinkColor		

TABLE A.3 **JavaScript Object Table** *(continued)*

Object	Properties	Methods	Event Handlers
FileUpload	form	blur	onblur
	name	focus	onclick
	type	select	ondblclick
	value		onfocus
			onkeydown
			onkeypress
			onkeyup
			onmousedown
			onmousemove
			onmouseout
			onmouseover
			onmouseup
			onselect
Form	action	reset	onclick
	Button	submit	ondblclick
	Checkbox		onkeydown
	elements		onkeypress
	encoding		onkeyup
	encType		onmousedown
	FileUpload		onmousemove
	Hidden		onmouseout
	length		onmouseover
	method		onmouseup
	name		onreset
	Password		onsubmit
	Radio		
	Reset		
	Select		
	Submit		
	target		
	Text		
	Textarea		
forms array	length	none	none
Hidden	form	none	none
	maxLength		
	name		
	readOnly		
	size		
	type		
	value		

Table continues on next page

TABLE A.3 JavaScript Object Table *(continued)*

Object	Properties	Methods	Event Handlers
History	length	back forward go	none
history array	length	none	none
Image	align alt border complete height href hspace isMap lowsrc name src useMap vspace width x y	none	onabort onblur onclick ondblclick onerror onkeydown onkeypress onkeyup onload onmousedown onmousemove onmouseout onmouseover onmouseup onreset onresize onsubmit
images array	length	none	none
Link	hash host hostname href name pathname port protocol rel rev search target	none	onblur onclick ondblclick onkeydown onkeypress onkeyup onmousedown onmousemove onmouseout onmouseover onmouseup
links array	length	none	none
location	hash host hostname href pathname port protocol search	assign reload replace	none

Object	Properties	Methods	Event Handlers
Math	E LN2 LN10 LOG2E LOG10E PI SQRT1_2 SQRT2	abs acos asin atan atan2 ceil cos exp floor log max min pow random round sin sqrt tan	none
MimeType	description enabledPlugin suffixes type	none	none
mimeTypes array	length	none	none
navigator	appCodeName appName appVersion cookieEnabled MimeType mimeTypes platform Plugin plugins userAgent	javaEnabled taintEnabled	none
Number	MAX_VALUE MIN_VALUE NaN NEGATIVE_INFINITY POSITIVE_INFINITY	toExponential toFixed toLocaleString toPrecision toString valueOf	none

Table continues on next page

TABLE A.3 **JavaScript Object Table** *(continued)*

Object	Properties	Methods	Event Handlers
Object	attributes	appendChild	onblur
	childNodes	blur	onchange
	children	click	onclick
	className	cloneNode	oncontextmenu
	clientHeight	focus	ondblclick
	clientLeft	getAttribute	onfocus
	clientTop	getAttributeNode	onkeydown
	clientWidth	getElementsByTagName	onkeypress
	dir	getExpression	onkeyup
	firstChild	hasChildNodes	onmousedown
	id	insertBefore	onmousemove
	innerHTML	item	onmouseout
	lang	releaseCapture	onmouseover
	language	removeAttribute	onmouseup
	lastChild	removeAttributeNode	onreadystatechange
	length	removeChild	onresize
	localName	replaceChild	onscroll
	namespaceURI	scrollIntoView	
	nextSibling	setAttribute	
	nodeName		
	nodeType		
	nodeValue		
	offsetHeight		
	offsetLeft		
	offsetParent		
	offsetTop		
	offsetWidth		
	ownerDocument		
	parentNode		
	prefix		
	previousSibling		
	readyState		
	scrollHeight		
	scrollLeft		
	scrollTop		
	scrollWidth		
	sourceIndex		
	style		
	tabIndex		
	tagName		
	title		

Object	Properties	Methods	Event Handlers
Option	defaultSelected form index selected text value	remove	none
options array	length	none	none
Password	defaultValue form maxLength name readOnly size type value	blur focus select	onblur onchange onclick ondblclick onfocus onkeydown onkeypress onkeyup onmousedown onmousemove onmouseout onmouseover onmouseup onselect
Plugin	description filename length name	refresh	none
plugins array	length	none	none
Radio	checked defaultChecked form name type value	blur click focus	onblur onchange onclick ondblclick onfocus onkeydown onkeypress onkeyup onmousedown onmousemove onmouseout onmouseover onmouseup
radio array	length	none	none

Table continues on next page

TABLE A.3 JavaScript Object Table *(continued)*

Object	Properties	Methods	Event Handlers
RegExp	constructor	compile	none
	global	exec	
	ignoreCase	test	
	input	toSource	
	lastIndex	toString	
	lastMatch	valueOf	
	lastParen		
	leftContext		
	multiline		
	rightContext		
	source		
	$1		
	$2		
	$3		
	$4		
	$5		
	$6		
	$7		
	$8		
	$9		
	$_		
	$*		
	$&		
	$+		
	$`		
	$'		
Reset	form	blur	onblur
	name	click	onclick
	type	focus	ondblclick
	value		onfocus
			onkeydown
			onkeypress
			onkeyup
			onmousedown
			onmousemove
			onmouseout
			onmouseover
			onmouseup

Object	Properties	Methods	Event Handlers
screen	availHeight availWidth colorDepth height pixelDepth width	none	none
Script	defer event htmlFor language src text type	none	
Select	form length multiple name Option options selectedIndex size type value	blur focus	onblur onchange onclick ondblclick onfocus onkeydown onkeypress onkeyup onmousedown onmousemove onmouseout onmouseover onmouseup onresize

Table continues on next page

Object	Properties	Methods	Event Handlers
String	length	anchor	none
		big	
		blink	
		bold	
		charAt	
		charCodeAt	
		concat	
		fixed	
		fontcolor	
		fontsize	
		fromCharCode	
		indexOf	
		italics	
		lastIndexOf	
		link	
		localeCompare	
		match	
		replace	
		search	
		slice	
		small	
		split	
		strike	
		sub	
		substr	
		substring	
		sup	
		toLocaleLowerCase	
		toLocaleUpperCase	
		toLowerCase	
		toString	
		toUpperCase	
		valueOf	

TABLE A.3 JavaScript Object Table *(continued)*

Object	Properties	Methods	Event Handlers
Style	background	none	none
	backgroundAttachment		
	backgroundColor		
	backgroundImage		
	backgroundPosition		
	backgroundRepeat		
	border		
	borderBottom		
	borderBottomColor		
	borderBottomStyle		
	borderBottomWidth		
	borderColor		
	borderLeft		
	borderLeftColor		
	borderLeftStyle		
	borderLeftWidth		
	borderRight		
	borderRightColor		
	borderRightStyle		
	borderRightWidth		
	borderStyle		
	borderTop		
	borderTopColor		
	borderTopStyle		
	borderTopWidth		
	borderWidth		
	bottom		
	clear		
	clip		
	color		
	cssText		
	cursor		
	direction		
	display		
	font		
	fontFamily		
	fontSize		
	fontStyle		
	fontVariant		
	fontWeight		

Table continues on next page

Object	Properties	Methods	Event Handlers
Style (*continued*)	height	none	none
	left		
	lineHeight		
	listStyle		
	listStyleImage		
	listStylePosition		
	listStyleType		
	margin		
	marginBottom		
	marginLeft		
	marginRight		
	marginTop		
	overflow		
	padding		
	paddingBottom		
	paddingLeft		
	paddingRight		
	paddingTop		
	pageBreakAfter		
	pageBreakBefore		
	position		
	right		
	tableLayout		
	textAlign		
	textIndent		
	textTransform		
	top		
	unicodeBidi		
	verticalAlign		
	visibility		
	whiteSpace		
	width		
	wordSpacing		
	zIndex		
StyleSheet	cssRules	none	none
	disabled		
	href		
	media		
	parentStyleSheet		
	title		
	type		

TABLE A.3 JavaScript Object Table *(continued)*

Object	Properties	Methods	Event Handlers
Submit	form	blur	onblur
	name	click	onclick
	type	focus	ondblclick
	value		onfocus
			onkeydown
			onkeypress
			onkeyup
			onmousedown
			onmousemove
			onmouseout
			onmouseover
			onmouseup
Text	defaultValue	blur	onblur
	disabled	click	onchange
	form	focus	onclick
	maxLength	select	ondblclick
	name		onfocus
	readOnly		onkeydown
	size		onkeypress
	type		onkeyup
	value		onmousedown
			onmousemove
			onmouseout
			onmouseover
			onmouseup
			onselect
Textarea	cols	blur	onblur
	defaultValue	click	onchange
	form	focus	onclick
	name	select	ondblclick
	readOnly		onfocus
	rows		onkeydown
	type		onkeypress
	value		onkeyup
	wrap		onmousedown
			onmousemove
			onmouseout
			onmouseover
			onmouseup
			onselect

Table continues on next page

Object	Properties	Methods	Event Handlers
window	closed	alert	onblur
	defaultStatus	blur	onerror
	document	clearInterval	onfocus
	event	clearTimeout	onload
	external	close	onmove
	frames	confirm	onresize
	history	focus	onunload
	length	moveBy	
	location	moveTo	
	name	open	
	navigator	print	
	opener	prompt	
	parent	resizeBy	
	screen	resizeTo	
	self	scroll	
	status	scrollBy	
	top	scrollTo	
		setInterval	
		setTimeout	
XMLHttpRequest	readyState	abort	onload
	response	addEventListener	onloadend
	responseText	getAllResponseHeaders	onloadstart
	responseXML	getResponseHeader	onreadystatechange
	status	open	ontimeout
	statusText	overrideMimeType	
	timeout	send	
	upload	setRequestHeader	
	withCredentials		

B

JavaScript Reserved Words

Reserved words are words that have special meaning to JavaScript. Therefore, they cannot be used as variable or function names.

You'll recognize many of the reserved words from previous chapters, but others will be unfamiliar. Some of the latter group are future reserved words; that is, it's expected that they might be used in future editions of ECMAScript. They're being set aside now so that you won't have to revise your code when revisions are released.

ECMAScript Edition 3 Reserved Words

These words are part of the JavaScript language as of ES3.

break	for	throw
case	function	try
catch	if	typeof
continue	in	var
default	instanceof	void
delete	new	while
do	return	with
else	switch	
finally	this	

ES3 Future Reserved Words

abstract	final	protected
boolean	float	public
byte	goto	short
char	implements	static
class	import	super
const	int	synchronized
debugger	interface	throws
double	long	transient
enum	native	volatile
export	package	
extends	private	

ECMAScript Edition 5 Reserved Words

This is ES5's list of reserved words. It's similar to that of ES3, but given that browsers primarily support ES3, we recommend that you keep both lists in mind.

break	finally	this
case	for	throw
catch	function	try
continue	if	typeof
debugger	in	var
default	instanceof	void
delete	new	while
do	return	with
else	switch	

ES5 Future Reserved Words

class	interface	super
const	let	yield
enum	package	
export	private	
extends	protected	
implements	public	
import	static	

Other identifiers to avoid

These (along with the object names used in Appendix A) aren't officially reserved, but as they are part of the JavaScript language, you shouldn't use them as function or variable names. If you do, abandon all hope; the results will be unpredictable.

In addition, most browsers are case-sensitive, which means that they differentiate between **Document** and **document**. Internet Explorer is only sometimes case-sensitive, which means that, for example, it may not understand any difference between **Document** and **document**. Consequently, be aware that just because it works in one browser doesn't mean that it'll always work in others. Test, test, test.

abstract	get	prototype
arguments	goto	RangeError
Array	has	ReferenceError
Boolean	include	RegExp
byte	Infinity	rounding
call	int	set
cast	internal	short
char	intrinsic	standard
Date	is	strict
decimal	isFinite	String
decodeURI	isNaN	synchronized
decodeURIComponent	JSON	SyntaxError
double	like	throws
dynamic	long	to
each	Math	transient
encodeURI	namespace	true
encodeURIComponent	NaN	type
Error	native	TypeError
eval	null	uint
EvalError	Number	undefined
false	Object	URIError
final	override	use
float	parseFloat	volatile
Function	parseInt	xml
generator	precision	

Cascading Style Sheets Reference

This appendix lists CSS 3 properties as defined by the W3C at **w3.org/Style/CSS/current-work**.

Work on CSS 2 began in the mid-1990s and was published as a standard in May 1998. Work on CSS 2.1 began shortly thereafter, with the goal of clarifying CSS 2 so that it was closer to what browser makers actually implemented. Unfortunately, what often happens to committees happened with the people working on the CSS 2.1 spec, and it wasn't standardized until June 2011.

Work began on CSS 3 shortly after CSS 2 shipped. It involved breaking the original specification into modules so that no single part would hold up shipping other parts. It's also suffered some pangs over the years, and as of this writing, only a few of the modules have been formally published.

There is some good news, though: browser makers have forged ahead to implement CSS 3 in their browsers, so much of it can actually be used today. This appendix includes most (but not all) of what's in CSS 3. What is actually usable will change over time, and the best way we've found to learn the current status of any property/browser/version combination is by checking out the tables at **caniuse.com/#cats=CSS**.

Because this is a book about JavaScript, we've only touched on a few of the cool things you can do with CSS. If you want to learn more, we recommend *Styling Web Pages with CSS: Visual QuickProject Guide* by Tom Negrino and Dori Smith (hey, that's us!).

TABLE C.1 Basic Concepts

Property Name	Value
In HTML	\<link\>
	\<style\>...\</style\>
	\<x style="declaration;"\>
Grouping	x, y, z {declaration;}
Contextual selectors	x y z {declaration;}
Class selector	.class
ID selector	#id
At-rules	@import
	@media
	@page
	@font-face
Important	!important

TABLE C.2 Pseudo-Elements and Pseudo-Classes

Property Name	Value
after	:after
anchor	a:active
	a:focus
	a:hover
	a:link
	a:visited
before	:before
first	:first
first-child	:first-child
left	:left
paragraph	p:first-letter
	p:first-line
right	:right

TABLE C.3 Page Properties

Property Name	Value
orphans	\<integer\>
page-break-after	auto
	always
	avoid
	left
	right
page-break-before	auto
	always
	avoid
	left
	right
page-break-inside	avoid
widows	auto
	\<integer\>

TABLE C.4 User Interface Properties

Property Name	Value
box-sizing	content-box
	padding-box
	border-box
cursor	<url>
	auto
	crosshair
	default
	pointer
	move
	e-resize
	ne-resize
	nw-resize
	n-resize
	se-resize
	sw-resize
	s-resize
	w-resize
	ew-resize
	ns-resize
	nesw-resize
	nwse-resize
	col-resize
	row-resize
	all-scroll
	zoom-in
	zoom-out
	text
	wait
	cell
	help
	progress
	context-menu
	vertical-text
	alias
	copy
	no-drop
	not-allowed
	none

TABLE C.4 *(continued)*

Property Name	Value
outline	<outline-color>
	<outline-style>
	<outline-width>
outline-color	<color>
	invert
outline-style	<border-style>
	auto
outline-width	<border-width>
resize	none
	both
	horizontal
	vertical
text-overflow	clip
	ellipsis
	<string>

TABLE C.5 Visual Effects Properties

Property Name	Value
max-lines	none
	<integer>
overflow	<overflow-x>
	<overflow-y>
overflow-x	visible
	hidden
	scroll
	auto
	paged-x
	paged-y
	paged-x-controls
	paged-y-controls
	fragments
overflow-y	visible
	hidden
	scroll
	auto
	paged-x
	paged-y
	paged-x-controls
	paged-y-controls
	fragments

TABLE C.6 Background and Border Properties

Property Name	Value
background	<background-color>
	<background-image>
	<background-position> → / <background-size>
	<background-repeat>
	<background- → attachment>
	<background-clip>
	<background-origin>
background-attachment	scroll
	fixed
	local
background-clip	border-box
	padding-box
	content-box
background-color	<color>
background-image	<url>
	none
background-origin	border-box
	padding-box
	content-box
background-position	<percentage>
	<length>
	top
	center
	bottom
	left
	right
background-repeat	repeat
	repeat-x
	repeat-y
	no-repeat
	space
	round
background-size	<percentage>
	<length>
	contain
	cover
	auto

TABLE C.6 *(continued)*

Property Name	Value
border	\<border-width\>
	\<border-style\>
	\<border-color\>
border-bottom	\<border-bottom-width\>
	\<border-bottom-style\>
	\<border-bottom-color\>
border-bottom-color	\<border-color\>
border-bottom-right-radius	\<border-radius\>
border-bottom-left-radius	\<border-radius\>
border-bottom-style	\<border-style\>
border-bottom-width	\<border-width\>
border-color	\<color\>
border-image	\<border-image-source\>
	\<border-image-slice\>
	\<border-image-width\>
	\<border-image-outset\>
	\<border-image-repeat\>
border-image-outset	\<length\>
	\<number\>
border-image-repeat	stretch
	repeat
	round
	space
border-image-slice	\<number\>
	\<percentage\>
border-image-source	none
	\<url\>
border-image-width	\<length\>
	\<percentage\>
	\<number\>
	auto
border-left	\<border-left-width\>
	\<border-left-style\>
	\<border-left-color\>
border-left-color	\<border-color\>

TABLE C.6 *(continued)*

Property Name	Value
border-left-style	\<border-style\>
border-left-width	\<border-width\>
border-radius	\<length\>
	\<percentage\>
border-right	\<border-right-width\>
	\<border-right-style\>
	\<border-right-color\>
border-right-color	\<border-color\>
border-right-style	\<border-style\>
border-right-width	\<border-width\>
border-style	none
	hidden
	dotted
	dashed
	solid
	double
	groove
	ridge
	inset
	outset
border-top	\<border-top-width\>
	\<border-top-style\>
	\<border-top-color\>
border-top-color	\<border-color\>
border-top-left-radius	\<border-radius\>
border-top-right-radius	\<border-radius\>
border-top-style	\<border-style\>
border-top-width	\<border-width\>
border-width	\<length\>
	thin
	medium
	thick
box-shadow	none
	\<length\>
	\<color\>
	inset

TABLE C.7 Table Properties

Property Name	Value
caption-side	top
	bottom
table-layout	auto
	fixed
border-collapse	collapse
	separate
border-spacing	<length>
empty-cells	show
	hide
border-style	none
	hidden
	dotted
	dashed
	solid
	double
	groove
	ridge
	inset
	outset
vertical-align	baseline
	sub
	super
	top
	text-top
	middle
	bottom
	text-bottom
	<percentage>
	<length>

TABLE C.8 Font Properties

Property Name	Value
font	<font-style>
	<font-variant>
	<font-weight>
	<font-stretch>
	<font-size> / <line-height>
	<font-family>
	caption
	icon
	menu
	message-box
	small-caption
	status-bar
font-family	<family-name>
	cursive
	fantasy
	monospace
	sans-serif
	serif
font-kerning	auto
	normal
	none
font-size	<absolute-size> (xx-small–xx-large)
	<relative-size> (smaller–larger)
	<length>
	<percentage>
font-size-adjust	none
	number
font-stretch	normal
	ultra-condensed
	extra-condensed
	condensed
	semi-condensed
	semi-expanded
	expanded
	extra-expanded
	ultra-expanded

TABLE C.8 *(continued)*

Property Name	Value
font-style	normal
	italic
	oblique
font-synthesis	none
	<weight>
	<style>
font-variant	none
	ruby
	<font-variant-caps>
	<font-variant-ligatures>
	<font-variant-numeric>
font-variant-caps	normal
	small-caps
	all-small-caps
	petite-caps
	all-petite-caps
	unicase
	titling-caps
font-variant-ligatures	normal
	none
	common-ligatures
	no-common-ligatures
	discretionary-ligatures
	no-discretionary-ligatures
	historical-ligatures
	no-historical-ligatures
	contextual
	no-contextual
font-variant-numeric	normal
	lining-nums
	oldstyle-nums
	proportional-nums
	tabular-nums
	diagonal-fractions
	stacked-fractions
	ordinal
	slashed-zero

TABLE C.8 *(continued)*

Property Name	Value
font-variant-position	normal
	sub
	super
font-weight	normal
	bold
	100 – 900
src	<url>

TABLE C.9 Units

Property Name	Value
Angle	deg
	grad
	rad
	turn
Image	<url>
Length Units	ch
	em
	ex
	px
	in
	cm
	mm
	pt
	pc
	rem
	vh
	vmax
	vmin
	vw
Resolution	dpi
	dpcm
	dppx
Time	s
	ms
URL	<url>

TABLE C.10 Text Properties

Property Name	Value
hanging-punctuation	none
	first
	force-end
	allow-end
	last
hyphens	none
	manual
	auto
letter-spacing	normal
	<length>
line-break	auto
	loose
	normal
	strict
overflow-wrap	normal
	break-word
tab-size	<integer>
	<length>
text-align	left
	right
	center
	justify
	start
	end
	match-parent
text-align-last	auto
	start
	end
	left
	right
	center
	justify
text-decoration	<text-decoration-line>
	<text-decoration-color>
	<text-decoration-style>
text-decoration-color	<color>

TABLE C.10 *(continued)*

Property Name	Value
text-decoration-line	none
	underline
	overline
	line-through
	blink
text-decoration-skip	none
	objects
	spaces
	ink
	edges
	box-decoration
text-decoration-style	solid
	double
	dotted
	dashed
	wavy
text-emphasis-color	<color>
text-emphasis-position	over
	under
	right
	left
text-emphasis-style	none
	filled
	open
	dot
	circle
	double-circle
	triangle
	sesame
	<string>
text-indent	<length>
	<percentage>
	each-line
	hanging
text-justify	auto
	none
	inter-word
	distribute

TABLE C.10 *(continued)*

Property Name	Value
text-shadow	none
	<length>
	<color>
text-transform	capitalize
	uppercase
	lowercase
	full-width
	none
text-underline-position	auto
	under
	left
	right
white-space	normal
	pre
	nowrap
	pre-wrap
	pre-line
word-break	normal
	keep-all
	break-all
word-spacing	normal
	<length>
	<percentage>
word-wrap	normal
	break-word

TABLE C.11 Box Properties

Property Name	Value
clear	none
	left
	right
	both
float	left
	right
	none
margin	<length>
	<percentage>
margin-bottom	<length>
	<percentage>
margin-left	<length>
	<percentage>
margin-right	<length>
	<percentage>
margin-top	<length>
	<percentage>
width	<length>
	<percentage>
	auto
min-width	<length>
	<percentage>
max-width	<length>
	<percentage>
	none
height	<length>
	<percentage>
	auto
min-height	<length>
	<percentage>
max-height	<length>
	<percentage>
	none

TABLE C.11 *(continued)*

Property Name	Value
overflow	visible
	hidden
	scroll
	auto
	no-display
	no-content
overflow-style	auto
	scrollbar
	panner
	move
	marquee
overflow-x	visible
	hidden
	scroll
	auto
	no-display
	no-content
overflow-y	visible
	hidden
	scroll
	auto
	no-display
	no-content
padding	<length>
	<percentage>
padding-bottom	<length>
	<percentage>
padding-left	<length>
	<percentage>
padding-right	<length>
	<percentage>
padding-top	<length>
	<percentage>
rotation	<angle>
visibility	collapse
	visible
	hidden

TABLE C.12 Visual Formatting Properties

Property Name	Value
display	block
	inline
	inline-block
	list-item
	table
	inline-table
	table-row-group
	table-header-group
	table-footer-group
	table-row
	table-column-group
	table-column
	table-cell
	table-caption
	none
left	auto
	<length>
	<percentage>
right	auto
	<length>
	<percentage>
top	auto
	<length>
	<percentage>
bottom	auto
	<length>
	<percentage>
float	left
	right
	none
clear	none
	left
	right
	both
direction	ltr
	rtl

TABLE C.12 (continued)

Property Name	Value
unicode-bidi	normal
	embed
	bidi-override
line-height	normal
	<number>
	<length>
	<percentage>
	none
position	static
	absolute
	relative
	fixed
z-index	auto
	<integer>

TABLE C.13 List Properties

Property Name	Value
counter-reset	<identifier><integer>
	none
counter-set	<identifier><integer>
	none
counter-increment	<identifier><integer>
	none
list-style	<list-style-type>
	<list-style-position>
	<list-style-image>
list-style-image	<image>
	none
list-style-position	inside
	outside
list-style-type	disc
	circle
	square
	disclosure-open
	disclosure-closed
	decimal
	decimal-leading-zero
	hebrew
	lower-roman
	upper-roman
	lower-greek
	lower-alpha
	lower-latin
	upper-alpha
	upper-latin
	armenian
	georgian
	<string>
	none

TABLE C.14 Generated Content Properties

Property Name	Value
content	<string>
	<url>
	<identifier>
	<counters>
	inhibit
	open-quote
	close-quote
	no-open-quote
	no-close-quote
	none
	normal
counter-increment	<identifier>
	<integer>
	none
counter-reset	<identifier>
	<integer>
	none
quotes	<string>
	none

TABLE C.15 Color Properties

Property Name	Value
color	#000
	#000000
	hsl(HHH,S%,L%)
	rgb(RRR,GGG,BBB)
	rgb(R%,G%,B%)
	rgba(RRR,GGG,BBB, → <alphavalue>)
	rgba(R%,G%,B%, → <alphavalue>)
	transparent
	currentColor
	<keyword>
opacity	<alphavalue>

D

Where to Learn More

Once you've worked through this book, you should be well on your way to spicing up your websites with JavaScript. But there's a lot more to learn about the JavaScript language, and you'll probably have questions as you write your own code.

The best place to get those questions answered is online, as you might expect. There are many resources on the web that can help you deepen your understanding of JavaScript.

In this appendix, we'll point you to several of the most helpful JavaScript-oriented websites, and we'll even mention a few other books that we found helpful.

But first, a gentle reminder: the Net is not a static, unchanging place. Websites can and often do change the addresses of their pages, so it's possible that the URLs we list will become out of date by the time you use them. We're just reporting the URLs; we have no control over them. Sometimes, entire websites disappear. If you find a link that's become stale, check our companion website at **javascriptworld.com** to see if we have posted a new location for the page you were looking for.

Finding Help Online

The original JavaScript documentation is found at Mozilla's website, but there's a lot of good information at sites from Microsoft and at independent JavaScript pages as well. Here are some of the best:

Browser vendors

Since Netscape developed JavaScript, it's no surprise that the Mozilla project, the creator of Mozilla and Firefox (the successors to Netscape's browser), has lots of great information about the language and further development.

JavaScript Center

developer.mozilla.org/en/javascript

This site is designed for all levels of JavaScript users and includes links to tools and documentation . The documentation includes the Core JavaScript Reference (covering JavaScript 1.5), which gives you a rundown on the basics of the language, and definitions and explanations of the concepts used in JavaScript. It suffers from a moderately geeky difficulty level and sketchy examples, but you should be able to puzzle it out once you've digested this book. Also found here are the Core JavaScript Guide and explanations of what was added in JavaScript from versions 1.6 on.

Venkman Debugger

developer.mozilla.org/en/venkman

When you need to debug your JavaScript, it certainly would be nice to have a good tool to use to help you. Wish no longer; Venkman, the JavaScript debugger from

Ⓐ Mozilla's JavaScript section of their Developer Center is a good place for you to start furthering your knowledge of JavaScript.

B Microsoft gives you the lowdown on JScript, Microsoft's variant of JavaScript.

C To learn the latest about Safari (on Mac, Windows, or iOS), you want to go Surfin' Safari.

the Mozilla project, is a pretty good tool that works with Firefox, Thunderbird, and Mozilla, and it allows you to step through your code, setting breakpoints, inspecting objects and variables as the script executes, and working with JavaScript source code.

Mozilla Hacks—the web developer blog

hacks.mozilla.org

The blog itself says that it is a "key resource for people developing for the Open Web, talking about news and in-depth descriptions of technologies and features"—and that's just what it does.

Microsoft's JScript Language

msdn.microsoft.com/hbxc2t98.aspx

Microsoft's own version of JavaScript—called JScript—has its own pages on the Microsoft Developer Network site **B**, where you can learn about its similarities to (and differences from) Mozilla's JavaScript. You'll find a detailed JScript Language Reference and the JScript User's Guide.

Surfin' Safari

webkit.org/blog/

This site **C** isn't just about JavaScript, but it is all about Apple's Safari browser and its WebKit rendering engine—which aren't just for the Mac anymore. Here's where you can get information straight from Apple employees about what upcoming versions of Safari will and won't do. You'll also find links to downloadable nightly builds of WebKit, giving you features long before Apple ships them to the public.

Weblogs, elsewhere

There are many weblogs devoted to JavaScript; here are a couple of our favorites, but they by no means form an exhaustive list.

DailyJS

`dailyjs.com`

JavaScript blogs come and JavaScript blogs go, but one that just keeps chugging along is DailyJS. Check it out for always-new JavaScript news and links.

QuirksMode

`quirksmode.org/blog/`

Peter-Paul Koch is a JavaScript developer in the Netherlands. The best thing about his site  is that he keeps it amazingly up to date with the latest news about browsers and their JavaScript capabilities. It's not a tutorial site, but along with the blog there is a great deal of basic information that will be helpful to the beginning scripter.

D Peter-Paul Koch's QuirksMode site often has JavaScript information well ahead of any others.

Offline Resources

Books

Though the authors would naturally like to think that the book you've got in your hands is all you'll ever need to become a JavaScript expert, they recognize that you might just want a bit more information after you've eagerly devoured this book. There are approximately a zillion JavaScript books on the market; here (in no particular order) are some of the books that we think are the best.

JavaScript: The Definitive Guide

Written by David Flanagan and published by O'Reilly Media, this is an exhaustive reference to the JavaScript language. Not for the faint of heart, this is where the experts turn to look up those weird operators and nail down that odd syntax. After a lengthy wait, the sixth edition of this book has finally arrived, bringing its knowledge base up to date.

ppk on JavaScript

Peter-Paul Koch is one of the acknowledged masters of JavaScript. In this book from New Riders, he uses real-world script examples he created for paying clients to take you through a journey that is both theoretical and practical.

Pro JavaScript Techniques

John Resig (of jQuery fame) wrote this book to help intermediate-level JavaScripters become advanced scripters. Not for the novice, it's a good book to take you onward from where this book ends.

Troubleshooting Tips

When you first start writing code, it may feel like you're running into trouble with every line—but happily, there are many online resources to help you through that rocky beginning. Here are some of our favorites.

The missing add-ons

Firebug Debugger

getfirebug.com

If you like Mozilla's Venkman (or even if you don't), you'll love Firebug . You can use it with Firefox to debug not just your scripts, but your HTML and CSS as well. It's free, with good documentation, handy logging, and all the breakpoint and DOM support you could want.

If the only thing missing to make your (scripting) life complete is similar functionality for IE, Safari, and Opera, then you need to check out Firebug Lite at **getfirebug.com/lite.html** . It doesn't have all the functionality of its big brother, but it's very handy to have a single common interface when trying to track down a random bug.

Ⓐ Firebug, an add-on to Firefox, gives you an extraordinary amount of control and a lot of ways to examine your code.

Ⓑ If you aren't running Firefox, you can still run Firebug Lite—shown here inside Safari on the same page as Ⓐ.

JSHint

jshint.com

If you're like us, the first thing you do if you have trouble with HTML and CSS is run to a validator. If you've wished for something similar with JavaScript, you may have heard of JSLint, a code-checking tool. And if, like us (and many other JavaScript developers), you found that JSLint just wasn't designed for real-world use, then what you want is JSHint. It's designed both for checking code and for flexibility, and it has none of JSLint's "my way or the highway" rigid enforcement.

Can I Use…

caniuse.com/#cats=JS_API

If you're writing cutting-edge JavaScript, you may run into trouble due to browser incompatibilities. When that happens, check out this site, and you'll find tables upon tables letting you know which browsers do (and don't) support the functionality you're trying to use.

Online pastebins

Ever wish you could use your browser not just for testing your code, but also for writing it—after all, why should you have to keep toggling back and forth? That's part of what pastebins are all about—the ability to write and run in the same window.

The other handy benefit is being able to save your files and show them to other people (that is, you have something to point to while yelling for help). And even better—they can make changes to your code as well, helping you to find and fix those sneaky bugs.

There are numerous pastebin sites online, some of which support HTML, CSS, and JavaScript. Here are two we (and others) like:

JSBin

`jsbin.com`

JSFiddle

`jsfiddle.net`

Index

B

back button, 117, 330

background color, changing page's, 447, 448–450

background properties (CSS), 498

backslash (\), 123, 174, 177

banners, 104–107, 113–114

bar graph generator, 306–314

Bare Bones Software, 20

BBEdit, 20, 172

beta property, 432

binary math, 70, 74, 75–76

binary values, 70, 71

Bingo cards

  adding interactivity to, 68–70

  applying styles to, 52, 68–70

  avoiding duplicate numbers in, 62–63, 64

  checking for winning state, 71–74

  creating skeleton for, 50–51

  limiting range of values in, 59

  possible winning patterns for, 75

  range of allowable numbers for, 52, 59

  using loop to create table for, 53–54

bit.ly, 465

bits, 70, 71, 75–76

bitwise arithmetic, 70, 72, 75–76

Blackberry devices, 437. *See also* mobile devices

blind users, 296

Blink, 472

block-level elements, 18

blog.jquery.com, 384

blogs

  DailyJS, 510

  jQuery, 384

  Mozilla Hacks, 509

  QuirksMode, 510

  Safari, 509

blur() method, 132

body scripts, 23

<body> tags, 22, 23

bookmarklets, 441–468

  for changing page's styles, 448–450

  for converting kilometers to miles, 461–462

for converting RGB values to hex, 459–460

creating

  in Chrome, 444

  in Firefox, 442

  in Internet Explorer, 445

  in Safari, 443

defined, 441

for displaying ISO Latin characters, 456–458

for doing complex calculations, 463–464

and IE security, 446

for looking up words, 451–453

for mailing webpages, 467

origin of, 443

repositioning, 443

for resetting page background, 447

for resizing pages, 468

for shortening URLs, 465

troubleshooting, 468

use of semicolons in, 441, 450

use of single *vs.* double quotes in, 447

for validating pages, 466

for viewing images, 454–455

vs. other JavaScript code, 441

bookmarklets.com, 443

books

  Dreamweaver: Visual QuickStart Guide, 20, 138

  HTML and CSS: Visual QuickStart Guide, 2, 430

  JavaScript, The Definitive Guide, 511

  ppk on JavaScript, 511

  Pro JavaScript Techniques, 511

  Styling Web Pages with CSS: Visual QuickProject Guide, 496

Boolean values, 15, 61, 63, 70, 77, 217

border properties (CSS), 499

box properties (CSS), 504

braces ({ }), 25, 34, 175, 177

brackets ([ ]), 174, 177

browser compatibility, 412

browser detection, 58

browser objects, 11. *See also* objects

browser security settings, 129

browser windows, 128

GestureEvent object, 432
gesturestart event, 432
getAllResponseHeaders() method, 333
getDate() method, 283
getDay() method, 283
getElementById() method, 27
getElementsByTagName() method, 245, 246, 247
getfirebug.com, 512
getFullYear() method, 277, 283
getHours() method, 265, 283
getMilliseconds() method, 283
getMinutes() method, 283
getMonth() method, 283
getResponseHeader() method, 333
getSeconds() method, 283
getTime() method, 277, 283
getTimezoneOffset() method, 283
getUTCDate() method, 283
getUTCDay() method, 283
getUTCFullYear() method, 283
getUTCHours() method, 283
getUTCMilliseconds() method, 283
getUTCMinutes() method, 283
getUTCMonth() method, 283
getUTCSeconds() method, 283
getYear() method, 277, 283
GIF images, 90, 104, 105
global property, 185
Global Statistics, StatCounter's, 314
Gmail, 10, 325
GMT. See Greenwich Mean Time
goo.gl, 465
Google
  and Ajax, 10
  Android emulator, 431
  Calendar, 10
  Docs, 10
  Gmail, 10, 325
  Instant, 361
  Maps, 9, 10, 325, 440
  Maps Mania, 10
googlemapsmania.blogspot.com, 10
graphics. See also images
  animating, 81
  displaying, 111

preparing for rollovers, 90
programs, 459
Greenwich Mean Time (GMT), 266, 283, 284
grep, 171
gs.statcounter.com, 314

H

<h1>...<h6> tags, 22
hash symbol (#), 19
<head> tags, 22, 23
header scripts, 23
hexadecimal, converting RGB values to, 459–460
hide() method, 387
highlighting new elements, 386–388
hijacking pages, 117
hit counters, 230
hover() method, 374
href attribute, 22, 440
HTML
  and Ajax, 9, 327
  attributes, 22, 49, 82, 116, 134
  and case, 90
  and CSS, 17
  evolution of, 1
  forms, 133
  recommended book on, 2, 430
  separating JavaScript from, 41, 43
  tags, 22, 49, 82, 116, 134
  tools for writing, 20
  and W3C validation, 17
  writing JavaScript-friendly, 17–19
HTML and CSS: Visual QuickStart Guide, 2, 430
.html file extension, 20
HTML Source mode, 20
<html> tags, 22
Hyslop, Bruce, 2, 430

I

id attribute
  and frames, 116, 119
  and images, 82, 103
  manipulating cell contents with, 51
  purpose of, 18, 19
identifier property, 432

select-and-go, 135–138
sliding, 286–288
sortable tabs in, 398–400
metaKey property, 432
meta characters, 176
methods
combining with objects/properties, 12–13
defined, 12
for **DeviceMotionEvent** object, 432
for **DeviceOrientationEvent** object, 432
distinguishing from properties, 12
for **GestureEvent** object, 432
for **Math** object, 54, 481
reference, 473–490
for **RegExp** object, 185
for strings, 185
for **TouchEvent** object, 432
use of parentheses in, 12
for **XMLHttpRequest** object, 333, 490
Microsoft
and ECMAScript, 472
Excel (*See* Excel)
Internet Explorer (*See* Internet Explorer)
and Java, 3
and JScript, 5, 42, 471
JScript Language site, 509
Windows (*See* Windows)
Word (*See* Word)
min() method, 54
mobile apps, launching, 440
mobile devices, 425–440
changing orientation, 426–430
debugging, 431
differentiating, 436–437
font considerations, 437
handling touch events, 433–435
help building websites for, 384
launching apps for, 440
locating, 438–440
popularity of, 425
mobile events, 432
modal dialogs, 392–393
modifiers, regular expression, 177
month/day pop-up menus, 140–141
MooTools, 373

mouse click codes, 203
mouse event handlers, 201–208
onclick, 208
oncontextmenu, 201–203
ondblclick, 2070
onmousedown, 201–203
onmousemove, 204–206, 207
onmouseout, 207, 375
onmouseover, 207, 353
onmouseup, 204, 208
Mozilla, 58, 470, 508–509
Mozilla Hacks blog, 509
MSIE. *See* Internet Explorer
multi-level conditionals, 43–45, 276
multiline property, 185
My Yahoo, 10

N

name attribute, 116, 119, 134
navigation menus, 135
Navigator, Netscape
and ECMAScript, 472
and JavaScript, 1, 5, 42, 470
and LiveScript, 5, 470
and Year 2000 Problem, 277
nested **if** statements, 43
Netscape
Communicator (*See* Communicator)
and external JavaScript files, 28
JavaScript Guide, 443
Navigator (*See* Navigator)
and rollovers, 84, 90
node manipulation, 241, 242–243, 260
nodes, 241–260
adding, 244–245
defined, 13
deleting, 246–250
and the DOM, 13, 241–243
inserting, 251–253
replacing, 254–256
types of, 13, 243
vs. **innerHTML**, 245
non-breaking space (** **), 51
<noscript> tags, 32
Notepad, 20

null values, 15, 35
number sign (#), 19
numbers
  random, 54, 347
  validating, 189–190
numeric values, 15

O

object detection, 57–58
object literals, 257–260
  sample scripts, 258–259, 371, 375
  similarity to CSS, 257
  use of **this** with, 260
  vs. standard procedural JavaScript, 257, 260
object table, 473–490
<object> tags, 4
object values, 15
object-based languages, 11
object-oriented languages, 11
objects
  combining with properties/methods, 12–13
  defined, 11
  detecting, 57–58
  displaying/hiding, 280
  methods of, 12
  moving, 281–282
  naming, 11
  properties of, 12
  reference, 473–490
offline resources, 511
onabort events, 14, 199
onbeforeunload events, 198–199
onblur events, 14, 200, 210–211
onchange events, 14, 209, 211
onclick events, 14, 38, 208, 210
oncontextmenu events, 201–203
ondblclick events, 208
onDOMContentLoaded events, 200
onerror events, 14, 200
one-up calendars, 404–405
onfocus events, 14, 200, 212
onkeydown events, 213–215
onkeypress events, 215
onkeyup events, 215
online pastebins, 514

online resources, 508–510, 512–514
onload events, 14, 195–197, 333
onloadend events, 333
onloadstart events, 333
onmousedown events, 201–203
onmousemove events, 204–206, 207
onmouseout events, 14, 90, 207
onmouseover events, 14, 90, 207, 353
onmouseup events, 204, 208
onmove events, 199
onpagehide events, 138
onpageshow events, 138
onreadystatechange events, 333
onreset events, 209
onresize events, 199
onscroll events, 200
onselect events, 14, 209
onsubmit events, 14, 209
ontimeout events, 333
onunload events, 14, 136, 198
open() method, 128, 130, 333
Opera, 58, 512
operators, 15–16, 70, 171
<option> tags, 134
or (|) comparison, 16, 70, 74, 76, 177
orientationChange event, 432
orientation changes, 426–430
OS X
  alert boxes, 32
  and daylight saving time, 271
  dictionary/thesaurus window, 453
  and Java, 3
  text editors, 20
outline-style menus, 285
overrideMimeType() method, 333

P

pageX property, 432
pageY property, 432
page properties (CSS), 496
paragraphs, 245
parameters, passing, 35, 55
parentheses. *See* ( ) (parentheses)
parse() method, 269, 283
parseInt() method, 228, 240

passing information, 55–56
password-checking script, 142, 147–148
pastebins, 514
period (.), 12, 19, 177
Perl, 7, 172
phone numbers, formatting/validating, 188–190
phones. *See also* mobile devices
  app for dialing, 440
  differentiating between, 436–437
  font considerations, 437
  free simulators, 431
  handling orientation changes, 426–430
  locating, 438–440
Photoshop, 306, 459
PHP, 7, 172
plugins, jQuery, 384, 411, 413, 420–424
plugins.jquery.com, 384, 413
plus sign (+), 15, 53, 174, 177
PNG images, 105
pop-up killers, 127
pop-up menus, 140–141
pop-up windows, 127, 195, 198, 278
portrait orientation, 426, 427
postal codes, validating, 162–165
pow() method, 54
ppk on JavaScript, 511
preventDefault() method, 217
Pro JavaScript Techniques, 511
programming languages, 2, 3, 172
progressive enhancement, 42
prompt() method, 35
properties
  combining with objects/methods, 12–13
  defined, 12
  for **DeviceMotionEvent** object, 432
  for **DeviceOrientationEvent** object, 432
  distinguishing from methods, 12
  for **GestureEvent** object, 432
  reference
    CSS, 496–506
    JavaScript, 473–490
  for **RegExp** object, 185
  touch, 432
  for **TouchEvent** object, 432
  for **XMLHttpRequest** object, 333, 490

Prototype, 373
pseudo-classes (CSS), 496
pseudo-elements (CSS), 496
pull-down menus, 289–296
Python, 172

Q

question mark (?), 34, 175, 177
QuirksMode blog, 510
quotes. *See* " (quotes)

R

radio buttons, 156–158
random images, 111–114
random() method, 54, 112, 347
random numbers, 54, 127, 347
ready() method, 368
readyState property, 333, 334
redirection, 21, 37–38
RegExp object, 171, 185, 484
regular expressions, 171–192
  alternate names for, 171
  defined, 171
  extracting strings with, 180–182
  formatting strings with, 183–190
  modifiers for, 177
  purpose of, 171
  replacing elements with, 191–192
  sorting strings with, 186–187
  special characters for, 177
  validating email addresses with, 173–176
  validating file names with, 178–179
  validating strings with, 188–190
  validating URLs with, 178–179
removeEventListener() method, 217
replace() method, 117, 185
replaceChild() method, 254
reserved words, 491–494
Resig, John, 384, 511
resizable dialogs, 393
resizeTo() method, 468
resizing windows, 468

resources
  books
    CSS, 2, 430, 496
    Dreamweaver, 138
    HTML, 2, 430
    JavaScript, 511
    `@media` queries, 430
  websites
    Android SDK, 431
    Bare Bones Software, 20
    `bit.ly`, 465
    `bookmarklets.com`, 443
    `caniuse.com`, 496, 513
    `dailyjs.com`, 510
    Dojo, 373
    ECMA International, 472
    Firebug Debugger, 512
    font-compatibility list, 437
    Google Maps Mania, 10
    `is.gd`, 465
    `java.com`, 3
    JavaScript Center, 508
    `javascriptworld.com`, 2, 507
    jQuery, 384
    jQuery Mobile, 384
    jQuery plugins, 413
    JSBin, 514
    JScript Language, 509
    JSFiddle, 514
    JSHint, 513
    `jsperf.com`, 366
    Modernizr, 373
    MooTools, 373
    Mozilla Hacks, 509
    Prototype, 373
    QuirksMode, 510
    Resig, John (`ejohn.org`), 384
    `slidesjs.com`, 422
    StatCounter's Global Statistics, 314
    Surfin' Safari, 509
    `tablesorter.com`, 383
    `tinyURL.com`, 465
    toolkits, 373
    URL-shortening services, 465
    Venkman Debugger, 508–509

W3C validation tool, 17, 466
Web Standards Project, 42
Wikipedia, 373
Willison, Simon (simonwillison.net), 197
Xcode developer tools, 431
YUI, 373
`response` property, 333
`responseText` property, 333, 335
`responseXML` property, 333, 335
right-click codes, 203
`rightContext` property, 185
rollovers, 83–103
  browser considerations, 84, 90
  building three-state, 91–92, 191
  checking whether image exists, 362–364
  defined, 6, 81
  preparing images for, 90
`rotation` property, 432
`rotationRate` property, 432
`round()` method, 54
RSS feeds, 340

S

Safari
  and alert boxes, 32
  blog, 509
  and browser detection, 58
  creating bookmarklets in, 443
  debugger, 512
  and debugging mobile devices, 431
  development tools, 431
  and DOM-2, 242
  and ECMAScript, 472
  and external JavaScript files, 28
  and iPhone, 80
  iPhone/iPad Simulator, 431
  and JavaScript toolkits, 373
  and `onkeydown` events, 214
  and `onload` events, 136, 138
  and page caching, 136, 138
  performing word lookups in, 453
  viewing document tree structure in, 13
  Web Inspector, 431
  window defaults, 130

Unix, 3, 20
unobtrusive scripting, 41, 42
unordered lists, 288, 398
upload property, 333
URLs. *See also* links
  shortening, 465
  updates to this book's, 507
  validating, 178–179
user interface, jQuery. *See* jQuery UI
user interface properties (CSS), 497
users
  alerting, 31–32
  allowing control of scripts by, 66–67
  confirming choices of, 33–34
  prompting for response, 35–36
  redirecting with links, 37–38
UT (Universal Time). *See* Greenwich Mean
    Time
UTC() method, 284
UTC (Coordinated Universal Time).
    See Greenwich Mean Time

V

validating
  email addresses, 166–170, 173–176
  file names, 178–179
  forms, 151–155, 209
  JavaScript, 512
  phone numbers, 188–190
  strings, 171, 188–190
  URLs, 178–179
  webpages, 17, 466
  zip codes, 162–165
validator.w3.org, 17, 466
value attribute, 134
valueOf() method, 185, 284
values
  adding, 15
  assigning to variables, 16
  binary, 70, 71
  checking variables against multiple, 43
  comparing, 16, 70
  literal, 16
  passing to functions, 55–56
  types of, 15

var keyword, 35, 36
variables
  assigning values to, 16
  checking against multiple values, 43
  comparing values of, 16
  declaring, 35
  defined, 15
  defining scope of, 36, 450
  naming, 15, 182, 494
  use of equals sign with, 15
Venkman Debugger, 508–509
verifying email addresses, 170
Vista, 446
visual effects properties (CSS), 498
visual formatting properties (CSS), 505
visually-impaired users, 296
void() method, 447, 450

W

W3C
  and CSS 3 properties, 495
  deprecation of attributes by, 24
  and DOM scripting, 42
  and DOM-2, 242
  and DOM-3, 243
  and **innerHTML** property, 28
  and node manipulation, 241, 242, 243
  validation tool, 17, 466
web
  browsers (*See* browsers)
  dynamic nature of, 1, 325
  sites (*See* websites)
  standard layout language for, 17
  standards, 17, 42, 373, 466
Web 2.0, 328, 342, 385
Web Inspector, Safari, 431
Web Standards Project, 42
web-based applications
  and Ajax, 9, 10
  and JavaScript, 6
  and jQuery, 413
web-based email, 10
web-based slideshows, 108–110, 414–416
webkitCompassAccuracy property, 432
webkitCompassHeading property, 432